INFERNO

Dante Alighieri

Inferno

Translated by Henry Wadsworth Longfellow

Edited and with a Preface by Matthew Pearl

Introduction by Lino Pertile

THE MODERN LIBRARY

NEW YORK

2003 Modern Library Paperback Edition

Preface copyright © 2003 by Matthew Pearl
Introduction copyright © 2003 by Lino Pertile
Biographical note copyright © 1996 by Random House, Inc.

LIBRARY OF CONGRESS CATALOGING-IN-PUBLICATION DATA
Dante Alighieri, 1265–1321.
[Inferno. English]
Inferno / Dante Alighieri ; translated by Henry Wadsworth Longfellow ; edited and with a
preface by Matthew Pearl ; introduction by Lino Pertile.
p.   cm.
ISBN 0-8129-6721-6
I. Longfellow, Henry Wadsworth, 1807–1882. II. Title.

PQ4315.2 .L65   2003
851'.1—dc21
2002026565

Modern Library website address: www.modernlibrary.com

Printed in the United States of America

4   6   8   9   7   5

DANTE ALIGHIERI

Dante Alighieri, the Italian poet whose great poem the *Divine Comedy* has exerted a profound effect on Western literature and thought, was born in Florence in May 1265. He came from a noble though impoverished family, descendants of the city's Roman founders. Relatively little is known with certainty about Dante's early life, but it is noteworthy that he grew up during the restless period that followed decades of blood rivalry between two Florentine political groups, the Guelphs and the Ghibellines. His childhood was doubtless colored by stories of this partisan strife from which, as Machiavelli later wrote, "there resulted more murders, banishments, and destruction of families than ever in any city known to history."

Dante probably received his early schooling from the Franciscans and the Dominicans; later, he studied rhetoric with the Guelph statesman and scholar Brunetto Latini. Another significant mentor was the aristocratic poet Guido Cavalcanti, who strongly influenced his early work. For the young Dante, writing poetry became an important expression of his passion for art and learning, and of his abiding concern with the nature of love and spiritual fulfillment. A Florentine woman of exceptional beauty, Beatrice Portinari, provided a powerful stimulus to the poet's artistic development. Dante idealized her as the "bringer of blessings," a beatific guide capable of pointing him toward inner perfection sought by every noble mind. Following her untimely death in 1290, Dante, overcome with grief, celebrated her grace and virtue in *La vita nuova* (1292–94), a small "book of memory" written in verse and prose. He then sought renewal in an extensive study of theology and philosophy.

In 1295 Dante entered public life and within a few years emerged as a prominent figure in Florentine politics. By then he had entered into an arranged marriage with Gemma Donati, a gentlewoman with whom he had several children. In the summer of 1300 Dante was named one of the six governing magistrates of Florence. During this time he was involved in the clash between two hostile factions of the Guelph party, the Whites and the Blacks. Aligning himself with the White Guelphs, Dante campaigned to preserve the independence of Florence and repeatedly opposed the machinations of Pope Boniface VIII, who was attempting to place all of Tuscany under papal control. In 1301, however, the Black Guelphs seized power, and Dante was banished at once on trumped-up charges of graft, embezzlement, and other transgressions. Later sentenced to death by fire if he returned to Florence, Dante never entered his native city again.

Dante's remaining years were spent with a series of patrons in various courts of Italy. Two uncompleted works date from his early period of exile. *De vulgari eloquentia* (1303–4), a scholarly tract in Latin on the eloquence of the Italian vernacular, is generally acknowledged to be the key to Dante's artistic inquiries. *Il convivio* (1304–7), a glorification of moral philosophy, is viewed as the cornerstone of his investigations into knowledge and wisdom. Perhaps as early as 1306, Dante began to compose the *Divine Comedy,* the greatest poem of the Middle Ages and the first masterpiece of world literature written in a modern European language. The Latin treatise *De monarchia* (1312–13), a practical guide calling for the restoration of peace in Europe under a secular ruler in Rome, is a statement of the poet's political theories. In his final years Dante was given asylum in Ravenna, where he completed the *Divine Comedy* shortly before his death in September 1321.

CONTENTS

PREFACE

Matthew Pearl

For most of his life, Henry Wadsworth Longfellow avoided the *Inferno*. As a professor of modern languages at Harvard, Longfellow must have been doubly aggrieved when administrators discharged the department's Italian instructor, Pietro Bachi—not only because the dismissal represented another casualty in the university's long-standing assault on the department, but also because it had been Bachi who relieved Longfellow of the task of teaching *Inferno* ("with all its horrors," said Longfellow). This had freed his lecture hours for *Purgatorio* and *Paradiso*, the other canticles of Dante Alighieri's *Divine Comedy*. So it was with a sense of relief that Longfellow reported in his journal in May 1847, the term after Bachi's departure: "Finished the *Inferno* with my class; and am not sorry."

It was maddening to be invested in the field of modern languages in the middle of the nineteenth century. Longfellow, sharing a contemporary's assessment that Americans were still colonists in culture, delighted in strolling along the crowded wharves and hearing the sailors converse in their native tongues. But the specter of Harvard faculty members spreading the "low" languages of foreigners intensified an already stubborn preference among administrators for the study of ancient languages. This tension, highly charged by divergent ideas of America's intellectual future, generated some memorable positions, such as a Harvard committee's conclusion that the simplistic grammatical structures and base literature of modern languages would irreparably harm a student's capacity for disciplined learning.

Italian was among the more suspect "living" languages. In an age of comfortable anti-Catholicism, Unitarian Boston Brahmins balked at Papist loyalties and incense-scented "superstitions" reported to be propagated in cathedrals. No doubt poor Pietro Bachi's status as an Italian immigrant lent more momentum to his removal than did his officially cited impropriety: insolvency (hardly surprising, considering what Harvard paid its foreign-born instructors). With every restriction the Harvard Corporation inflicted on the department of modern languages, new leverage was awarded to the Latin and Greek departments: an extra vote at faculty meetings, a more prestigious classroom on campus, and so on. At other elite universities where reformers managed to offer new languages, administrators similarly insured against a drift of power away from the traditional and established.

So we face an understandable but still quite provocative historical void: the poetry of Dante, who died in exile in 1321, had failed to enter significantly into the American consciousness by the mid-nineteenth century. Hard on the trail of an original "American" literature, the literary trendsetters of Boston and New York had little energy to devote to a medieval poet's mythic-Catholic afterlife. Moreover, ruffled by London's frequent scoffing at the state of American letters, they would have particularly shied away from finding Dante through the mediation of the several available British translations.

In and away from Harvard Yard, Longfellow tested means of assailing what he called this "citadel of Unbelief." In *Voices of the Night*, Longfellow's first collection of poetry, he included three translated selections from *Purgatorio*, though without contextualizing their source. Some extensive background material on Dante was incorporated into his prose work *Drift-Wood*, but the chapters disappeared from later editions, as though fading away from lack of attention. Longfellow proposed a plan to use the Harvard chapel in the summertime to deliver a series of free public lectures on Dante, ambitiously evoking (as one literary historian noted) Boccaccio's unveiling of the *Divine Comedy* to the Florentines in the fourteenth century. But Harvard summarily refused, and the sight of the empty chapel that summer surely reminded Longfellow of the public's continued exclusion from Dante's "medieval miracle of song."

Weary of the severe restraints placed on his professorship, Longfellow resigned in 1854 to dedicate his time to writing poetry. When he would again seek out Dante, the intent would be more personal than vocational; it would come amid groping desperation. On July 9, 1861, his wife, Fanny Longfellow, died when her clothes caught fire from a flake of hot sealing wax. Longfellow smothered the flames with a rug and his own body, but her burns proved fatal. Longfellow's face had been burned too, necessitating the leonine beard that has become the distinguishing feature of his public persona, an image of old-world contentment and quaintness that, colluding with careless readings of his work, has long become its own cast-iron caricature. (Interesting to think that his wife of eighteen years would not have recognized the man we have been so sure we know.) In the aftermath of the accident, Longfellow feared his physical recovery. "Then," he said, "then I shall have to take up the great burden, and I do not know how I shall bear it."

He was distressed at the idea of writing poetry—of writing anything at all. His private journal proved too demanding an outlet of expression, waiting to tear his wounds further. "What is the use of this Record? What I feel and suffer, I cannot record. It would only redouble my sorrows." Here, Longfellow sounds not unlike the infernal shades hesitant to relive their nostalgia and deprivation with their interviewer, Dante.

The *Divine Comedy,* this epical autobiographical pilgrimage from Hell to Heaven, somehow held out a promise to Longfellow. We may never reconstruct the full psychological thrust behind the task, but for the next six years Longfellow was consumed by a translation project he had occasionally begun as a professor. He turned to Dante as though he had no choice in the matter. "I have taken refuge in this translation of the *Divine Comedy,*" he informed a friend. "I have done this work," he told another, "when I could do nothing else."

Longfellow, though famously undemonstrative by nature, did nothing to hide the intense emotional life of his Dante translation from friends or readers. In fact, he composed six sonnets, first published in *The Atlantic Monthly* and then printed on the flyleaves of the translation's three volumes, not on the subject of Dante, but rather "On Translating Dante"—on Longfellow's own process. Thus, channeling an audacious tradition that belonged more to pioneer epic translators of the seventeenth century, the first poetry in Longfellow's Dante comes from the translator. The opening sonnet imagines the act of translating Dante as entering a cathedral (conjuring up the Catholic institutions that so many contemporaries feared), not primarily as a metaphor for the awesome structural design of the *Comedy*, but as an intimate revelation of the translator's need to escape pain, to enact a spiritual release.

> So, as I enter here from day to day,
> And leave my burden at this minster gate,
> Kneeling in prayer, and not ashamed to pray

That biographical events adorn Longfellow's translation of the *Divine Comedy* is only natural to Dante's poem, which dares to make the poet the character in jeopardy. Dante must contend with precarious physical and psychological assaults in Hell, as well as the threat that he will dwell there permanently if he cannot rediscover eternal over material desires, transcendent instead of physical sorrows.

In something of a performance of Dante's first canticle, Longfellow translated the thirty-four cantos of *Inferno* in thirty-four consecutive days, beginning in March 1863. Dante may have written each canto on a single sheet; likewise, Longfellow frames his translation in single units of time. This was the only one of the three canticles of the *Comedy* for which the translator worked in such a distinct, almost devotional pattern. It is worth observing that Longfellow first plotted this passage through *Inferno* on the day that he received terrifying news: his eldest son, Charley, had secretly enlisted in the Union army.

Facing this new potential violence to his family, Longfellow conducted *Inferno* through an agonizing month of outward helplessness. Though he could not protect his son on distant battlefields, he could confront and co-opt lyrically organized contours of suffering and hope by inhabiting Dante's voice. "I do not grow at all weary of my work. On the contrary, the great undulations of Dante's verse lift me and bear me onward in spite of myself," Longfellow writes on the day set aside for *Inferno* 23 (where Virgil, compared by Dante to "a mother who by noise is wakened," seizes the pilgrim Dante in his arms, carrying him away from a pursuing regiment of cruel demons). As

Longfellow translated Dante, Dante's poem translated unspeakable emotions into representational form for Longfellow, even to the point of granting new ritual incantation, a literary "paternoster" (a type of comfort mentioned in his translation's opening sonnet). Three times over a five-year period, Longfellow copied out the same Italian lines from *Inferno* on May 10, the anniversary of his marriage proposal to Fanny: "Nessun maggior dolore / che ricordarsi del tempo felice / nella miseria" ("There is no greater sorrow than to be mindful of the happy time in misery") (5, 121–123).

Longfellow's immersion in Dante provided not only a framework for renewed private expression, but for personal relationships as well. After a period of seclusion from the social world (starting with his physical inability to attend Fanny's funeral), Longfellow gradually accepted the company of a small number of scholars with professional stakes in Dante's poetry. The "Dante Club" gathered every Wednesday at Longfellow's house to read and critique a canto or two of the host's translation before supper. These friends recognized well enough the profound process Longfellow had discovered in Dante; Charles Eliot Norton called the endeavor Longfellow's "restorative labor." That the Dante Club collaborated to commemorate the six-hundredth anniversary of Dante's birth and also held a translation session for Longfellow's sixtieth birthday helps elucidate the dual project at hand: a rebirth of sorts for two poets.

The first American translation of the *Divine Comedy*, invigorated by the anticipation of a new Longfellow work and by publisher J. T. Fields's masterful fanfare, became the literary event of 1867, with four printings in its first year of publication.

Later critics downplayed the gripping emotional partnership between poet and translator, suggesting that the work was perfunctory and bookish, one of countless enterprises exemplifying Longfellow's "wise economy of time." To have acknowledged the complete experience at work would have unsettled the image of a cold-blooded Longfellow formulated as early as 1856, when one British writer arrogantly added to a profile of Longfellow's placidness, "there is no hell in his future." As the cultural emphasis on an author's individuality grew, there was also some principled backlash against the collegial involvement that had helped complete the translation. Other commentators blamed the members of the Dante Club for not sufficiently championing Longfellow's version in subsequent decades when alternatives appeared.

In truth, if Longfellow's supporters showed any hesitancy, it may have revealed a need to come to terms for themselves with Dante's raw power and hard depictions of justice. Indeed, in a letter to Harriet Beecher Stowe shortly after the publication of Longfellow's work, Dr. Oliver Wendell Holmes felt it necessary in speaking of his Dante Club participation to stress (probably inaccurately) how few sessions he had attended for *Inferno,* which he nervously described in terms of "the hideousness, the savagery, of that medieval nightmare!" Longfellow would have understood this recoil; he had once explained his impulse to retreat from *Inferno* by noting, "I know of no book so fearfully expressive of human passions as this." At a time when the nation sought ascension from its own fearful abyss, Longfellow's translation boldly met Dante's demand for a rehabilitating self-communion, and opened up the same opportunity and challenge to American readers.

INTRODUCTION

Lino Pertile

On May 22, 1838, concluding an unpublished lecture on the *Divine Comedy,* Henry Wadsworth Longfellow wrote:

> All great poets, too, must be read in their native tongue. It is almost mockery, —cruel mockery to translate them. How true is this of Cary's translation of Dante. For the most part it is faithful to the original; and yet gives no better idea of Dante, than some portraits do of the persons they represent, and yet are so faithful—so horribly like!
>
> To understand Dante, then, it is absolutely necessary to understand the Italian Language. This may seem a truism, but it is not. For I mean not only Dante's language, but the language of all Italian literature, as modified by time. That we may not only know, but feel the power of each unusual and quaint epithet, the magic of each old word, even as in the writings of Shakespeare. Thus alone can we perceive and recognize the exceeding beauty of each sweet face and image, which from the printed page "peeps under the eaves of our eyelids."

Twenty-nine years later, in 1867, Longfellow published his complete version of Dante's great poem with the Boston publisher Ticknor and Fields.

Having started with the uncompromising notion that to translate is to betray, Longfellow resorted to turning Dante into his own English when he discovered that his admiration and love for the Italian poet could be assuaged in no other way. In earlier years Longfellow may have translated for utilitarian reasons in the context of his teaching. In the despair of the 1860s translating Dante's poetry became for him a way of keeping himself alive as a poet. I suspect also that Dante's moral strength in the face of his stinging exile may have become a source of energy and courage, a model through which Longfellow could bear his loneliness and temper the rawness of his untimely widowhood.

How true was Longfellow to his own condition that to understand Dante it is absolutely necessary to understand the Italian language? How good was his Italian? If we judge it by the problems he had in placing a simple Italian inscription on the copy of his translation of the *Inferno* he sent to Florence in 1865, his ability to express himself in Italian must have been modest. However, this does not mean that his understanding of the written language was inadequate. Longfellow's translation is on the whole not only correct, but accurate and attentive to the semantic nuances of the original. Indeed, the literalness of his translation shows that he understood Dante's language so well that he felt duty-bound to render into English its extraordinary precision, richness, and variety.

Such punctilious adherence to the original text found a mixed reception when the translation was published. Professor George Ticknor, who preceded Longfellow to the Chair of Romance Languages at Harvard, thought it was done with "extraordinary strictness, and at the same time with grace and fluency": in other words, a beautiful and at the same time faithful translation, a notoriously impossible combination. However, the opinion of some was less favorable. Even William Dean Howells, a member of Longfellow's Dante Club, felt that in some passages Longfellow translated "into the English dictionary rather than the English language."

As one Dublin reviewer perceptively pointed out, the writer of *Evangeline* and *The Song of Hiawatha* would have had little trouble producing an English text more immediately pleasing and accessible to the American reader. If he did not, it was because he was convinced that overtranslating Dante's text would have made a "mockery" of the original. Ultimately, the quality of Longfellow's translation is a function of his appreciation of Dante's distinctive style. But what was the

"Dantesque" for Longfellow? An extract from John Ruskin's *Modern Painters*, with which Longfellow opens his notes to the third canto of *Inferno*, answers this question fully: "Milton's effort, in all that he tells us of his Inferno, is to make it indefinite; Dante's, to make it *definite*." In contrast with Milton's vagueness, Ruskin noted the topographic exactness of Dante's Inferno, the accuracy of both the huge overall structure and every detail of it. However, he also emphasized that "vagueness is not the sign of imagination, but of its absence." Reflecting this crucial distinction, Longfellow felt compelled, in order to do justice to the original text, to reproduce Dante's *definite* style, which in the first instance meant translating literally. One example will clarify the significance of this approach.

In *Inferno* 15, in a speech bristling with animal and agricultural metaphors, Brunetto Latini predicts to Dante that the people of Florence will turn against him, and exhorts him to face bravely their hostility; fortune will compensate him with much honor. Dante thanks Brunetto for the warning, and he adds:

> Tanto vogl' io che vi sia manifesto,
> pur che mia cosc̈ïenza non mi garra,
> ch'a la Fortuna, come vuol, son presto.
>   Non è nuova a li orecchi miei tal arra:
> però giri Fortuna la sua rota
> come le piace, e 'l villan la sua marra. (91–96)

The reader should not think that these lines were, or are, likely to be immediately transparent to an ordinary nineteenth- or twentieth-century Italian, for few Italians would know the meaning of the three rhyming words *garra, arra, marra*. *Garra* (for *garrisca*) is a subjunctive from *garrire*, which properly describes the squeaking of animals, especially birds, and therefore means "to chirp," "to twitter"; Dante uses it figuratively in the sense of *sgridare*, i.e., "scolding," "chiding": thus line 92 means "so long as my conscience does not scold me." *Arra* is the same as *caparra*, i.e., an "advance" or a "down payment" given to a seller to bind a bargain, technically an "earnest" (a word that derives from the Latin *arra*) but in this case, again figuratively, a prediction. Finally, *marra* is a wide and short hoe used in agriculture to loosen the soil. It is clear that what drives Dante's lexical selection, within the constraints of his rhyming scheme, is his desire to respond not only to Brunetto's meanings, but also to Brunetto's animal and rustic imagery. Thus Dante the character is shown to be no less able a speaker than his old teacher Brunetto. This ability to extend metaphors across entire passages and episodes is the foundation of both Dante's rich imagery and his *definite* language: to it we owe our impression of a language full of things rather than words.

Now, how should a translator deal with this kind of rich and definite language? A literal translation of the words requires the reader to make an effort not to miss the sense of Dante's discourse, but a freer rendering of the thoughts behind the words, while producing an immediately accessible text, misses the subtlety and power of Dante's imagery as well as its thematic and contextual referentiality. Faced with this dilemma, Longfellow chooses a literal translation not as a way of abdicating his own role as a poet, but rather as the only way of preserving in the English text something of the original energy and concreteness of the Italian:

> This much will I have manifest to you;
> Provided that my conscience do not chide me,
> For whatsoever Fortune I am ready.
>   Such hansel is not new unto mine ears;
> Therefore let Fortune turn her wheel around
> As it may please her, and the churl his mattock.

Compare this to Henry Francis Cary's 1814 translation:

> This only would I have thee clearly note:
> That, so my conscience have no plea against me,
> Do Fortune as she list, I stand prepared.
> Not new or strange such earnest to mine ear.
> Speed Fortune then her wheel, as likes her best;
> The clown his mattock; all things have their course.

Cary's search for some kind of classical rotundity ends up by adding half a line ("all things have their course") that not only mars the crispness of Dante's discourse but actually blurs its contextual meaning. If, on the other hand, Longfellow seems to translate "into the

English dictionary rather than the English language," as Howells put it, it is precisely because Dante himself does it, for not only does Dante write into, but he actually invents, the Italian dictionary.

———

Longfellow's "Notes" illustrate the quality of his attention to Dante's text. Like many lovers of Dante before and after him, Longfellow found commentators' pedantry rather tiresome. When Charon appears on the scene of *Inferno* 3, Longfellow remarks that Dante's mingling of pagan and Christian elements had caused much consternation, especially among Italian critics of the nineteenth century. Then, epitomizing his attitude toward such critics, he adds scathingly: "While the great Comedy is going on upon the scene above, with all its pomp and music, these critics in the pit keep up such a perpetual wrangling among themselves, as seriously to disturb the performance." And on April 20, 1864, as he began writing his own notes, he wrote:

> I wish somebody would pour a barrel of brandy into the grave of the Commentators, as the old bridegroom in the old Icelandic tale did into the grave of his friend the taper, to moisten the dry bones. I shall not be able to do that; but something like it perhaps. I have already begun to light up these footlights of the great Comedy and am not wholly dissatisfied with the effect. Will the oil hold out? I hope so.

Such protestations are not unusual among commentators of all ages who, nevertheless, caught by the poem's complicated web, regularly end up just as pedantic as any of their predecessors. Not Longfellow—he clearly knows all the major commentators, ancient and modern, but refuses to follow in their footsteps.

Rather than commentators, Longfellow utilizes what we would call firsthand witnesses. Brunetto Latini is one. A great scholar, writer, and teacher from Florence, Brunetto Latini (d. 1294) provides material for Longfellow's notes to canto 1, line 2, and to canto 4, line 118, as parallels respectively to Dante's forest and the meadow of the great spirits. Indeed Longfellow seems to love early narrative texts. In canto 4, line 129, he devotes a long note to the Saladin in which, not satisfied with a quotation from Richard Knolles's *History of the Turks,* he transcribes in full a novella about the Saladin from the *Cento novelle antiche* (now better known as *Il Novellino*), the earliest known collection of novellas written in Italian. Commenting on canto 6, where Dante recalls his meeting with the Florentine Ciacco, Longfellow offers Boccaccio's novella about the same Ciacco, *Decameron* IX, 8. When Cavalcante Cavalcanti mentions his son Guido (10, 63), Longfellow assembles a portrait of the latter by transcribing *Decameron* VI, 9, quoting an anecdote about him from Henry Edward Napier's *Florentine History*, and summarizing Sacchetti's novella 68. Indeed, his preferred sources for factual or historical information are not historians and chroniclers, but storytellers. Thus, his account of the origins of the White and Black factions among the Florentine Guelphs (10, 51) is taken from *Il Pecorone* (XIII, 1), a fourteenth-century collection of novellas by Ser Giovanni Fiorentino.

However, this interest in extended narratives does not mean that Longfellow neglects semantic details. In the first note to canto 2, he quotes at length Ruskin (*Modern Painters*) on Dante's use of the word *brown* (*bruno*). Similarly, the longest note to canto 4 is devoted to the word *enamel* (*smalto*, line 118): it includes a striking observation by Ruskin regarding the hardened, silent, and lifeless quality of Limbo's green enamel grass.

Another vivid and distinguishing feature of Longfellow's notes is his attention to the geographical contexts in which the events mentioned by Dante took place. To re-create this special sense of place, he quotes abundantly from travelers' descriptions and accounts. Thus we approach Francesca's Ravenna guided by the words of Jean-Jacques Ampère's *Voyage dantesque* (5, 97); we see the wood of the suicides through the description of "the fatal Maremma" given in Joseph Forsyth's *Italy* (13, 9); and we reach Venice and her famous Arsenal through George Stillman Hillard's *Six Months in Italy* (21, 7). Occasionally, a note discloses an inner landscape, too, as when Longfellow romantically glosses Dante's "heart's lake" (1, 20) as "The deep mountain tarn of his heart, dark with his own depth, and the shadows hanging over it."

However, what truly make his annotations the inspired work of a poet are Longfellow's references to Greek (especially Homer), Latin (Virgil, Ovid, Lucan, Statius, and others), and English poetry (from Chaucer and Gower to Shakespeare, Milton, Shelley, and Tennyson). Longfellow's modern quotations include not only such famous rewritings as Tennyson's "Ulysses," Chaucer's "Hugelin," and Milton's

Satan, but they also suggest subtler connections. The reading of Dante evokes other poetry: poets talk to one another crossing the ages in both directions. Thus the description of Beatrice (2, 56) evokes *King Lear,* act 5, scene 3 ("Her voice was ever soft, / Gentle, and low; an excellent thing in woman"), and Dante's "piaggia" (6, 69) suggests *King Henry VI,* Part III, act 1, scene 1 ("whose haughty spirit, winged with desire, / Will coast my crown"). Out of Dante's mention of the centaur Nessus (12, 68) springs, instead of an erudite note, an extract from *The Monkes Tale* (129–136) that tells how Nessus avenged himself of Hercules; and out of Chiron (12, 71), come a line from the *Iliad* (XI, 832) and a long quotation from *The Tanglewood Tales* of Hawthorne, once Longfellow's college classmate, who lends the fable of Chiron "a humorous turn." Thus Longfellow lights up the footlights of the great Comedy, and the oil holds out through the end.

Traditionally, the notes to Dante's *Divine Comedy,* often much longer and much harder to digest than the poem itself, are a formidable stumbling block for readers new and experienced alike—the safest sleeping potion for generations of Italian high school students. On the contrary, Longfellow's notes are never pedantic. They form an original and personal commentary that tells us a great deal about Longfellow himself, and not only as a reader of Dante. On the surface, their energy and creativity may seem to contradict the literal submissiveness of the translation. But in fact Longfellow's notes underscore the creative nature of the translator's enterprise, for, as he reaches down to the roots of Dante's meanings, Longfellow finds himself again in touch with the very sources of his own poetry. The result is a unique book in which two great poets, one from fourteenth-century Tuscany, the other from nineteenth-century America, speak to us today with a single strong and moving voice.

———

Lino Pertile is a professor of Romance languages and literature, and Master of Eliot House, at Harvard University. A graduate of the University of Padua, where he studied classics and French, he has taught Italian literature in France, Italy, and the United Kingdom. Professor Pertile has published extensively on Dante. His books include the critical edition of the sixteenth-century commentary on Dante *Annotationi nel Dante fatte con M. Triphon Gabriele* and *La puttana e il gigante: dal Cantico dei Cantici al Paradiso terrestre di Dante.* Other recent books he has coedited and contributed to include *The New Italian Novel, The Cambridge History of Italian Literature,* and *In amicizia: Essays in Honour of Giulio Lepschy.* The completion of his two current projects, both on Dante, is being considerably delayed by his love affairs with Eliot House and the Charles River.

A NOTE ON THE TEXT

Ticknor and Fields first published Longfellow's translation of Dante's *Inferno* on April 13, 1867 (followed separately by *Purgatorio* and *Paradiso*). The volume contained four main sections: Longfellow's sonnets; the thirty-four cantos of *Inferno;* Longfellow's "Notes" covering each of those cantos; and finally his "Illustrations," selected excerpts and essays related to Dante's poem. This edition reproduces the 1867 version of the translation, thus presenting *Inferno* as it would have been seen by readers of the first complete American translation. The "Notes" and "Illustrations" incorporate later additions and alterations found in subsequent editions published during Longfellow's lifetime.

The "Notes" also include eighteen additions that Longfellow expressed a desire to include before his death in 1882. His onetime student Charles Eliot Norton, a Dante scholar and translator, integrated most of these notes into an 1886 edition, but in doing so changed some wording and abridged Longfellow's presentation. The Modern Library edition restores these later notes in full for the first time, conforming as closely as possible to the original notes in the Longfellow papers of Houghton Library, Harvard University (MS Am 1340 [109]); sources used in the writing of the Preface and Introduction included Longfellow's lectures on Dante, which can be found at Houghton MS Am 1340 (106), and Longfellow's original journals from 1860–1869 at MS Am 1340 (209 and 210).

I follow here the footing of thy feete
That with thy meaning so I may the rather meete

Oft have I seen at some cathedral door
    A laborer, pausing in the dust and heat,
    Lay down his burden, and with reverent feet
    Enter, and cross himself, and on the floor
Kneel to repeat his paternoster o'er;
    Far off the noises of the world retreat;
    The loud vociferations of the street
    Become an undistinguishable roar.
So, as I enter here from day to day,
    And leave my burden at this minster gate,
    Kneeling in prayer, and not ashamed to pray,
The tumult of the time disconsolate
    To inarticulate murmurs dies away,
    While the eternal ages watch and wait.

How strange the sculptures that adorn these towers!
  This crowd of statues, in whose folded sleeves
  Birds build their nests; while canopied with leaves
  Parvis and portal bloom like trellised bowers,
And the vast minster seems a cross of flowers!
  But fiends and dragons on the gargoyled eaves
  Watch the dead Christ between the living thieves,
  And, underneath, the traitor Judas lowers!
Ah! from what agonies of heart and brain,
  What exultations trampling on despair,
  What tenderness, what tears, what hate of wrong,
What passionate outcry of a soul in pain,
  Uprose this poem of the earth and air,
  This mediæval miracle of song!

INFERNO

Canto I

Midway upon the journey of our life
    I found myself within a forest dark,
    For the straightforward pathway had been lost.
Ah me! how hard a thing it is to say
    What was this forest savage, rough, and stern,   5
    Which in the very thought renews the fear.
So bitter is it, death is little more;
    But of the good to treat, which there I found,
    Speak will I of the other things I saw there.
I cannot well repeat how there I entered,   10
    So full was I of slumber at the moment
    In which I had abandoned the true way.
But after I had reached a mountain's foot,
    At that point where the valley terminated,
    Which had with consternation pierced my heart,   15
Upward I looked, and I beheld its shoulders,
    Vested already with that planet's rays
    Which leadeth others right by every road.
Then was the fear a little quieted
    That in my heart's lake had endured throughout   20
    The night, which I had passed so piteously.

And even as he, who, with distressful breath,
    Forth issued from the sea upon the shore,
    Turns to the water perilous and gazes;
So did my soul, that still was fleeing onward,   25
    Turn itself back to re-behold the pass
    Which never yet a living person left.
After my weary body I had rested,
    The way resumed I on the desert slope,
    So that the firm foot ever was the lower.   30
And lo! almost where the ascent began,
    A panther light and swift exceedingly,
    Which with a spotted skin was covered o'er!
And never moved she from before my face,
    Nay, rather did impede so much my way,   35
    That many times I to return had turned.
The time was the beginning of the morning,
    And up the sun was mounting with those stars
    That with him were, what time the Love Divine
At first in motion set those beauteous things;   40
    So were to me occasion of good hope,
    The variegated skin of that wild beast,
The hour of time, and the delicious season;
    But not so much, that did not give me fear
    A lion's aspect which appeared to me.   45
He seemed as if against me he were coming
    With head uplifted, and with ravenous hunger,
    So that it seemed the air was afraid of him;
And a she-wolf, that with all hungerings
    Seemed to be laden in her meagreness,   50
    And many folk has caused to live forlorn!
She brought upon me so much heaviness,
    With the affright that from her aspect came,
    That I the hope relinquished of the height.
And as he is who willingly acquires,   55
    And the time comes that causes him to lose,
    Who weeps in all his thoughts and is despondent,

E'en such made me that beast withouten peace,
  Which, coming on against me by degrees,
  Thrust me back thither where the sun is silent.   60
While I was rushing downward to the lowland,
  Before mine eyes did one present himself,
  Who seemed from long-continued silence hoarse.
When I beheld him in the desert vast,
  "Have pity on me," unto him I cried,   65
  "Whiche'er thou art, or shade or real man!"
He answered me: "Not man; man once I was,
  And both my parents were of Lombardy,
  And Mantuans by country both of them.
Sub Julio was I born, though it was late,   70
  And lived at Rome under the good Augustus,
  During the time of false and lying gods.
A Poet was I, and I sang that just
  Son of Anchises, who came forth from Troy,
  After that Ilion the superb was burned.   75
But thou, why goest thou back to such annoyance?
  Why climb'st thou not the Mount Delectable,
  Which is the source and cause of every joy?"
"Now, art thou that Virgilius and that fountain
  Which spreads abroad so wide a river of speech?"   80
  I made response to him with bashful forehead.
"O, of the other poets honor and light,
  Avail me the long study and great love
  That have impelled me to explore thy volume!
Thou art my master, and my author thou,   85
  Thou art alone the one from whom I took
  The beautiful style that has done honor to me.
Behold the beast, for which I have turned back;
  Do thou protect me from her, famous Sage,
  For she doth make my veins and pulses tremble."   90
"Thee it behoves to take another road,"
  Responded he, when he beheld me weeping,
  "If from this savage place thou wouldst escape;

Because this beast, at which thou criest out,
    Suffers not any one to pass her way,   95
    But so doth harass him, that she destroys him;
And has a nature so malign and ruthless,
    That never doth she glut her greedy will,
    And after food is hungrier than before.
Many the animals with whom she weds,   100
    And more they shall be still, until the Greyhound
    Comes, who shall make her perish in her pain.
He shall not feed on either earth or pelf,
    But upon wisdom, and on love and virtue;
    'Twixt Feltro and Feltro shall his nation be;   105
Of that low Italy shall he be the saviour,
    On whose account the maid Camilla died,
    Euryalus, Turnus, Nisus, of their wounds;
Through every city shall he hunt her down,
    Until he shall have driven her back to Hell,   110
    There from whence envy first did let her loose.
Therefore I think and judge it for thy best
    Thou follow me, and I will be thy guide,
    And lead thee hence through the eternal place,
Where thou shalt hear the desperate lamentations,   115
    Shalt see the ancient spirits disconsolate,
    Who cry out each one for the second death;
And thou shalt see those who contented are
    Within the fire, because they hope to come,
    Whene'er it may be, to the blessed people;   120
To whom, then, if thou wishest to ascend,
    A soul shall be for that than I more worthy;
    With her at my departure I will leave thee;
Because that Emperor, who reigns above,
    In that I was rebellious to his law,   125
    Wills that through me none come into his city.
He governs everywhere, and there he reigns;
    There is his city and his lofty throne;
    O happy he whom thereto he elects!"

And I to him: "Poet, I thee entreat,   130
   By that same God whom thou didst never know,
   So that I may escape this woe and worse,
Thou wouldst conduct me there where thou hast said,
   That I may see the portal of Saint Peter,
   And those thou makest so disconsolate."   135
Then he moved on, and I behind him followed.

CANTO II

Day was departing, and the embrowned air
   Released the animals that are on earth
   From their fatigues; and I the only one
Made myself ready to sustain the war,
   Both of the way and likewise of the woe,   5
   Which memory that errs not shall retrace.
O Muses, O high genius, now assist me!
   O memory, that didst write down what I saw,
   Here thy nobility shall be manifest!
And I began: "Poet, who guidest me,   10
   Regard my manhood, if it be sufficient,
   Ere to the arduous pass thou dost confide me.
Thou sayest, that of Silvius the parent,
   While yet corruptible, unto the world
   Immortal went, and was there bodily.   15
But if the adversary of all evil
   Was courteous, thinking of the high effect
   That issue would from him, and who, and what,
To men of intellect unmeet it seems not;
   For he was of great Rome, and of her empire   20
   In the empyreal heaven as father chosen;

The which and what, wishing to speak the truth,
　　Were stablished as the holy place, wherein
　　Sits the successor of the greatest Peter.
Upon this journey, whence thou givest him vaunt,　　　　25
　　Things did he hear, which the occasion were
　　Both of his victory and the papal mantle.
Thither went afterwards the Chosen Vessel,
　　To bring back comfort thence unto that Faith,
　　Which of salvation's way is the beginning.　　　　30
But I, why thither come, or who concedes it?
　　I not Æneas am, I am not Paul,
　　Nor I, nor others, think me worthy of it.
Therefore, if I resign myself to come,
　　I fear the coming may be ill-advised;　　　　35
　　Thou 'rt wise, and knowest better than I speak."
And as he is, who unwills what he willed,
　　And by new thoughts doth his intention change,
　　So that from his design he quite withdraws,
Such I became, upon that dark hillside,　　　　40
　　Because, in thinking, I consumed the emprise,
　　Which was so very prompt in the beginning.
"If I have well thy language understood,"
　　Replied that shade of the Magnanimous,
　　"Thy soul attainted is with cowardice,　　　　45
Which many times a man encumbers so,
　　It turns him back from honored enterprise,
　　As false sight doth a beast, when he is shy.
That thou mayst free thee from this apprehension,
　　I'll tell thee why I came, and what I heard　　　　50
　　At the first moment when I grieved for thee.
Among those was I who are in suspense,
　　And a fair, saintly Lady called to me
　　In such wise, I besought her to command me.
Her eyes were shining brighter than the Star;　　　　55
　　And she began to say, gentle and low,
　　With voice angelical, in her own language:

'O spirit courteous of Mantua,
   Of whom the fame still in the world endures,
   And shall endure, long-lasting as the world;   60
A friend of mine, and not the friend of fortune,
   Upon the desert slope is so impeded
   Upon his way, that he has turned through terror,
And may, I fear, already be so lost,
   That I too late have risen to his succor,   65
   From that which I have heard of him in Heaven.
Bestir thee now, and with thy speech ornate,
   And with what needful is for his release,
   Assist him so, that I may be consoled.
Beatrice am I, who do bid thee go;   70
   I come from there, where I would fain return;
   Love moved me, which compelleth me to speak.
When I shall be in presence of my Lord,
   Full often will I praise thee unto him.'
   Then paused she, and thereafter I began: 75
'O Lady of virtue, thou alone through whom
   The human race exceedeth all contained
   Within the heaven that has the lesser circles,
So grateful unto me is thy commandment,
   To obey, if 't were already done, were late;   80
   No farther need'st thou ope to me thy wish.
But the cause tell me why thou dost not shun
   The here descending down into this centre,
   From the vast place thou burnest to return to.'
'Since thou wouldst fain so inwardly discern,   85
   Briefly will I relate,' she answered me,
   'Why I am not afraid to enter here.
Of those things only should one be afraid
   Which have the power of doing others harm;
   Of the rest, no; because they are not fearful.   90
God in his mercy such created me
   That misery of yours attains me not,
   Nor any flame assails me of this burning.

A gentle Lady is in Heaven, who grieves
 At this impediment, to which I send thee,   95
 So that stern judgment there above is broken.
In her entreaty she besought Lucìa,
 And said, "Thy faithful one now stands in need
 Of thee, and unto thee I recommend him."
Lucìa, foe of all that cruel is,   100
 Hastened away, and came unto the place
 Where I was sitting with the ancient Rachel.
"Beatrice," said she, "the true praise of God,
 Why succorest thou not him, who loved thee so,
 For thee he issued from the vulgar herd?   105
Dost thou not hear the pity of his plaint?
 Dost thou not see the death that combats him
 Beside that flood, where ocean has no vaunt?"
Never were persons in the world so swift
 To work their weal and to escape their woe,   110
 As I, after such words as these were uttered,
Came hither downward from my blessed seat,
 Confiding in thy dignified discourse,
 Which honors thee, and those who've listened to it.'
After she thus had spoken unto me,   115
 Weeping, her shining eyes she turned away;
 Whereby she made me swifter in my coming;
And unto thee I came, as she desired;
 I have delivered thee from that wild beast,
 Which barred the beautiful mountain's short ascent. 120
What is it, then? Why, why dost thou delay?
 Why is such baseness bedded in thy heart?
 Daring and hardihood why hast thou not,
Seeing that three such Ladies benedight
 Are caring for thee in the court of Heaven,   125
 And so much good my speech doth promise thee?"
Even as the flowerets, by nocturnal chill,
 Bowed down and closed, when the sun whitens them,
 Uplift themselves all open on their stems;

Such I became with my exhausted strength, 130
  And such good courage to my heart there coursed,
  That I began, like an intrepid person:
"O she compassionate, who succored me,
  And courteous thou, who hast obeyed so soon
  The words of truth which she addressed to thee! 135
Thou hast my heart so with desire disposed
  To the adventure, with these words of thine,
  That to my first intent I have returned.
Now go, for one sole will is in us both,
  Thou Leader, and thou Lord, and Master thou." 140
  Thus said I to him; and when he had moved,
I entered on the deep and savage way.

Canto III

"Through me the way is to the city dolent;
    Through me the way is to eternal dole;
    Through me the way among the people lost.
Justice incited my sublime Creator;
    Created me divine Omnipotence,   5
    The highest Wisdom and the primal Love.
Before me there were no created things,
    Only eterne, and I eternal last.
    All hope abandon, ye who enter in!"
These words in sombre color I beheld   10
    Written upon the summit of a gate;
    Whence I: "Their sense is, Master, hard to me!"
And he to me, as one experienced:
    "Here all suspicion needs must be abandoned,
    All cowardice must needs be here extinct.   15
We to the place have come, where I have told thee
    Thou shalt behold the people dolorous
    Who have foregone the good of intellect."
And after he had laid his hand on mine
    With joyful mien, whence I was comforted,   20
    He led me in among the secret things.

There sighs, complaints, and ululations loud
 Resounded through the air without a star,
 Whence I, at the beginning, wept thereat.
Languages diverse, horrible dialects,   25
 Accents of anger, words of agony,
 And voices high and hoarse, with sound of hands,
Made up a tumult that goes whirling on
 Forever in that air forever black,
 Even as the sand doth, when the whirlwind breathes.   30
And I, who had my head with horror bound,
 Said: "Master, what is this which now I hear?
 What folk is this, which seems by pain so vanquished?"
And he to me: "This miserable mode
 Maintain the melancholy souls of those   35
 Who lived withouten infamy or praise.
Commingled are they with that caitiff choir
 Of Angels, who have not rebellious been,
 Nor faithful were to God, but were for self.
The heavens expelled them, not to be less fair;   40
 Nor them the nethermore abyss receives,
 For glory none the damned would have from them."
And I: "O Master, what so grievous is
 To these, that maketh them lament so sore?"
 He answered: "I will tell thee very briefly.   45
These have no longer any hope of death;
 And this blind life of theirs is so debased,
 They envious are of every other fate.
No fame of them the world permits to be;
 Misericord and Justice both disdain them.   50
 Let us not speak of them, but look, and pass."
And I, who looked again, beheld a banner,
 Which, whirling round, ran on so rapidly,
 That of all pause it seemed to me indignant;
And after it there came so long a train   55
 Of people, that I ne'er would have believed
 That ever Death so many had undone.

When some among them I had recognized,
    I looked, and I beheld the shade of him
    Who made through cowardice the great refusal. 60
Forthwith I comprehended, and was certain,
    That this the sect was of the caitiff wretches
    Hateful to God and to his enemies.
These miscreants, who never were alive,
    Were naked, and were stung exceedingly 65
    By gadflies and by hornets that were there.
These did their faces irrigate with blood,
    Which, with their tears commingled, at their feet
    By the disgusting worms was gathered up.
And when to gazing farther I betook me,
    People I saw on a great river's bank; 70
    Whence said I: "Master, now vouchsafe to me,
That I may know who these are, and what law
    Makes them appear so ready to pass over,
    As I discern athwart the dusky light." 75
And he to me: "These things shall all be known
    To thee, as soon as we our footsteps stay
    Upon the dismal shore of Acheron."
Then with mine eyes ashamed and downward cast,
    Fearing my words might irksome be to him, 80
    From speech refrained I till we reached the river.
And lo! towards us coming in a boat
    An old man, hoary with the hair of eld,
    Crying: "Woe unto you, ye souls depraved!
Hope nevermore to look upon the heavens; 85
    I come to lead you to the other shore,
    To the eternal shades in heat and frost.
And thou, that yonder standest, living soul,
    Withdraw thee from these people, who are dead!"
    But when he saw that I did not withdraw, 90
He said: "By other ways, by other ports
    Thou to the shore shalt come, not here, for passage;
    A lighter vessel needs must carry thee."

And unto him the Guide: "Vex thee not, Charon;
    It is so willed there where is power to do   95
    That which is willed; and farther question not."
Thereat were quieted the fleecy cheeks
    Of him the ferryman of the livid fen,
    Who round about his eyes had wheels of flame.
But all those souls who weary were and naked   100
    Their color changed and gnashed their teeth together,
    As soon as they had heard those cruel words.
God they blasphemed and their progenitors,
    The human race, the place, the time, the seed
    Of their engendering and of their birth!   105
Thereafter all together they drew back,
    Bitterly weeping, to the accursed shore,
    Which waiteth every man who fears not God.
Charon the demon, with the eyes of glede,
    Beckoning to them, collects them all together,   110
    Beats with his oar whoever lags behind.
As in the autumn-time the leaves fall off,
    First one and then another, till the branch
    Unto the earth surrenders all its spoils;
In similar wise the evil seed of Adam   115
    Throw themselves from that margin one by one,
    At signals, as a bird unto its lure.
So they depart across the dusky wave,
    And ere upon the other side they land,
    Again on this side a new troop assembles.   120
"My son," the courteous Master said to me,
    "All those who perish in the wrath of God
    Here meet together out of every land;
And ready are they to pass o'er the river,
    Because celestial Justice spurs them on,   125
    So that their fear is turned into desire.
This way there never passes a good soul;
    And hence if Charon doth complain of thee,
    Well mayst thou know now what his speech imports."

This being finished, all the dusk champaign   130
   Trembled so violently, that of that terror
   The recollection bathes me still with sweat.
The land of tears gave forth a blast of wind,
   And fulminated a vermilion light,
   Which overmastered in me every sense,   135
And as a man whom sleep hath seized I fell.

CANTO IV

Broke the deep lethargy within my head
    A heavy thunder, so that I upstarted,
    Like to a person who by force is wakened;
And round about I moved my rested eyes,
    Uprisen erect, and steadfastly I gazed,   5
    To recognize the place wherein I was.
True is it, that upon the verge I found me
    Of the abysmal valley dolorous,
    That gathers thunder of infinite ululations.
Obscure, profound it was, and nebulous,   10
    So that by fixing on its depths my sight
    Nothing whatever I discerned therein.
"Let us descend now into the blind world,"
    Began the Poet, pallid utterly;
    "I will be first, and thou shalt second be."   15
And I, who of his color was aware,
    Said: "How shall I come, if thou art afraid,
    Who 'rt wont to be a comfort to my fears?"
And he to me: "The anguish of the people
    Who are below here in my face depicts   20
    That pity which for terror thou hast taken.

Let us go on, for the long way impels us."
    Thus he went in, and thus he made me enter
    The foremost circle that surrounds the abyss.
There, in so far as I had power to hear,   25
    Were lamentations none, but only sighs,
    That tremulous made the everlasting air.
And this arose from sorrow without torment,
    Which the crowds had, that many were and great,
    Of infants and of women and of men.   30
To me the Master good: "Thou dost not ask
    What spirits these, which thou beholdest, are?
    Now will I have thee know, ere thou go farther,
That they sinned not; and if they merit had,
    'T is not enough, because they had not baptism,   35
    Which is the portal of the Faith thou holdest;
And if they were before Christianity,
    In the right manner they adored not God;
    And among such as these am I myself.
For such defects, and not for other guilt,   40
    Lost are we, and are only so far punished,
    That without hope we live on in desire."
Great grief seized on my heart when this I heard,
    Because some people of much worthiness
    I knew, who in that Limbo were suspended.   45
"Tell me, my Master, tell me, thou my Lord,"
    Began I, with desire of being certain
    Of that Faith which o'ercometh every error,
"Came any one by his own merit hence,
    Or by another's, who was blessed thereafter?"   50
    And he, who understood my covert speech,
Replied: "I was a novice in this state,
    When I saw hither come a Mighty One,
    With sign of victory incoronate.
Hence he drew forth the shade of the First Parent,   55
    And that of his son Abel, and of Noah,
    Of Moses the lawgiver, and the obedient

Abraham, patriarch, and David, king,
    Israel with his father and his children,
    And Rachel, for whose sake he did so much,   60
And others many, and he made them blessed;
    And thou must know, that earlier than these
    Never were any human spirits saved."
We ceased not to advance because he spake,
    But still were passing onward through the forest,   65
    The forest, say I, of thick-crowded ghosts.
Not very far as yet our way had gone
    This side the summit, when I saw a fire
    That overcame a hemisphere of darkness.
We were a little distant from it still,   70
    But not so far that I in part discerned not
    That honorable people held that place.
"O thou who honorest every art and science,
    Who may these be, which such great honor have,
    That from the fashion of the rest it parts them?"   75
And he to me: "The honorable name,
    That sounds of them above there in thy life,
    Wins grace in Heaven, that so advances them."
In the mean time a voice was heard by me:
    "All honor be to the pre-eminent Poet;   80
    His shade returns again, that was departed."
After the voice had ceased and quiet was,
    Four mighty shades I saw approaching us;
    Semblance had they nor sorrowful nor glad.
To say to me began my gracious Master: 85
    "Him with that falchion in his hand behold,
    Who comes before the three, even as their lord.
That one is Homer, Poet sovereign;
    He who comes next is Horace, the satirist;
    The third is Ovid, and the last is Lucan.   90
Because to each of these with me applies
    The name that solitary voice proclaimed,
    They do me honor, and in that do well."

Thus I beheld assemble the fair school
    Of that lord of the song pre-eminent,   95
    Who o'er the others like an eagle soars.
When they together had discoursed somewhat,
    They turned to me with signs of salutation,
    And on beholding this, my Master smiled;
And more of honor still, much more, they did me,   100
    In that they made me one of their own band;
    So that the sixth was I, 'mid so much wit.
Thus we went on as far as to the light,
    Things saying 't is becoming to keep silent,
    As was the saying of them where I was.   105
We came unto a noble castle's foot,
    Seven times encompassëd with lofty walls,
    Defended round by a fair rivulet;
This we passed over even as firm ground;
    Through portals seven I entered with these Sages;   110
    We came into a meadow of fresh verdure.
People were there with solemn eyes and slow,
    Of great authority in their countenance;
    They spake but seldom, and with gentle voices.
Thus we withdrew ourselves upon one side   115
    Into an opening luminous and lofty,
    So that they all of them were visible.
There opposite, upon the green enamel,
    Were pointed out to me the mighty spirits,
    Whom to have seen I feel myself exalted.   120
I saw Electra with companions many,
    'Mongst whom I knew both Hector and Æneas,
    Cæsar in armor with gerfalcon eyes;
I saw Camilla and Penthesilea
    On the other side, and saw the King Latinus,   125
    Who with Lavinia his daughter sat;
I saw that Brutus who drove Tarquin forth,
    Lucretia, Julia, Marcia, and Cornelia,
    And saw alone, apart, the Saladin.

When I had lifted up my brows a little,   130
   The Master I beheld of those who know,
   Sit with his philosophic family.
All gaze upon him, and all do him honor.
   There I beheld both Socrates and Plato,
   Who nearer him before the others stand;   135
Democritus, who puts the world on chance,
   Diogenes, Anaxagoras, and Thales,
   Zeno, Empedocles, and Heraclitus;
Of qualities I saw the good collector,
   Hight Dioscorides; and Orpheus saw I,   140
   Tully and Livy, and moral Seneca,
Euclid, geometrician, and Ptolemy,
   Galen, Hippocrates, and Avicenna,
   Averroes, who the great Comment made.
I cannot all of them portray in full,   145
   Because so drives me onward the long theme,
   That many times the word comes short of fact.
The sixfold company in two divides;
   Another way my sapient Guide conducts me
   Forth from the quiet to the air that trembles;   150
And to a place I come where nothing shines.

CANTO V

Thus I descended out of the first circle
    Down to the second, that less space begirds,
    And so much greater dole, that goads to wailing.
There standeth Minos horribly, and snarls;
    Examines the transgressions at the entrance;   5
    Judges, and sends according as he girds him.
I say, that when the spirit evil-born
    Cometh before him, wholly it confesses;
    And this discriminator of transgressions
Seeth what place in Hell is meet for it;   10
    Girds himself with his tail as many times
    As grades he wishes it should be thrust down.
Always before him many of them stand;
    They go by turns each one unto the judgment;
    They speak, and hear, and then are downward hurled.   15
"O thou, that to this dolorous hostelry
    Comest," said Minos to me, when he saw me,
    Leaving the practice of so great an office,
"Look how thou enterest, and in whom thou trustest;
    Let not the portal's amplitude deceive thee."   20
    And unto him my Guide: "Why criest thou too?

Do not impede his journey fate-ordained;
    It is so willed there where is power to do
    That which is willed; and ask no further question."
And now begin the dolesome notes to grow   25
    Audible unto me; now am I come
    There where much lamentation strikes upon me.
I came into a place mute of all light,
    Which bellows as the sea does in a tempest,
    If by opposing winds 't is combated.   30
The infernal hurricane that never rests
    Hurtles the spirits onward in its rapine;
    Whirling them round, and smiting, it molests them.
When they arrive before the precipice,
    There are the shrieks, the plaints, and the laments,   35
    There they blaspheme the puissance divine.
I understood that unto such a torment
    The carnal malefactors were condemned,
    Who reason subjugate to appetite.
And as the wings of starlings bear them on   40
    In the cold season in large band and full,
    So doth that blast the spirits maledict;
It hither, thither, downward, upward, drives them;
    No hope doth comfort them forevermore,
    Not of repose, but even of lesser pain.   45
And as the cranes go chanting forth their lays,
    Making in air a long line of themselves,
    So saw I coming, uttering lamentations,
Shadows borne onward by the aforesaid stress.
    Whereupon said I: "Master, who are those   50
    People, whom the black air so castigates?"
"The first of those, of whom intelligence
    Thou fain wouldst have," then said he unto me,
    "The empress was of many languages.
To sensual vices she was so abandoned,   55
    That lustful she made licit in her law,
    To remove the blame to which she had been led.

She is Semiramis, of whom we read
    That she succeeded Ninus, and was his spouse;
    She held the land which now the Sultan rules.   60
The next is she who killed herself for love,
    And broke faith with the ashes of Sichæus;
    Then Cleopatra the voluptuous."
Helen I saw, for whom so many ruthless
    Seasons revolved; and saw the great Achilles,   65
    Who at the last hour combated with Love.
Paris I saw, Tristan; and more than a thousand
    Shades did he name and point out with his finger,
    Whom Love had separated from our life.
After that I had listened to my Teacher,   70
    Naming the dames of eld and cavaliers,
    Pity prevailed, and I was nigh bewildered.
And I began: "O Poet, willingly
    Speak would I to those two, who go together,
    And seem upon the wind to be so light."   75
And he to me: "Thou 'lt mark, when they shall be
    Nearer to us; and then do thou implore them
    By love which leadeth them, and they will come."
Soon as the wind in our direction sways them,
    My voice uplift I: "O ye weary souls!   80
    Come speak to us, if no one interdicts it."
As turtle-doves, called onward by desire,
    With open and steady wings to the sweet nest
    Fly through the air by their volition borne,
So came they from the band where Dido is,   85
    Approaching us athwart the air malign,
    So strong was the affectionate appeal.
"O living creature gracious and benignant,
    Who visiting goest through the purple air
    Us, who have stained the world incarnadine,   90
If were the King of the Universe our friend,
    We would pray unto him to give thee peace,
    Since thou hast pity on our woe perverse.

Of what it pleases thee to hear or speak,
   That will we hear, and we will speak to you,   95
   While silent is the wind, as it is now.
Sitteth the city, wherein I was born,
   Upon the sea-shore where the Po descends
   To rest in peace with all his retinue.
Love, that on gentle heart doth swiftly seize,   100
   Seized this man for the person beautiful
   That was ta'en from me, and still the mode offends me.
Love, that exempts no one beloved from loving,
   Seized me with pleasure of this man so strongly,
   That, as thou seest, it doth not yet desert me;   105
Love has conducted us unto one death;
   Caïna waiteth him who quenched our life!"
   These words were borne along from them to us.
As soon as I had heard those souls tormented,
   I bowed my face, and so long held it down   110
   Until the Poet said to me: "What thinkest?"
When I made answer, I began: "Alas!
   How many pleasant thoughts, how much desire,
   Conducted these unto the dolorous pass!"
Then unto them I turned me, and I spake,   115
   And I began: "Thine agonies, Francesca,
   Sad and compassionate to weeping make me.
But tell me, at the time of those sweet sighs,
   By what and in what manner Love conceded,
   That you should know your dubious desires?"   120
And she to me: "There is no greater sorrow
   Than to be mindful of the happy time
   In misery, and that thy Teacher knows.
But, if to recognize the earliest root
   Of love in us thou hast so great desire,   125
   I will do even as he who weeps and speaks.
One day we reading were for our delight
   Of Launcelot, how Love did him enthrall.
   Alone we were and without any fear.

Full many a time our eyes together drew 130
    That reading, and drove the color from our faces;
    But one point only was it that o'ercame us.
Whenas we read of the much longed-for smile
    Being by such a noble lover kissed,
    This one, who ne'er from me shall be divided, 135
Kissed me upon the mouth all palpitating.
    Galeotto was the book and he who wrote it.
    That day no farther did we read therein."
And all the while one spirit uttered this,
    The other one did weep so, that, for pity, 140
    I swooned away as if I had been dying,
And fell, even as a dead body falls.

Canto VI

At the return of consciousness, that closed
    Before the pity of those two relations,
    Which utterly with sadness had confused me,
New torments I behold, and new tormented
    Around me, whichsoever way I move,   5
    And whichsoever way I turn, and gaze.
In the third circle am I of the rain
    Eternal, maledict, and cold, and heavy;
    Its law and quality are never new.
Huge hail, and water sombre-hued, and snow,   10
    Athwart the tenebrous air pour down amain;
    Noisome the earth is, that receiveth this.
Cerberus, monster cruel and uncouth,
    With his three gullets like a dog is barking
    Over the people that are there submerged.   15
Red eyes he has, and unctuous beard and black,
    And belly large, and armed with claws his hands;
    He rends the spirits, flays, and quarters them.
Howl the rain maketh them like unto dogs;
    One side they make a shelter for the other;   20
    Oft turn themselves the wretched reprobates.

When Cerberus perceived us, the great worm!
    His mouths he opened, and displayed his tusks;
    Not a limb had he that was motionless.
And my Conductor, with his spans extended,   25
    Took of the earth, and with his fists well filled,
    He threw it into those rapacious gullets.
Such as that dog is, who by barking craves,
    And quiet grows soon as his food he gnaws,
    For to devour it he but thinks and struggles,   30
The like became those muzzles filth-begrimed
    Of Cerberus the demon, who so thunders
    Over the souls that they would fain be deaf.
We passed across the shadows, which subdues
    The heavy rain-storm, and we placed our feet   35
    Upon their vanity that person seems.
They all were lying prone upon the earth,
    Excepting one, who sat upright as soon
    As he beheld us passing on before him.
"O thou that art conducted through this Hell,"   40
    He said to me, "recall me, if thou canst;
    Thyself wast made before I was unmade."
And I to him: "The anguish which thou hast
    Perhaps doth draw thee out of my remembrance,
    So that it seems not I have ever seen thee.   45
But tell me who thou art, that in so doleful
    A place art put, and in such punishment,
    If some are greater, none is so displeasing."
And he to me: "Thy city, which is full
    Of envy so that now the sack runs over,   50
    Held me within it in the life serene.
You citizens were wont to call me Ciacco;
    For the pernicious sin of gluttony
    I, as thou seest, am battered by this rain.
And I, sad soul, am not the only one,   55
    For all these suffer the like penalty
    For the like sin"; and word no more spake he.

I answered him: "Ciacco, thy wretchedness
   Weighs on me so that it to weep invites me;
   But tell me, if thou knowest, to what shall come   60
The citizens of the divided city;
   If any there be just; and the occasion
   Tell me why so much discord has assailed it."
And he to me: "They, after long contention,
   Will come to bloodshed; and the rustic party   65
   Will drive the other out with much offence.
Then afterwards behoves it this one fall
   Within three suns, and rise again the other
   By force of him who now is on the coast.
High will it hold its forehead a long while,   70
   Keeping the other under heavy burdens,
   Howe'er it weeps thereat and is indignant.
The just are two, and are not understood there;
   Envy and Arrogance and Avarice
   Are the three sparks that have all hearts enkindled."   75
Here ended he his tearful utterance;
   And I to him: "I wish thee still to teach me,
   And make a gift to me of further speech.
Farinata and Tegghiaio, once so worthy,
   Jacopo Rusticucci, Arrigo, and Mosca,   80
   And others who on good deeds set their thoughts,
Say where they are, and cause that I may know them;
   For great desire constraineth me to learn
   If Heaven doth sweeten them, or Hell envenom."
And he: "They are among the blacker souls;   85
   A different sin downweighs them to the bottom;
   If thou so far descendest, thou canst see them.
But when thou art again in the sweet world,
   I pray thee to the mind of others bring me;
   No more I tell thee and no more I answer."   90
Then his straightforward eyes he turned askance,
   Eyed me a little, and then bowed his head;
   He fell therewith prone like the other blind.

And the Guide said to me: "He wakes no more
    This side the sound of the angelic trumpet;   95
    When shall approach the hostile Potentate,
Each one shall find again his dismal tomb,
    Shall reassume his flesh and his own figure,
    Shall hear what through eternity re-echoes."
So we passed onward o'er the filthy mixture   100
    Of shadows and of rain with footsteps slow,
    Touching a little on the future life.
Wherefore I said: "Master, these torments here,
    Will they increase after the mighty sentence,
    Or lesser be, or will they be as burning?"   105
And he to me: "Return unto thy science,
    Which wills, that as the thing more perfect is,
    The more it feels of pleasure and of pain.
Albeit that this people maledict
    To true perfection never can attain,   110
    Hereafter more than now they look to be."
Round in a circle by that road we went,
    Speaking much more, which I do not repeat;
    We came unto the point where the descent is;
There we found Plutus the great enemy.   115

Canto VII

"Papë Satàn, Papë Satàn, Aleppë!"
    Thus Plutus with his clucking voice began;
    And that benignant Sage, who all things knew,
Said, to encourage me: "Let not thy fear
    Harm thee; for any power that he may have   5
    Shall not prevent thy going down this crag."
Then he turned round unto that bloated lip,
    And said: "Be silent, thou accursed wolf;
    Consume within thyself with thine own rage.
Not causeless is this journey to the abyss;   10
    Thus is it willed on high, where Michael wrought
    Vengeance upon the proud adultery."
Even as the sails inflated by the wind
    Together fall involved when snaps the mast,
    So fell the cruel monster to the earth.   15
Thus we descended into the fourth chasm,
    Gaining still farther on the dolesome shore
    Which all the woe of the universe insacks.
Justice of God, ah! who heaps up so many
    New toils and sufferings as I beheld?   20
    And why doth our transgression waste us so?

As doth the billow there upon Charybdis,
    That breaks itself on that which it encounters,
    So here the folk must dance their roundelay.
Here saw I people, more than elsewhere, many,   25
    On one side and the other, with great howls,
    Rolling weights forward by main-force of chest.
They clashed together, and then at that point
    Each one turned backward, rolling retrograde,
    Crying, "Why keepest?" and, "Why squanderest thou?"   30
Thus they returned along the lurid circle
    On either hand unto the opposite point,
    Shouting their shameful metre evermore.
Then each, when he arrived there, wheeled about
    Through his half-circle to another joust;   35
    And I, who had my heart pierced as it were,
Exclaimed: "My Master, now declare to me
    What people these are, and if all were clerks,
    These shaven crowns upon the left of us."
And he to me: "All of them were asquint   40
    In intellect in the first life, so much
    That there with measure they no spending made.
Clearly enough their voices bark it forth,
    Whene'er they reach the two points of the circle,
    Where sunders them the opposite defect.   45
Clerks those were who no hairy covering
    Have on the head, and Popes and Cardinals,
    In whom doth avarice practise its excess."
And I: "My Master, among such as these
    I ought forsooth to recognize some few,   50
    Who were infected with these maladies."
And he to me: "Vain thought thou entertainest;
    The undiscerning life which made them sordid
    Now makes them unto all discernment dim.
Forever shall they come to these two buttings;   55
    These from the sepulchre shall rise again
    With the fist closed, and these with tresses shorn.

Ill giving and ill keeping the fair world
   Have ta'en from them, and placed them in this scuffle;
   Whate'er it be, no words adorn I for it.   60
Now canst thou, Son, behold the transient farce
   Of goods that are committed unto Fortune,
   For which the human race each other buffet;
For all the gold that is beneath the moon,
   Or ever has been, of these weary souls   65
   Could never make a single one repose."
"Master," I said to him, "now tell me also
   What is this Fortune which thou speakest of,
   That has the world's goods so within its clutches?"
And he to me: "O creatures imbecile,   70
   What ignorance is this which doth beset you?
   Now will I have thee learn my judgment of her.
He whose omniscience everything transcends
   The heavens created, and gave who should guide them,
   That every part to every part may shine,   75
Distributing the light in equal measure;
   He in like manner to the mundane splendors
   Ordained a general ministress and guide,
That she might change at times the empty treasures
   From race to race, from one blood to another,   80
   Beyond resistance of all human wisdom.
Therefore one people triumphs, and another
   Languishes, in pursuance of her judgment,
   Which hidden is, as in the grass a serpent.
Your knowledge has no counterstand against her;   85
   She makes provision, judges, and pursues
   Her governance, as theirs the other gods.
Her permutations have not any truce;
   Necessity makes her precipitate,
   So often cometh who his turn obtains.   90

And this is she who is so crucified
  Even by those who ought to give her praise,
  Giving her blame amiss, and bad repute.
But she is blissful, and she hears it not;
  Among the other primal creatures gladsome   95
  She turns her sphere, and blissful she rejoices.
Let us descend now unto greater woe;
  Already sinks each star that was ascending
  When I set out, and loitering is forbidden."
We crossed the circle to the other bank,   100
  Near to a fount that boils, and pours itself
  Along a gully that runs out of it.
The water was more sombre far than perse;
  And we, in company with the dusky waves,
  Made entrance downward by a path uncouth.   105
A marsh it makes, which has the name of Styx,
  This tristful brooklet, when it has descended
  Down to the foot of the malign gray shores.
And I, who stood intent upon beholding,
  Saw people mud-besprent in that lagoon,   110
  All of them naked and with angry look.
They smote each other not alone with hands,
  But with the head and with the breast and feet,
  Tearing each other piecemeal with their teeth.
Said the good Master: "Son, thou now beholdest   115
  The souls of those whom anger overcame;
  And likewise I would have thee know for certain
Beneath the water people are who sigh
  And make this water bubble at the surface,
  As the eye tells thee wheresoe'er it turns.   120
Fixed in the mire they say, 'We sullen were
  In the sweet air, which by the sun is gladdened,
  Bearing within ourselves the sluggish reek;

Now we are sullen in this sable mire.'
    This hymn do they keep gurgling in their throats,   125
    For with unbroken words they cannot say it."
Thus we went circling round the filthy fen
    A great arc 'twixt the dry bank and the swamp,
    With eyes turned unto those who gorge the mire;
Unto the foot of a tower we came at last.   130

Canto VIII

I say, continuing, that long before
   We to the foot of that high tower had come,
   Our eyes went upward to the summit of it,
By reason of two flamelets we saw placed there,
   And from afar another answer them,   5
   So far, that hardly could the eye attain it.
And, to the sea of all discernment turned,
   I said: "What sayeth this, and what respondeth
   That other fire? and who are they that made it?"
And he to me: "Across the turbid waves   10
   What is expected thou canst now discern,
   If reek of the morass conceal it not."
Cord never shot an arrow from itself
   That sped away athwart the air so swift,
   As I beheld a very little boat   15
Come o'er the water tow'rds us at that moment,
   Under the guidance of a single pilot,
   Who shouted, "Now art thou arrived, fell soul?"
"Phlegyas, Phlegyas, thou criest out in vain
   For this once," said my Lord; "thou shalt not have us   20
   Longer than in the passing of the slough."

As he who listens to some great deceit
    That has been done to him, and then resents it,
    Such became Phlegyas, in his gathered wrath.
My Guide descended down into the boat,   25
    And then he made me enter after him,
    And only when I entered seemed it laden.
Soon as the Guide and I were in the boat,
    The antique prow goes on its way, dividing
    More of the water than 't is wont with others.   30
While we were running through the dead canal,
    Uprose in front of me one full of mire,
    And said, "Who 'rt thou that comest ere the hour?"
And I to him: "Although I come, I stay not;
    But who art thou that hast become so squalid?"   35
    "Thou seest that I am one who weeps," he answered.
And I to him: "With weeping and with wailing,
    Thou spirit maledict, do thou remain;
    For thee I know, though thou art all defiled."
Then stretched he both his hands unto the boat;   40
    Whereat my wary Master thrust him back,
    Saying, "Away there with the other dogs!"
Thereafter with his arms he clasped my neck;
    He kissed my face, and said: "Disdainful soul,
    Blessed be she who bore thee in her bosom.   45
That was an arrogant person in the world;
    Goodness is none, that decks his memory;
    So likewise here his shade is furious.
How many are esteemed great kings up there,
    Who here shall be like unto swine in mire,   50
    Leaving behind them horrible dispraises!"
And I: "My Master, much should I be pleased,
    If I could see him soused into this broth,
    Before we issue forth out of the lake."

And he to me: "Ere unto thee the shore 55
   Reveal itself, thou shalt be satisfied;
   Such a desire 't is meet thou shouldst enjoy."
A little after that, I saw such havoc
   Made of him by the people of the mire,
   That still I praise and thank my God for it. 60
They all were shouting, "At Philippo Argenti!"
   And that exasperate spirit Florentine
   Turned round upon himself with his own teeth.
We left him there, and more of him I tell not;
   But on mine ears there smote a lamentation, 65
   Whence forward I intent unbar mine eyes.
And the good Master said: "Even now, my son,
   The city draweth near whose name is Dis,
   With the grave citizens, with the great throng."
And I: "Its mosques already, Master, clearly 70
   Within there in the valley I discern
   Vermilion, as if issuing from the fire
They were." And he to me: "The fire eternal
   That kindles them within makes them look red,
   As thou beholdest in this nether Hell." 75
Then we arrived within the moats profound,
   That circumvallate that disconsolate city;
   The walls appeared to me to be of iron.
Not without making first a circuit wide,
   We came unto a place where loud the pilot 80
   Cried out to us, "Debark, here is the entrance."
More than a thousand at the gates I saw
   Out of the Heavens rained down, who angrily
   Were saying, "Who is this that without death
Goes through the kingdom of the people dead?" 85
   And my sagacious Master made a sign
   Of wishing secretly to speak with them.

A little then they quelled their great disdain,
  And said: "Come thou alone, and he begone
  Who has so boldly entered these dominions.   90
Let him return alone by his mad road;
  Try, if he can; for thou shalt here remain,
  Who hast escorted him through such dark regions."
Think, Reader, if I was discomforted
  At utterance of the accursed words;   95
  For never to return here I believed.
"O my dear Guide, who more than seven times
  Hast rendered me security, and drawn me
  From imminent peril that before me stood,
Do not desert me," said I, "thus undone;   100
  And if the going farther be denied us,
  Let us retrace our steps together swiftly."
And that Lord, who had led me thitherward,
  Said unto me: "Fear not; because our passage
  None can take from us, it by Such is given.   105
But here await me, and thy weary spirit
  Comfort and nourish with a better hope;
  For in this nether world I will not leave thee."
So onward goes and there abandons me
  My Father sweet, and I remain in doubt,   110
  For No and Yes within my head contend.
I could not hear what he proposed to them;
  But with them there he did not linger long,
  Ere each within in rivalry ran back.
They closed the portals, those our adversaries,   115
  On my Lord's breast, who had remained without
  And turned to me with footsteps far between.
His eyes cast down, his forehead shorn had he
  Of all its boldness, and he said, with sighs,
  "Who has denied to me the dolesome houses?"   120
And unto me: "Thou, because I am angry,
  Fear not, for I will conquer in the trial,
  Whatever for defence within be planned.

This arrogance of theirs is nothing new;
    For once they used it at less secret gate,   125
    Which finds itself without a fastening still.
O'er it didst thou behold the dead inscription;
    And now this side of it descends the steep,
    Passing across the circles without escort,
One by whose means the city shall be opened."   130

Canto IX

That hue which cowardice brought out on me,
    Beholding my Conductor backward turn,
    Sooner repressed within him his new color.
He stopped attentive, like a man who listens,
    Because the eye could not conduct him far   5
    Through the black air, and through the heavy fog.
"Still it behoveth us to win the fight,"
    Began he; "Else . . . Such offered us herself . . .
    O how I long that some one here arrive!"
Well I perceived, as soon as the beginning   10
    He covered up with what came afterward,
    That they were words quite different from the first;
But none the less his saying gave me fear,
    Because I carried out the broken phrase,
    Perhaps to a worse meaning than he had.   15
"Into this bottom of the doleful conch
    Doth any e'er descend from the first grade,
    Which for its pain has only hope cut off?"
This question put I; and he answered me:
    "Seldom it comes to pass that one of us   20
    Maketh the journey upon which I go.

True is it, once before I here below
   Was conjured by that pitiless Erictho,
   Who summoned back the shades unto their bodies.
Naked of me short while the flesh had been,   25
   Before within that wall she made me enter,
   To bring a spirit from the circle of Judas;
That is the lowest region and the darkest,
   And farthest from the heaven which circles all.
   Well know I the way; therefore be reassured.   30
This fen, which a prodigious stench exhales,
   Encompasses about the city dolent,
   Where now we cannot enter without anger."
And more he said, but not in mind I have it;
   Because mine eye had altogether drawn me   35
   Tow'rds the high tower with the red-flaming summit,
Where in a moment saw I swift uprisen
   The three infernal Furies stained with blood,
   Who had the limbs of women and their mien,
And with the greenest hydras were begirt;   40
   Small serpents and cerastes were their tresses,
   Wherewith their horrid temples were entwined.
And he who well the handmaids of the Queen
   Of everlasting lamentation knew,
   Said unto me: "Behold the fierce Erinnys.   45
This is Megæra, on the left-hand side;
   She who is weeping on the right, Alecto;
   Tisiphone is between"; and then was silent.
Each one her breast was rending with her nails;
   They beat them with their palms, and cried so loud,   50
   That I for dread pressed close unto the Poet.
"Medusa come, so we to stone will change him!"
   All shouted looking down; "in evil hour
   Avenged we not on Theseus his assault!"
"Turn thyself round, and keep thine eyes close shut,   55
   For if the Gorgon appear, and thou shouldst see it,
   No more returning upward would there be."

Thus said the Master; and he turned me round
    Himself, and trusted not unto my hands
    So far as not to blind me with his own.   60
O ye who have undistempered intellects,
    Observe the doctrine that conceals itself
    Beneath the veil of the mysterious verses!
And now there came across the turbid waves
    The clangor of a sound with terror fraught,   65
    Because of which both of the margins trembled;
Not otherwise it was than of a wind
    Impetuous on account of adverse heats,
    That smites the forest, and, without restraint,
The branches rends, beats down, and bears away;   70
    Right onward, laden with dust, it goes superb,
    And puts to flight the wild beasts and the shepherds.
Mine eyes he loosed, and said: "Direct the nerve
    Of vision now along that ancient foam,
    There yonder where that smoke is most intense."   75
Even as the frogs before the hostile serpent
    Across the water scatter all abroad,
    Until each one is huddled in the earth,
More than a thousand ruined souls I saw,
    Thus fleeing from before one who on foot   80
    Was passing o'er the Styx with soles unwet.
From off his face he fanned that unctuous air,
    Waving his left hand oft in front of him,
    And only with that anguish seemed he weary.
Well I perceived one sent from Heaven was he,   85
    And to the Master turned; and he made sign
    That I should quiet stand, and bow before him.
Ah! how disdainful he appeared to me!
    He reached the gate, and with a little rod
    He opened it, for there was no resistance.   90

"O banished out of Heaven, people despised!"
    Thus he began upon the horrid threshold;
    "Whence is this arrogance within you couched?
Wherefore recalcitrate against that will,
    From which the end can never be cut off,   95
    And which has many times increased your pain?
What helpeth it to butt against the fates?
    Your Cerberus, if you remember well,
    For that still bears his chin and gullet peeled."
Then he returned along the miry road,   100
    And spake no word to us, but had the look
    Of one whom other care constrains and goads
Than that of him who in his presence is;
    And we our feet directed tow'rds the city,
    After those holy words all confident.   105
Within we entered without any contest;
    And I, who inclination had to see
    What the condition such a fortress holds,
Soon as I was within, cast round mine eye,
    And see on every hand an ample plain,   110
    Full of distress and torment terrible.
Even as at Arles, where stagnant grows the Rhone,
    Even as at Pola near to the Quarnaro,
    That shuts in Italy and bathes its borders,
The sepulchres make all the place uneven;   115
    So likewise did they there on every side,
    Saving that there the manner was more bitter;
For flames between the sepulchres were scattered,
    By which they so intensely heated were,
    That iron more so asks not any art.   120
All of their coverings uplifted were,
    And from them issued forth such dire laments,
    Sooth seemed they of the wretched and tormented.

And I: "My Master, what are all those people
    Who, having sepulture within those tombs, 125
    Make themselves audible by doleful sighs?"
And he to me: "Here are the Heresiarchs,
    With their disciples of all sects, and much
    More than thou thinkest laden are the tombs.
Here like together with its like is buried; 130
    And more and less the monuments are heated."
    And when he to the right had turned, we passed
Between the torments and high parapets.

Canto X

Now onward goes, along a narrow path
    Between the torments and the city wall,
    My Master, and I follow at his back.
"O power supreme, that through these impious circles
    Turnest me," I began, "as pleases thee,   5
    Speak to me, and my longings satisfy;
The people who are lying in these tombs,
    Might they be seen? already are uplifted
    The covers all, and no one keepeth guard."
And he to me: "They all will be closed up   10
    When from Jehosaphat they shall return
    Here with the bodies they have left above.
Their cemetery have upon this side
    With Epicurus all his followers,
    Who with the body mortal make the soul;   15
But in the question thou dost put to me,
    Within here shalt thou soon be satisfied,
    And likewise in the wish thou keepest silent."
And I: "Good Leader, I but keep concealed
    From thee my heart, that I may speak the less,   20
    Nor only now hast thou thereto disposed me."

"O Tuscan, thou who through the city of fire
    Goest alive, thus speaking modestly,
    Be pleased to stay thy footsteps in this place.
Thy mode of speaking makes thee manifest   25
    A native of that noble fatherland,
    To which perhaps I too molestful was."
Upon a sudden issued forth this sound
    From out one of the tombs; wherefore I pressed,
    Fearing, a little nearer to my Leader.   30
And unto me he said: "Turn thee; what dost thou?
    Behold there Farinata who has risen;
    From the waist upwards wholly shalt thou see him."
I had already fixed mine eyes on his,
    And he uprose erect with breast and front   35
    E'en as if Hell he had in great despite.
And with courageous hands and prompt my Leader
    Thrust me between the sepulchres towards him,
    Exclaiming, "Let thy words explicit be."
As soon as I was at the foot of his tomb,   40
    Somewhat he eyed me, and, as if disdainful,
    Then asked of me, "Who were thine ancestors?"
I, who desirous of obeying was,
    Concealed it not, but all revealed to him;
    Whereat he raised his brows a little upward.   45
Then said he: "Fiercely adverse have they been
    To me, and to my fathers, and my party;
    So that two several times I scattered them."
"If they were banished, they returned on all sides,"
    I answered him, "the first time and the second;   50
    But yours have not acquired that art aright."
Then there uprose upon the sight, uncovered
    Down to the chin, a shadow at his side;
    I think that he had risen on his knees.
Round me he gazed, as if solicitude   55
    He had to see if some one else were with me;
    But after his suspicion was all spent,

Weeping, he said to me: "If through this blind
    Prison thou goest by loftiness of genius,
    Where is my son? and why is he not with thee?"   60
And I to him: "I come not of myself;
    He who is waiting yonder leads me here,
    Whom in disdain perhaps your Guido had."
His language and the mode of punishment
    Already unto me had read his name;   65
    On that account my answer was so full.
Up starting suddenly, he cried out: "How
    Saidst thou,—he had? Is he not still alive?
    Does not the sweet light strike upon his eyes?"
When he became aware of some delay,   70
    Which I before my answer made, supine
    He fell again, and forth appeared no more.
But the other, magnanimous, at whose desire
    I had remained, did not his aspect change,
    Neither his neck he moved, nor bent his side.   75
"And if," continuing his first discourse,
    "They have that art," he said, "not learned aright,
    That more tormenteth me, than doth this bed.
But fifty times shall not rekindled be
    The countenance of the Lady who reigns here,   80
    Ere thou shalt know how heavy is that art;
And as thou wouldst to the sweet world return,
    Say why that people is so pitiless
    Against my race in each one of its laws?"
Whence I to him: "The slaughter and great carnage   85
    Which have with crimson stained the Arbia, cause
    Such orisons in our temple to be made."
After his head he with a sigh had shaken,
    "There I was not alone," he said, "nor surely
    Without a cause had with the others moved.   90
But there I was alone, where every one
    Consented to the laying waste of Florence,
    He who defended her with open face."

"Ah! so hereafter may your seed repose,"
  I him entreated, "solve for me that knot,   95
  Which has entangled my conceptions here.
It seems that you can see, if I hear rightly,
  Beforehand whatsoe'er time brings with it,
  And in the present have another mode."
"We see, like those who have imperfect sight,   100
  The things," he said, "that distant are from us;
  So much still shines on us the Sovereign Ruler.
When they draw near, or are, is wholly vain
  Our intellect, and if none brings it to us,
  Not anything know we of your human state.   105
Hence thou canst understand, that wholly dead
  Will be our knowledge from the moment when
  The portal of the future shall be closed."
Then I, as if compunctious for my fault,
  Said: "Now, then, you will tell that fallen one,   110
  That still his son is with the living joined.
And if just now, in answering, I was dumb,
  Tell him I did it because I was thinking
  Already of the error you have solved me."
And now my Master was recalling me,   115
  Wherefore more eagerly I prayed the spirit
  That he would tell me who was with him there.
He said: "With more than a thousand here I lie;
  Within here is the second Frederick,
  And the Cardinal, and of the rest I speak not."   120
Thereon he hid himself; and I towards
  The ancient poet turned my steps, reflecting
  Upon that saying, which seemed hostile to me.
He moved along; and afterward, thus going,
  He said to me, "Why art thou so bewildered?"   125
  And I in his inquiry satisfied him.
"Let memory preserve what thou hast heard
  Against thyself," that Sage commanded me,
  "And now attend here"; and he raised his finger.

"When thou shalt be before the radiance sweet   130
    Of her whose beauteous eyes all things behold,
    From her thou 'lt know the journey of thy life."
Unto the left hand then he turned his feet;
    We left the wall, and went towards the middle,
    Along a path that strikes into a valley,   135
Which even up there unpleasant made its stench.

CANTO XI

Upon the margin of a lofty bank
    Which great rocks broken in a circle made,
    We came upon a still more cruel throng;
And there, by reason of the horrible
    Excess of stench the deep abyss throws out,   5
    We drew ourselves aside behind the cover
Of a great tomb, whereon I saw a writing,
    Which said: "Pope Anastasius I hold,
    Whom out of the right way Photinus drew."
"Slow it behoveth our descent to be,   10
    So that the sense be first a little used
    To the sad blast, and then we shall not heed it."
The Master thus; and unto him I said,
    "Some compensation find, that the time pass not
    Idly"; and he: "Thou seest I think of that.   15
My son, upon the inside of these rocks,"
    Began he then to say, "are three small circles,
    From grade to grade, like those which thou art leaving.
They all are full of spirits maledict;
    But that hereafter sight alone suffice thee,   20
    Hear how and wherefore they are in constraint.

Of every malice that wins hate in Heaven,
    Injury is the end; and all such end
    Either by force or fraud afflicteth others.
But because fraud is man's peculiar vice,   25
    More it displeases God; and so stand lowest
    The fraudulent, and greater dole assails them.
All the first circle of the Violent is;
    But since force may be used against three persons,
    In three rounds 't is divided and constructed.   30
To God, to ourselves, and to our neighbor can we
    Use force; I say on them and on their things,
    As thou shalt hear with reason manifest.
A death by violence, and painful wounds,
    Are to our neighbor given; and in his substance   35
    Ruin, and arson, and injurious levies;
Whence homicides, and he who smites unjustly,
    Marauders, and freebooters, the first round
    Tormenteth all in companies diverse.
Man may lay violent hands upon himself   40
    And his own goods; and therefore in the second
    Round must perforce without avail repent
Whoever of your world deprives himself,
    Who games, and dissipates his property,
    And weepeth there, where he should jocund be.   45
Violence can be done the Deity,
    In heart denying and blaspheming Him,
    And by disdaining Nature and her bounty.
And for this reason doth the smallest round
    Seal with its signet Sodom and Cahors,   50
    And who, disdaining God, speaks from the heart.
Fraud, wherewithal is every conscience stung,
    A man may practise upon him who trusts,
    And him who doth no confidence imburse.
This latter mode, it would appear, dissevers   55
    Only the bond of love which Nature makes;
    Wherefore within the second circle nestle

Hypocrisy, flattery, and who deals in magic,
　　Falsification, theft, and simony,
　　Panders, and barrators, and the like filth.　　　　60
By the other mode, forgotten is that love
　　Which Nature makes, and what is after added,
　　From which there is a special faith engendered.
Hence in the smallest circle, where the point is
　　Of the Universe, upon which Dis is seated,　　　　65
　　Whoe'er betrays forever is consumed."
And I: "My Master, clear enough proceeds
　　Thy reasoning, and full well distinguishes
　　This cavern and the people who possess it.
But tell me, those within the fat lagoon,　　　　　　70
　　Whom the wind drives, and whom the rain doth beat,
　　And who encounter with such bitter tongues,
Wherefore are they inside of the red city
　　Not punished, if God has them in his wrath,
　　And if he has not, wherefore in such fashion?"　　75
And unto me he said: "Why wanders so
　　Thine intellect from that which it is wont?
　　Or, sooth, thy mind where is it elsewhere looking?
Hast thou no recollection of those words
　　With which thine Ethics thoroughly discusses　　80
　　The dispositions three, that Heaven abides not,—
Incontinence, and Malice, and insane
　　Bestiality? and how Incontinence
　　Less God offendeth, and less blame attracts?
If thou regardest this conclusion well,　　　　　　85
　　And to thy mind recallest who they are
　　That up outside are undergoing penance,
Clearly wilt thou perceive why from these felons
　　They separated are, and why less wroth
　　Justice divine doth smite them with its hammer."　90
"O Sun, that healest all distempered vision,
　　Thou dost content me so, when thou resolvest,
　　That doubting pleases me no less than knowing!

Once more a little backward turn thee," said I,
    "There where thou sayest that usury offends   95
    Goodness divine, and disengage the knot."
"Philosophy," he said, "to him who heeds it,
    Noteth, not only in one place alone,
    After what manner Nature takes her course
From Intellect Divine, and from its art;   100
    And if thy Physics carefully thou notest,
    After not many pages shalt thou find,
That this your art as far as possible
    Follows, as the disciple doth the master;
    So that your art is, as it were, God's grandchild.   105
From these two, if thou bringest to thy mind
    Genesis at the beginning, it behoves
    Mankind to gain their life and to advance;
And since the usurer takes another way,
    Nature herself and in her follower   110
    Disdains he, for elsewhere he puts his hope.
But follow, now, as I would fain go on,
    For quivering are the Fishes on the horizon,
    And the Wain wholly over Caurus lies,
And far beyond there we descend the crag."   115

CANTO XII

The place where to descend the bank we came
    Was alpine, and from what was there, moreover,
    Of such a kind that every eye would shun it.
Such as that ruin is which in the flank
    Smote, on this side of Trent, the Adige,   5
    Either by earthquake or by failing stay,
For from the mountain's top, from which it moved,
    Unto the plain the cliff is shattered so,
    Some path 't would give to him who was above;
Even such was the descent of that ravine,   10
    And on the border of the broken chasm
    The infamy of Crete was stretched along,
Who was conceived in the fictitious cow;
    And when he us beheld, he bit himself,
    Even as one whom anger racks within.   15
My Sage towards him shouted: "Peradventure
    Thou think'st that here may be the Duke of Athens,
    Who in the world above brought death to thee?
Get thee gone, beast, for this one cometh not
    Instructed by thy sister, but he comes   20
    In order to behold your punishments."

As is that bull who breaks loose at the moment
   In which he has received the mortal blow,
   Who cannot walk, but staggers here and there,
The Minotaur beheld I do the like;   25
   And he, the wary, cried: "Run to the passage;
   While he is wroth, 't is well thou shouldst descend."
Thus down we took our way o'er that discharge
   Of stones, which oftentimes did move themselves
   Beneath my feet, from the unwonted burden.   30
Thoughtful I went; and he said: "Thou art thinking
   Perhaps upon this ruin, which is guarded
   By that brute anger which just now I quenched.
Now will I have thee know, the other time
   I here descended to the nether Hell,   35
   This precipice had not yet fallen down.
But truly, if I well discern, a little
   Before His coming who the mighty spoil
   Bore off from Dis, in the supernal circle,
Upon all sides the deep and loathsome valley   40
   Trembled so, that I thought the Universe
   Was thrilled with love, by which there are who think
The world ofttimes converted into chaos;
   And at that moment this primeval crag
   Both here and elsewhere made such overthrow.   45
But fix thine eyes below; for draweth near
   The river of blood, within which boiling is
   Whoe'er by violence doth injure others."
O blind cupidity, O wrath insane,
   That spurs us onward so in our short life,   50
   And in the eternal then so badly steeps us!
I saw an ample moat bent like a bow,
   As one which all the plain encompasses,
   Conformable to what my Guide had said.
And between this and the embankment's foot   55
   Centaurs in file were running, armed with arrows,
   As in the world they used the chase to follow.

Beholding us descend, each one stood still,
    And from the squadron three detached themselves,
    With bows and arrows in advance selected;   60
And from afar one cried: "Unto what torment
    Come ye, who down the hillside are descending?
    Tell us from there; if not, I draw the bow."
My Master said: "Our answer will we make
    To Chiron, near you there; in evil hour,   65
    That will of thine was evermore so hasty."
Then touched he me, and said: "This one is Nessus,
    Who perished for the lovely Dejanira,
    And for himself, himself did vengeance take.
And he in the midst, who at his breast is gazing,   70
    Is the great Chiron, who brought up Achilles;
    That other Pholus is, who was so wrathful.
Thousands and thousands go about the moat
    Shooting with shafts whatever soul emerges
    Out of the blood, more than his crime allots."   75
Near we approached unto those monsters fleet;
    Chiron an arrow took, and with the notch
    Backward upon his jaws he put his beard.
After he had uncovered his great mouth,
    He said to his companions: "Are you ware   80
    That he behind moveth whate'er he touches?
Thus are not wont to do the feet of dead men."
    And my good Guide, who now was at his breast,
    Where the two natures are together joined,
Replied: "Indeed he lives, and thus alone   85
    Me it behoves to show him the dark valley;
    Necessity, and not delight, impels us.
Some one withdrew from singing Halleluja,
    Who unto me committed this new office;
    No thief is he, nor I a thievish spirit.   90
But by that virtue through which I am moving
    My steps along this savage thoroughfare,
    Give us some one of thine, to be with us,

And who may show us where to pass the ford,
    And who may carry this one on his back;   95
    For 't is no spirit that can walk the air."
Upon his right breast Chiron wheeled about,
    And said to Nessus: "Turn and do thou guide them,
    And warn aside, if other band may meet you."
We with our faithful escort onward moved,   100
    Along the brink of the vermilion boiling,
    Wherein the boiled were uttering loud laments.
People I saw within up to the eyebrows,
    And the great Centaur said: "Tyrants are these,
    Who dealt in bloodshed and in pillaging.   105
Here they lament their pitiless mischiefs; here
    Is Alexander, and fierce Dionysius
    Who upon Sicily brought dolorous years.
That forehead there which has the hair so black
    Is Azzolin; and the other who is blond,   110
    Obizzo is of Esti, who, in truth,
Up in the world was by his step-son slain."
    Then turned I to the Poet; and he said,
    "Now he be first to thee, and second I."
A little farther on the Centaur stopped   115
    Above a folk, who far down as the throat
    Seemed from that boiling stream to issue forth.
A shade he showed us on one side alone,
    Saying: "He cleft asunder in God's bosom
    The heart that still upon the Thames is honored."   120
Then people saw I, who from out the river
    Lifted their heads and also all the chest;
    And many among these I recognized.
Thus ever more and more grew shallower
    That blood, so that the feet alone it covered;   125
    And there across the moat our passage was.
"Even as thou here upon this side beholdest
    The boiling stream, that aye diminishes,"
    The Centaur said, "I wish thee to believe

That on this other more and more declines   130
   Its bed, until it reunites itself
   Where it behoveth tyranny to groan.
Justice divine, upon this side, is goading
   That Attila, who was a scourge on earth,
   And Pyrrhus, and Sextus; and forever milks   135
The tears which with the boiling it unseals
   In Rinier da Corneto and Rinier Pazzo,
   Who made upon the highways so much war."
Then back he turned, and passed again the ford.

Canto XIII

Not yet had Nessus reached the other side,
    When we had put ourselves within a wood,
    That was not marked by any path whatever.
Not foliage green, but of a dusky color,
    Not branches smooth, but gnarled and intertangled,   5
    Not apple-trees were there, but thorns with poison.
Such tangled thickets have not, nor so dense,
    Those savage wild-beasts, that in hatred hold
    'Twixt Cecina and Corneto the tilled places.
There do the hideous Harpies make their nests,   10
    Who chased the Trojans from the Strophades,
    With sad announcement of impending doom;
Broad wings have they, and necks and faces human,
    And feet with claws, and their great bellies fledged;
    They make laments upon the wondrous trees.   15
And the good Master: "Ere thou enter farther,
    Know that thou art within the second round,"
    Thus he began to say, "and shalt be, till
Thou comest out upon the horrible sand;
    Therefore look well around, and thou shalt see   20
    Things that will credence give unto my speech."

I heard on all sides lamentations uttered,
    And person none beheld I who might make them,
    Whence, utterly bewildered, I stood still.
I think he thought that I perhaps might think   25
    So many voices issued through those trunks
    From people who concealed themselves for us;
Therefore the Master said: "If thou break off
    Some little spray from any of these trees,
    The thoughts thou hast will wholly be made vain."   30
Then stretched I forth my hand a little forward,
    And plucked a branchlet off from a great thorn;
    And the trunk cried, "Why dost thou mangle me?"
After it had become embrowned with blood,
    It recommenced its cry: "Why dost thou rend me?   35
    Hast thou no spirit of pity whatsoever?
Men once we were, and now are changed to trees;
    Indeed, thy hand should be more pitiful,
    Even if the souls of serpents we had been."
As out of a green brand, that is on fire   40
    At one of the ends, and from the other drips
    And hisses with the wind that is escaping;
So from that splinter issued forth together
    Both words and blood; whereat I let the tip
    Fall, and stood like a man who is afraid.   45
"Had he been able sooner to believe,"
    My Sage made answer, "O thou wounded soul,
    What only in my verses he has seen,
Not upon thee had he stretched forth his hand;
    Whereas the thing incredible has caused me   50
    To put him to an act which grieveth me.
But tell him who thou wast, so that by way
    Of some amends thy fame he may refresh
    Up in the world, to which he can return."
And the trunk said: "So thy sweet words allure me,   55
    I can not silent be; and you be vexed not,
    That I a little to discourse am tempted.

I am the one who both keys had in keeping
  Of Frederick's heart, and turned them to and fro
  So softly in unlocking and in locking,   60
That from his secrets most men I withheld;
  Fidelity I bore the glorious office
  So great, I lost thereby my sleep and pulses.
The courtesan who never from the dwelling
  Of Cæsar turned aside her strumpet eyes,   65
  Death universal and the vice of courts,
Inflamed against me all the other minds,
  And they, inflamed, did so inflame Augustus,
  That my glad honors turned to dismal mournings.
My spirit, in disdainful exultation,   70
  Thinking by dying to escape disdain,
  Made me unjust against myself, the just.
I, by the roots unwonted of this wood,
  Do swear to you that never broke I faith
  Unto my lord, who was so worthy of honor;   75
And to the world if one of you return,
  Let him my memory comfort, which is lying
  Still prostrate from the blow that envy dealt it."
Waited awhile, and then: "Since he is silent,"
  The Poet said to me, "lose not the time,   80
  But speak, and question him, if more may please thee."
Whence I to him: "Do thou again inquire
  Concerning what thou think'st will satisfy me;
  For I can not, such pity is in my heart."
Therefore he recommenced: "So may the man   85
  Do for thee freely what thy speech implores,
  Spirit incarcerate, again be pleased
To tell us in what way the soul is bound
  Within these knots; and tell us, if thou canst,
  If any from such members e'er is freed."   90
Then blew the trunk amain, and afterward
  The wind was into such a voice converted:
  "With brevity shall be replied to you.

When the exasperated soul abandons
  The body whence it rent itself away,   95
  Minos consigns it to the seventh abyss.
It falls into the forest, and no part
  Is chosen for it; but where Fortune hurls it,
  There like a grain of spelt it germinates.
It springs a sapling, and a forest tree;   100
  The Harpies, feeding then upon its leaves,
  Do pain create, and for the pain an outlet.
Like others for our spoils shall we return;
  But not that any one may them revest,
  For 't is not just to have what one casts off.   105
Here we shall drag them, and along the dismal
  Forest our bodies shall suspended be,
  Each to the thorn of his molested shade."
We were attentive still unto the trunk,
  Thinking that more it yet might wish to tell us,   110
  When by a tumult we were overtaken,
In the same way as he is who perceives
  The boar and chase approaching to his stand,
  Who hears the crashing of the beasts and branches;
And two behold! upon our left-hand side,   115
  Naked and scratched, fleeing so furiously,
  That of the forest every fan they broke.
He who was in advance: "Now help, Death, help!"
  And the other one, who seemed to lag too much,
  Was shouting: "Lano, were not so alert   120
Those legs of thine at joustings of the Toppo!"
  And then, perchance because his breath was failing,
  He grouped himself together with a bush.
Behind them was the forest full of black
  She-mastiffs, ravenous, and swift of foot   125
  As greyhounds, who are issuing from the chain.
On him who had crouched down they set their teeth,
  And him they lacerated piece by piece,
  Thereafter bore away those aching members.

Thereat my Escort took me by the hand,   130
    And led me to the bush, that all in vain
    Was weeping from its bloody lacerations.
"O Jacopo," it said, "of Sant' Andrea,
    What helped it thee of me to make a screen?
    What blame have I in thy nefarious life?"   135
When near him had the Master stayed his steps,
    He said: "Who wast thou, that through wounds so many
    Art blowing out with blood thy dolorous speech?"
And he to us: "O souls, that hither come
    To look upon the shameful massacre   140
    That has so rent away from me my leaves,
Gather them up beneath the dismal bush;
    I of that city was which to the Baptist
    Changed its first patron, wherefore he for this
Forever with his art will make it sad.   145
    And were it not that on the pass of Arno
    Some glimpses of him are remaining still,
Those citizens, who afterwards rebuilt it
    Upon the ashes left by Attila,
    In vain had caused their labor to be done.   150
Of my own house I made myself a gibbet."

CANTO XIV

Because the charity of my native place
    Constrained me, gathered I the scattered leaves,
    And gave them back to him, who now was hoarse.
Then came we to the confine, where disparted
    The second round is from the third, and where   5
    A horrible form of Justice is beheld.
Clearly to manifest these novel things,
    I say that we arrived upon a plain,
    Which from its bed rejecteth every plant;
The dolorous forest is a garland to it   10
    All round about, as the sad moat to that;
    There close upon the edge we stayed our feet.
The soil was of an arid and thick sand,
    Not of another fashion made than that
    Which by the feet of Cato once was pressed.   15
Vengeance of God, O how much oughtest thou
    By each one to be dreaded, who doth read
    That which was manifest unto mine eyes!
Of naked souls beheld I many herds,
    Who all were weeping very miserably,   20
    And over them seemed set a law diverse.

Supine upon the ground some folk were lying;
 And some were sitting all drawn up together,
 And others went about continually.
Those who were going round were far the more,   25
 And those were less who lay down to their torment,
 But had their tongues more loosed to lamentation.
O'er all the sand-waste, with a gradual fall,
 Were raining down dilated flakes of fire,
 As of the snow on Alp without a wind.   30
As Alexander, in those torrid parts
 Of India, beheld upon his host
 Flames fall unbroken till they reached the ground,
Whence he provided with his phalanxes
 To trample down the soil, because the vapor   35
 Better extinguished was while it was single;
Thus was descending the eternal heat,
 Whereby the sand was set on fire, like tinder
 Beneath the steel, for doubling of the dole.
Without repose forever was the dance   40
 Of miserable hands, now there, now here,
 Shaking away from off them the fresh gleeds.
"Master," began I, "thou who overcomest
 All things except the demons dire, that issued
 Against us at the entrance of the gate,   45
Who is that mighty one who seems to heed not
 The fire, and lieth lowering and disdainful,
 So that the rain seems not to ripen him?"
And he himself, who had become aware
 That I was questioning my Guide about him,   50
 Cried: "Such as I was living, am I, dead!
If Jove should weary out his smith, from whom
 He seized in anger the sharp thunderbolt,
 Wherewith upon the last day I was smitten,
And if he wearied out by turns the others   55
 In Mongibello at the swarthy forge,
 Vociferating, 'Help, good Vulcan, help!'

Even as he did there at the fight of Phlegra,
    And shot his bolts at me with all his might,
    He would not have thereby a joyous vengeance."   60
Then did my Leader speak with such great force,
    That I had never heard him speak so loud:
    "O Capaneus, in that is not extinguished
Thine arrogance, thou punished art the more;
    Not any torment, saving thine own rage,   65
    Would be unto thy fury pain complete."
Then he turned round to me with better lip,
    Saying: "One of the Seven Kings was he
    Who Thebes besieged, and held, and seems to hold
God in disdain, and little seems to prize him;   70
    But, as I said to him, his own despites
    Are for his breast the fittest ornaments.
Now follow me, and mind thou do not place
    As yet thy feet upon the burning sand,
    But always keep them close unto the wood."   75
Speaking no word, we came to where there gushes
    Forth from the wood a little rivulet,
    Whose redness makes my hair still stand on end.
As from the Bulicamë springs the brooklet,
    The sinful women later share among them,   80
    So downward through the sand it went its way.
The bottom of it, and both sloping banks,
    Were made of stone, and the margins at the side;
    Whence I perceived that there the passage was.
"In all the rest which I have shown to thee   85
    Since we have entered in within the gate
    Whose threshold unto no one is denied,
Nothing has been discovered by thine eyes
    So notable as is the present river,
    Which all the little flames above it quenches."   90
These words were of my Leader; whence I prayed him
    That he would give me largess of the food,
    For which he had given me largess of desire.

"In the mid-sea there sits a wasted land,"
    Said he thereafterward, "whose name is Crete,   95
    Under whose king the world of old was chaste.
There is a mountain there, that once was glad
    With waters and with leaves, which was called Ida;
    Now 't is deserted, as a thing worn out.
Rhea once chose it for the faithful cradle   100
    Of her own son; and to conceal him better,
    Whene'er he cried, she there had clamors made.
A grand old man stands in the mount erect,
    Who holds his shoulders turned tow'rds Damietta,
    And looks at Rome as if it were his mirror.   105
His head is fashioned of refined gold,
    And of pure silver are the arms and breast;
    Then he is brass as far down as the fork.
From that point downward all is chosen iron,
    Save that the right foot is of kiln-baked clay,   110
And more he stands on that than on the other.
Each part, except the gold, is by a fissure
    Asunder cleft, that dripping is with tears,
    Which gathered together perforate that cavern.
From rock to rock they fall into this valley;   115
    Acheron, Styx, and Phlegethon they form;
    Then downward go along this narrow sluice
Unto that point where is no more descending.
    They form Cocytus; what that pool may be
    Thou shalt behold, so here 't is not narrated."   120
And I to him: "If so the present runnel
    Doth take its rise in this way from our world,
    Why only on this verge appears it to us?"
And he to me: "Thou knowest the place is round,
    And notwithstanding thou hast journeyed far,   125
    Still to the left descending to the bottom,
Thou hast not yet through all the circle turned.
    Therefore if something new appear to us,
    It should not bring amazement to thy face."

And I again: "Master, where shall be found   130
   Lethe and Phlegethon, for of one thou 'rt silent,
   And sayest the other of this rain is made?"
"In all thy questions truly thou dost please me,"
   Replied he; "but the boiling of the red
   Water might well solve one of them thou makest.   135
Thou shalt see Lethe, but outside this moat,
   There where the souls repair to lave themselves,
   When sin repented of has been removed."
Then said he: "It is time now to abandon
   The wood; take heed that thou come after me;   140
   A way the margins make that are not burning,
And over them all vapors are extinguished."

Canto XV

Now bears us onward one of the hard margins,
    And so the brooklet's mist o'ershadows it,
    From fire it saves the water and the dikes.
Even as the Flemings, 'twixt Cadsand and Bruges,
    Fearing the flood that tow'rds them hurls itself,   5
    Their bulwarks build to put the sea to flight;
And as the Paduans along the Brenta,
    To guard their villas and their villages,
    Or ever Chiarentana feel the heat;
In such similitude had those been made,   10
    Albeit not so lofty nor so thick,
    Whoever he might be, the master made them.
Now were we from the forest so remote,
    I could not have discovered where it was,
    Even if backward I had turned myself,   15
When we a company of souls encountered,
    Who came beside the dike, and every one
    Gazed at us, as at evening we are wont
To eye each other under a new moon,
    And so towards us sharpened they their brows   20
    As an old tailor at the needle's eye.

Thus scrutinized by such a family,
   By some one I was recognized, who seized
   My garment's hem, and cried out, "What a marvel!"
And I, when he stretched forth his arm to me,   25
   On his baked aspect fastened so mine eyes,
   That the scorched countenance prevented not
His recognition by my intellect;
   And bowing down my face unto his own,
   I made reply, "Are you here, Ser Brunetto?"   30
And he: "May 't not displease thee, O my son,
   If a brief space with thee Brunetto Latini
   Backward return and let the trail go on."
I said to him: "With all my power I ask it;
   And if you wish me to sit down with you,   35
   I will, if he please, for I go with him."
"O son," he said, "whoever of this herd
   A moment stops, lies then a hundred years,
   Nor fans himself when smiteth him the fire.
Therefore go on; I at thy skirts will come,   40
   And afterward will I rejoin my band,
   Which goes lamenting its eternal doom."
I did not dare to go down from the road
   Level to walk with him; but my head bowed
   I held as one who goeth reverently.   45
And he began: "What fortune or what fate
   Before the last day leadeth thee down here?
   And who is this that showeth thee the way?"
"Up there above us in the life serene,"
   I answered him, "I lost me in a valley,   50
   Or ever yet my age had been completed.
But yestermorn I turned my back upon it;
   This one appeared to me, returning thither,
   And homeward leadeth me along this road."
And he to me: "If thou thy star do follow,   55
   Thou canst not fail thee of a glorious port,
   If well I judged in the life beautiful.

And if I had not died so prematurely,
    Seeing Heaven thus benignant unto thee,
    I would have given thee comfort in the work.   60
But that ungrateful and malignant people,
    Which of old time from Fesole descended,
    And smacks still of the mountain and the granite,
Will make itself, for thy good deeds, thy foe;
    And it is right; for among crabbed sorbs   65
    It ill befits the sweet fig to bear fruit.
Old rumor in the world proclaims them blind;
    A people avaricious, envious, proud;
    Take heed that of their customs thou do cleanse thee.
Thy fortune so much honor doth reserve thee,   70
    One party and the other shall be hungry
    For thee; but far from goat shall be the grass.
Their litter let the beasts of Fesole
    Make of themselves, nor let them touch the plant,
    If any still upon their dunghill rise,   75
In which may yet revive the consecrated
    Seed of those Romans, who remained there when
    The nest of such great malice it became."
"If my entreaty wholly were fulfilled,"
    Replied I to him, "not yet would you be   80
    In banishment from human nature placed;
For in my mind is fixed, and touches now
    My heart the dear and good paternal image
    Of you, when in the world from hour to hour
You taught me how a man becomes eternal;   85
    And how much I am grateful, while I live
    Behoves that in my language be discerned.
What you narrate of my career I write,
    And keep it to be glossed with other text
    By a Lady who can do it, if I reach her.   90
This much will I have manifest to you;
    Provided that my conscience do not chide me,
    For whatsoever Fortune I am ready.

Such hansel is not new unto mine ears;
   Therefore let Fortune turn her wheel around   95
   As it may please her, and the churl his mattock."
My Master thereupon on his right cheek
   Did backward turn himself, and looked at me;
   Then said: "He listeneth well who noteth it."
Nor speaking less on that account, I go   100
   With Ser Brunetto, and I ask who are
   His most known and most eminent companions.
And he to me: "To know of some is well;
   Of others it were laudable to be silent,
   For short would be the time for so much speech.   105
Know then, in sum, that all of them were clerks,
   And men of letters great and of great fame,
   In the world tainted with the selfsame sin.
Priscian goes yonder with that wretched crowd,
   And Francis of Accorso; and thou hadst seen there,   110
   If thou hadst had a hankering for such scurf,
That one, who by the Servant of the Servants
   From Arno was transferred to Bacchiglione,
   Where he has left his sin-excited nerves.
More would I say, but coming and discoursing   115
   Can be no longer; for that I behold
   New smoke uprising yonder from the sand.
A people comes with whom I may not be;
   Commended unto thee be my Tesoro,
   In which I still live, and no more I ask."   120
Then he turned round, and seemed to be of those
   Who at Verona run for the Green Mantle
   Across the plain; and seemed to be among them
The one who wins, and not the one who loses.

Canto XVI

Now was I where was heard the reverberation
    Of water falling into the next round,
    Like to that humming which the beehives make,
When shadows three together started forth,
    Running, from out a company that passed   5
    Beneath the rain of the sharp martyrdom.
Towards us came they, and each one cried out:
    "Stop, thou; for by thy garb to us thou seemest
    To be some one of our depraved city."
Ah me! what wounds I saw upon their limbs,   10
    Recent and ancient by the flames burnt in!
    It pains me still but to remember it.
Unto their cries my Teacher paused attentive;
    He turned his face towards me, and "Now wait,"
    He said; "to these we should be courteous.   15
And if it were not for the fire that darts
    The nature of this region, I should say
    That haste were more becoming thee than them."
As soon as we stood still, they recommenced
    The old refrain, and when they overtook us,   20
    Formed of themselves a wheel, all three of them.

As champions stripped and oiled are wont to do,
  Watching for their advantage and their hold,
  Before they come to blows and thrusts between them,
Thus, wheeling round, did every one his visage   25
  Direct to me, so that in opposite wise
  His neck and feet continual journey made.
And, "If the misery of this soft place
  Bring in disdain ourselves and our entreaties,"
  Began one, "and our aspect black and blistered,   30
Let the renown of us thy mind incline
  To tell us who thou art, who thus securely
  Thy living feet dost move along through Hell.
He in whose footprints thou dost see me treading,
  Naked and skinless though he now may go,   35
  Was of a greater rank than thou dost think;
He was the grandson of the good Gualdrada;
  His name was Guidoguerra, and in life
  Much did he with his wisdom and his sword.
The other, who close by me treads the sand,   40
  Tegghiaio Aldobrandi is, whose fame
  Above there in the world should welcome be.
And I, who with them on the cross am placed,
  Jacopo Rusticucci was; and truly
  My savage wife, more than aught else, doth harm me."   45
Could I have been protected from the fire,
  Below I should have thrown myself among them,
  And think the Teacher would have suffered it;
But as I should have burned and baked myself,
  My terror overmastered my good will,   50
  Which made me greedy of embracing them.
Then I began: "Sorrow and not disdain
  Did your condition fix within me so,
  That tardily it wholly is stripped off,
As soon as this my Lord said unto me   55
  Words, on account of which I thought within me
  That people such as you are were approaching.

I of your city am; and evermore
    Your labors and your honorable names
    I with affection have retraced and heard.   60
I leave the gall, and go for the sweet fruits
    Promised to me by the veracious Leader;
    But to the centre first I needs must plunge."
"So may the soul for a long while conduct
    Those limbs of thine," did he make answer then,   65
    "And so may thy renown shine after thee,
Valor and courtesy, say if they dwell
    Within our city, as they used to do,
    Or if they wholly have gone out of it;
For Guglielmo Borsier, who is in torment   70
    With us of late, and goes there with his comrades,
    Doth greatly mortify us with his words."
"The new inhabitants and the sudden gains,
    Pride and extravagance have in thee engendered,
    Florence, so that thou weep'st thereat already!"   75
In this wise I exclaimed with face uplifted;
    And the three, taking that for my reply,
    Looked at each other, as one looks at truth.
"If other times so little it doth cost thee,"
    Replied they all, "to satisfy another,   80
    Happy art thou, thus speaking at thy will!
Therefore, if thou escape from these dark places,
    And come to rebehold the beauteous stars,
    When it shall pleasure thee to say, 'I was,'
See that thou speak of us unto the people."   85
    Then they broke up the wheel, and in their flight
    It seemed as if their agile legs were wings.
Not an Amen could possibly be said
    So rapidly as they had disappeared;
    Wherefore the Master deemed best to depart.   90
I followed him, and little had we gone,
    Before the sound of water was so near us,
    That speaking we should hardly have been heard.

Even as that stream which holdeth its own course
   The first from Monte Veso tow'rds the East,   95
   Upon the left-hand slope of Apennine,
Which is above called Acquacheta, ere
   It down descendeth into its low bed,
   And at Forlì is vacant of that name,
Reverberates there above San Benedetto   100
   From Alps, by falling at a single leap,
   Where for a thousand there were room enough;
Thus downward from a bank precipitate,
   We found resounding that dark-tinted water,
   So that it soon the ear would have offended.   105
I had a cord around about me girt,
   And therewithal I whilom had designed
   To take the panther with the painted skin.
After I this had all from me unloosed,
   As my Conductor had commanded me,   110
   I reached it to him, gathered up and coiled,
Whereat he turned himself to the right side,
   And at a little distance from the verge,
   He cast it down into that deep abyss.
"It must needs be some novelty respond,"   115
   I said within myself, "to the new signal
   The Master with his eye is following so."
Ah me! how very cautious men should be
   With those who not alone behold the act,
   But with their wisdom look into the thoughts!   120
He said to me: "Soon there will upward come
   What I await; and what thy thought is dreaming
   Must soon reveal itself unto thy sight."
Aye to that truth which has the face of falsehood,
   A man should close his lips as far as may be,   125
   Because without his fault it causes shame;
But here I can not; and, Reader, by the notes
   Of this my Comedy to thee I swear,
   So may they not be void of lasting favor,

Athwart that dense and darksome atmosphere 130
    I saw a figure swimming upward come,
    Marvellous unto every steadfast heart,
Even as he returns who goeth down
    Sometimes to clear an anchor, which has grappled
    Reef, or aught else that in the sea is hidden, 135
Who upward stretches, and draws in his feet.

Canto XVII

"Behold the monster with the pointed tail,
    Who cleaves the hills, and breaketh walls and weapons,
    Behold him who infecteth all the world."
Thus unto me my Guide began to say,
    And beckoned him that he should come to shore,   5
    Near to the confine of the trodden marble;
And that uncleanly image of deceit
    Came up and thrust ashore its head and bust,
    But on the border did not drag its tail.
The face was as the face of a just man,   10
    Its semblance outwardly was so benign,
    And of a serpent all the trunk beside.
Two paws it had, hairy unto the armpits;
    The back, and breast, and both the sides it had
    Depicted o'er with nooses and with shields.   15
With colors more, groundwork or broidery
    Never in cloth did Tartars make nor Turks,
    Nor were such tissues by Arachne laid.
As sometimes wherries lie upon the shore,
    That part are in the water, part on land;   20
    And as among the guzzling Germans there,

The beaver plants himself to wage his war;
  So that vile monster lay upon the border,
  Which is of stone, and shutteth in the sand.
His tail was wholly quivering in the void,   25
  Contorting upwards the envenomed fork,
  That in the guise of scorpion armed its point.
The Guide said: "Now perforce must turn aside
  Our way a little, even to that beast
  Malevolent, that yonder coucheth him."   30
We therefore on the right-hand side descended,
  And made ten steps upon the outer verge,
  Completely to avoid the sand and flame;
And after we are come to him, I see
  A little farther off upon the sand   35
  A people sitting near the hollow place.
Then said to me the Master: "So that full
  Experience of this round thou bear away,
  Now go and see what their condition is.
There let thy conversation be concise;   40
  Till thou returnest I will speak with him,
  That he concede to us his stalwart shoulders."
Thus farther still upon the outermost
  Head of that seventh circle all alone
  I went, where sat the melancholy folk.   45
Out of their eyes was gushing forth their woe;
  This way, that way, they helped them with their hands
  Now from the flames and now from the hot soil.
Not otherwise in summer do the dogs,
  Now with the foot, now with the muzzle, when   50
  By fleas, or flies, or gadflies, they are bitten.
When I had turned mine eyes upon the faces
  Of some, on whom the dolorous fire is falling,
  Not one of them I knew; but I perceived
That from the neck of each there hung a pouch,   55
  Which certain color had, and certain blazon;
  And thereupon it seems their eyes are feeding.

And as I gazing round me come among them,
    Upon a yellow pouch I azure saw
    That had the face and posture of a lion.   60
Proceeding then the current of my sight,
    Another of them saw I, red as blood,
    Display a goose more white than butter is.
And one, who with an azure sow and gravid
    Emblazoned had his little pouch of white,   65
    Said unto me: "What dost thou in this moat?
Now get thee gone; and since thou 'rt still alive,
    Know that a neighbor of mine, Vitaliano,
    Will have his seat here on my left-hand side.
A Paduan am I with these Florentines;   70
    Full many a time they thunder in mine ears,
    Exclaiming, 'Come the sovereign cavalier,
He who shall bring the satchel with three goats' ";
    Then twisted he his mouth, and forth he thrust
    His tongue, like to an ox that licks its nose.   75
And fearing lest my longer stay might vex
    Him who had warned me not to tarry long,
    Backward I turned me from those weary souls.
I found my Guide, who had already mounted
    Upon the back of that wild animal,   80
    And said to me: "Now be both strong and bold.
Now we descend by stairways such as these;
    Mount thou in front, for I will be midway,
    So that the tail may have no power to harm thee."
Such as he is who has so near the ague   85
    Of quartan that his nails are blue already,
    And trembles all, but looking at the shade;
Even such became I at those proffered words;
    But shame in me his menaces produced,
    Which maketh servant strong before good master.   90
I seated me upon those monstrous shoulders;
    I wished to say, and yet the voice came not
    As I believed, "Take heed that thou embrace me."

But he, who other times had rescued me
    In other peril, soon as I had mounted, 95
    Within his arms encircled and sustained me,
And said: "Now, Geryon, bestir thyself;
    The circles large, and the descent be little;
    Think of the novel burden which thou hast."
Even as the little vessel shoves from shore, 100
    Backward, still backward, so he thence withdrew;
    And when he wholly felt himself afloat,
There where his breast had been he turned his tail,
    And that extended like an eel he moved,
    And with his paws drew to himself the air. 105
A greater fear I do not think there was
    What time abandoned Phaeton the reins,
    Whereby the heavens, as still appears, were scorched;
Nor when the wretched Icarus his flanks
    Felt stripped of feathers by the melting wax, 110
    His father crying, "An ill way thou takest!"
Than was my own, when I perceived myself
    On all sides in the air, and saw extinguished
    The sight of everything but of the monster.
Onward he goeth, swimming slowly, slowly; 115
    Wheels and descends, but I perceive it only
    By wind upon my face and from below.
I heard already on the right the whirlpool
    Making a horrible crashing under us;
    Whence I thrust out my head with eyes cast downward. 120
Then was I still more fearful of the abyss;
    Because I fires beheld, and heard laments,
    Whereat I, trembling, all the closer cling.
I saw then, for before I had not seen it,
    The turning and descending, by great horrors 125
    That were approaching upon divers sides.
As falcon who has long been on the wing,
    Who, without seeing either lure or bird,
    Maketh the falconer say, "Ah me, thou stoopest,"

Descendeth weary, whence he started swiftly,   130
   Thorough a hundred circles, and alights
   Far from his master, sullen and disdainful;
Even thus did Geryon place us on the bottom,
   Close to the bases of the rough-hewn rock,
   And being disencumbered of our persons,   135
He sped away as arrow from the string.

Canto XVIII

There is a place in Hell called Malebolge,
    Wholly of stone and of an iron color,
    As is the circle that around it turns.
Right in the middle of the field malign
    There yawns a well exceeding wide and deep,   5
    Of which its place the structure will recount.
Round, then, is that enclosure which remains
    Between the well and foot of the high, hard bank,
    And has distinct in valleys ten its bottom.
As where for the protection of the walls   10
    Many and many moats surround the castles,
    The part in which they are a figure forms,
Just such an image those presented there;
    And as about such strongholds from their gates
    Unto the outer bank are little bridges,   15
So from the precipice's base did crags
    Project, which intersected dikes and moats,
    Unto the well that truncates and collects them.
Within this place, down shaken from the back
    Of Geryon, we found us; and the Poet   20
    Held to the left, and I moved on behind.

Upon my right hand I beheld new anguish,
    New torments, and new wielders of the lash,
    Wherewith the foremost Bolgia was replete.
Down at the bottom were the sinners naked;   25
    This side the middle came they facing us,
    Beyond it, with us, but with greater steps;
Even as the Romans, for the mighty host,
    The year of Jubilee, upon the bridge,
    Have chosen a mode to pass the people over;   30
For all upon one side towards the Castle
    Their faces have, and go unto Saint Peter's;
    On the other side they go towards the Mountain.
This side and that, along the livid stone
    Beheld I hornëd demons with great scourges,   35
    Who cruelly were beating them behind.
Ah me! how they did make them lift their legs
    At the first blows! and sooth not any one
    The second waited for, nor for the third.
While I was going on, mine eyes by one   40
    Encountered were; and straight I said: "Already
    With sight of this one I am not unfed."
Therefore I stayed my feet to make him out,
    And with me the sweet Guide came to a stand,
    And to my going somewhat back assented;   45
And he, the scourged one, thought to hide himself,
    Lowering his face, but little it availed him;
    For said I: "Thou that castest down thine eyes,
If false are not the features which thou bearest,
    Thou art Venedico Caccianimico;   50
    But what doth bring thee to such pungent sauces?"
And he to me: "Unwillingly I tell it;
    But forces me thine utterance distinct,
    Which makes me recollect the ancient world.
I was the one who the fair Ghisola   55
    Induced to grant the wishes of the Marquis,
    Howe'er the shameless story may be told.

Not the sole Bolognese am I who weeps here;
 Nay, rather is this place so full of them,
 That not so many tongues to-day are taught   60
'Twixt Reno and Savena to say *sipa;*
 And if thereof thou wishest pledge or proof,
 Bring to thy mind our avaricious heart."
While speaking in this manner, with his scourge
 A demon smote him, and said: "Get thee gone, 65
 Pander, there are no women here for coin."
I joined myself again unto mine Escort;
 Thereafterward with footsteps few we came
 To where a crag projected from the bank.
This very easily did we ascend,   70
 And turning to the right along its ridge,
 From those eternal circles we departed.
When we were there, where it is hollowed out
 Beneath, to give a passage to the scourged,
 The Guide said: "Wait, and see that on thee strike 75
The vision of those others evil-born,
 Of whom thou hast not yet beheld the faces,
 Because together with us they have gone."
From the old bridge we looked upon the train
 Which tow'rds us came upon the other border, 80
 And which the scourges in like manner smite.
And the good Master, without my inquiring,
 Said to me: "See that tall one who is coming
 And for his pain seems not to shed a tear;
Still what a royal aspect he retains!   85
 That Jason is, who by his heart and cunning
 The Colchians of the Ram made destitute.
He by the isle of Lemnos passed along
 After the daring women pitiless
 Had unto death devoted all their males.   90
There with his tokens and with ornate words
 Did he deceive Hypsipyle, the maiden
 Who first, herself, had all the rest deceived.

There did he leave her pregnant and forlorn;
    Such sin unto such punishment condemns him,   95
    And also for Medea is vengeance done.
With him go those who in such wise deceive;
    And this sufficient be of the first valley
    To know, and those that in its jaws it holds."
We were already where the narrow path   100
    Crosses athwart the second dike, and forms
    Of that a buttress for another arch.
Thence we heard people, who are making moan
    In the next Bolgia, snorting with their muzzles,
    And with their palms beating upon themselves.   105
The margins were encrusted with a mould
    By exhalation from below, that sticks there,
    And with the eyes and nostrils wages war.
The bottom is so deep, no place suffices
    To give us sight of it, without ascending   110
    The arch's back, where most the crag impends.
Thither we came, and thence down in the moat
    I saw a people smothered in a filth
    That out of human privies seemed to flow;
And whilst below there with mine eye I search,   115
    I saw one with his head so foul with ordure,
    It was not clear if he were clerk or layman.
He screamed to me: "Wherefore art thou so eager
    To look at me more than the other foul ones?"
    And I to him: "Because, if I remember,   120
I have already seen thee with dry hair,
    And thou 'rt Alessio Interminei of Lucca;
    Therefore I eye thee more than all the others."
And he thereon, belaboring his pumpkin:
    "The flatteries have submerged me here below,   125
    Wherewith my tongue was never surfeited."
Then said to me the Guide: "See that thou thrust
    Thy visage somewhat farther in advance,
    That with thine eyes thou well the face attain

Of that uncleanly and dishevelled drab,   130
    Who there doth scratch herself with filthy nails,
    And crouches now, and now on foot is standing.
Thais the harlot is it, who replied
    Unto her paramour, when he said, 'Have I
    Great gratitude from thee?'—'Nay, marvellous';   135
And herewith let our sight be satisfied."

Canto XIX

O Simon Magus, O forlorn disciples,
    Ye who the things of God, which ought to be
    The brides of holiness, rapaciously
For silver and for gold do prostitute,
    Now it behoves for you the trumpet sound,   5
    Because in this third Bolgia ye abide.
We had already on the following tomb
    Ascended to that portion of the crag
    Which o'er the middle of the moat hangs plumb.
Wisdom supreme, O how great art thou showest   10
    In heaven, in earth, and in the evil world,
    And with what justice doth thy power distribute!
I saw upon the sides and on the bottom
    The livid stone with perforations filled,
    All of one size, and every one was round.   15
To me less ample seemed they not, nor greater
    Than those that in my beautiful Saint John
    Are fashioned for the place of the baptizers,
And one of which, not many years ago,
    I broke for some one, who was drowning in it;   20
    Be this a seal all men to undeceive.

Out of the mouth of each one there protruded
    The feet of a transgressor, and the legs
    Up to the calf, the rest within remained.
In all of them the soles were both on fire;   25
    Wherefore the joints so violently quivered,
    They would have snapped asunder withes and bands.
Even as the flame of unctuous things is wont
    To move upon the outer surface only,
    So likewise was it there from heel to point.   30
"Master, who is that one who writhes himself,
    More than his other comrades quivering,"
    I said, "and whom a redder flame is sucking?"
And he to me: "If thou wilt have me bear thee
    Down there along that bank which lowest lies,   35
    From him thou 'lt know his errors and himself."
And I: "What pleases thee, to me is pleasing;
    Thou art my Lord, and knowest that I depart not
    From thy desire, and knowest what is not spoken."
Straightway upon the fourth dike we arrived;   40
    We turned, and on the left-hand side descended
    Down to the bottom full of holes and narrow.
And the good Master yet from off his haunch
    Deposed me not, till to the hole he brought me
    Of him who so lamented with his shanks.   45
"Whoe'er thou art, that standest upside down,
    O doleful soul, implanted like a stake,"
    To say began I, "if thou canst, speak out."
I stood even as the friar who is confessing
    The false assassin, who, when he is fixed,   50
    Recalls him, so that death may be delayed.
And he cried out: "Dost thou stand there already,
    Dost thou stand there already, Boniface?
    By many years the record lied to me.
Art thou so early satiate with that wealth,   55
    For which thou didst not fear to take by fraud
    The beautiful Lady, and then work her woe?"

Such I became, as people are who stand,
    Not comprehending what is answered them,
    As if bemocked, and know not how to answer.   60
Then said Virgilius: "Say to him straightway,
    I am not he, I am not he thou thinkest."
    And I replied as was imposed on me.
Whereat the spirit writhed with both his feet,
    Then, sighing, with a voice of lamentation   65
    Said to me: "Then what wantest thou of me?
If who I am thou carest so much to know,
    That thou on that account hast crossed the bank,
    Know that I vested was with the great mantle;
And truly was I son of the She-bear,   70
    So eager to advance the cubs, that wealth
    Above, and here myself, I pocketed.
Beneath my head the others are dragged down
    Who have preceded me in simony,
    Flattened along the fissure of the rock.   75
Below there I shall likewise fall, whenever
    That one shall come who I believed thou wast,
    What time the sudden question I proposed.
But longer I my feet already toast,
    And here have been in this way upside down,   80
    Than he will planted stay with reddened feet;
For after him shall come of fouler deed
    From tow'rds the west a Pastor without law,
    Such as befits to cover him and me.
New Jason will he be, of whom we read   85
    In Maccabees; and as his king was pliant,
    So he who governs France shall be to this one."
I do not know if I were here too bold,
    That him I answered only in this metre:
    "I pray thee tell me now how great a treasure   90

Our Lord demanded of Saint Peter first,
    Before he put the keys into his keeping?
    Truly he nothing asked but 'Follow me.'
Nor Peter nor the rest asked of Matthias
    Silver or gold, when he by lot was chosen   95
    Unto the place the guilty soul had lost.
Therefore stay here, for thou art justly punished,
    And keep safe guard o'er the ill-gotten money,
    Which caused thee to be valiant against Charles.
And were it not that still forbids it me   100
    The reverence for the keys superlative
    Thou hadst in keeping in the gladsome life,
I would make use of words more grievous still;
    Because your avarice afflicts the world,
    Trampling the good and lifting the depraved.   105
The Evangelist you Pastors had in mind,
    When she who sitteth upon many waters
    To fornicate with kings by him was seen;
The same who with the seven heads was born,
    And power and strength from the ten horns received,   110
    So long as virtue to her spouse was pleasing.
Ye have made yourselves a god of gold and silver;
    And from the idolater how differ ye,
    Save that he one, and ye a hundred worship?
Ah, Constantine! of how much ill was mother,   115
    Not thy conversion, but that marriage-dower
    Which the first wealthy Father took from thee!"
And while I sang to him such notes as these,
    Either that anger or that conscience stung him,
    He struggled violently with both his feet.   120
I think in sooth that it my Leader pleased,
    With such contented lip he listened ever
    Unto the sound of the true words expressed.

Therefore with both his arms he took me up,
    And when he had me all upon his breast,   125
    Remounted by the way where he descended.
Nor did he tire to have me clasped to him;
    But bore me to the summit of the arch
    Which from the fourth dike to the fifth is passage.
There tenderly he laid his burden down,   130
    Tenderly on the crag uneven and steep,
    That would have been hard passage for the goats:
Thence was unveiled to me another valley.

Canto XX

Of a new pain behoves me to make verses
    And give material to the twentieth canto
    Of the first song, which is of the submerged.
I was already thoroughly disposed
    To peer down into the uncovered depth,   5
    Which bathed itself with tears of agony;
And people saw I through the circular valley,
    Silent and weeping, coming at the pace
    Which in this world the Litanies assume.
As lower down my sight descended on them,   10
    Wondrously each one seemed to be distorted
    From chin to the beginning of the chest;
For tow'rds the reins the countenance was turned,
    And backward it behoved them to advance,
    As to look forward had been taken from them.   15
Perchance indeed by violence of palsy
    Some one has been thus wholly turned awry;
    But I ne'er saw it, nor believe it can be.
As God may let thee, Reader, gather fruit
    From this thy reading, think now for thyself   20
    How I could ever keep my face unmoistened,

When our own image near me I beheld,
    Distorted so, the weeping of the eyes
    Along the fissure bathed the hinder parts.
Truly I wept, leaning upon a peak   25
    Of the hard crag, so that my Escort said
    To me: "Art thou, too, of the other fools?
Here pity lives when it is wholly dead;
    Who is a greater reprobate than he
    Who feels compassion at the doom divine?   30
Lift up, lift up thy head, and see for whom
    Opened the earth before the Thebans' eyes;
    Wherefore they all cried: 'Whither rushest thou,
Amphiaraus? Why dost leave the war?'
    And downward ceased he not to fall amain   35
    As far as Minos, who lays hold on all.
See, he has made a bosom of his shoulders!
    Because he wished to see too far before him
    Behind he looks, and backward makes his way:
Behold Tiresias, who his semblance changed,   40
    When from a male a female he became,
    His members being all of them transformed;
And afterwards was forced to strike once more
    The two entangled serpents with his rod,
    Ere he could have again his manly plumes.   45
That Aruns is, who backs the other's belly,
    Who in the hills of Luni, there where grubs
    The Carrarese who houses underneath,
Among the marbles white a cavern had
    For his abode; whence to behold the stars   50
    And sea, the view was not cut off from him.
And she there, who is covering up her breasts,
    Which thou beholdest not, with loosened tresses,
    And on that side has all the hairy skin,

Was Manto, who made quest through many lands,   55
    Afterwards tarried there where I was born;
    Whereof I would thou list to me a little.
After her father had from life departed,
    And the city of Bacchus had become enslaved,
    She a long season wandered through the world.   60
Above in beauteous Italy lies a lake
    At the Alp's foot that shuts in Germany
    Over Tyrol, and has the name Benaco.
By a thousand springs, I think, and more, is bathed,
    'Twixt Garda and Val Camonica, Pennino,   65
    With water that grows stagnant in that lake.
Midway a place is where the Trentine Pastor,
    And he of Brescia, and the Veronese
    Might give his blessing, if he passed that way.
Sitteth Peschiera, fortress fair and strong,   70
    To front the Brescians and the Bergamasks,
    Where round about the bank descendeth lowest.
There of necessity must fall whatever
    In bosom of Benaco cannot stay,
    And grows a river down through verdant pastures.   75
Soon as the water doth begin to run,
    No more Benaco is it called, but Mincio,
    Far as Governo, where it falls in Po.
Not far it runs before it finds a plain
    In which it spreads itself, and makes it marshy,   80
    And oft 't is wont in summer to be sickly.
Passing that way the virgin pitiless
    Land in the middle of the fen descried,
    Untilled and naked of inhabitants;
There to escape all human intercourse,   85
    She with her servants stayed, her arts to practise,
    And lived, and left her empty body there.

The men, thereafter, who were scattered round,
 Collected in that place, which was made strong
 By the lagoon it had on every side;   90
They built their city over those dead bones,
 And, after her who first the place selected,
 Mantua named it, without other omen.
Its people once within more crowded were,
 Ere the stupidity of Casalodi   95
 From Pinamonte had received deceit.
Therefore I caution thee, if e'er thou hearest
 Originate my city otherwise,
 No falsehood may the verity defraud."
And I: "My master, thy discourses are   100
 To me so certain, and so take my faith,
 That unto me the rest would be spent coals.
But tell me of the people who are passing,
 If any one note-worthy thou beholdest,
 For only unto that my mind reverts."   105
Then said he to me: "He who from the cheek
 Thrusts out his beard upon his swarthy shoulders
 Was, at the time when Greece was void of males,
So that there scarce remained one in the cradle,
 An augur, and with Calchas gave the moment,   110
 In Aulis, when to sever the first cable.
Eryphylus his name was, and so sings
 My lofty Tragedy in some part or other;
 That knowest thou well, who knowest the whole of it.
The next, who is so slender in the flanks,   115
 Was Michael Scott, who of a verity
 Of magical illusions knew the game.
Behold Guido Bonatti, behold Asdente,
 Who now unto his leather and his thread
 Would fain have stuck, but he too late repents.   120
Behold the wretched ones, who left the needle,
 The spool and rock, and made them fortune-tellers;
 They wrought their magic spells with herb and image.

But come now, for already holds the confines
    Of both the hemispheres, and under Seville   125
    Touches the ocean-wave, Cain and the thorns,
And yesternight the moon was round already;
    Thou shouldst remember well it did not harm thee
    From time to time within the forest deep."
Thus spake he to me, and we walked the while.   130

CANTO XXI

From bridge to bridge thus, speaking other things
    Of which my Comedy cares not to sing,
    We came along, and held the summit, when
We halted to behold another fissure
    Of Malebolge and other vain laments;   5
    And I beheld it marvellously dark.
As in the Arsenal of the Venetians
    Boils in the winter the tenacious pitch
    To smear their unsound vessels o'er again,
For sail they cannot; and instead thereof   10
    One makes his vessel new, and one recaulks
    The ribs of that which many a voyage has made;
One hammers at the prow, one at the stern,
    This one makes oars, and that one cordage twists,
    Another mends the mainsail and the mizzen;   15
Thus, not by fire, but by the art divine,
    Was boiling down below there a dense pitch
    Which upon every side the bank belimed.
I saw it, but I did not see within it
    Aught but the bubbles that the boiling raised,   20
    And all swell up and resubside compressed.

The while below there fixedly I gazed,
    My Leader, crying out: "Beware, beware!"
    Drew me unto himself from where I stood.
Then I turned round, as one who is impatient   25
    To see what it behoves him to escape,
    And whom a sudden terror doth unman,
Who, while he looks, delays not his departure;
    And I beheld behind us a black devil,
    Running along upon the crag, approach.   30
Ah, how ferocious was he in his aspect!
    And how he seemed to me in action ruthless,
    With open wings and light upon his feet!
His shoulders, which sharp-pointed were and high,
    A sinner did encumber with both haunches,   35
    And he held clutched the sinews of the feet.
From off our bridge, he said: "O Malebranche,
    Behold one of the elders of Saint Zita;
    Plunge him beneath, for I return for others
Unto that town, which is well furnished with them.   40
    All there are barrators, except Bonturo;
    No into Yes for money there is changed."
He hurled him down, and over the hard crag
    Turned round, and never was a mastiff loosened
    In so much hurry to pursue a thief.   45
The other sank, and rose again face downward;
    But the demons, under cover of the bridge,
    Cried: "Here the Santo Volto has no place!
Here swims one otherwise than in the Serchio;
    Therefore, if for our gaffs thou wishest not,   50
    Do not uplift thyself above the pitch."
They seized him then with more than a hundred rakes;
    They said: "It here behoves thee to dance covered,
    That, if thou canst, thou secretly mayest pilfer."
Not otherwise the cooks their scullions make   55
    Immerse into the middle of the caldron
    The meat with hooks, so that it may not float.

Said the good Master to me: "That it be not
    Apparent thou art here, crouch thyself down
    Behind a jag, that thou mayest have some screen;   60
And for no outrage that is done to me
    Be thou afraid, because these things I know,
    For once before was I in such a scuffle."
Then he passed on beyond the bridge's head,
    And as upon the sixth bank he arrived,   65
    Need was for him to have a steadfast front.
With the same fury, and the same uproar,
    As dogs leap out upon a mendicant,
    Who on a sudden begs, where'er he stops,
They issued from beneath the little bridge,   70
    And turned against him all their grappling-irons;
    But he cried out: "Be none of you malignant!
Before those hooks of yours lay hold of me,
    Let one of you step forward, who may hear me,
    And then take counsel as to grappling me."   75
They all cried out: "Let Malacoda go";
    Whereat one started, and the rest stood still,
    And he came to him, saying: "What avails it?"
"Thinkest thou, Malacoda, to behold me
    Advanced into this place," my Master said,   80
    "Safe hitherto from all your skill of fence,
Without the will divine, and fate auspicious?
    Let me go on, for it in Heaven is willed
    That I another show this savage road."
Then was his arrogance so humbled in him,   85
    That he let fall his grapnel at his feet,
    And to the others said: "Now strike him not."
And unto me my Guide: "O thou, who sittest
    Among the splinters of the bridge crouched down,
    Securely now return to me again."   90
Wherefore I started and came swiftly to him;
    And all the devils forward thrust themselves,
    So that I feared they would not keep their compact.

And thus beheld I once afraid the soldiers
    Who issued under safeguard from Caprona,   95
    Seeing themselves among so many foes.
Close did I press myself with all my person
    Beside my Leader, and turned not mine eyes
    From off their countenance, which was not good.
They lowered their rakes, and "Wilt thou have me hit him,"   100
    They said to one another, "on the rump?"
    And answered: "Yes; see that thou nick him with it."
But the same demon who was holding parley
    With my Conductor turned him very quickly,
    And said: "Be quiet, be quiet, Scarmiglione";   105
Then said to us: "You can no farther go
    Forward upon this crag, because is lying
    All shattered, at the bottom, the sixth arch.
And if it still doth please you to go onward,
    Pursue your way along upon this rock;   110
    Near is another crag that yields a path.
Yesterday, five hours later than this hour,
    One thousand and two hundred sixty-six
    Years were complete, that here the way was broken.
I send in that direction some of mine   115
    To see if any one doth air himself;
    Go ye with them; for they will not be vicious.
Step forward Alichino and Calcabrina,"
    Began he to cry out, "and thou, Cagnazzo;
    And Barbariccia do thou guide the ten.   120
Come forward, Libicocco and Draghignazzo,
    And tuskëd Ciriatto and Graffiacane,
    And Farfarello and mad Rubicante;
Search ye all round about the boiling pitch;
    Let these be safe as far as the next crag,   125
    That all unbroken passes o'er the dens."
"O me! what is it, Master, that I see?
    Pray let us go," I said, "without an escort,
    If thou knowest how, since for myself I ask none.

If thou art as observant as thy wont is,   130
    Dost thou not see that they do gnash their teeth,
    And with their brows are threatening woe to us?"
And he to me: "I will not have thee fear;
    Let them gnash on, according to their fancy,
    Because they do it for those boiling wretches."   135
Along the left-hand dike they wheeled about;
    But first had each one thrust his tongue between
    His teeth towards their leader for a signal;
And he had made a trumpet of his rump.

Canto XXII

I have erewhile seen horsemen moving camp,
    Begin the storming, and their muster make,
    And sometimes starting off for their escape;
Vaunt-couriers have I seen upon your land,
    O Aretines, and foragers go forth,   5
    Tournaments stricken, and the joustings run,
Sometimes with trumpets and sometimes with bells,
    With kettle-drums, and signals of the castles,
    And with our own, and with outlandish things,
But never yet with bagpipe so uncouth   10
    Did I see horsemen move, nor infantry,
    Nor ship by any sign of land or star.
We went upon our way with the ten demons;
    Ah, savage company! but in the church
    With saints, and in the tavern with the gluttons!   15
Ever upon the pitch was my intent,
    To see the whole condition of that Bolgia,
    And of the people who therein were burned.
Even as the dolphins, when they make a sign
    To mariners by arching of the back,   20
    That they should counsel take to save their vessel,

Thus sometimes, to alleviate his pain,
    One of the sinners would display his back,
    And in less time conceal it than it lightens.
As on the brink of water in a ditch   25
    The frogs stand only with their muzzles out,
    So that they hide their feet and other bulk,
So upon every side the sinners stood;
    But ever as Barbariccia near them came,
    Thus underneath the boiling they withdrew.   30
I saw, and still my heart doth shudder at it,
    One waiting thus, even as it comes to pass
    One frog remains, and down another dives;
And Graffiacan, who most confronted him,
    Grappled him by his tresses smeared with pitch,   35
    And drew him up, so that he seemed an otter.
I knew, before, the names of all of them,
    So had I noted them when they were chosen,
    And when they called each other, listened how.
"O Rubicante, see that thou do lay   40
    Thy claws upon him, so that thou mayst flay him,"
    Cried all together the accursed ones.
And I: "My Master, see to it, if thou canst,
    That thou mayst know who is the luckless wight,
    Thus come into his adversaries' hands."   45
Near to the side of him my Leader drew,
    Asked of him whence he was; and he replied:
    "I in the kingdom of Navarre was born;
My mother placed me servant to a lord,
    For she had borne me to a ribald knave,   50
    Destroyer of himself and of his things.
Then I domestic was of good King Thibault;
    I set me there to practise barratry,
    For which I pay the reckoning in this heat."
And Ciriatto, from whose mouth projected,   55
    On either side, a tusk, as in a boar,
    Caused him to feel how one of them could rip.

Among malicious cats the mouse had come;
  But Barbariccia clasped him in his arms,
  And said: "Stand ye aside, while I enfork him." 60
And to my Master he turned round his head;
  "Ask him again," he said, "if more thou wish
  To know from him, before some one destroy him."
The Guide: "Now tell then of the other culprits;
  Knowest thou any one who is a Latian, 65
  Under the pitch?" And he: "I separated
Lately from one who was a neighbor to it;
  Would that I still were covered up with him,
  For I should fear not either claw nor hook!"
And Libicocco: "We have borne too much"; 70
  And with his grapnel seized him by the arm,
  So that, by rending, he tore off a tendon.
Eke Draghignazzo wished to pounce upon him
  Down at the legs; whence their Decurion
  Turned round and round about with evil look. 75
When they again somewhat were pacified,
  Of him, who still was looking at his wound,
  Demanded my Conductor without stay:
"Who was that one, from whom a luckless parting
  Thou sayest thou hast made, to come ashore?" 80
  And he replied: "It was the Friar Gomita,
He of Gallura, vessel of all fraud,
  Who had the enemies of his Lord in hand,
  And dealt so with them each exults thereat;
Money he took, and let them smoothly off, 85
  As he says; and in other offices
  A barrator was he, not mean but sovereign.
Foregathers with him one Don Michael Zanche
  Of Logodoro; and of Sardinia
  To gossip never do their tongues feel tired. 90
O me! see that one, how he grinds his teeth;
  Still farther would I speak, but am afraid
  Lest he to scratch my itch be making ready."

And the grand Provost, turned to Farfarello,
    Who rolled his eyes about as if to strike,   95
    Said: "Stand aside there, thou malicious bird."
"If you desire either to see or hear,"
    The terror-stricken recommenced thereon,
    "Tuscans or Lombards, I will make them come.
But let the Malebranche cease a little,   100
    So that these may not their revenges fear,
    And I, down sitting in this very place,
For one that I am will make seven come,
    When I shall whistle, as our custom is
    To do whenever one of us comes out."   105
Cagnazzo at these words his muzzle lifted,
    Shaking his head, and said: "Just hear the trick
    Which he has thought of, down to throw himself!"
Whence he, who snares in great abundance had,
    Responded: "I by far too cunning am,   110
    When I procure for mine a greater sadness."
Alichin held not in, but running counter
    Unto the rest, said to him: "If thou dive,
    I will not follow thee upon the gallop,
But I will beat my wings above the pitch;   115
    The height be left, and be the bank a shield,
    To see if thou alone dost countervail us."
O thou who readest, thou shalt hear new sport!
    Each to the other side his eyes averted;
    He first, who most reluctant was to do it.   120
The Navarrese selected well his time;
    Planted his feet on land, and in a moment
    Leaped, and released himself from their design.
Whereat each one was suddenly stung with shame,
    But he most who was cause of the defeat;   125
    Therefore he moved, and cried: "Thou art o'ertaken."
But little it availed, for wings could not
    Outstrip the fear; the other one went under,
    And, flying, upward he his breast directed.

Not otherwise the duck upon a sudden   130
 Dives under, when the falcon is approaching,
 And upward he returneth cross and weary.
Infuriate at the mockery, Calcabrina
 Flying behind him followed close, desirous
 The other should escape, to have a quarrel.   135
And when the barrator had disappeared,
 He turned his talons upon his companion,
 And grappled with him right above the moat.
But sooth the other was a doughty sparhawk
 To clapperclaw him well; and both of them   140
 Fell in the middle of the boiling pond.
A sudden intercessor was the heat;
 But ne'ertheless of rising there was naught,
 To such degree they had their wings belimed.
Lamenting with the others, Barbariccia   145
 Made four of them fly to the other side
 With all their gaffs, and very speedily
This side and that they to their posts descended;
 They stretched their hooks towards the pitch-ensnared,
 Who were already baked within the crust,   150
And in this manner busied did we leave them.

Canto XXIII

Silent, alone, and without company
    We went, the one in front, the other after,
    As go the Minor Friars along their way.
Upon the fable of *Æsop* was directed
    My thought, by reason of the present quarrel,   5
    Where he has spoken of the frog and mouse;
For *mo* and *issa* are not more alike
    Than this one is to that, if well we couple
    End and beginning with a steadfast mind.
And even as one thought from another springs,   10
    So afterward from that was born another,
    Which the first fear within me double made.
Thus did I ponder: "These on our account
    Are laughed to scorn, with injury and scoff
    So great, that much I think it must annoy them.   15
If anger be engrafted on ill-will,
    They will come after us more merciless
    Than dog upon the leveret which he seizes,"
I felt my hair stand all on end already
    With terror, and stood backwardly intent,   20
    When said I: "Master, if thou hidest not

Thyself and me forthwith, of Malebranche
    I am in dread; we have them now behind us;
    I so imagine them, I already feel them."
And he: "If I were made of leaded glass,   25
    Thine outward image I should not attract
    Sooner to me than I imprint the inner.
Just now thy thoughts came in among my own,
    With similar attitude and similar face,
    So that of both one counsel sole I made.   30
If peradventure the right bank so slope
    That we to the next Bolgia can descend,
    We shall escape from the imagined chase."
Not yet he finished rendering such opinion,
    When I beheld them come with outstretched wings,   35
    Not far remote, with will to seize upon us.
My Leader on a sudden seized me up,
    Even as a mother who by noise is wakened,
    And close beside her sees the enkindled flames,
Who takes her son, and flies, and does not stop,   40
    Having more care of him than of herself,
    So that she clothes her only with a shift;
And downward from the top of the hard bank
    Supine he gave him to the pendent rock,
    That one side of the other Bolgia walls.   45
Ne'er ran so swiftly water through a sluice
    To turn the wheel of any land-built mill,
    When nearest to the paddles it approaches,
As did my Master down along that border,
    Bearing me with him on his breast away,   50
    As his own son, and not as a companion.
Hardly the bed of the ravine below
    His feet had reached, ere they had reached the hill
    Right over us; but he was not afraid;
For the high Providence, which had ordained   55
    To place them ministers of the fifth moat,
    The power of thence departing took from all.

A painted people there below we found,
  Who went about with footsteps very slow,
  Weeping and in their semblance tired and vanquished.   60
They had on mantles with the hoods low down
  Before their eyes, and fashioned of the cut
  That in Cologne they for the monks are made.
Without, they gilded are so that it dazzles;
  But inwardly all leaden and so heavy   65
  That Frederick used to put them on of straw.
O everlastingly fatiguing mantle!
  Again we turned us, still to the left hand
  Along with them, intent on their sad plaint;
But owing to the weight, that weary folk   70
  Came on so tardily, that we were new
  In company at each motion of the haunch.
Whence I unto my Leader: "See thou find
  Some one who may by deed or name be known,
  And thus in going move thine eye about."   75
And one, who understood the Tuscan speech,
  Cried to us from behind: "Stay ye your feet,
  Ye, who so run athwart the dusky air!
Perhaps thou 'lt have from me what thou demandest."
  Whereat the Leader turned him, and said: "Wait,   80
  And then according to his pace proceed."
I stopped, and two beheld I show great haste
  Of spirit, in their faces, to be with me;
  But the burden and the narrow way delayed them.
When they came up, long with an eye askance   85
  They scanned me without uttering a word.
  Then to each other turned, and said together:
"He by the action of his throat seems living;
  And if they dead are, by what privilege
  Go they uncovered by the heavy stole?"   90
Then said to me: "Tuscan, who to the college
  Of miserable hypocrites art come,
  Do not disdain to tell us who thou art."

And I to them: "Born was I, and grew up
   In the great town on the fair river of Arno,   95
   And with the body am I've always had.
But who are ye, in whom there trickles down
   Along your cheeks such grief as I behold?
   And what pain is upon you, that so sparkles?"
And one replied to me: "These orange cloaks   100
   Are made of lead so heavy, that the weights
   Cause in this way their balances to creak.
Frati Gaudenti were we, and Bolognese;
   I Catalano, and he Loderingo
   Named, and together taken by thy city,   105
As the wont is to take one man alone,
   For maintenance of its peace; and we were such
   That still it is apparent round Gardingo."
"O Friars," began I, "your iniquitous . . ."
   But said no more; for to mine eyes there rushed   110
   One crucified with three stakes on the ground.
When me he saw, he writhed himself all over,
   Blowing into his beard with suspirations;
   And the Friar Catalan, who noticed this,
Said to me: "This transfixed one, whom thou seest,   115
   Counselled the Pharisees that it was meet
   To put one man to torture for the people.
Crosswise and naked is he on the path,
   As thou perceivest; and he needs must feel,
   Whoever passes, first how much he weighs;   120
And in like mode his father-in-law is punished
   Within this moat, and the others of the council,
   Which for the Jews was a malignant seed."
And thereupon I saw Virgilius marvel
   O'er him who was extended on the cross   125
   So vilely in eternal banishment.
Then he directed to the Friar this voice:
   "Be not displeased, if granted thee, to tell us
   If to the right hand any pass slope down

By which we two may issue forth from here,   130
    Without constraining some of the black angels
    To come and extricate us from this deep."
Then he made answer: "Nearer than thou hopest
    There is a rock, that forth from the great circle
    Proceeds, and crosses all the cruel valleys,   135
Save that at this 't is broken, and does not bridge it;
    You will be able to mount up the ruin,
    That sidelong slopes and at the bottom rises."
The Leader stood awhile with head bowed down;
    Then said: "The business badly he recounted   140
    Who grapples with his hook the sinners yonder."
And the Friar: "Many of the Devil's vices
    Once heard I at Bologna, and among them,
    That he's a liar and the father of lies."
Thereat my Leader with great strides went on,   145
    Somewhat disturbed with anger in his looks;
    Whence from the heavy-laden I departed
After the prints of his beloved feet.

CANTO XXIV

In that part of the youthful year wherein
    The Sun has locks beneath Aquarius tempers,
    And now the nights draw near to half the day,
What time the hoar-frost copies on the ground
    The outward semblance of her sister white,   5
    But little lasts the temper of her pen,
The husbandman, whose forage faileth him,
    Rises, and looks, and seeth the champaign
    All gleaming white, whereat he beats his flank,
Returns in doors, and up and down laments,   10
    Like a poor wretch, who knows not what to do;
    Then he returns, and hope revives again,
Seeing the world has changed its countenance
    In little time, and takes his shepherd's crook,
    And forth the little lambs to pasture drives.   15
Thus did the Master fill me with alarm,
    When I beheld his forehead so disturbed,
    And to the ailment came as soon the plaster.
For as we came unto the ruined bridge,
    The Leader turned to me with that sweet look   20
    Which at the mountain's foot I first beheld.

His arms he opened, after some advisement
    Within himself elected, looking first
    Well at the ruin, and laid hold of me.
And even as he who acts and meditates,   25
    For aye it seems that he provides beforehand,
    So upward lifting me towards the summit
Of a huge rock, he scanned another crag,
    Saying: "To that one grapple afterwards,
    But try first if 't is such that it will hold thee."   30
This was no way for one clothed with a cloak;
    For hardly we, he light, and I pushed upward,
    Were able to ascend from jag to jag.
And had it not been, that upon that precinct
    Shorter was the ascent than on the other,   35
    He I know not, but I had been dead beat.
But because Malebolge tow'rds the mouth
    Of the profoundest well is all inclining,
    The structure of each valley doth import
That one bank rises and the other sinks.   40
    Still we arrived at length upon the point
    Wherefrom the last stone breaks itself asunder.
The breath was from my lungs so milked away,
    When I was up, that I could go no farther,
    Nay, I sat down upon my first arrival.   45
"Now it behoves thee thus to put off sloth,"
    My Master said; "for sitting upon down,
    Or under quilt, one cometh not to fame,
Withouten which whoso his life consumes
    Such vestige leaveth of himself on earth,   50
    As smoke in air or in the water foam.
And therefore raise thee up, o'ercome the anguish
    With spirit that o'ercometh every battle,
    If with its heavy body it sink not.
A longer stairway it behoves thee mount;   55
    'T is not enough from these to have departed;
    Let it avail thee, if thou understand me."

Then I uprose, showing myself provided
 Better with breath than I did feel myself,
 And said: "Go on, for I am strong and bold."   60
Upward we took our way along the crag,
 Which jagged was, and narrow, and difficult,
 And more precipitous far than that before.
Speaking I went, not to appear exhausted;
 Whereat a voice from the next moat came forth,   65
 Not well adapted to articulate words.
I know not what it said, though o'er the back
 I now was of the arch that passes there;
 But he seemed moved to anger who was speaking.
I was bent downward, but my living eyes   70
 Could not attain the bottom, for the dark;
 Wherefore I: "Master, see that thou arrive
At the next round, and let us descend the wall;
 For as from hence I hear and understand not,
 So I look down and nothing I distinguish."   75
"Other response," he said, "I make thee not,
 Except the doing; for the modest asking
 Ought to be followed by the deed in silence."
We from the bridge descended at its head,
 Where it connects itself with the eighth bank,   80
 And then was manifest to me the Bolgia;
And I beheld therein a terrible throng
 Of serpents, and of such a monstrous kind,
 That the remembrance still congeals my blood.
Let Lybia boast no longer with her sand;   85
 For if Chelydri, Jaculi, and Phareæ
 She breeds, with Cenchri and with Amphisbæna,
Neither so many plagues nor so malignant
 E'er showed she with all Ethiopia,
 Nor with whatever on the Red Sea is!   90
Among this cruel and most dismal throng
 People were running naked and affrighted,
 Without the hope of hole or heliotrope.

They had their hands with serpents bound behind them;
   These riveted upon their reins the tail   95
   And head, and were in front of them entwined.
And lo! at one who was upon our side
   There darted forth a serpent, which transfixed him
   There where the neck is knotted to the shoulders.
Nor *O* so quickly e'er, nor *I* was written,   100
   As he took fire, and burned; and ashes wholly
   Behoved it that in falling he became.
And when he on the ground was thus destroyed,
   The ashes drew together, and of themselves
   Into himself they instantly returned.   105
Even thus by the great sages 't is confessed
   The phœnix dies, and then is born again,
   When it approaches its five-hundredth year;
On herb or grain it feeds not in its life,
   But only on tears of incense and amomum,   110
   And nard and myrrh are its last winding-sheet.
And as he is who falls, and knows not how,
   By force of demons who to earth down drag him,
   Or other oppilation that binds man,
When he arises and around him looks,   115
   Wholly bewildered by the mighty anguish
   Which he has suffered, and in looking sighs;
Such was that sinner after he had risen.
   Justice of God! O how severe it is,
   That blows like these in vengeance poureth down!   120
The Guide thereafter asked him who he was;
   Whence he replied: "I rained from Tuscany
   A short time since into this cruel gorge.
A bestial life, and not a human, pleased me,
   Even as the mule I was; I'm Vanni Fucci,   125
   Beast, and Pistoia was my worthy den."
And I unto the Guide: "Tell him to stir not,
   And ask what crime has thrust him here below,
   For once a man of blood and wrath I saw him."

And the sinner, who had heard, dissembled not,   130
    But unto me directed mind and face,
    And with a melancholy shame was painted.
Then said: "It pains me more that thou hast caught me
    Amid this misery where thou seest me,
    Than when I from the other life was taken.   135
What thou demandest I cannot deny;
    So low am I put down because I robbed
    The sacristy of the fair ornaments,
And falsely once 't was laid upon another;
    But that thou mayst not such a sight enjoy,   140
    If thou shalt e'er be out of the dark places,
Thine ears to my announcement ope and hear:
    Pistoia first of Neri groweth meagre;
    Then Florence doth renew her men and manners;
Mars draws a vapor up from Val di Magra,   145
    Which is with turbid clouds enveloped round,
    And with impetuous and bitter tempest
Over Campo Picen shall be the battle;
    When it shall suddenly rend the mist asunder,
    So that each Bianco shall thereby be smitten.   150
And this I've said that it may give thee pain."

CANTO XXV

At the conclusion of his words, the thief
   Lifted his hands aloft with both the figs,
   Crying: "Take that, God, for at thee I aim them."
From that time forth the serpents were my friends;
   For one entwined itself about his neck   5
   As if it said: "I will not thou speak more";
And round his arms another, and rebound him,
   Clinching itself together so in front,
   That with them he could not a motion make.
Pistoia, ah, Pistoia! why resolve not   10
   To burn thyself to ashes and so perish,
   Since in ill-doing thou thy seed excellest?
Through all the sombre circles of this Hell,
   Spirit I saw not against God so proud,
   Not he who fell at Thebes down from the walls!   15
He fled away, and spake no further word;
   And I beheld a Centaur full of rage
   Come crying out: "Where is, where is the scoffer?"
I do not think Maremma has so many
   Serpents as he had all along his back,   20
   As far as where our countenance begins.

Upon the shoulders, just behind the nape,
   With wings wide open was a dragon lying,
   And he sets fire to all that he encounters.
My Master said: "That one is Cacus, who   25
   Beneath the rock upon Mount Aventine
   Created oftentimes a lake of blood.
He goes not on the same road with his brothers,
   By reason of the fraudulent theft he made
   Of the great herd, which he had near to him;   30
Whereat his tortuous actions ceased beneath
   The mace of Hercules, who peradventure
   Gave him a hundred, and he felt not ten."
While he was speaking thus, he had passed by,
   And spirits three had underneath us come,   35
   Of which nor I aware was, nor my Leader,
Until what time they shouted: "Who are you?"
   On which account our story made a halt,
   And then we were intent on them alone.
I did not know them; but it came to pass,   40
   As it is wont to happen by some chance,
   That one to name the other was compelled,
Exclaiming: "Where can Cianfa have remained?"
   Whence I, so that the Leader might attend,
   Upward from chin to nose my finger laid.   45
If thou art, Reader, slow now to believe
   What I shall say, it will no marvel be,
   For I who saw it hardly can admit it.
As I was holding raised on them my brows,
   Behold! a serpent with six feet darts forth   50
   In front of one, and fastens wholly on him.
With middle feet it bound him round the paunch,
   And with the forward ones his arms it seized;
   Then thrust its teeth through one cheek and the other;
The hindermost it stretched upon his thighs,   55
   And put its tail through in between the two,
   And up behind along the reins outspread it.

Ivy was never fastened by its barbs
    Unto a tree so, as this horrible reptile
    Upon the other's limbs entwined its own. 60
Then they stuck close, as if of heated wax
    They had been made, and intermixed their color;
    Nor one nor other seemed now what he was;
E'en as proceedeth on before the flame
    Upward along the paper a brown color, 65
    Which is not black as yet, and the white dies.
The other two looked on, and each of them
    Cried out: "O me, Agnello, how thou changest!
    Behold, thou now art neither two nor one."
Already the two heads had one become, 70
    When there appeared to us two figures mingled
    Into one face, wherein the two were lost.
Of the four lists were fashioned the two arms,
    The thighs and legs, the belly and the chest
    Members became that never yet were seen. 75
Every original aspect there was cancelled;
    Two and yet none did the perverted image
    Appear, and such departed with slow pace.
Even as a lizard, under the great scourge
    Of days canicular, exchanging hedge, 80
    Lightning appeareth if the road it cross;
Thus did appear, coming towards the bellies
    Of the two others, a small fiery serpent,
    Livid and black as is a peppercorn.
And in that part whereat is first received 85
    Our ailment, it one of them transfixed;
    Then downward fell in front of him extended.
The one transfixed looked at it, but said naught;
    Nay, rather with feet motionless he yawned,
    Just as if sleep or fever had assailed him. 90
He at the serpent gazed, and it at him;
    One through the wound, the other through the mouth
    Smoked violently, and the smoke commingled.

Henceforth be silent Lucan, where he mentions
    Wretched Sabellus and Nassidius,   95
    And wait to hear what now shall be shot forth.
Be silent Ovid, of Cadmus and Arethusa;
    For if him to a snake, her to a fountain,
    Converts he fabling, that I grudge him not;
Because two natures never front to front   100
    Has he transmuted, so that both the forms
    To interchange their matter ready were.
Together they responded in such wise,
    That to a fork the serpent cleft his tail,
    And eke the wounded drew his feet together.   105
The legs together with the thighs themselves
    Adhered so, that in little time the juncture
    No sign whatever made that was apparent.
He with the cloven tail assumed the figure
    The other one was losing, and his skin   110
    Became elastic, and the other's hard.
I saw the arms draw inward at the armpits,
    And both feet of the reptile, that were short,
    Lengthen as much as those contracted were.
Thereafter the hind feet, together twisted,   115
    Became the member that a man conceals,
    And of his own the wretch had two created.
While both of them the exhalation veils
    With a new color, and engenders hair
    On one of them and depilates the other,   120
The one uprose and down the other fell,
    Though turning not away their impious lamps,
    Underneath which each one his muzzle changed.
He who was standing drew it tow'rds the temples,
    And from excess of matter, which came thither,   125
    Issued the ears from out the hollow cheeks;
What did not backward run and was retained
    Of that excess made to the face a nose,
    And the lips thickened far as was befitting.

He who lay prostrate thrusts his muzzle forward,   130
   And backward draws the ears into his head,
   In the same manner as the snail its horns;
And so the tongue, which was entire and apt
   For speech before, is cleft, and the bi-forked
   In the other closes up, and the smoke ceases.   135
The soul, which to a reptile had been changed,
   Along the valley hissing takes to flight,
   And after him the other speaking sputters.
Then did he turn upon him his new shoulders,
   And said to the other: "I'll have Buoso run,   140
   Crawling as I have done, along this road."
In this way I beheld the seventh ballast
   Shift and reshift, and here be my excuse
   The novelty, if aught my pen transgress.
And notwithstanding that mine eyes might be   145
   Somewhat bewildered, and my mind dismayed,
   They could not flee away so secretly
But that I plainly saw Puccio Sciancato;
   And he it was who sole of three companions,
   Which came in the beginning, was not changed;   150
The other was he whom thou, Gaville, weepest.

Canto XXVI

Rejoice, O Florence, since thou art so great,
   That over sea and land thou beatest thy wings,
   And throughout Hell thy name is spread abroad!
Among the thieves five citizens of thine
   Like these I found, whence shame comes unto me,   5
   And thou thereby to no great honor risest.
But if when morn is near our dreams are true,
   Feel shalt thou in a little time from now
   What Prato, if none other, craves for thee.
And if it now were, it were not too soon;   10
   Would that it were, seeing it needs must be,
   For 't will aggrieve me more the more I age.
We went our way, and up along the stairs
   The bourns had made us to descend before,
   Remounted my Conductor and drew me.   15
And following the solitary path
   Among the rocks and ridges of the crag,
   The foot without the hand sped not at all.
Then sorrowed I, and sorrow now again,
   When I direct my mind to what I saw,
   And more my genius curb than I am wont,   20

That it may run not unless virtue guide it;
    So that if some good star, or better thing,
    Have given me good, I may myself not grudge it.
As many as the hind (who on the hill   25
    Rests at the time when he who lights the world
    His countenance keeps least concealed from us,
Whileas the fly gives place unto the gnat)
    Seeth the glow-worms down along the valley,
    Perchance there where he ploughs and makes his vintage;   30
With flames as manifold resplendent all
    Was the eighth Bolgia, as I grew aware
    As soon as I was where the depth appeared.
And such as he who with the bears avenged him
    Beheld Elijah's chariot at departing,   35
    What time the steeds to heaven erect uprose,
For with his eye he could not follow it
    So as to see aught else than flame alone,
    Even as a little cloud ascending upward,
Thus each along the gorge of the intrenchment   40
    Was moving; for not one reveals the theft,
    And every flame a sinner steals away.
I stood upon the bridge uprisen to see,
    So that, if I had seized not on a rock,
    Down had I fallen without being pushed.   45
And the Leader, who beheld me so attent,
    Exclaimed: "Within the fires the spirits are;
    Each swathes himself with that wherewith he burns."
"My Master," I replied, "by hearing thee
    I am more sure; but I surmised already   50
    It might be so, and already wished to ask thee
Who is within that fire, which comes so cleft
    At top, it seems uprising from the pyre
    Where was Eteocles with his brother placed."
He answered me: "Within there are tormented   55
    Ulysses and Diomed, and thus together
    They unto vengeance run as unto wrath.

And there within their flame do they lament
    The ambush of the horse, which made the door
    Whence issued forth the Romans' gentle seed;   60
Therein is wept the craft, for which being dead
    Deidamia still deplores Achilles,
    And pain for the Palladium there is borne."
"If they within those sparks possess the power
    To speak," I said, "thee, Master, much I pray,   65
    And re-pray, that the prayer be worth a thousand,
That thou make no denial of awaiting
    Until the hornëd flame shall hither come;
    Thou seest that with desire I lean towards it."
And he to me: "Worthy is thy entreaty   70
    Of much applause, and therefore I accept it;
    But take heed that thy tongue restrain itself.
Leave me to speak, because I have conceived
    That which thou wishest; for they might disdain
    Perchance, since they were Greeks, discourse of thine."   75
When now the flame had come unto that point,
    Where to my Leader it seemed time and place,
    After this fashion did I hear him speak:
"O ye, who are twofold within one fire,
    If I deserved of you, while I was living,   80
    If I deserved of you or much or little
When in the world I wrote the lofty verses,
    Do not move on, but one of you declare
    Whither, being lost, he went away to die."
Then of the antique flame the greater horn,   85
    Murmuring, began to wave itself about
    Even as a flame doth which the wind fatigues.
Thereafterward, the summit to and fro
    Moving as if it were the tongue that spake,
    It uttered forth a voice, and said: "When I   90
From Circe had departed, who concealed me
    More than a year there near unto Gaëta,
    Or ever yet Æneas named it so,

Nor fondness for my son, nor reverence
   For my old father, nor the due affection   95
   Which joyous should have made Penelope,
Could overcome within me the desire
   I had to be experienced of the world,
   And of the vice and virtue of mankind;
But I put forth on the high open sea   100
   With one sole ship, and that small company
   By which I never had deserted been.
Both of the shores I saw as far as Spain,
   Far as Morocco, and the isle of Sardes,
   And the others which that sea bathes round about.   105
I and my company were old and slow
   When at that narrow passage we arrived
   Where Hercules his landmarks set as signals,
That man no farther onward should adventure.
   On the right hand behind me left I Seville,   110
   And on the other already had left Ceuta.
'O brothers, who amid a hundred thousand
   Perils,' I said, 'have come unto the West,
   To this so inconsiderable vigil
Which is remaining of your senses still,   115
   Be ye unwilling to deny the knowledge,
   Following the sun, of the unpeopled world.
Consider ye the seed from which ye sprang;
   Ye were not made to live like unto brutes,
   But for pursuit of virtue and of knowledge.'   120
So eager did I render my companions,
   With this brief exhortation, for the voyage,
   That then I hardly could have held them back.
And having turned our stern unto the morning,
   We of the oars made wings for our mad flight,   125
   Evermore gaining on the larboard side.
Already all the stars of the other pole
   The night beheld, and ours so very low
   It did not rise above the ocean floor.

Five times rekindled and as many quenched   130
    Had been the splendor underneath the moon,
    Since we had entered into the deep pass,
When there appeared to us a mountain, dim
    From distance, and it seemed to me so high
    As I had never any one beheld.   135
Joyful were we, and soon it turned to weeping;
    For out of the new land a whirlwind rose,
    And smote upon the fore part of the ship.
Three times it made it whirl with all the waters,
    At the fourth time it made the stern uplift,   140
    And the prow downward go, as pleased Another,
Until the sea above us closed again."

Canto XXVII

Already was the flame erect and quiet,
    To speak no more, and now departed from us
    With the permission of the gentle Poet;
When yet another, which behind it came,
    Caused us to turn our eyes upon its top   5
    By a confusëd sound that issued from it.
As the Sicilian bull (that bellowed first
    With the lament of him, and that was right,
    Who with his file had modulated it)
Bellowed so with the voice of the afflicted,   10
    That, notwithstanding it was made of brass,
    Still it appeared with agony transfixed;
Thus, by not having any way or issue
    At first from out the fire, to its own language
    Converted were the melancholy words.   15
But afterwards, when they had gathered way
    Up through the point, giving it that vibration
    The tongue had given them in their passage out,
We heard it said: "O thou, at whom I aim
    My voice, and who but now wast speaking Lombard,   20
    Saying, 'Now go thy way, no more I urge thee,'

Because I come perchance a little late,
    To stay and speak with me let it not irk thee;
    Thou seest it irks not me, and I am burning.
If thou but lately into this blind world   25
    Hast fallen down from that sweet Latian land,
    Wherefrom I bring the whole of my transgression,
Say, have the Romagnuoli peace or war,
    For I was from the mountains there between
    Urbino and the yoke whence Tiber bursts."   30
I still was downward bent and listening,
    When my Conductor touched me on the side,
    Saying: "Speak thou: this one a Latian is."
And I, who had beforehand my reply
    In readiness, forthwith began to speak: 35
    "O soul, that down below there art concealed,
Romagna thine is not and never has been
    Without war in the bosom of its tyrants;
    But open war I none have left there now.
Ravenna stands as it long years has stood;   40
    The Eagle of Polenta there is brooding,
    So that she covers Cervia with her vans.
The city which once made the long resistance,
    And of the French a sanguinary heap,
    Beneath the Green Paws finds itself again;   45
Verrucchio's ancient Mastiff and the new,
    Who made such bad disposal of Montagna,
    Where they are wont make wimbles of their teeth.
The cities of Lamone and Santerno
    Governs the Lioncel of the white lair,   50
    Who changes sides 'twixt summer-time and winter;
And that of which the Savio bathes the flank,
    Even as it lies between the plain and mountain,
    Lives between tyranny and a free state.
Now I entreat thee tell us who thou art;   55
    Be not more stubborn than the rest have been,
    So may thy name hold front there in the world."

After the fire a little more had roared
   In its own fashion, the sharp point it moved
   This way and that, and then gave forth such breath: 60
"If I believed that my reply were made
   To one who to the world would e'er return,
   This flame without more flickering would stand still;
But inasmuch as never from this depth
   Did any one return, if I hear true,   65
   Without the fear of infamy I answer,
I was a man of arms, then Cordelier,
   Believing thus begirt to make amends;
   And truly my belief had been fulfilled
But for the High Priest, whom may ill betide,   70
   Who put me back into my former sins;
   And how and wherefore I will have thee hear.
While I was still the form of bone and pulp
   My mother gave to me, the deeds I did
   Were not those of a lion, but a fox.   75
The machinations and the covert ways
   I knew them all, and practised so their craft,
   That to the ends of earth the sound went forth.
When now unto that portion of mine age
   I saw myself arrived, when each one ought   80
   To lower the sails, and coil away the ropes,
That which before had pleased me then displeased me;
   And penitent and confessing I surrendered,
   Ah woe is me! and it would have bestead me;
The Leader of the modern Pharisees   85
   Having a war near unto Lateran,
   And not with Saracens nor with the Jews,
For each one of his enemies was Christian,
   And none of them had been to conquer Acre,
   Nor merchandising in the Sultan's land,   90
Nor the high office, nor the sacred orders,
   In him regarded, nor in me that cord
   Which used to make those girt with it more meagre;

But even as Constantine sought out Sylvester
    To cure his leprosy, within Soracte,   95
    So this one sought me out as an adept
To cure him of the fever of his pride.
    Counsel he asked of me, and I was silent,
    Because his words appeared inebriate.
And then he said: 'Be not thy heart afraid;   100
    Henceforth I thee absolve; and thou instruct me
    How to raze Palestrina to the ground.
Heaven have I power to lock and to unlock,
    As thou dost know; therefore the keys are two,
    The which my predecessor held not dear.'   105
Then urged me on his weighty arguments
    There, where my silence was the worst advice;
    And said I: 'Father, since thou washest me
Of that sin into which I now must fall,
    The promise long with the fulfilment short   110
    Will make thee triumph in thy lofty seat.'
Francis came afterward, when I was dead,
    For me; but one of the black Cherubim
    Said to him: 'Take him not; do me no wrong;
He must come down among my servitors,   115
    Because he gave the fraudulent advice
    From which time forth I have been at his hair;
For who repents not cannot be absolved,
    Nor can one both repent and will at once,
    Because of the contradiction which consents not.'   120
O miserable me! how I did shudder
    When he seized on me, saying: 'Peradventure
    Thou didst not think that I was a logician!'
He bore me unto Minos, who entwined
    Eight times his tail about his stubborn back,   125
    And after he had bitten it in great rage,
Said: 'Of the thievish fire a culprit this';
    Wherefore, here where thou seest, am I lost,
    And vested thus in going I bemoan me."

When it had thus completed its recital,   130
    The flame departed uttering lamentations,
    Writhing and flapping its sharp-pointed horn.
Onward we passed, both I and my Conductor,
    Up o'er the crag above another arch,
    Which the moat covers, where is paid the fee   135
By those who, sowing discord, win their burden.

Canto XXVIII

Who ever could, e'en with untrammelled words,
　　Tell of the blood and of the wounds in full
　　Which now I saw, by many times narrating?
Each tongue would for a certainty fall short
　　By reason of our speech and memory,　　　　　　　　5
　　That have small room to comprehend so much.
If were again assembled all the people
　　Which formerly upon the fateful land
　　Of Puglia were lamenting for their blood
Shed by the Romans and the lingering war　　　　　　10
　　That of the rings made such illustrious spoils,
　　As Livy has recorded, who errs not,
With those who felt the agony of blows
　　By making counterstand to Robert Guiscard,
　　And all the rest, whose bones are gathered still　　15
At Ceperano, where a renegade
　　Was each Apulian, and at Tagliacozzo,
　　Where without arms the old Alardo conquered,
And one his limb transpierced, and one lopped off,
　　Should show, it would be nothing to compare　　　20
　　With the disgusting mode of the ninth Bolgia.

A cask by losing centre-piece or cant
    Was never shattered so, as I saw one
    Rent from the chin to where one breaketh wind.
Between his legs were hanging down his entrails;   25
    His heart was visible, and the dismal sack
    That maketh excrement of what is eaten.
While I was all absorbed in seeing him,
    He looked at me, and opened with his hands
    His bosom, saying: "See now how I rend me;   30
How mutilated, see, is Mahomet;
    In front of me doth Ali weeping go,
    Cleft in the face from forelock unto chin;
And all the others whom thou here beholdest,
    Disseminators of scandal and of schism   35
    While living were, and therefore are cleft thus.
A devil is behind here, who doth cleave us
    Thus cruelly, unto the falchion's edge
    Putting again each one of all this ream,
When we have gone around the doleful road;   40
    By reason that our wounds are closed again
    Ere any one in front of him repass.
But who art thou, that musest on the crag,
    Perchance to postpone going to the pain
    That is adjudged upon thine accusations?"   45
"Nor death hath reached him yet, nor guilt doth bring him,"
    My Master made reply, "to be tormented;
    But to procure him full experience,
Me, who am dead, behoves it to conduct him
    Down here through Hell, from circle unto circle;   50
    And this is true as that I speak to thee."
More than a hundred were there when they heard him,
    Who in the moat stood still to look at me,
    Through wonderment oblivious of their torture.
"Now say to Fra Dolcino, then, to arm him,   55
    Thou, who perhaps wilt shortly see the sun,
    If soon he wish not here to follow me,

So with provisions, that no stress of snow
    May give the victory to the Novarese,
    Which otherwise to gain would not be easy."   60
After one foot to go away he lifted,
    This word did Mahomet say unto me,
    Then to depart upon the ground he stretched it.
Another one, who had his throat pierced through,
    And nose cut off close underneath the brows,   65
    And had no longer but a single ear,
Staying to look in wonder with the others,
    Before the others did his gullet open,
    Which outwardly was red in every part,
And said: "O thou, whom guilt doth not condemn,   70
    And whom I once saw up in Latian land,
    Unless too great similitude deceive me,
Call to remembrance Pier da Medicina,
    If e'er thou see again the lovely plain
    That from Vercelli slopes to Marcabò,   75
And make it known to the best two of Fano,
    To Messer Guido and Angiolello likewise,
    That if foreseeing here be not in vain,
Cast over from their vessel shall they be,
    And drowned near unto the Cattolica,   80
    By the betrayal of a tyrant fell.
Between the isles of Cyprus and Majorca
    Neptune ne'er yet beheld so great a crime,
    Neither of pirates nor Argolic people.
That traitor, who sees only with one eye,   85
    And holds the land, which some one here with me
    Would fain be fasting from the vision of,
Will make them come unto a parley with him;
    Then will do so, that to Focara's wind
    They will not stand in need of vow or prayer."   90
And I to him: "Show to me and declare,
    If thou wouldst have me bear up news of thee,
    Who is this person of the bitter vision."

Then did he lay his hand upon the jaw
    Of one of his companions, and his mouth   95
    Oped, crying: "This is he, and he speaks not.
This one, being banished, every doubt submerged
    In Cæsar by affirming the forearmed
    Always with detriment allowed delay."
O how bewildered unto me appeared,   100
    With tongue asunder in his windpipe slit,
    Curio, who in speaking was so bold!
And one, who both his hands dissevered had,
    The stumps uplifting through the murky air,
    So that the blood made horrible his face,   105
Cried out: "Thou shalt remember Mosca also,
    Who said, alas! 'A thing done has an end!'
    Which was an ill seed for the Tuscan people";
"And death unto thy race," thereto I added;
    Whence he, accumulating woe on woe,   110
    Departed, like a person sad and crazed.
But I remained to look upon the crowd;
    And saw a thing which I should be afraid,
    Without some further proof, even to recount,
If it were not that conscience reassures me,   115
    That good companion which emboldens man
    Beneath the hauberk of its feeling pure.
I truly saw, and still I seem to see it,
    A trunk without a head walk in like manner
    As walked the others of the mournful herd.   120
And by the hair it held the head dissevered,
    Hung from the hand in fashion of a lantern,
    And that upon us gazed and said: "O me!"
It of itself made to itself a lamp,
    And they were two in one, and one in two;   125
    How that can be, He knows who so ordains it.
When it was come close to the bridge's foot,
    It lifted high its arm with all the head,
    To bring more closely unto us its words,

Which were: "Behold now the sore penalty,   130
    Thou, who dost breathing go the dead beholding;
    Behold if any be as great as this.
And so that thou may carry news of me,
    Know that Bertram de Born am I, the same
    Who gave to the Young King the evil comfort.   135
I made the father and the son rebellious;
    Achitophel not more with Absalom
    And David did with his accursed goadings.
Because I parted persons so united,
    Parted do I now bear my brain, alas!   140
    From its beginning, which is in this trunk.
Thus is observed in me the counterpoise."

CANTO XXIX

The many people and the divers wounds
    These eyes of mine had so inebriated,
    That they were wishful to stand still and weep;
But said Virgilius: "What dost thou still gaze at?
    Why is thy sight still riveted down there   5
    Among the mournful, mutilated shades?
Thou hast not done so at the other Bolge;
    Consider, if to count them thou believest,
    That two-and-twenty miles the valley winds,
And now the moon is underneath our feet;   10
    Henceforth the time allotted us is brief,
    And more is to be seen than what thou seest."
"If thou hadst," I made answer thereupon,
    "Attended to the cause for which I looked,
    Perhaps a longer stay thou wouldst have pardoned."   15
Meanwhile my Guide departed, and behind him
    I went, already making my reply,
    And superadding: "In that cavern where
I held mine eyes with such attention fixed,
    I think a spirit of my blood laments   20
    The sin which down below there costs so much."

Then said the Master: "Be no longer broken
    Thy thought from this time forward upon him;
    Attend elsewhere, and there let him remain;
For him I saw below the little bridge,   25
    Pointing at thee, and threatening with his finger
    Fiercely, and heard him called Geri del Bello.
So wholly at that time wast thou impeded
    By him who formerly held Altaforte,
    Thou didst not look that way; so he departed."   30
"O my Conductor, his own violent death,
    Which is not yet avenged for him," I said,
    "By any who is sharer in the shame,
Made him disdainful; whence he went away,
    As I imagine, without speaking to me,   35
    And thereby made me pity him the more."
Thus did we speak as far as the first place
    Upon the crag, which the next valley shows
    Down to the bottom, if there were more light.
When we were now right over the last cloister   40
    Of Malebolge, so that its lay-brothers
    Could manifest themselves unto our sight,
Divers lamentings pierced me through and through,
    Which with compassion had their arrows barbed,
    Whereat mine ears I covered with my hands.   45
What pain would be, if from the hospitals
    Of Valdichiana, 'twixt July and September,
    And of Maremma and Sardinia
All the diseases in one moat were gathered,
    Such was it here, and such a stench came from it   50
    As from putrescent limbs is wont to issue.
We had descended on the furthest bank
    From the long crag, upon the left hand still,
    And then more vivid was my power of sight
Down tow'rds the bottom, where the ministress   55
    Of the high Lord, Justice infallible,
    Punishes forgers, which she here records.

I do not think a sadder sight to see
   Was in Ægina the whole people sick,
   (When was the air so full of pestilence,   60
The animals, down to the little worm,
   All fell, and afterwards the ancient people,
   According as the poets have affirmed,
Were from the seed of ants restored again,)
   Than was it to behold through that dark valley   65
   The spirits languishing in divers heaps.
This on the belly, that upon the back
   One of the other lay, and others crawling
   Shifted themselves along the dismal road.
We step by step went onward without speech,   70
   Gazing upon and listening to the sick
   Who had not strength enough to lift their bodies.
I saw two sitting leaned against each other,
   As leans in heating platter against platter,
   From head to foot bespotted o'er with scabs;   75
And never saw I plied a currycomb
   By stable-boy for whom his master waits,
   Or him who keeps awake unwillingly,
As every one was plying fast the bite
   Of nails upon himself, for the great rage   80
   Of itching which no other succor had.
And the nails downward with them dragged the scab,
   In fashion as a knife the scales of bream,
   Or any other fish that has them largest.
"O thou, that with thy fingers dost dismail thee,"   85
   Began my Leader unto one of them,
   "And makest of them pincers now and then,
Tell me if any Latian is with those
   Who are herein; so may thy nails suffice thee
   To all eternity unto this work."   90
"Latians are we, whom thou so wasted seest,
   Both of us here," one weeping made reply;
   "But who art thou, that questionest about us?"

And said the Guide: "One am I who descends
    Down with this living man from cliff to cliff,   95
    And I intend to show Hell unto him."
Then broken was their mutual support,
    And trembling each one turned himself to me,
    With others who had heard him by rebound.
Wholly to me did the good Master gather,   100
    Saying: "Say unto them whate'er thou wishest."
    And I began, since he would have it so:
"So may your memory not steal away
    In the first world from out the minds of men,
    But so may it survive 'neath many suns,   105
Say to me who ye are, and of what people;
    Let not your foul and loathsome punishment
    Make you afraid to show yourselves to me."
"I of Arezzo was," one made reply,
    "And Albert of Siena had me burned;   110
    But what I died for does not bring me here.
'T is true I said to him, speaking in jest,
    That I could rise by flight into the air,
    And he who had conceit, but little wit,
Would have me show to him the art; and only   115
    Because no Dædalus I made him, made me
    Be burned by one who held him as his son.
But unto the last Bolgia of the ten,
    For alchemy, which in the world I practised,
    Minos, who cannot err, has me condemned."   120
And to the Poet said I: "Now was ever
    So vain a people as the Sienese?
    Not for a certainty the French by far."
Whereat the other leper, who had heard me,
    Replied unto my speech: "Taking out Stricca,   125
    Who knew the art of moderate expenses,
And Niccolò, who the luxurious use
    Of cloves discovered earliest of all
    Within that garden where such seed takes root;

And taking out the band, among whom squandered   130
   Caccia d' Ascian his vineyards and vast woods,
   And where his wit the Abbagliáto proffered!
But, that thou know who thus doth second thee
   Against the Sienese, make sharp thine eye
   Tow'rds me, so that my face well answer thee,   135
And thou shalt see I am Capocchio's shade,
   Who metals falsified by alchemy;
   Thou must remember, if I well descry thee,
How I a skilful ape of nature was."

CANTO XXX

'T was at the time when Juno was enraged,
   For Semele, against the Theban blood,
   As she already more than once had shown,
So reft of reason Athamas became,
   That, seeing his own wife with children twain   5
   Walking encumbered upon either hand,
He cried: "Spread out the nets, that I may take
   The lioness and her whelps upon the passage";
   And then extended his unpitying claws,
Seizing the first, who had the name Learchus,   10
   And whirled him round, and dashed him on a rock;
   And she, with the other burthen, drowned herself; —
And at the time when fortune downward hurled
   The Trojans' arrogance, that all things dared,
   So that the king was with his kingdom crushed,   15
Hecuba sad, disconsolate, and captive,
   When lifeless she beheld Polyxena,
   And of her Polydorus on the shore
Of ocean was the dolorous one aware,
   Out of her senses like a dog she barked,   20
   So much the anguish had her mind distorted;

But not of Thebes the furies nor the Trojan
   Were ever seen in any one so cruel
   In goading beasts, and much more human members,
As I beheld two shadows pale and naked,   25
   Who, biting, in the manner ran along
   That a boar does, when from the sty turned loose.
One to Capocchio came, and by the nape
   Seized with its teeth his neck, so that in dragging
   It made his belly grate the solid bottom.   30
And the Aretine, who trembling had remained,
   Said to me: "That mad sprite is Gianni Schicchi,
   And raving goes thus harrying other people."
"O," said I to him, "so may not the other
   Set teeth on thee, let it not weary thee   35
   To tell us who it is, ere it dart hence."
And he to me: "That is the ancient ghost
   Of the nefarious Myrrha, who became
   Beyond all rightful love her father's lover.
She came to sin with him after this manner,   40
   By counterfeiting of another's form;
   As he who goeth yonder undertook,
That he might gain the lady of the herd,
   To counterfeit in himself Buoso Donati,
   Making a will and giving it due form."   45
And after the two maniacs had passed
   On whom I held mine eye, I turned it back
   To look upon the other evil-born.
I saw one made in fashion of a lute,
   If he had only had the groin cut off   50
   Just at the point at which a man is forked.
The heavy dropsy, that so disproportions
   The limbs with humors, which it ill concocts,
   That the face corresponds not to the belly,
Compelled him so to hold his lips apart   55
   As does the hectic, who because of thirst
   One tow'rds the chin, the other upward turns.

"O ye, who without any torment are,
 And why I know not, in the world of woe,"
 He said to us, "behold, and be attentive   60
Unto the misery of Master Adam;
 I had while living much of what I wished,
 And now, alas! a drop of water crave.
The rivulets, that from the verdant hills
 Of Cassentin descend down into Arno,   65
 Making their channels to be cold and moist,
Ever before me stand, and not in vain;
 For far more doth their image dry me up
 Than the disease which strips my face of flesh.
The rigid justice that chastises me   70
 Draweth occasion from the place in which
 I sinned, to put the more my sighs in flight.
There is Romena, where I counterfeited
 The currency imprinted with the Baptist,
 For which I left my body burned above.   75
But if I here could see the tristful soul
 Of Guido, or Alessandro, or their brother,
 For Branda's fount I would not give the sight.
One is within already, if the raving
 Shades that are going round about speak truth;   80
 But what avails it me, whose limbs are tied?
If I were only still so light, that in
 A hundred years I could advance one inch,
 I had already started on the way,
Seeking him out among this squalid folk,   85
 Although the circuit be eleven miles,
 And be not less than half a mile across.
For them am I in such a family;
 They did induce me into coining florins,
 Which had three carats of impurity."   90
And I to him: "Who are the two poor wretches
 That smoke like unto a wet hand in winter,
 Lying there close upon thy right-hand confines?"

"I found them here," replied he, "when I rained
    Into this chasm, and since they have not turned,   95
    Nor do I think they will for evermore.
One the false woman is who accused Joseph,
    The other the false Sinon, Greek of Troy;
    From acute fever they send forth such reek."
And one of them, who felt himself annoyed   100
    At being, peradventure, named so darkly,
    Smote with the fist upon his hardened paunch.
It gave a sound, as if it were a drum;
    And Master Adam smote him in the face,
    With arm that did not seem to be less hard,   105
Saying to him: "Although be taken from me
    All motion, for my limbs that heavy are,
    I have an arm unfettered for such need."
Whereat he answer made: "When thou didst go
    Unto the fire, thou hadst it not so ready;   110
    But hadst it so and more when thou wast coining."
The dropsical: "Thou sayest true in that;
    But thou wast not so true a witness there,
    Where thou wast questioned of the truth at Troy."
"If I spake false, thou falsifiedst the coin,"   115
    Said Sinon; "and for one fault I am here,
    And thou for more than any other demon."
"Remember, perjurer, about the horse,"
    He made reply who had the swollen belly,
    "And rueful be it thee the whole world knows it."   120
"Rueful to thee the thirst be wherewith cracks
    Thy tongue," the Greek said, "and the putrid water
    That hedges so thy paunch before thine eyes."
Then the false-coiner: "So is gaping wide
    Thy mouth for speaking evil, as 't is wont;   125
    Because if I have thirst, and humor stuff me,
Thou hast the burning and the head that aches,
    And to lick up the mirror of Narcissus
    Thou wouldst not want words many to invite thee."

In listening to them was I wholly fixed,   130
    When said the Master to me: "Now just look,
    For little wants it that I quarrel with thee."
When him I heard in anger speak to me,
    I turned me round towards him with such shame
    That still it eddies through my memory.   135
And as he is who dreams of his own harm,
    Who dreaming wishes it may be a dream,
    So that he craves what is, as if it were not;
Such I became, not having power to speak,
    For to excuse myself I wished, and still   140
    Excused myself, and did not think I did it.
"Less shame doth wash away a greater fault,"
    The Master said, "than this of thine has been;
    Therefore thyself disburden of all sadness,
And make account that I am aye beside thee,   145
    If e'er it come to pass that fortune bring thee
    Where there are people in a like dispute;
For a base wish it is to wish to hear it."

Canto XXXI

One and the self-same tongue first wounded me,
    So that it tinged the one cheek and the other,
    And then held out to me the medicine;
Thus do I hear that once Achilles' spear,
    His and his father's, used to be the cause   5
    First of a sad and then a gracious boon.
We turned our backs upon the wretched valley,
    Upon the bank that girds it round about,
    Going across it without any speech.
There it was less than night, and less than day,   10
    So that my sight went little in advance;
    But I could hear the blare of a loud horn,
So loud it would have made each thunder faint,
    Which, counter to it following its way,
    Mine eyes directed wholly to one place.   15
After the dolorous discomfiture
    When Charlemagne the holy emprise lost,
    So terribly Orlando sounded not.
Short while my head turned thitherward I held
    When many lofty towers I seemed to see,   20
    Whereat I: "Master, say, what town is this?"

And he to me: "Because thou peerest forth
    Athwart the darkness at too great a distance,
    It happens that thou errest in thy fancy.
Well shalt thou see, if thou arrivest there,   25
    How much the sense deceives itself by distance;
    Therefore a little faster spur thee on."
Then tenderly he took me by the hand,
    And said: "Before we farther have advanced,
    That the reality may seem to thee   30
Less strange, know that these are not towers, but giants,
    And they are in the well, around the bank,
    From navel downward, one and all of them."
As, when the fog is vanishing away,
    Little by little doth the sight refigure   35
    What'er the mist that crowds the air conceals,
So, piercing through the dense and darksome air,
    More and more near approaching tow'rd the verge,
    My error fled, and fear came over me;
Because as on its circular parapets   40
    Montereggione crowns itself with towers,
    E'en thus the margin which surrounds the well
With one half of their bodies turreted
    The horrible giants, whom Jove menaces
    E'en now from out the heavens when he thunders.   45
And I of one already saw the face,
    Shoulders, and breast, and great part of the belly,
    And down along his sides both of the arms.
Certainly Nature, when she left the making
    Of animals like these, did well indeed,   50
    By taking such executors from Mars;
And if of elephants and whales she doth not
    Repent her, whosoever looketh subtly
    More just and more discreet will hold her for it;
For where the argument of intellect   55
    Is added unto evil will and power,
    No rampart can the people make against it.

His face appeared to me as long and large
 As is at Rome the pine-cone of Saint Peter's,
 And in proportion were the other bones;   60
So that the margin, which an apron was
 Down from the middle, showed so much of him
 Above it, that to reach up to his hair
Three Frieslanders in vain had vaunted them;
 For I beheld thirty great palms of him   65
 Down from the place where man his mantle buckles.
"Raphel mai amech izabi almi,"
 Began to clamor the ferocious mouth,
 To which were not befitting sweeter psalms.
And unto him my Guide: "Soul idiotic,   70
 Keep to thy horn, and vent thyself with that,
 When wrath or other passion touches thee.
Search round thy neck, and thou wilt find the belt
 Which keeps it fastened, O bewildered soul,
 And see it, where it bars thy mighty breast."   75
Then said to me: "He doth himself accuse;
 This one is Nimrod, by whose evil thought
 One language in the world is not still used.
Here let us leave him and not speak in vain;
 For even such to him is every language   80
 As his to others, which to none is known."
Therefore a longer journey did we make,
 Turned to the left, and a crossbow-shot off
 We found another far more fierce and large.
In binding him, who might the master be   85
 I cannot say; but he had pinioned close
 Behind the right arm, and in front the other,
With chains, that held him so begirt about
 From the neck down, that on the part uncovered
 It wound itself as far as the fifth gyre.   90
"This proud one wished to make experiment
 Of his own power against the Supreme Jove,"
 My Leader said, "whence he has such a guerdon.

Ephialtes is his name; he showed great prowess,
    What time the giants terrified the Gods;   95
    The arms he wielded never more he moves."
And I to him: "If possible, I should wish
    That of the measureless Briareus
    These eyes of mine might have experience."
Whence he replied: "Thou shalt behold Antæus   100
    Close by here, who can speak and is unbound,
    Who at the bottom of all crime shall place us.
Much farther yon is he whom thou wouldst see,
    And he is bound, and fashioned like to this one,
    Save that he seems in aspect more ferocious."   105
There never was an earthquake of such might
    That it could shake a tower so violently,
    As Ephialtes suddenly shook himself.
Then was I more afraid of death than ever,
    For nothing more was needful than the fear,   110
    If I had not beheld the manacles.
Then we proceeded farther in advance,
    And to Antæus came, who, full five ells
    Without the head, forth issued from the cavern.
"O thou, who in the valley fortunate,   115
    Which Scipio the heir of glory made,
    When Hannibal turned back with all his hosts,
Once brought'st a thousand lions for thy prey,
    And who, hadst thou been at the mighty war
    Among thy brothers, some it seems still think   120
The sons of Earth the victory would have gained;
    Place us below, nor be disdainful of it,
    There where the cold doth lock Cocytus up.
Make us not go to Tityus nor Typhœus;
    This one can give of that which here is longed for;   125
    Therefore stoop down, and do not curl thy lip.
Still in the world can he restore thy fame;
    Because he lives, and still expects long life,
    If to itself Grace call him not untimely."

So said the Master; and in haste the other   130
　His hands extended and took up my Guide,—
　Hands whose great pressure Hercules once felt.
Virgilius, when he felt himself embraced,
　Said unto me: "Draw nigh, that I may take thee";
　Then of himself and me one bundle made.   135
As seems the Carisenda, to behold
　Beneath the leaning side, when goes a cloud
　Above it so that opposite it hangs;
Such did Antæus seem to me, who stood
　Watching to see him stoop, and then it was   140
　I could have wished to go some other way.
But lightly in the abyss, which swallows up
　Judas with Lucifer, he put us down;
　Nor thus bowed downward made he there delay,
But, as a mast does in a ship, uprose.   145

Canto XXXII

If I had rhymes both rough and stridulous,
    As were appropriate to the dismal hole
    Down upon which thrust all the other rocks,
I would press out the juice of my conception
    More fully; but because I have them not,   5
    Not without fear I bring myself to speak;
For 't is no enterprise to take in jest,
    To sketch the bottom of all the universe,
    Nor for a tongue that cries Mamma and Babbo.
But may those Ladies help this verse of mine,   10
    Who helped Amphion in enclosing Thebes,
    That from the fact the word be not diverse.
O rabble ill-begotten above all,
    Who 're in the place to speak of which is hard,
    'T were better ye had here been sheep or goats!   15
When we were down within the darksome well,
    Beneath the giant's feet, but lower far,
    And I was scanning still the lofty wall,
I heard it said to me: "Look how thou steppest!
    Take heed thou do not trample with thy feet   20
    The heads of the tired, miserable brothers!"

Whereat I turned me round, and saw before me
   And underfoot a lake, that from the frost
   The semblance had of glass, and not of water.
So thick a veil ne'er made upon its current   25
   In winter-time Danube in Austria,
   Nor there beneath the frigid sky the Don,
As there was here; so that if Tambernich
   Had fallen upon it, or Pietrapana,
   E'en at the edge 't would not have given a creak.   30
And as to croak the frog doth place himself
   With muzzle out of water,—when is dreaming
   Of gleaning oftentimes the peasant-girl,—
Livid, as far down as where shame appears,
   Were the disconsolate shades within the ice,   35
   Setting their teeth unto the note of storks.
Each one his countenance held downward bent;
   From mouth the cold, from eyes the doleful heart
   Among them witness of itself procures.
When round about me somewhat I had looked,   40
   I downward turned me, and saw two so close,
   The hair upon their heads together mingled.
"Ye who so strain your breasts together, tell me,"
   I said, "who are you"; and they bent their necks,
   And when to me their faces they had lifted,   45
Their eyes, which first were only moist within,
   Gushed o'er the eyelids, and the frost congealed
   The tears between, and locked them up again.
Clamp never bound together wood with wood
   So strongly; whereat they, like two he-goats,   50
   Butted together, so much wrath o'ercame them.
And one, who had by reason of the cold
   Lost both his ears, still with his visage downward,
   Said: "Why dost thou so mirror thyself in us?
If thou desire to know who these two are,   55
   The valley whence Bisenzio descends
   Belonged to them and to their father Albert.

They from one body came, and all Caïna
  Thou shalt search through, and shalt not find a shade
  More worthy to be fixed in gelatine;   60
Not he in whom were broken breast and shadow
  At one and the same blow by Arthur's hand;
  Focaccia not; not he who me encumbers
So with his head I see no farther forward,
  And bore the name of Sassol Mascheroni;   65
  Well knowest thou who he was, if thou art Tuscan.
And that thou put me not to further speech,
  Know that I Camicion de' Pazzi was,
  And wait Carlino to exonerate me."
Then I beheld a thousand faces, made   70
  Purple with cold; whence o'er me comes a shudder,
  And evermore will come, at frozen ponds.
And while we were advancing tow'rds the middle,
  Where everything of weight unites together,
  And I was shivering in the eternal shade,   75
Whether 't were will, or destiny, or chance,
  I know not; but in walking 'mong the heads
  I struck my foot hard in the face of one.
Weeping he growled: "Why dost thou trample me?
  Unless thou comest to increase the vengeance   80
  Of Montaperti, why dost thou molest me?"
And I: "My Master, now wait here for me,
  That I through him may issue from a doubt;
  Then thou mayst hurry me, as thou shalt wish."
The Leader stopped; and to that one I said   85
  Who was blaspheming vehemently still:
  "Who art thou, that thus reprehendest others?"
"Now who art thou, that goest through Antenora
  Smiting," replied he, "other people's cheeks,
  So that, if thou wert living, 't were too much?"   90
"Living I am, and dear to thee it may be,"
  Was my response, "if thou demandest fame,
  That 'mid the other notes thy name I place."

And he to me: "For the reverse I long;
 Take thyself hence, and give me no more trouble;   95
 For ill thou knowest to flatter in this hollow."
Then by the scalp behind I seized upon him,
 And said: "It must needs be thou name thyself,
 Or not a hair remain upon thee here."
Whence he to me: "Though thou strip off my hair,   100
 I will not tell thee who I am, nor show thee,
 If on my head a thousand times thou fall."
I had his hair in hand already twisted,
 And more than one shock of it had pulled out,
 He barking, with his eyes held firmly down,   105
When cried another: "What doth ail thee, Bocca?
 Is 't not enough to clatter with thy jaws,
 But thou must bark? what devil touches thee?"
"Now," said I, "I care not to have thee speak,
 Accursed traitor; for unto thy shame   110
 I will report of thee veracious news."
"Begone," replied he, "and tell what thou wilt,
 But be not silent, if thou issue hence,
 Of him who had just now his tongue so prompt;
He weepeth here the silver of the French;   115
 'I saw,' thus canst thou phrase it, 'him of Duera
 There where the sinners stand out in the cold.'
If thou shouldst questioned be who else was there,
 Thou hast beside thee him of Beccaria,
 Of whom the gorget Florence slit asunder;   120
Gianni del Soldanier, I think, may be
 Yonder with Ganellon, and Tebaldello
 Who oped Faenza when the people slept."
Already we had gone away from him,
 When I beheld two frozen in one hole,   125
 So that one head a hood was to the other;
And even as bread through hunger is devoured,
 The uppermost on the other set his teeth,
 There where the brain is to the nape united.

Not in another fashion Tydeus gnawed   130
    The temples of Menalippus in disdain,
    Than that one did the skull and the other things.
"O thou, who showest by such bestial sign
    Thy hatred against him whom thou art eating,
    Tell me the wherefore," said I, "with this compact,   135
That if thou rightfully of him complain,
    In knowing who ye are, and his transgression,
    I in the world above repay thee for it,
If that wherewith I speak be not dried up."

Canto XXXIII

His mouth uplifted from his grim repast,
    That sinner, wiping it upon the hair
    Of the same head that he behind had wasted.
Then he began: "Thou wilt that I renew
    The desperate grief, which wrings my heart already   5
    To think of only, ere I speak of it;
But if my words be seed that may bear fruit
    Of infamy to the traitor whom I gnaw,
    Speaking and weeping shalt thou see together.
I know not who thou art, nor by what mode   10
    Thou hast come down here; but a Florentine
    Thou seemest to me truly, when I hear thee.
Thou hast to know I was Count Ugolino,
    And this one was Ruggieri the Archbishop;
    Now I will tell thee why I am such a neighbor.   15
That, by effect of his malicious thoughts,
    Trusting in him I was made prisoner,
    And after put to death, I need not say;
But ne'ertheless what thou canst not have heard,
    That is to say, how cruel was my death,   20
    Hear shalt thou, and shalt know if he has wronged me.

A narrow perforation in the mew,
    Which bears because of me the title of Famine,
    And in which others still must be locked up,
Had shown me through its opening many moons   25
    Already, when I dreamed the evil dream
    Which of the future rent for me the veil.
This one appeared to me as lord and master,
    Hunting the wolf and whelps upon the mountain
    For which the Pisans cannot Lucca see.   30
With sleuth-hounds gaunt, and eager, and well trained,
    Gualandi with Sismondi and Lanfranchi
    He had sent out before him to the front.
After brief course seemed unto me forespent
    The father and the sons, and with sharp tushes   35
    It seemed to me I saw their flanks ripped open.
When I before the morrow was awake,
    Moaning amid their sleep I heard my sons
    Who with me were, and asking after bread.
Cruel indeed art thou, if yet thou grieve not,   40
    Thinking of what my heart foreboded me,
    And weep'st thou not, what art thou wont to weep at?
They were awake now, and the hour drew nigh
    At which our food used to be brought to us,
    And through his dream was each one apprehensive;   45
And I heard locking up the under door
    Of the horrible tower; whereat without a word
    I gazed into the faces of my sons.
I wept not, I within so turned to stone;
    They wept; and darling little Anselm mine   50
    Said: 'Thou dost gaze so, father, what doth ail thee?'
Still not a tear I shed, nor answer made
    All of that day, nor yet the night thereafter,
    Until another sun rose on the world.
As now a little glimmer made its way   55
    Into the dolorous prison, and I saw
    Upon four faces my own very aspect,

Both of my hands in agony I bit;
    And, thinking that I did it from desire
    Of eating, on a sudden they uprose,   60
And said they: 'Father, much less pain 't will give us
    If thou do eat of us; thyself didst clothe us
    With this poor flesh, and do thou strip it off.'
I calmed me then, not to make them more sad.
    That day we all were silent, and the next.   65
    Ah! obdurate earth, wherefore didst thou not open?
When we had come unto the fourth day, Gaddo
    Threw himself down outstretched before my feet,
    Saying, 'My father, why dost thou not help me?'
And there he died; and, as thou seest me,   70
    I saw the three fall one by one, between
    The fifth day and the sixth; whence I betook me,
Already blind, to groping over each,
    And three days called them after they were dead;
    Then hunger did what sorrow could not do."   75
When he had said this, with his eyes distorted,
    The wretched skull resumed he with his teeth,
    Which, as a dog's, upon the bone were strong.
Ah! Pisa, thou opprobium of the people
    Of the fair land there where the *Sì* doth sound,   80
    Since slow to punish thee thy neighbors are,
Let the Capraia and Gorgona move,
    And make a hedge across the mouth of Arno,
    That every person in thee it may drown!
For if Count Ugolino had the fame   85
    Of having in thy castles thee betrayed,
    Thou shouldst not on such cross have put his sons.
Guiltless of any crime, thou modern Thebes!
    Their youth made Uguccione and Brigata,
    And the other two my song doth name above!   90
We passed still farther onward, where the ice
    Another people ruggedly enswathes,
    Not downward turned, but all of them reversed.

Weeping itself there does not let them weep,
    And grief that finds a barrier in the eyes   95
    Turns itself inward to increase the anguish
Because the earliest tears a cluster form,
    And, in the manner of a crystal visor,
    Fill all the cup beneath the eyebrow full.
And notwithstanding that, as in a callus,   100
    Because of cold all sensibility
    Its station had abandoned in my face,
Still it appeared to me I felt some wind;
    Whence I: "My Master, who sets this in motion?
    Is not below here every vapor quenched?"   105
Whence he to me: "Full soon shalt thou be where
    Thine eye shall answer make to thee of this,
    Seeing the cause which raineth down the blast."
And one of the wretches of the frozen crust
    Cried out to us: "O souls so merciless   110
    That the last post is given unto you,
Lift from mine eyes the rigid veils, that I
    May vent the sorrow which impregns my heart
    A little, e'er the weeping recongeal."
Whence I to him: "If thou wouldst have me help thee,   115
    Say who thou wast; and if I free thee not,
    May I go to the bottom of the ice."
Then he replied: "I am Friar Alberigo;
    He am I of the fruit of the bad garden,
    Who here a date am getting for my fig."   120
"O," said I to him, "now art thou, too, dead?"
    And he to me: "How may my body fare
    Up in the world, no knowledge I possess.
Such an advantage has this Ptolomæa,
    That oftentimes the soul descendeth here   125
    Sooner than Atropos in motion sets it.
And, that thou mayest more willingly remove
    From off my countenance these glassy tears,
    Know that as soon as any soul betrays

As I have done, his body by a demon   130
    Is taken from him, who thereafter rules it,
    Until his time has wholly been revolved.
Itself down rushes into such a cistern;
    And still perchance above appears the body
    Of yonder shade, that winters here behind me.   135
This thou shouldst know, if thou hast just come down;
    It is Ser Branca d' Oria, and many years
    Have passed away since he was thus locked up.
"I think," said I to him, "thou dost deceive me;
    For Branca d' Oria is not dead as yet,   140
    And eats, and drinks, and sleeps, and puts on clothes."
"In moat above," said he, "of Malebranche,
    There where is boiling the tenacious pitch,
    As yet had Michel Zanche not arrived,
When this one left a devil in his stead   145
    In his own body and one near of kin,
    Who made together with him the betrayal.
But hitherward stretch out thy hand forthwith,
    Open mine eyes"; —and open them I did not,
    And to be rude to him was courtesy.   150
Ah, Genoese! ye men at variance
    With every virtue, full of every vice!
    Wherefore are ye not scattered from the world?
For with the vilest spirit of Romagna
    I found of you one such, who for his deeds   155
    In soul already in Cocytus bathes,
And still above in body seems alive!

CANTO XXXIV

"*Vexilla Regis prodeunt Inferni*
   Towards us; therefore look in front of thee,"
   My Master said, "if thou discernest him."
As, when there breathes a heavy fog, or when
   Our hemisphere is darkening into night,   5
   Appears far off a mill the wind is turning,
Methought that such a building then I saw;
   And, for the wind, I drew myself behind
   My Guide, because there was no other shelter.
Now was I, and with fear in verse I put it,   10
   There where the shades were wholly covered up,
   And glimmered through like unto straws in glass.
Some prone are lying, others stand erect,
   This with the head, and that one with the soles;
   Another, bow-like, face to feet inverts.   15
When in advance so far we had proceeded,
   That it my Master pleased to show to me
   The creature who once had the beauteous semblance,
He from before me moved and made me stop,
   Saying: "Behold Dis, and behold the place   20
   Where thou with fortitude must arm thyself."

How frozen I became and powerless then,
    Ask it not, Reader, for I write it not,
    Because all language would be insufficient.
I did not die, and I alive remained not;   25
    Think for thyself now, hast thou aught of wit,
    What I became, being of both deprived.
The Emperor of the kingdom dolorous
    From his mid-breast forth issued from the ice;
    And better with a giant I compare   30
Than do the giants with those arms of his;
    Consider now how great must be that whole,
    Which unto such a part conforms itself.
Were he as fair once, as he now is foul,
    And lifted up his brow against his Maker,   35
    Well may proceed from him all tribulation.
O, what a marvel it appeared to me,
    When I beheld three faces on his head!
    The one in front, and that vermilion was;
Two were the others, that were joined with this   40
    Above the middle part of either shoulder,
    And they were joined together at the crest;
And the right-hand one seemed 'twixt white and yellow;
    The left was such to look upon as those
    Who come from where the Nile falls valley-ward.   45
Underneath each came forth two mighty wings,
    Such as befitting were so great a bird;
    Sails of the sea I never saw so large.
No feathers had they, but as of a bat
    Their fashion was; and he was waving them,   50
    So that three winds proceeded forth therefrom.
Thereby Cocytus wholly was congealed.
    With six eyes did he weep, and down three chins
    Trickled the tear-drops and the bloody drivel.
At every mouth he with his teeth was crunching   55
    A sinner, in the manner of a brake,
    So that he three of them tormented thus.

To him in front the biting was as naught
    Unto the clawing, for sometimes the spine
    Utterly stripped of all the skin remained.   60
"That soul up there which has the greatest pain,"
    The Master said, "is Judas Iscariot;
    With head inside, he plies his legs without.
Of the two others, who head downward are,
    The one who hangs from the black jowl is Brutus;   65
    See how he writhes himself, and speaks no word.
And the other, who so stalwart seems, is Cassius.
    But night is reascending, and 't is time
    That we depart, for we have seen the whole."
As seemed him good, I clasped him round the neck,   70
    And he the vantage seized of time and place,
    And when the wings were opened wide apart,
He laid fast hold upon the shaggy sides;
    From fell to fell descended downward then
    Between the thick hair and the frozen crust.   75
When we were come to where the thigh revolves
    Exactly on the thickness of the haunch,
    The Guide, with labor and with hard-drawn breath,
Turned round his head where he had had his legs,
    And grappled to the hair, as one who mounts,   80
    So that to Hell I thought we were returning.
"Keep fast thy hold, for by such stairs as these,"
    The Master said, panting as one fatigued,
    "Must we perforce depart from so much evil."
Then through the opening of a rock he issued,   85
    And down upon the margin seated me;
    Then tow'rds me he outstretched his wary step.
I lifted up mine eyes and thought to see
    Lucifer in the same way I had left him;
    And I beheld him upward hold his legs.   90
And if I then became disquieted,
    Let stolid people think who do not see
    What the point is beyond which I had passed.

"Rise up," the Master said, "upon thy feet;
  The way is long, and difficult the road,   95
  And now the sun to middle-tierce returns."
It was not any palace corridor
  There where we were, but dungeon natural,
  With floor uneven and unease of light.
"Ere from the abyss I tear myself away,   100
  My Master," said I when I had arisen,
  "To draw me from an error speak a little;
Where is the ice? and how is this one fixed
  Thus upside down? and how in such short time
  From eve to morn has the sun made his transit?"   105
And he to me: "Thou still imaginest
  Thou art beyond the centre, where I grasped
  The hair of the fell worm, who mines the world.
That side thou wast, so long as I descended;
  When round I turned me, thou didst pass the point   110
  To which things heavy draw from every side,
And now beneath the hemisphere art come
  Opposite that which overhangs the vast
  Dry-land, and 'neath whose cope was put to death
The Man who without sin was born and lived.   115
  Thou hast thy feet upon the little sphere
  Which makes the other face of the Judecca.
Here it is morn when it is evening there;
  And he who with his hair a stairway made us
  Still fixed remaineth as he was before.   120
Upon this side he fell down out of heaven;
  And all the land, that whilom here emerged,
  For fear of him made of the sea a veil,
And came to our hemisphere; and peradventure
  To flee from him, what on this side appears   125
  Left the place vacant here, and back recoiled."
A place there is below, from Beelzebub
  As far receding as the tomb extends,
  Which not by sight is known, but by the sound

Of a small rivulet, that there descendeth   130
   Through chasm within the stone, which it has gnawed
   With course that winds about and slightly falls.
The Guide and I into that hidden road
   Now entered, to return to the bright world;
   And without care of having any rest   135
We mounted up, he first and I the second,
   Till I beheld through a round aperture
   Some of those beauteous things which Heaven doth bear;
Thence we came forth to rebehold the stars.

Notes

THE DIVINE COMEDY.—The *Vita Nuova* of Dante closes with these words: "After this sonnet there appeared to me a wonderful vision, in which I beheld things that made me propose to say no more of this blessed one, until I shall be able to treat of her more worthily. And to attain thereunto, truly I strive with all my power, as she knoweth. So that if it shall be the pleasure of Him, through whom all things live, that my life continue somewhat longer, I hope to say of her what never yet was said of any woman. And then may it please Him, who is the Sire of courtesy, that my soul may depart to look upon the glory of its Lady, that is to say, of the blessed Beatrice, who in glory gazes into the face of Him, *qui est per omnia sæcula benedictus.*"

In these lines we have the earliest glimpse of the *Divine Comedy*, as it rose in the author's mind.

Whoever has read the *Vita Nuova* will remember the stress which Dante lays upon the mystic numbers Nine and Three; his first meeting with Beatrice at the beginning of her ninth year, and the end of his; his nine days' illness, and the thought of her death which came to him on the ninth day; her death on the ninth day of the ninth month, "computing by the Syrian method," and in that year of our Lord "when the perfect number ten was nine times completed in that century" which was the thirteenth. Moreover, he says the number nine was friendly to her, because the nine heavens were in conjunction at her birth; and that she was herself the number nine, "that is, a miracle whose root is the wonderful Trinity."

Following out this idea, we find the *Divine Comedy* written in *terza rima*, or threefold rhyme, divided into three parts, and each part again subdivided in its structure into three. The whole number of cantos is one hundred, the perfect number ten multiplied into itself; but if we count the first canto of the *Inferno* as a Prelude, which it really is, each part will consist of thirty-three cantos, making ninety-nine in all; and so the favorite mystic numbers reappear.

The three divisions of the *Inferno* are minutely described and explained by Dante in Canto XI. They are separated from each other by great spaces in the infernal abyss. The sins punished in them are,—I. Incontinence. II. Malice. III. Bestiality.

I. INCONTINENCE: 1. The Wanton. 2. The Gluttonous. 3. The Avaricious and Prodigal. 4. The Irascible and the Sullen.

II. MALICE: 1. The Violent against their neighbor, in person or property. 2. The Violent against themselves, in person or property. 3. The Violent against God, or against Nature, the daughter of God, or against Art, the daughter of Nature.

III. BESTIALITY: first subdivision: 1. Seducers. 2. Flatterers. 3. Simoniacs. 4. Soothsayers. 5. Barrators. 6. Hypocrites. 7. Thieves. 8. Evil counsellors. 9. Schismatics. 10. Falsifiers.

Second subdivision: 1. Traitors to their kindred. 2. Traitors to their country. 3. Traitors to their friends. 4. Traitors to their lords and benefactors.

The *Divine Comedy* is not strictly an allegorical poem in the sense in which the *Faerie Queene* is; and yet it is full of allegorical symbols and figurative meanings. In a letter to Can Grande della Scala, Dante writes: "It is to be remarked, that the sense of this work is not simple, but on the contrary one may say manifold. For one sense is that which is derived from the letter, and another is that which is derived from the things signified by the letter. The first is called literal, the second allegorical or moral. . . . The subject, then, of the whole work, taken literally, is the condition of souls after death, simply considered. For on this and around this the whole action of the work turns. But if the work be taken allegorically, the subject is man, how by actions of merit or demerit, through freedom of the will, he justly deserves reward or punishment."

It may not be amiss here to refer to what are sometimes called the sources of the *Divine Comedy*. Foremost among them must be placed the Eleventh Book of the *Odyssey*, and the Sixth of the *Æneid;* and to the latter Dante seems to point significantly in choosing Virgil for his Guide, his Master, his Author, from whom he took "the beautiful style that did him honor."

Next to these may be mentioned Cicero's *Vision of Scipio*, of which Chaucer says: —

> Chapiters seven it had, of Heven, and Hell,
> And Earthe, and soules that therein do dwell.

Then follow the popular legends which were current in Dante's age; an age when the end of all things was thought to be near at hand, and the wonders of the invisible world had laid fast hold on the imaginations of men. Prominent among these is the *Vision of Frate Alberico* who calls himself "the humblest servant of the servants of the Lord"; and who

> Saw in dreame at point-devyse
> Heaven, Earthe, Hell, and Paradyse.

This vision was written in Latin in the latter half of the twelfth century, and contains a description of Hell, Purgatory, and Paradise, with its Seven Heavens. It is for the most part a tedious tale, and bears evident marks of having been written by a friar of some monastery, when the afternoon sun was shining into his sleepy eyes. He seems, however, to have looked upon his own work with a not unfavorable opinion; for he concludes the Epistle Introductory with the words of St. John: "If any man shall add unto these things, God shall add unto him the plagues that are written in this book; and if any man shall take away from these things, God shall take away his part from the good things written in this book."

It is not impossible that Dante may have taken a few hints also from the *Tesoretto* of his teacher, Ser Brunetto Latini. See Canto XV. Note 30.

See upon this subject, Cancellieri, *Osservazioni Sopra l'Originalità di Dante;*— Wright, *St. Patrick's Purgatory, an Essay on the Legends of Purgatory, Hell, and Paradise, current during the Middle Ages;*—Ozanam, *Dante et la Philosophie Catholique au Treizième Siècle;*—Labitte, *La Divine Comédie avant Dante,* published as an Introduction to the translation of Brizeux;—and Delepierre, *Le Livre des Visions, ou l'Enfer et le Ciel décrits par ceux qui les ont vus.* See also the Illustrations at the end of this volume.

CANTO I

1. The action of the poem begins on Good Friday of the year 1300, at which time Dante, who was born in 1265, had reached the middle of the Scriptural threescore years and ten. It ends on the first Sunday after Easter, making in all ten days.

2. The dark forest of human life, with its passions, vices, and perplexities of all kinds; politically the state of Florence with its factions Guelf and Ghibelline. Dante, *Convito,* IV. 25, says: "Thus the adolescent, who enters into the erroneous forest of this life, would not know how to keep the right way if he were not guided by his elders."

   Brunetto Latini, *Tesoretto,* II. 75: —

   > Pensando a capo chino
   >   Perdei il gran cammino,
   > E tenni alla traversa
   >   D' una selva diversa.

   Spenser, *Faerie Queene,* IV. ii. 45: —

   > Seeking adventures in the salvage wood.

13. Bunyan, in his *Pilgrim's Progress,* which is a kind of Divine Comedy in prose, says: "I beheld then that they all went on till they came to the foot of the hill Difficulty.... But the narrow way lay right up the hill, and the name of the going up the side of the hill is called Difficulty.... They went then till they came to the Delectable Mountains, which mountains belong to the Lord of that hill of which we have spoken before."

14. Bunyan, *Pilgrim's Progress:* "But now in this valley of Humiliation poor Christian was hard put to it; for he had gone but a little way before he spied a foul fiend coming over the field to meet him; his name is Apollyon. Then did Christian begin to be afraid, and to cast in his mind whether to go back or stand his ground.... Now at the end of this valley was another, called the valley of the Shadow of Death; and Christian must needs go through it, because the way to the Celestial City lay through the midst of it."

17. The sun, with all its symbolical meanings. This is the morning of Good Friday.

    In the Ptolemaic system the sun was one of the planets.

20. The deep mountain tarn of his heart, dark with its own depth, and the shadows hanging over it.

27. *Jeremiah* ii. 6: "That led us through the wilderness, through a land of deserts and of pits, through a land of drought, and of the shadow of death, through a land that no man passed through, and where no man dwelt."

    In his note upon this passage Mr. Wright quotes Spenser's lines, *Faerie Queene,* I. v. 31,—

    There creature never passed
    That back returned without heavenly grace.

30. Climbing the hillside slowly, so that he rests longest on the foot that is lowest.

31. *Jeremiah* v. 6: "Wherefore a lion out of the forest shall slay them, a wolf of the evenings shall spoil them, a leopard shall watch over their cities: every one that goeth out thence shall be torn in pieces."

32. Worldly Pleasure; and politically Florence, with its factions of Bianchi and Neri.

36. *Più volte volto.* Dante delights in a play upon words as much as Shakespeare.

38. The stars of Aries. Some philosophers and fathers think the world was created in Spring.

45. Ambition; and politically the royal house of France.

48. Some editions read *temesse,* others *tremesse.*

49. Avarice; and politically the Court of Rome, or temporal power of the Popes.

60. Dante as a Ghibelline and Imperialist is in opposition to the Guelfs, Pope Boniface VIII., and the King of France, Philip the Fair, and is banished from Florence, out of the sunshine, and into "the dry wind that blows from dolorous poverty."

    Cato speaks of the "silent moon" in *De Re Rustica,* XXIX., *Evehito luna silenti;* and XL., *Vites inseri luna silenti.* Also Pliny, XVI. 39, has *Silens luna;* and Milton, in *Samson Agonistes,* "Silent as the moon."

63. The long neglect of classic studies in Italy before Dante's time.

70. Born under Julius Cæsar, but too late to grow up to manhood during his Imperial reign. He flourished later under Augustus.

79. In this passage Dante but expresses the universal veneration felt for Virgil during the Middle Ages, and especially in Italy. Petrarch's copy of Virgil is still preserved in the Ambrosian Library at Milan; and at the beginning of it he has recorded in a Latin note the time of his first meeting with Laura, and the date of her death, which, he says, "I write in this book, rather than elsewhere, because it comes often under my eye."

    In the popular imagination Virgil became a mythical personage and a mighty magician. See the story of *Virgilius* in Thom's *Early Prose Romances,* II. Dante selects him for his guide, as symbolizing human science or Philosophy. "I say and affirm," he remarks, *Convito,* V. 16, "that the lady with whom I became enamored after my first love was the most beautiful and modest daughter of the Emperor of the Universe, to whom Pythagoras gave the name of Philosophy."

87. Dante seems to have been already conscious of the fame which his *Vita Nuova* and *Canzoni* had given him.

101. The greyhound is Can Grande della Scala, Lord of Verona, Imperial Vicar, Ghibelline, and friend of Dante. Verona is between Feltro in the Marca Trivigiana, and Montefeltro in Romagna. Boccaccio, *Decamerone,* I. 7, speaks of him as "one of the most notable and magnificent lords that had been known in Italy, since the Emperor Frederick the Second." To him Dante dedicated the *Paradiso.* Some commentators think the *Veltro* is not Can Grande, but Ugguccione della Faggiola. See Troya, *Del Veltro Allegorico di Dante.*

106. The plains of Italy, in contradistinction to the mountains; the *humilemque Italiam* of Virgil, *Æneid,* III. 522: "And now the stars being chased away, blushing Aurora appeared, when far off we espy the hills obscure, and lowly Italy."

116. I give preference to the reading, *Vedrai gli antichi spiriti dolenti.*

122. Beatrice.

CANTO II

1. The evening of Good Friday.

   Dante, *Convito*, III. 2, says: "Man is called by philosophers the divine animal." Chaucer's *Assemble of Foules:* ——

   > The daie gan failen, and the darke night
   > That reveth bestes from hir businesse
   > Berafte me my boke for lacke of light.

   Mr. Ruskin, *Modern Painters*, III. 240, speaking of Dante's use of the word *"bruno,"* says: ——

   "In describing a simple twilight—not a Hades twilight, but an ordinarily fair evening—(*Inf.* II. 1), he says, the 'brown' air took the animals away from their fatigues; —the waves under Charon's boat are 'brown' (*Inf.* III. 117); and Lethe, which is perfectly clear and yet dark, as with oblivion, is 'bruna-bruna,' 'brown, *exceeding* brown.' Now, clearly in all these cases no *warmth* is meant to be mingled in the color. Dante had never seen one of our bog-streams, with its porter-colored foam; and there can be no doubt that, in calling Lethe brown, he means that it was dark slate-gray, inclining to black; as, for instance, our clear Cumberland lakes, which, looked straight down upon where they are deep, seem to be lakes of ink. I am sure this is the color he means; because no clear stream or lake on the Continent ever looks brown, but blue or green; and Dante, by merely taking away the pleasant color, would get at once to this idea of grave clear gray. So, when he was talking of twilight, his eye for color was far too good to let him call it *brown* in our sense. Twilight is not brown, but purple, golden, or dark gray; and this last was what Dante meant. Farther, I find that this negation of color is always the means by which Dante subdues his tones. Thus the fatal inscription on the Hades gate is written in 'obscure color,' and the air which torments the passionate spirits is 'aer nero,' *black* air (*Inf.* V. 51), called presently afterwards (line 81) malignant air, just as the gray cliffs are called malignant cliffs."

13. Æneas, founder of the Roman Empire. Virgil, *Æneid*, B. VI.

24. "That is," says Boccaccio, *Comento*, "St. Peter the Apostle, called the greater on account of his papal dignity, and to distinguish him from many other holy men of the same name."

28. St. Paul. *Acts*, ix. 15: "He is a chosen vessel unto me." Also, 2 *Corinthians*, xii. 3, 4: "And I knew such a man, whether in the body, or out of the body,

I cannot tell; God knoweth; how that he was caught up into Paradise, and heard unspeakable words, which it is not lawful for a man to utter."

42. Shakespeare, *Macbeth*, IV. 1: —

> The flighty purpose never is o'ertook
> Unless the deed go with it.

52. Suspended in Limbo; neither in pain nor in glory.

55. Brighter than the star; than "that star which is brightest," comments Boccaccio. Others say the Sun, and refer to Dante's *Canzone*, beginning: —

> The star of beauty which doth measure time,
> The lady seems, who has enamored me,
> Placed in the heaven of Love.

56. Shakespeare, *King Lear*, V. 3: —

> Her voice was ever soft,
> Gentle, and low; an excellent thing in woman.

67. This passage will recall Minerva transmitting the message of Juno to Achilles, *Iliad*, II.: "Go thou forthwith to the army of the Achæans, and hesitate not; but restrain each man with thy persuasive words, nor suffer them to drag to the sea their double-oared ships."

70. Beatrice Portinari, Dante's first love, the inspiration of his song and in his mind the symbol of the Divine. He says of her in the *Vita Nuova*: "This most gentle lady, of whom there has been discourse in what precedes, reached such favor among the people, that when she passed along the way persons ran to see her, which gave me wonderful delight. And when she was near any one, such modesty took possession of his heart, that he did not dare to raise his eyes or to return her salutation; and to this, should any one doubt it, many, as having experienced it, could bear witness for me. She, crowned and clothed with humility, took her way, displaying no pride in that which she saw and heard. Many, when she had passed, said, 'This is not a woman, rather is she one of the most beautiful angels of heaven.' Others said, 'She is a miracle. Blessed be the Lord who can perform such a marvel.' I say, that she showed herself so gentle and so full of all beauties, that those who looked on her felt within themselves a pure and sweet delight, such as they could not tell in words."— C. E. Norton, *The New Life*, 51, 52.

78. The heaven of the moon, which contains or encircles the earth.

84. The ampler circles of Paradise.

94. Divine Mercy.

97. St. Lucia, emblem of enlightening Grace.

102. Rachel, emblem of Divine Contemplation. See *Par.* XXXII. 9.

108. *Beside that flood, where ocean has no vaunt;* "That is," says Boccaccio, *Comento,* "the sea cannot boast of being more impetuous or more dangerous than that."

127. This simile has been imitated by Chaucer, Spenser, and many more. Jeremy Taylor says: —

> "So have I seen the sun kiss the frozen earth, which was bound up with the images of death, and the colder breath of the north; and then the waters break from their enclosures, and melt with joy, and run in useful channels; and the flies do rise again from their little graves in walls, and dance awhile in the air, to tell that there is joy within, and that the great mother of creatures will open the stock of her new refreshment, become useful to mankind, and sing praises to her Redeemer."

> Rossetti, *Spirito Antipapale del Secolo di Dante,* translated by Miss Ward, II. 216, makes this political application of the lines: "The *Florentines,* called *Sons of Flora,* are compared to *flowers;* and Dante calls the two parties who divided the city *white and black flowers,* and himself *white-flower,*— the name by which he was called by many. Now he makes use of a very abstruse comparison, to express how he became, from a Guelph or *Black,* a Ghibelline or *White.* He describes himself as a *flower,* first bent and closed by the night frosts, and then *blanched* or *whitened* by the sun (the symbol of reason), which opens its leaves; and what produces the effect of the sun on him is a speech of Virgil's, persuading him to follow his guidance."

CANTO III

1. This canto begins with a repetition of sounds like the tolling of a funeral bell: *dolente . . . dolore!*

> Ruskin, *Modern Painters,* III. 215, speaking of the Inferno, says: —

> "Milton's effort, in all that he tells us of his Inferno, is to make it indefinite; Dante's, to make it *definite.* Both, indeed, describe it as entered through gates; but, within the gate, all is wild and fenceless with Milton, having indeed its four rivers,—the last vestige of the mediæval tradition,—but rivers which flow through a waste of mountain and moorland, and by 'many a frozen, many a fiery Alp.' But Dante's Inferno is accurately separated into circles drawn with well-pointed compasses;

mapped and properly surveyed in every direction, trenched in a thoroughly good style of engineering from depth to depth, and divided, in the '*accurate* middle' (*dritto mezzo*) of its deepest abyss, into a concentric series of ten moats and embankments, like those about a castle, with bridges from each embankment to the next; precisely in the manner of those bridges over Hiddekel and Euphrates, which Mr. Macaulay thinks so innocently designed, apparently not aware that he is also laughing at Dante. These larger fosses are of rock, and the bridges also; but as he goes further into detail, Dante tells us of various minor fosses and embankments, in which he anxiously points out to us not only the formality, but the neatness and perfectness, of the stonework. For instance, in describing the river Phlegethon, he tells us that it was 'paved with stone at the bottom, and at the sides, and *over the edges of the sides*,' just as the water is at the baths of Bulicame; and for fear we should think this embankment at all *larger* than it really was, Dante adds, carefully, that it was made just like the embankments of Ghent or Bruges against the sea, or those in Lombardy which bank the Brenta, only 'not so high, nor so wide,' as any of these. And besides the trenches, we have two well-built castles; one like Ecbatana, with seven circuits of wall (and surrounded by a fair stream), wherein the great poets and sages of antiquity live; and another, a great fortified city with walls of iron, red-hot, and a deep fosse round it, and full of 'grave citizens,'—the city of Dis.

"Now, whether this be in what we moderns call 'good taste,' or not, I do not mean just now to inquire,—Dante having nothing to do with taste, but with the facts of what he had seen; only, so far as the imaginative faculty of the two poets is concerned, note that Milton's vagueness is not the sign of imagination, but of its absence, so far as it is significative in the matter. For it does not follow, because Milton did not map out his Inferno as Dante did, that he *could* not have done so if he had chosen; only it was the easier and less imaginative process to leave it vague than to define it. Imagination is always the seeing and asserting faculty; that which obscures or conceals may be judgment, or feeling, but not invention. The invention, whether good or bad, is in the accurate engineering, not in the fog and uncertainty."

18. Aristotle says: "The good of the intellect is the highest beatitude"; and Dante in the *Convito*: "The True is the good of the intellect." In other words, the knowledge of God is intellectual good.

"It is a most just punishment," says St. Augustine, "that man should lose that freedom which man could not use, yet had power to keep, if he would, and that he who had knowledge to do what was right, and did not do it, should be deprived of the knowledge of what was right; and that he who would not do righteously, when he had the power, should lose the power to do it when he had the will."

22. The description given of the Mouth of Hell by Frate Alberico, *Visio,* 9, is in the grotesque spirit of the Mediæval Mysteries.

"After all these things, I was led to the Tartarean Regions, and to the mouth of the Infernal Pit, which seemed like unto a well; regions full of horrid darkness, of fetid exhalations, of shrieks and loud howlings. Near this Hell there was a Worm of immeasurable size, bound with a huge chain, one end of which seemed to be fastened in Hell. Before the mouth of this Hell there stood a great multitude of souls, which he absorbed at once, as if they were flies; so that, drawing in his breath, he swallowed them all together; then, breathing, exhaled them all on fire, like sparks."

36. The reader will here be reminded of Bunyan's town of Fair-speech.

"*Christian.* Pray who are your kindred there, if a man may be so bold.

"*By-ends.* Almost the whole town; and in particular my Lord Turn-about, my Lord Timeserver, my Lord Fair-speech, from whose ancestors that town first took its name; also Mr. Smoothman, Mr. Facing-both-ways, Mr. Anything,—and the parson of our parish, Mr. Two-tongues, was my mother's own brother by father's side. . . .

"There Christian stepped a little aside to his fellow Hopeful, saying, 'It runs in my mind that this is one By-ends of Fair-speech; and if it be he, we have as very a knave in our company as dwelleth in all these parts.'"

42. Dryden, *The Hind and the Panther,* Part I. 341, says: —

> If, as our dreaming Platonists report,
> There could be spirits of a middle sort,
> Too black for heav'n, and yet too white for hell,
> Who just dropped half way down, nor lower fell.
> So pois'd, so gently she descends from high,
> It seems a soft dismission from the sky.

Many commentators and translators interpret *alcuna* in its usual significance of *some:* "For some glory the damned would have from them." This would be a reason why these pusillanimous ghosts should not be sent into the profounder abyss, but no reason why they should not be received there. This is strengthened by what comes afterwards, 1. 63. These souls were "hateful to God, and to his enemies." They were not good enough for Heaven, nor bad enough for Hell. "So then, because thou art lukewarm, and neither cold nor hot, I will spew thee out of my mouth." *Revelation* iii. 16.

Macchiavelli represents this scorn of inefficient mediocrity in an epigram on Peter Soderini: —

> The night that Peter Soderini died
> He at the mouth of Hell himself presented.
> "What, you come into Hell? poor ghost demented,
> Go to the Babies' Limbo!" Pluto cried.

The same idea is intensified in the old ballad of *Carle of Kelly-Burn Brees,* Cromek, p. 37: —

> She's nae fit for heaven, an' she'll ruin a' hell.

52. This restless flag is an emblem of the shifting and unstable minds of its followers.

59. Generally supposed to be Pope Celestine V., whose great refusal, or abdication, of the papal office is thus described by Boccaccio in his *Comento:* —

"Being a simple man and of a holy life, living as a hermit in the mountains of Morrone in Abruzzo, above Selmona, he was elected Pope in Perugia after the death of Pope Niccola d' Ascoli; and his name being Peter, he was called Celestine. Considering his simplicity, Cardinal Messer Benedetto Gatano, a very cunning man, of great courage and desirous of being Pope, managing astutely, began to show him that he held this high office much to the prejudice of his own soul, inasmuch as he did not feel himself competent for it;—others pretend that he contrived with some private servants of his to have voices heard in the chamber of the aforesaid Pope, which, as if they were voices of angels sent from heaven, said, 'Resign, Celestine! Resign, Celestine!'—moved by which, and being an idiotic man, he took counsel with Messer Benedetto aforesaid, as to the best method of resigning."

Celestine having relinquished the papal office, this "Messer Benedetto aforesaid" was elected Pope, under the title of Boniface VIII. His greatest misfortune was that he had Dante for an adversary.

Gower gives this legend of Pope Celestine in his *Confessio Amantis,* Book II., as an example of "the vice of supplantacion." He says: —

> This clerk, when he hath herd the form,
> How he the pope shuld enform,

Toke of the cardinal his leve
And goth him home, till it was eve.
And prively the trompe he hadde
Til that the pope was abedde.
And at midnight when he knewe
The pope slepte, then he blewe
Within his trompe through the wall
And tolde in what maner he shall
His papacie leve, and take
His first estate.

Milman, *Hist. Latin Christianity*, VI. 194, speaks thus upon the subject: —

"The abdication of Celestine V. was an event unprecedented in the annals of the Church, and jarred harshly against some of the first principles of the Papal authority. It was a confession of common humanity, of weakness below the ordinary standard of men in him whom the Conclave, with more than usual certitude, as guided by the special interposition of the Holy Ghost, had raised to the spiritual throne of the world. The Conclave had been, as it seemed, either under an illusion as to this declared manifestation of the Holy Spirit, or had been permitted to deceive itself. Nor was there less incongruity in a Pope, whose office invested him in something at least approaching to infallibility, acknowledging before the world his utter incapacity, his undeniable fallibility. That idea, formed out of many conflicting conceptions, yet forcibly harmonized by long, traditionary reverence, of unerring wisdom, oracular truth, authority which it was sinful to question or limit, was strangely disturbed and confused, not as before by too overweening ambition, or even awful yet still unacknowledged crime, but by avowed weakness, bordering on imbecility. His profound piety hardly reconciled the confusion. A saint after all made but a bad Pope.

"It was viewed, in his own time, in a different light by different minds. The monkish writers held it up as the most noble example of monastic, of Christian perfection. Admirable as was his election, his abdication was even more to be admired. It was an example of humility stupendous to all, imitable by few. The divine approval was said to be shown by a miracle which followed directly on his resignation; but the scorn of man has been expressed by the undying verse of Dante, who condemned him who was guilty of the baseness of the 'great refusal' to that circle of hell where are those disdained alike by mercy and justice, on whom the poet will not condescend to look. This sentence, so accordant with the stirring and passionate soul of the great Florentine, has been feebly counteracted, if counteracted, by the praise of Petrarch in his declamation on the beauty of a solitary life, for which the lyrist professed a somewhat hollow and poetic admiration. Assuredly there was no magnanimity contemptuous of the Papal greatness in the abdication of Celestine; it was the weariness, the conscious inefficiency, the regret of a man suddenly wrenched away from all his habits, pursuits, and avocations, and unnaturally compelled or tempted to assume an uncongenial dignity. It was the cry of passionate feebleness to be released from an insupportable burden. Compassion is the highest emotion of sympathy which it would have desired or could deserve."

A writer in the *North British Review,* XL. 87, speaking of this passage, says: —

"The common interpretation is, that Celestine the Fifth, who abdicated the Papacy in 1294, is the person indicated. But we may safely conclude that Dante knew better than to consign a man to eternal pain for having declined the path of ambition. Our MS. annotator has written on the margin: 'The reference is probably to *Matt.* xix. 22.' And there cannot be the slightest doubt of it. A young man came asking our Lord, 'What good thing shall I do, that I may have eternal life? Jesus said unto him, If thou wilt be perfect, go and sell that thou hast, and give to the poor, and thou shalt have treasure in heaven; and come, follow me. But when the young man heard that saying, he went away sorrowful, for he had great possessions.' It is the only instance recorded in the Gospels in which 'Jesus looking on a man and loving him,' asked him to become his friend and companion, but the glorious invitation was declined. Certainly nothing that ever happened in this world could so justly be called 'the great refusal.' And it is touchingly characteristic of the deep purity and spirituality of Dante's mind that he so regarded it."

75. Spenser's "misty dampe of misconceyving night."
82. Virgil, *Æneid,* VI., Davidson's translation: —

"A grim ferryman guards these floods and rivers, Charon, of frightful slovenliness; on whose chin a load of gray hair neglected lies; his eyes are flame: his vestments hang from his shoulders by a knot, with filth overgrown. Himself thrusts on the barge with a pole, and tends the sails, and wafts over the bodies in his iron-colored boat, now in years: but the god is of fresh and green old age. Hither the whole tribe in swarms come pouring to the banks, matrons and men, the souls of magnanimous heroes who had gone through life, boys and unmarried maids, and young men who had been stretched on the funeral pile before the eyes of their parents; as numerous as withered leaves fall in the woods with the first cold of autumn, or as numerous as birds flock to the land from deep ocean, when the chilling year drives them beyond sea, and sends them to sunny climes. They stood praying to cross the flood the first, and were stretching forth their hands with fond desire to gain the further bank: but the sullen boatman admits sometimes these, sometimes those; while others to a great distance removed, he debars from the banks."

And Shakespeare, *Richard III.*, I. 4: —

> I passed, methought, the melancholy flood
> With that grim ferryman which poets write of,
> Unto the kingdom of perpetual night.

87. Shakespeare, *Measure for Measure*, III. 1: —

> This sensible warm motion to become
> A kneaded clod; and the delighted spirit
> To bathe in fiery floods, or to reside
> In thrilling regions of thick-ribbed ice;
> To be imprisoned in the viewless winds,
> And blown with restless violence round about
> The pendent world; or to be worse than worst
> Of those that lawless and incertain thoughts
> Imagine howling.

89. Virgil, *Æneid*, VI.: "This is the region of Ghosts, of Sleep and drowsy Night; to waft over the bodies of the living in my Stygian boat is not permitted."

93. The souls that were to be saved assembled at the mouth of the Tiber, where they were received by the celestial pilot, or ferryman, who transported them to the shores of Purgatory, as described in *Purg.* II.

94. Many critics, and foremost among them Padre Pompeo Venturi, blame Dante for mingling together things Pagan and Christian. But they should remember how through all the Middle Ages human thought was wrestling with the old traditions; how many Pagan observances passed into Christianity in those early days; what reverence Dante had for Virgil and the classics; and how many Christian nations still preserve some traces of Paganism in the names of the stars, the months, and the days. Padre Pompeo should not have forgotten that he, though a Christian, bore a Pagan name, which perhaps is as evident a *brutto miscuglio* in a learned Jesuit, as any which he has pointed out in Dante.

Upon him and other commentators of the Divine Poem, a very amusing chapter might be written. While the great Comedy is going on upon the scene above, with all its pomp and music, these critics in the pit keep up such a perpetual wrangling among themselves, as seriously to disturb the performance. Biagioli is the most violent of all, particularly against Venturi, whom he calls an "infamous dirty dog," *sozzo can vituperato,* an epithet hardly permissible in the most heated literary controversy. Whereupon in return Zani de' Ferranti calls Biagioli "an inurbane grammarian," and a "most ungrateful ingrate,"—*quel grammatico inurbano . . . ingrato ingratissimo.*

Any one who is desirous of tracing out the presence of Paganism in Christianity will find the subject amply discussed by Middleton in his *Letter from Rome.*

109. Dryden's *Aeneïs,* B. VI.: —

His eyes like hollow furnaces on fire.

112. Homer, *Iliad,* VI.: "As is the race of leaves, such is that of men; some leaves the wind scatters upon the ground, and others the budding wood produces, for they come again in the season of Spring. So is the race of men, one springs up and the other dies."

See also Note 82 of this canto.

Mr. Ruskin, *Modern Painters,* III. 160, says: —

"When Dante describes the spirits falling from the bank of Acheron 'as dead leaves flutter from a bough,' he gives the most perfect image possible of their utter lightness, feebleness, passiveness, and scattering agony of despair, without, however, for an instant losing his own clear perception that *these* are souls, and *those* are leaves: he makes no confusion of one with the other."

Shelley in his *Ode to the West Wind* inverts this image, and compares the dead leaves to ghosts: —

O wild West Wind! thou breath of Autumn's being!
Thou from whose presence the leaves dead
Are driven like ghosts, from an enchanter fleeing,
Yellow, and black, and pale, and hectic red,
Pestilence-stricken multitudes.

Canto IV

1. Dante is borne across the river Acheron in his sleep, he does not tell us how, and awakes on the brink of "the dolorous valley of the abyss." He now enters the First Circle of the Inferno; the Limbo of the Unbaptized, the border land, as the name denotes.

   Frate Alberico in § 2 of his *Vision* says, that the divine punishments are tempered to extreme youth and old age.

   "Man is first a little child, then grows and reaches adolescence, and attains to youthful vigor; and, little by little growing weaker, declines into old age; and at every step of life the sum of his sins increases. So likewise the little children are punished least, and more and more the adolescents and the youths; until, their sins decreasing with the long-continued torments, punishment also begins to decrease, as if by a kind of old age *(veluti quadam senectute)*."

10. Frate Alberico, in § 9: "The darkness was so dense and impenetrable that it was impossible to see anything there."

28. Mental, not physical pain; what the French theologians call *la peine du dam,* the privation of the sight of God.

30. Virgil, *Æneid,* VI.: "Forthwith are heard voices, loud wailings, and weeping ghosts of infants, in the first opening of the gate; whom, bereaved of sweet life out of the course of nature, and snatched from the breast, a black day cut off, and buried in an untimely grave."

53. The descent of Christ into Limbo. Neither here nor elsewhere in the *Inferno* does Dante mention the name of Christ.

72. The reader will not fail to observe how Dante makes the word *honor,* in its various forms, ring and reverberate through these lines,—*orrevol, onori, orranza, onrata, onorata!*

86. Dante puts the sword into the hand of Homer as a symbol of his warlike epic, which is a Song of the Sword.

93. Upon this line Boccaccio, *Comento,* says: "A proper thing it is to honor every man, but especially those who are of one and the same profession, as these were with Virgil."

100. Another assertion of Dante's consciousness of his own power as a poet.

106. This is the Noble Castle of human wit and learning, encircled with its seven scholastic walls, the *Trivium,* Logic, Grammar, Rhetoric, and the *Quadrivium,* Arithmetic, Astronomy, Geometry, Music.

   The fair rivulet is Eloquence, which Dante does not seem to consider a very profound matter, as he and Virgil pass over it as if it were dry ground.

118. Of this word "enamel" Mr. Ruskin, *Modern Painters,* III. 227, remarks: —

"The first instance I know of its right use, though very probably it had been so employed before, is in Dante. The righteous spirits of the pre-Christian ages are seen by him, though in the Inferno, yet in a place open, luminous, and high, walking upon the 'green enamel.'

"I am very sure that Dante did not use this phrase as we use it. He knew well what enamel was; and his readers, in order to understand him thoroughly, must remember what it is,—a vitreous paste, dissolved in water, mixed with metallic oxides, to give it the opacity and the color required, spread in a moist state on metal, and afterwards hardened by fire, so as never to change. And Dante means, in using this metaphor of the grass of the Inferno, to mark that it is laid as a tempering and cooling substance over the dark, metallic, gloomy ground; but yet so hardened by the fire, that it is not any more fresh or living grass, but a smooth, silent, lifeless bed of eternal green. And we know how *hard* Dante's idea of it was; because afterwards, in what is perhaps the most awful passage of the whole *Inferno,* when the three furies rise at the top of the burning tower, and, catching sight of Dante, and not being able to get at him, shriek wildly for the Gorgon to come up, too, that they may turn him into stone, the word *stone* is not hard enough for them. Stone might crumble away after it was made, or something with life might grow upon it; no, it shall not be stone; they will make enamel of him; nothing can grow out of that; it is dead forever."

And yet just before, line 111, Dante speaks of this meadow as a "meadow of fresh verdure."

Compare Brunetto's *Tesoretto,* XIII.

Or va mastro Brunetto
Per lo cammino stretto,
Cercando di vedere,
E toccare, e sapere
Ciò, che gli è destinato.
E non fui guari andato,
Ch' i' fui nella diserta,
Dov' i' non trovai certa
Nè strada, nè sentiero.
Deh che paese fero
Trovai in quelle parti!
Che s' io sapessi d' arti
Quivi mi bisognava,
Chè quanto più mirava,

Più mi parea selvaggio.
    Quivi non ha viaggio,
Quivi non ha persone,
    Quivi non ha magione,
Non bestia, non uccello,
    Non fiume, non ruscello,
Non formica, nè mosca,
    Nè cosa, ch' i' conosca.
E io pensando forte,
    Dottai ben della morte.
E non è maraviglia;
    Chè ben trecento miglia
Girava d' ogni lato
    Quel paese snagiato.
Ma sì m' assicurai
    Quando mi ricordai
Del sicuro segnale,
    Che contra tutto male
Mi dà securamento:
    E io presi ardimento,
Quasi per avventura
    Per una valle scura,
Tanto, ch' al terzo giorno
    I' mi trovai d' intorno
Un grande pian giocondo,
    Lo più gaio del mondo,
E lo più dilettoso.
    Ma ricontar non oso
Ciò, ch' io trovai, e vidi,
    Se Dio mi guardi, e guidi.
Io non sarei creduto
    Di ciò, ch' i' ho veduto;
Ch' i' vidi Imperadori,
    E Re, e gran signori,
E mastri di scienze,
    Che dittavan sentenze;
E vidi tante cose,
    Che già 'n rime, nè 'n prose
Non le poria ritrare.

128. In the *Convito*, IV. 28, Dante makes Marcia, Cato's wife, a symbol of the noble soul: *"Per la quale Marzia s' intende la nobile anima."*

129. The Saladin of the Crusades. See Gibbon, Chap. LIX. Dante also makes
mention of him, as worthy of affectionate remembrance, in the *Convito*,
IV. 2. Mr. Cary quotes the following passage from Knolles's *History of the
Turks*, page 57: —

"About this time (1193) died the great Sultan Saladin, the greatest ter-
ror of the Christians, who, mindful of man's fragility and the vanity of
worldly honors, commanded at the time of his death no solemnity to be
used at his burial, but only his shirt in manner of an ensign, made fast
unto the point of a lance, to be carried before his dead body as an ensign,
a plain priest going before, and crying aloud unto the people in this sort,
'Saladin, Conqueror of the East, of all the greatness and riches he had in
his life, carrieth not with him anything more than his shirt.' A sight wor-
thy so great a king, as wanted nothing to his eternal commendation more
than the true knowledge of his salvation in Christ Jesus. He reigned
about sixteen years with great honor."

The following story of Saladin is from the *Cento Novelle Antiche*.
Roscoe's *Italian Novelists*, I. 18: —

"On another occasion the great Saladin, in the career of victory, pro-
claimed a truce between the Christian armies and his own. During this
interval he visited the camp and the cities belonging to his enemies,
with the design, should he approve of the customs and manners of the
people, of embracing the Christian faith. He observed their tables spread
with the finest damask coverings ready prepared for the feast, and he
praised their magnificence. On entering the tents of the king of France
during a festival, he was much pleased with the order and ceremony with
which everything was conducted, and the courteous manner in which he
feasted his nobles; but when he approached the residence of the poorer
class, and perceived them devouring their miserable pittance upon the
ground, he blamed the want of gratitude which permitted so many faith-
ful followers of their chief to fare so much worse than the rest of their
Christian brethren.

"Afterwards, several of the Christian leaders returned with the Sultan
to observe the manners of the Saracens. They appeared much shocked
on seeing all ranks of people take their meals sitting upon the ground.
The Sultan led them into a grand pavilion where he feasted his court,
surrounded with the most beautiful tapestries, and rich foot-cloths, on
which were wrought large embroidered figures of the cross. The Chris-
tian chiefs trampled them under their feet with the utmost indifference,
and even rubbed their boots, and spat upon them.

"On perceiving this, the Sultan turned towards them in the greatest
anger, exclaiming: 'And do you who pretend to preach the cross treat it

thus ignominiously? Gentlemen, I am shocked at your conduct. Am I to suppose from this that the worship of your Deity consists only in words, not in actions? Neither your manners nor your conduct please me.' And on this he dismissed them, breaking off the truce and commencing hostilities more warmly than before."

137. Diogenes, the cynic; Anaxagoras, the friend of Pericles; Thales of Miletus, one of the Seven Wise Men of Greece.

138. Zeno, the first of the Stoics; Empedocles, the poet, philosopher, and historian of Agrigentum, of whom Lucretius, *Nature of Things,* Good's Tr., I. 774, says: —

> Thus sung Empedocles, in honest fame
> First of his sect, whom Agrigentum bore
> In cloud-capt Sicily. . . . . . .
> . . . . A land in harvests rich,
> And rich in sages of illustrious fame.
> But naught so wondrous, so illustrious naught,
> So fair, so pure, so lovely, can it boast,
> Empedocles, as thou! whose song divine,
> By all rehearsed, so clears each mystic lore
> That scarce mankind believed thee born of man.

Heraclitus, the weeping philosopher. Lucretius, *Nature of Things,* Good's Tr., I. 693, says of him: —

> Hence those who deem the fabric of the world
> Educed from fire, itself, the source of all,
> Far wander from the truth. Thus deemed the sage,
> Chief of his sect, and fearless in the fight,
> Famed Heraclitus, by the learned esteemed
> Of doubtful phrase, mysterious; but revered
> By crowds of Grecians, flimsy and untaught.
> For such the obscure applaud; delighted most
> With systems dark, and most believing true
> The silver sounds that charm th' enchanted ear.

140. Dioscorides, the herbalist, celebrated for his work on the Materia Medica, describing the qualities or virtues of herbs, their poisons and antidotes.

143. Avicenna, an Arabian physician of Ispahan in the eleventh century. Born 980, died 1036.

144. Averrhoës, an Arabian scholar of the twelfth century, who translated the works of Aristotle, and wrote a commentary upon them. He was born in Cordova in 1149, and died in Morocco about 1200. He was the head of the Western School of philosophy, as Avicenna was of the Eastern.

CANTO V

In the Second Circle are found the souls of carnal sinners, whose punishment is

> To be imprisoned in the viewless winds,
> And blown with restless violence round about
> The pendent world.

2. The circles grow smaller and smaller as they descend.

4. Minos, the king of Crete, so renowned for justice as to be called the Favorite of the Gods, and after death made Supreme Judge in the Infernal Regions. Dante furnishes him with a tail, thus converting him, after the mediæval fashion, into a Christian demon.

21. Thou, too, as well as Charon, to whom Virgil has already made the same reply, Canto VI. 22.

28. In Canto I. 60, the sun is silent; here the light is dumb.

33. *Isaiah* xvii. 13: "And they shall flee far off, and shall be chased as the chaff of the mountains before the wind, and like a rolling thing before the whirlwind."

51. Gower, *Confessio Amantis,* VIII., gives a similar list "of gentil folke that whilom were lovers," seen by him as he lay in a swound and listened to the music

> Of bombarde and of clarionne
> With cornemuse and shalmele.

61. Queen Dido.

65. Achilles, being in love with Polyxena, a daughter of Priam, went unarmed to the temple of Apollo, where he was put to death by Paris.
    Gower, *Confessio Amantis,* IV., says: —

> For I have herde tell also
> Achilles left his armes so,
> Both of himself and of his men,
> At Troie for Polixenen

> Upon her love when he felle,
> That for no chaunce that befelle
> Among the Grekes or up or down
> He wolde nought ayen the town
> Ben armed for the love of her.

"I know not how," says Bacon in his Essay on Love, "but martial men are given to love; I think it is but as they are given to wine; for perils commonly ask to be paid in pleasure."

67. Paris of Troy, of whom Spenser says, *Faerie Queene,* III. ix. 34: —

> Most famous Worthy of the world, by whome
> That warre was kindled which did Troy inflame
> And stately towres of Ilion whilome
> Brought unto balefull ruine, was by name
> Sir Paris, far renowned through noble fame.

Tristan is the Sir Tristram of the Romances of Chivalry. See his adventures in the *Mort d'Arthure.* Also Thomas of Ercildoune's *Sir Tristram, a Metrical Romance.* His amours with Yseult or Ysonde bring him to this circle of the Inferno.

71. Shakespeare, Sonnet CVI.: —

> When in the chronicle of wasted time
> I see descriptions of the fairest wights,
> And beauty making beautiful old rhyme
> In praise of ladies dead and lovely knights.

See also the "wives and daughters of chieftains" that appear to Ulysses, in the *Odyssey,* Book XI.

Also Milton, *Paradise Regained,* II. 357: —

> And ladies of the Hesperides, that seemed
> Fairer than feigned of old, or fabled since
> Of fairy damsels met in forest wide
> By knights of Logres, or of Lyones,
> Lancelot, or Palleas, or Pellenore.

87. In the original, *l'aer perso,* the perse air. Dante, *Convito,* IV. 20, defines perse as "a color mixed of purple and black, but the black predominates."

Chaucer's "Doctour of Phisike" in the *Canterbury Tales,* Prologue 441, wore this color: —

> In sanguin and in perse he clad was alle,
> Lined with taffata and with sendalle.

The Glossary defines it, "skie colored, of a bluish gray." The word is again used, VII. 103, and *Purg.* IX. 97.

97. The city of Ravenna. "One reaches Ravenna," says Ampère, *Voyage Dantesque,* p. 311, "by journeying along the borders of a pine forest, which is seven leagues in length, and which seemed to me an immense funereal wood, serving as an avenue to the common tomb of those two great powers, Dante and the Roman Empire in the West. There is hardly room for any other memories than theirs. But other poetic names are attached to the Pine Woods of Ravenna. Not long ago Lord Byron evoked there the fantastic tales borrowed by Dryden from Boccaccio, and now he is himself a figure of the past, wandering in this melancholy place. I thought, in traversing it, that the singer of despair had ridden along this melancholy shore, trodden before him by the graver and slower footstep of the poet of the Inferno."

Quoting this line, Ampère remarks, *Voyage Dantesque,* p. 312: "We have only to cast our eyes upon the map to recognize the topographical exactitude of this last expression. In fact, in all the upper part of its course, the Po receives a multitude of affluents, which converge towards its bed. They are the Tessino, the Adda, the Olio, the Mincio, the Trebbia, the Bormida, the Taro;—names which recur so often in the history of the wars of the fifteenth and sixteenth centuries."

103. Here the word *love* is repeated, as the word *honor* was in Canto IV. 72. The verse murmurs with it, like the "moan of doves in immemorial elms."

St. Augustine says in his *Confessions,* III. 1: "I loved not yet, yet I loved to love.... I sought what I might love, in love with loving."

104. I think it is Coleridge who says: "The desire of man is for the woman, but the desire of woman is for the desire of man."

107. Caïna is in the lowest circle of the Inferno, where fratricides are punished.

116. Francesca, daughter of Guido da Polenta, Lord of Ravenna, and wife of Gianciotto Malatesta, son of the Lord of Rimini. The lover, Paul Malatesta, was the brother of the husband, who, discovering their amour, put them both to death with his own hand.

Carlyle, *Heroes and Hero Worship,* Lect. III., says: —

"Dante's painting is not graphic only, brief, true, and of a vividness as of fire in dark night; taken on the wider scale, it is every way noble, and the outcome of a great soul. Francesca and her Lover, what qualities in that! A thing woven as out of rainbows, on a ground of eternal black. A small flute-voice of infinite wail speaks there, into our very heart of hearts. A touch of womanhood in it too: *della bella persona, che mi fu tolta;* and how, even in the Pit of woe, it is a solace that *he* will never part from her! Saddest tragedy in these *alti guai.* And the racking winds, in that *aer bruno,* whirl them away again, to wail forever!—Strange to think: Dante was the friend of this poor Francesca's father; Francesca herself may have sat upon the Poet's knee, as a bright, innocent little child. Infinite pity, yet also infinite rigor of law: it is so Nature is made; it is so Dante discerned that she was made."

Later commentators assert that Dante's friend Guido was not the father of Francesca, but her nephew.

Boccaccio's account, translated from his Commentary by Leigh Hunt, *Stories from the Italian Poets,* Appendix II., is as follows: —

"You must know that this lady, Madonna Francesca, was daughter of Messer Guido the Elder, lord of Ravenna and of Cervia, and that a long and grievous war having been waged between him and the lords Malatesta of Rimini, a treaty of peace by certain mediators was at length concluded between them; the which, to the end that it might be the more firmly established, it pleased both parties to desire to fortify by relationship; and the matter of this relationship was so discoursed, that the said Messer Guido agreed to give his young and fair daughter in marriage to Gianciotto, the son of Messer Malatesta. Now, this being made known to certain of the friends of Messer Guido, one of them said to him: 'Take care what you do; for if you contrive not matters discreetly, such relationship will beget scandal. You know what manner of person your daughter is, and of how lofty a spirit; and if she see Gianciotto before the bond is tied, neither you nor any one else will have power to persuade her to marry him; therefore, if it so please you, it seems to me that it would be good to conduct the matter thus: namely, that Gianciotto should not come hither himself to marry her, but that a brother of his should come and espouse her in his name.'

"Gianciotto was a man of great spirit, and hoped, after his father's death, to become lord of Rimini; in the contemplation of which event, albeit he was rude in appearance and a cripple, Messer Guido desired him for a son-in-law above any one of his brothers. Discerning, therefore, the reasonableness of what his friend counselled, he secretly disposed matters according to his device; and a day being appointed, Polo, a brother of Gianciotto, came to Ravenna with full authority to espouse Madonna Francesca. Polo was a handsome man, very pleasant, and of a courteous breeding; and passing with other gentlemen over the court-yard of the palace of Messer Guido, a damsel who knew him pointed him out to Madonna Francesca through an opening in the casement, say-ing, 'That is he that is to be your husband'; and so indeed the poor lady believed, and incontinently placed in him her whole affection; and the ceremony of the marriage having been thus brought about, and the lady conveyed to Rimini, she became not aware of the deceit till the morning ensuing the marriage, when she beheld Gianciotto rise from her side; the which discovery moved her to such disdain, that she became not a whit the less rooted in her love for Polo. Nevertheless, that it grew to be un-lawful I never heard, except in what is written by this author (Dante), and possibly it might so have become; albeit I take what he says to have been an invention framed on the possibility, rather than anything which he knew of his own knowledge. Be this as it may, Polo and Madonna Francesca living in the same house, and Gianciotto being gone into a cer-tain neighboring district as governor, they fell into great companionship with one another, suspecting nothing; but a servant of Gianciotto's, not-ing it, went to his master and told him how matters looked; with the which Gianciotto, being fiercely moved, secretly returned to Rimini; and seeing Polo enter the room of Madonna Francesca the while he himself was arriving, went straight to the door, and, finding it locked inside, called to his lady to come out; for, Madonna Francesca and Polo having descried him, Polo thought to escape suddenly through an opening in the wall, by means of which there was a descent into another room; and therefore, thinking to conceal his fault either wholly or in part, he threw himself into the opening, telling the lady to go and open the door. But his hope did not turn out as he expected; for the hem of a mantle which he had on caught upon a nail, and the lady opening the door meantime, in the belief that all would be well by reason of Polo's not being there, Gianciotto caught sight of Polo as he was detained by the hem of the mantle, and straightway ran with his dagger in his hand to kill him; whereupon the lady, to prevent it, ran between them; but Gianciotto having lifted the dagger, and put the whole force of his arm into the blow, there came to pass what he had not desired,—namely, that he struck the dagger into the bosom of the lady before it could reach Polo; by which accident, being as one who had loved the lady better than himself, he withdrew the dagger and again struck at Polo, and slew him; and so leaving them both dead, he hastily went his way and betook him to his wonted affairs; and the next morning the two lovers, with many tears, were buried together in the same grave."

121. This thought is from Boethius, *De Consolat. Philos.*, Lib. II. Prosa 4: *"In omni adversitate fortunæ, infelicissimum genus est infortunii fuisse felicem et non esse."*

In the *Convito*, II. 16, Dante speaks of Boethius and Tully as having directed him "to the love, that is to the study, of this most gentle lady Philosophy." From this Venturi and Biagioli infer that, by the Teacher, Boethius is meant, not Virgil.

This interpretation, however, can hardly be accepted, as not in one place only, but throughout the *Inferno* and the *Purgatorio*, Dante proclaims Virgil as his Teacher, *il mio Dottore*. Lombardi thinks that Virgil had experience of this "greatest sorrow," finding himself also in "the infernal prison"; and that it is to this, in contrast with his happy life on earth, that Francesca alludes, and not to anything in his writings.

128. The Romance of Launcelot of the Lake. See Delvan, *Bibliotèque Bleue:* —

"Chap. 39. Comment Launcelot et la Reine Genièvre devisèrent de choses et d'autres, et surtout de choses amoureuses. . . .

"La Reine, voyant qu'il n'osait plus rien faire ni dire, le prit par le menton et le baisa assez longuement en présence de Gallehault."

The Romance was to these two lovers, what Galeotto (Gallehault or Sir Galahad) had been to Launcelot and Queen Guenever.

Leigh Hunt speaks of the episode of Francesca as standing in the *Inferno* "like a lily in the mouth of Tartarus."

142. Chaucer, *Knightes Tale:* —

The colde death, with mouth gaping upright.

CANTO VI

2. The sufferings of these two, and the pity it excited in him. As in Shakespeare, *Othello*, IV. 1: "But yet the pity of it, Iago!—O Iago, the pity of it, Iago!"

7. In this third circle are punished the Gluttons. Instead of the feasts of former days, the light, the warmth, the comfort, the luxury, and "the frolic wine" of dinner-tables, they have the murk and the mire, and the "rain eternal, maledict, and cold, and heavy"; and are barked at and bitten by the dog in the yard.

Of Gluttony, Chaucer says in *The Persones Tale*, p. 239: —

"He that is usant to this sinne of glotonie, he ne may no sinne withstond, he must be in servage of all vices, for it is the devils horde, ther he hideth him and resteth. This sinne hath many spices. The first is dronkennesse, that is the horrible sepulture of mannes reson: and there-fore whan a man is dronke, he hath lost his reson: and this is dedly sinne. But sothly, whan that a man is not wont to strong drinkes, and peraven-ture he knoweth not the strength of the drinke, or hath feblenesse in his hed, or hath travailled, thurgh which he drinketh the more, al be he so-denly caught with drinke, it is no dedly sinne, but venial. The second spice of glotonie is, that the spirit of a man wexeth all trouble for dronkennesse, and bereveth a man the discretion of his wit. The thridde spice of glotonie is, whan a man devoureth his mete, and hath not right-ful maner of eting. The fourthe is, whan thurgh the gret abundance of his mete, the humours in his body ben distempered. The fifthe is, foryetful-nesse by to moche drinking, for which sometime a man forgeteth by the morwe, what he did over eve."

52. It is a question whether *Ciacco,* Hog, is the real name of this person, or a nickname. Boccaccio gives him no other. He speaks of him, *Comento,* VI., as a noted diner-out in Florence, "who frequented the gentry and the rich, and particularly those who ate and drank sumptuously and deli-cately; and when he was invited by them to dine, he went; and likewise when he was not invited by them, he invited himself; and for this vice he was well known to all Florentines; though apart from this he was a well-bred man according to his condition, eloquent, affable, and of good feeling; on account of which he was welcomed by every gentleman."

The following story from the *Decamerone,* Gior. IX., Nov. viii., transla-tion of 1684, presents a lively picture of social life in Florence in Dante's time, and is interesting for the glimpse it gives, not only of Ciacco, but of Philippo Argenti, who is spoken of hereafter, Canto VIII. 61. The Corso Donati here mentioned is the Leader of the Neri. His violent death is predicted, *Purg.* XXIV. 82: —

"There dwelt sometime in Florence one that was generally called by the name of Ciacco, a man being the greatest Gourmand and grossest Feeder as ever was seen in any Countrey, all his means and procurements meerly unable to maintain expences for filling his belly. But otherwise he was of sufficient and commendable carriage, fairly demeaned, and well discoursing on any Argument: yet not as a curious and spruce Courtier, but rather a frequenter of rich mens Tables, where choice of good chear is seldom wanting, and such should have his Company, albeit not invited, he had the Courage to bid himself welcome.

"At the same time, and in our City of Florence also, there was another man named Biondello, very low of stature, yet comely formed, quick witted, more neat and brisk than a Butterflie, always wearing a wrought silk Cap on his head, and not a hair standing out of order, but the tuft flourishing above the forehead, and he such another trencher flie for the Table, as our forenamed Ciacco was. It so fell out on a morning in the Lent time, that he went into the Fish-market, where he bought two goodly Lampreys for Messer Viero de Cerchi, and was espyed by Ciacco, who, coming to Biondello, said, 'What is the meaning of this cost, and for whom is it?' Whereto Biondello thus answered, 'Yesternight three other Lampreys, far fairer than these, and a whole Sturgeon, were sent unto Messer Corso Donati, and being not sufficient to feed divers Gentlemen, whom he hath invited this day to dine with him, he caused me to buy these two beside: Dost not thou intend to make one of them?' 'Yes, I warrant thee,' replyed Ciacco, 'thou knowest I can invite my self thither, without any other bidding.'

"So parting, about the hour of dinner time Ciacco went to the house of Messer Corso, whom he found sitting and talking with certain of his Neighbours, but dinner was not as yet ready, neither were they come thither to dinner. Messer Corso demanded of Ciacco, what news with him, and whether he went? 'Why, Sir,' said Ciacco, 'I come to dine with you, and your good Company.' Whereto Messer Corso answered, That he was welcome: and his other friends being gone, dinner was served in, none else thereat present but Messer Corso and Ciacco: all the diet being a poor dish of Pease, a little piece of Tunny, and a few small fishes fryed, without any other dishes to follow after. Ciacco seeing no better fare, but being disappointed of his expectation, as longing to feed on the Lampreys and Sturgeon, and so to have made a full dinner indeed, was of a quick apprehension, and apparently perceived that Biondello had meerly gull'd him in a knavery, which did not a little vex him, and made him vow to be revenged on Biondello, as he could compass occasion afterward.

"Before many days were past, it was his fortune to meet with Biondello, who having told his jest to divers of his friends, and much good merryment made thereat: he saluted Ciacco in a kind manner, saying, 'How didst thou like the fat Lampreys and Sturgeon which thou fed'st on at the house of Messer Corso?' 'Well, Sir,' answered Ciacco, 'perhaps before Eight days pass over my head, thou shalt meet with as pleasing a dinner as I did.' So, parting away from Biondello, he met with a Porter, such as are usually sent on Errands; and hyring him to do a message for him, gave him a glass Bottle, and bringing him near to the Hall-house of Cavicciuli, shewed him there a Knight, called Signior Philippo Argenti, a man of huge stature, very cholerick, and sooner moved to Anger than other man. 'To him thou must go with this Bottle in thy hand, and say thus to him. Sir, Biondello sent me to you, and courteously entreateth you, that you would erubinate this glass Bottle with your best Claret Wine; because he would make merry with a few friends of his. But beware he lay no hand on thee, because he may be easily induced to misuse thee, and so my business be disappointed.' 'Well, Sir,' said the Porter, 'shall I say any thing else unto him?' 'No,' quoth Ciacco, 'only go and deliver this message, and when thou art returned, I'll pay thee for thy pains.' The Porter being gone to the house, delivered his message to the Knight, who, being a man of no great civil breeding, but very furious, presently conceived that Biondello, whom he knew well enough, sent this message in meer mockage of him, and, starting up with fierce looks, said, 'What erubination of Claret should I send him? and what have I to do with him or his drunken friends? Let him and thee go hang your selves together.' So he stept to catch hold on the Porter, but he being nimble and escaping from him, returned to Ciacco and told him the answer of Philippo. Ciacco, not a little contented, payed the Porter, tarried in no place till he met Biondello, to whom he said, 'When wast thou at the Hall of Cavicciuli?' 'Not a long while,' answered Biondello; 'but why dost thou demand such a question?' 'Because,' quoth Ciacco, 'Signior Philippo hath sought about for thee, yet know not I what he would have with thee.' 'Is it so,' replied Biondello, 'then I will walk thither presently, to understand his pleasure.'

"When Biondello was thus parted from him, Ciacco followed not far off behind him, to behold the issue of this angry business; and Signior Philippo, because he could not catch the Porter, continued much distempered, fretting and fuming, because he could not comprehend the meaning of the Porter's message, but only surmised that Biondello, by the procurement of some body else, had done this in scorn of him. While he remained thus deeply discontented, he espyed Biondello coming towards him, and meeting him by the way, he stept close to him and gave him a cruel blow on the Face, causing his Nose to fall out a bleeding. 'Alas, Sir,' said Biondello, 'wherefore do you strike me?' Signior Philippo, catching him by the hair of the head, trampled his Night Cap in the dirt, and his Cloak also, when, laying many violent blows on him, he said, 'Villanous Traitor as thou art, I'll teach thee what it is to erubinate with Claret, either thy self or any of thy cupping Companions. Am I a Child to be jested withal?'

"Nor was he more furious in words than in stroaks also, beating him about the Face, hardly leaving any hair on his head, and dragging him along in the mire, spoiling all his Garments, and he not able, from the first blow given, to speak a word in defence of himself. In the end Signior Philippo having extreamly beaten him, and many people gathering about them, to succour a man so much misused, the matter was at large related, and manner of the message sending. For which they all did greatly reprehend Biondello, considering he knew what kind of man Philippo was, not any way to be jested withal. Biondello in tears maintained that he never sent any such message for Wine, or intended it in the least degree; so, when the tempest was more mildly calmed, and Biondello, thus cruelly beaten and durtied, had gotten home to his own house, he could then remember that (questionless) this was occasioned by Ciacco.

"After some few days were passed over, and the hurts in his face indifferently cured, Biondello beginning to walk abroad again, chanced to meet with Ciacco, who, laughing heartily at him, said, 'Tell me, Biondello, how dost thou like the erubinating Claret of Signior Philippo?' 'As well,' quoth Biondello, 'as thou didst the Sturgeon and Lampreys at Messer Corso Donaties.' 'Why then,' said Ciacco, 'let these tokens continue familiar between thee and me, when thou wouldest bestow such another dinner on me, then will I erubinate thy Nose with a Bottle of the same Claret.' But Biondello perceived to his cost that he had met with the worser bargain, and Ciacco got cheer without any blows; and therefore desired a peacefull attonement, each of them always after abstaining from flouting one another."

Ginguené, *Hist. Lit. de l'Italie,* II. 53, takes Dante severely to task for wasting his pity upon poor Ciacco, but probably the poet had pleasant memories of him at Florentine banquets in the olden time. Nor is it remarkable that he should be mentioned only by his nickname. Mr. Forsyth calls Italy "the land of nicknames." He says in continuation, *Italy,* p. 145: —

"Italians have suppressed the surnames of their principal artists under various designations. Many are known only by the names of their birthplace, as Correggio, Bassano, etc. Some by those of their masters, as Il Salviati, Sansovino, etc. Some by their father's trade, as Andrea del Sarto, Tintoretto, etc. Some by their bodily defects, as Guercino, Cagnacci, etc. Some by the subjects in which they excelled, as M. Angelo delle battaglie, Agostino delle perspettive. A few (I can recollect only four) are known, each as the *prince* of his respective school, by their Christian names alone: Michael Angelo, Raphael, Guido, Titian."

65. The Bianchi are called the *Parte selvaggia,* because its leaders, the Cerchi, came from the forest lands of Val di Sieve. The other party, the Neri, were led by the Donati.

The following account of these factions is from Giovanni Florentino, a writer of the fourteenth century; *Il Pecorone* Gior. XIII. Nov. i., in Roscoe's *Italian Novelists,* I. 327.

"In the city of Pistoia, at the time of its greatest splendor, there flourished a noble family, called the Cancellieri, derived from Messer Cancelliere, who had enriched himself with his commercial transactions. He had numerous sons by two wives, and they were all entitled by their wealth to assume the title of Cavalieri, valiant and worthy men, and in all their actions magnanimous and courteous. And so fast did the various branches of this family spread, that in a short time they numbered a hundred men at arms, and being superior to every other, both in wealth and power, would have still increased, but that a cruel division arose between them, from some rivalship in the affections of a lovely and enchanting girl, and from angry words they proceeded to more angry blows. Separating into two parties, those descended from the first wife took the title of Cancellieri Bianchi, and the others, who were the offspring of the second marriage, were called Cancellieri Neri.

"Having at last come to action, the Neri were defeated, and wishing to adjust the affair as well as they yet could, they sent their relation, who had offended the opposite party, to entreat forgiveness on the part of the Neri, expecting that such submissive conduct would meet with the compassion it deserved. On arriving in the presence of the Bianchi, who conceived themselves the offended party, the young man, on bended knees, appealed to their feelings for forgiveness, observing, that he had placed himself in their power, that so they might inflict what punishment they judged proper; when several of the younger members of the offended party, seizing on him, dragged him into an adjoining stable, and ordered that his right hand should be severed from his body. In the utmost terror the youth, with tears in his eyes, besought them to have mercy, and to take a greater and nobler revenge, by pardoning one whom they had it in their power thus deeply to injure. But heedless of his prayers, they bound his hand by force upon the manger, and struck it off; a deed which excited the utmost tumult throughout Pistoia, and such indignation and reproaches from the injured party of the Neri, as to implicate the whole city in a division of interests between them and the Bianchi, which led to many desperate encounters.

"The citizens, fearful lest the faction might cause insurrections throughout the whole territory, in conjunction with the Guelfs, applied to the Florentines in order to reconcile them; on which the Florentines took possession of the place, and sent the partisans on both sides to the confines of Florence, whence it happened that the Neri sought refuge in the house of the Frescobaldi, and the Bianchi in that of the Cerchi nel Garbo, owing to the relationship which existed between them. The seeds of the same dissension being thus sown in Florence, the whole city became divided, the Cerchi espousing the interests of the Bianchi, and the Donati those of the Neri.

"So rapidly did this pestiferous spirit gain ground in Florence, as frequently to excite the greatest tumult; and from a peaceable and flourishing state, it speedily became a scene of rapine and devastation. In this stage Pope Boniface VIII. was made acquainted with the state of this ravaged and unhappy city, and sent the Cardinal Acqua Sparta on a mission to reform and pacify the enraged parties. But with his utmost efforts he was unable to make any impression, and accordingly, after declaring the place excommunicated, departed. Florence being thus exposed to the greatest perils, and in a continued state of insurrection, Messer Corso Donati, with the Spini, the Pazzi, the Tosinghi, the Cavicciuli, and the populace attached to the Neri faction, applied, with the consent of their leaders, to Pope Boniface. They entreated that he would employ his interest with the court of France to send a force to allay these feuds, and to quell the party of the Bianchi. As soon as this was reported in the city, Messer Donati was banished, and his property forfeited, and the other heads of the sect were proportionally fined and sent into exile. Messer Donati, arriving at Rome, so far prevailed with his Holiness, that he sent an embassy to Charles de Valois, brother to the king of France, declaring his wish that he should be made Emperor, and King of the Romans; under which persuasion Charles passed into Italy, reinstating Messer Donati and the Neri in the city of Florence. From this there only resulted worse evils, inasmuch as all the Bianchi, being the least powerful, were universally oppressed and robbed, and Charles, becoming the enemy of Pope Boniface, conspired his death, because the Pope had not fulfilled his promise of presenting him with an imperial crown. From which events it may be seen that this vile faction was the cause of discord in the cities of Florence and Pistoia, and of the other states of Tuscany; and no less to the same source was to be attributed the death of Pope Boniface VIII."

69. Charles de Valois, called Senzaterra, or Lackland, brother of Philip the Fair, king of France.

Che testè piaggia. Perhaps *piaggia* here means hovering over; in falconry, *coasting.*

Shakespeare, *Third Part of King Henry VI.* Act I. Sc. 1.

> Whose haughty spirit, winged with desire,
> Will coast my crown, and like an empty eagle
> Tire on the flesh of me and of my son.

Also in the *Roman de la Rose*, v. 1423.

> Mais le Dieu d'Amours m'a suivy,
> Et de loing m'estoit costoiant,
> Me regardant et espiant
> Comme le veneur fait la beste.

73. The names of these two remain unknown. Probably one of them was Dante's friend Guido Cavalcanti.

80. Of this Arrigo nothing whatever seems to be known, hardly even his name; for some commentators call him Arrigo dei Fisanti, and others Arrigo dei Fifanti. Of these other men of mark "who set their hearts on doing good," Farinata is among the Heretics, Canto X.; Tegghiaio and Rusticucci among the Sodomites, Canto XVI.; and Mosca among the Schismatics, Canto XXVIII.

106. The philosophy of Aristotle. The same doctrine is taught by St. Augustine: *"Cum fiet resurrectio carnis, et bonorum gaudia et tormenta malorum majora erunt."*

115. Plutus, the God of Riches, of which Lord Bacon says in his *Essays:* —

"I cannot call riches better than the baggage of virtue; the Roman word is better, 'impedimenta;' for as the baggage is to an army, so is riches to virtue; it cannot be spared nor left behind, but it hindereth the march; yea, and the care of it sometimes loseth or disturbeth the victory; of great riches there is no real use, except it be in the distribution; the rest is but conceit. . . . The personal fruition in any man cannot reach to feel great riches: there is a custody of them; or a power of dole and donative of them; or a fame of them; but no solid use to the owner."

Canto VII

1. In this Canto is described the punishment of the Avaricious and the Prodigal, with Plutus as their jailer. His outcry of alarm is differently interpreted by different commentators, and by none very satisfactorily. The curious student, groping among them for a meaning, is like Gower's young king, of whom he says, in his *Confessio Amantis:* —

> Of deepe ymaginations
> And straunge interpretations,
> Problemes and demaundes eke
> His wisedom was to finde and seke,
> Whereof he wolde in sondry wise

> Opposen hem, that weren wise;
> But none of hem it mighte bere
> Upon his word to give answere.

But nearly all agree, I believe, in construing the strange words into a cry of alarm or warning to Lucifer, that his realm is invaded by some unusual apparition.

Of all the interpretations given, the most amusing is that by Benvenuto Cellini, in his description of the Court of Justice in Paris, *Memoirs of Benvenuto Cellini*, Roscoe's Tr., Chap. XXII: —

"I stooped down several times to observe what passed: the words which I heard the judge utter, upon seeing two gentlemen who wanted to hear the trial, and whom the porter was endeavoring to keep out, were these: 'Be quiet, be quiet, Satan, get hence, and leave off disturbing us.' The terms were, *Paix, paix, Satan, allez, paix*. As I had by this time thoroughly learnt the French language, upon hearing these words, I recollected what Dante said, when he with his master, Virgil, entered the gates of hell; for Dante and Giotto the painter were together in France, and visited Paris with particular attention, where the court of justice may be considered as hell. Hence it is that Dante, who was likewise perfect master of the French, made use of that expression; and I have often been surprised, that it was never understood in that sense; so that I cannot help thinking, that the commentators on this author have often made him say things which he never so much as dreamed of."

Dante himself hardly seems to have understood the meaning of the words, though he suggests that Virgil did.

11. The overthrow of the Rebel Angels. St. Augustine says, *"Idolatria et quælibet noxia superstitio fornicatio est."*

24. Must dance the *Ridda*, a round dance of the olden time. It was a Roundelay, or singing and dancing together. Boccaccio's Monna Belcolore "knew better than any one how to play the tambourine and lead the Ridda."

27. As the word *honor* resounds in Canto IV., and the word *love* in Canto V., so here the words *rolling* and *turning* are the burden of the song, as if to suggest the motion of Fortune's wheel, so beautifully described a little later.

39. Clerks, clerics, or clergy. Boccaccio, *Comento*, remarks upon this passage: "Some maintain, that the clergy wear the tonsure in remembrance and reverence of St. Peter, on whom, they say, it was made by certain evil-minded men as a mark of madness; because not comprehending and not wishing to comprehend his holy doctrine, and seeing him fervently preaching before princes and people, who held that doctrine in detesta-

tion, they thought he acted as one out of his senses. Others maintain that the tonsure is worn as a mark of dignity, as a sign that those who wear it are more worthy than those who do not; and they call it *corona*, because, all the rest of the head being shaven, a single circle of hair should be left, which in form of a crown surrounds the whole head."

58. In like manner Chaucer, *Persones Tale*, pp. 227, 337, reproves ill-keeping and ill-giving.

"Avarice, after the description of Seint Augustine, is a likerousnesse in herte to have erthly thinges. Som other folk sayn, that avarice is for to purchase many erthly thinges, and nothing to yeve to hem that han nede. And understond wel, that avarice standeth not only in land ne catel, but som time in science and in glorie, and in every maner outrageous thing is avarice. . . .

"But for as moche as som folk ben unmesurable, men oughten for to avoid and eschue fool-largesse, the whiche men clepen waste. Certes, he that is fool-large, he yeveth not his catel, but he leseth his catel. Sothly, what thing that he yeveth for vaine-glory, as to minstrals, and to folk that bere his renome in the world, he hath do sinne thereof, and non almesse: certes, he leseth foule his good, that ne seketh with the yefte of his good nothing but sinne. He is like to an hors that seketh rather to drink drovy or troubled water, than for to drink water of the clere well. And for as moche as they yeven ther as they shuld nat yeven, to hem apperteineth thilke malison, that Crist shal yeve at the day of dome to hem that shul be dampned."

68. The Wheel of Fortune was one of the favorite subjects of art and song in the Middle Ages. On a large square of white marble set in the pavement of the nave of the Cathedral at Siena is the representation of a revolving wheel. Three boys are climbing and clinging at the sides and below; above is a dignified figure with a stern countenance, holding the sceptre and ball. At the four corners are inscriptions from Seneca, Euripides, Aristotle, and Epictetus. The same symbol may be seen also in the wheel-of-fortune windows of many churches; as, for example, that of San Zeno at Verona. See Knight, *Ecclesiastical Architecture*, II. plates v., vi.

In the following poem Guido Cavalcanti treats this subject in very much the same way that Dante does; and it is curious to observe how at particular times certain ideas seem to float in the air, and to become the property of every one who chooses to make use of them. From the similarity between this poem and the lines of Dante, one might infer that the two friends had discussed the matter in conversation, and afterwards that each had written out their common thought.

Cavalcanti's *Song of Fortune,* as translated by Rossetti, *Early Italian Poets,* p. 366, runs as follows: —

Lo! I am she who makes the wheel to turn;
Lo! I am she who gives and takes away;
Blamed idly, day by day,
In all mine acts by you, ye humankind.
For whoso smites his visage and doth mourn,
What time he renders back my gifts to me,
Learns then that I decree
No state which mine own arrows may not find.
Who clomb must fall:—this bear ye well in mind,
Nor say, because he fell, I did him wrong.
Yet mine is a vain song:
For truly ye may find out wisdom when
King Arthur's resting-place is found of men.

Ye make great marvel and astonishment
What time ye see the sluggard lifted up
And the just man to drop,
And ye complain on God and on my sway.
O humankind, ye sin in your complaint:
For He, that Lord who made the world to live,
Lets me not take or give
By mine own act, but as he wills I may.
Yet is the mind of man so castaway,
That it discerns not the supreme behest.
Alas! ye wretchedest,
And chide ye at God also? Shall not He
Judge between good and evil righteously?

Ah! had ye knowledge how God evermore,
With agonies of soul and grievous heats,
As on an anvil beats
On them that in this earth hold high estate,—
Ye would choose little rather than much store,
And solitude than spacious palaces;
Such is the sore disease
Of anguish that on all their days doth wait.
Behold if they be not unfortunate,
When oft the father dares not trust the son!
O wealth, with thee is won
A worm to gnaw forever on his soul
Whose abject life is laid in thy control!

If also ye take note what piteous death
They ofttimes make, whose hoards were manifold,
Who cities had and gold
And multitudes of men beneath their hand;
Then he among you that most angereth
Shall bless me saying, "Lo! I worship thee
That I was not as he
Whose death is thus accurst throughout the land.
But now your living souls are held in band
Of avarice, shutting you from the true light
Which shows how sad and slight
Are this world's treasured riches and array
That still change hands a hundred times a day.

For me,—could envy enter in my sphere,
Which of all human taint is clean and quit,—
I well might harbor it
When I behold the peasant at his toil.
Guiding his team, untroubled, free from fear,
He leaves his perfect furrow as he goes,
And gives his field repose
From thorns and tares and weeds that vex the soil:
Thereto he labors, and without turmoil
Entrusts his work to God, content if so
Such guerdon from it grow
That in that year his family shall live:
Nor care nor thought to other things will give.

But now ye may no more have speech of me,
For this mine office craves continual use:
Ye therefore deeply muse
Upon those things which ye have heard the while:
Yea, and even yet remember heedfully
How this my wheel a motion hath so fleet,
That in an eyelid's beat
Him whom it raised it maketh low and vile.
None was, nor is, nor shall be of such guile,
Who could, or can, or shall, I say, at length
Prevail against my strength.
But still those men that are my questioners
In bitter torment own their hearts perverse.

Song, that wast made to carry high intent
Dissembled in the garb of humbleness,—

With fair and open face
To Master Thomas let thy course be bent.
Say that a great thing scarcely may be pent
In little room: yet always pray that he
Commend us, thee and me,
To them that are more apt in lofty speech:
For truly one must learn ere he can teach.

74. This old Rabbinical tradition of the "Regents of the Planets" has been painted by Raphael, in the Capella Chigiana of the Church of Santa Maria del Popolo in Rome. See Mrs. Jameson, *Sacred and Legendary Art,* I. 45. She says: "As a perfect example of grand and poetical feeling I may cite the angels as 'Regents of the Planets' in the Capella Chigiana. The Cupola represents in a circle the creation of the solar system, according to the theological (or rather astrological) notions which then prevailed,—a hundred years before 'the starry Galileo and his woes.' In the centre is the Creator; around, in eight compartments, we have, first, the angel of the celestial sphere, who seems to be listening to the divine mandate, 'Let there be lights in the firmament of heaven'; then follow, in their order, the Sun, the Moon, Mercury, Venus, Mars, Jupiter, and Saturn. The name of each planet is expressed by its mythological representative; the Sun by Apollo, the Moon by Diana; and over each presides a grand, colossal winged spirit, seated or reclining on a portion of the zodiac as on a throne."

The old tradition may be found in Stehelin, *Rabbinical Literature,* I. 157. See *Cabala,* end of Vol. III.

98. Past midnight.

103. *Perse,* purple-black. See Canto V., Note 89.

115. "Is not this a cursed vice?" says Chaucer in *The Persones Tale,* p. 202, speaking of wrath. "Yes, certes. Alas! it benimmeth fro man his witte and his reson, and all his debonaire lif spirituel, that shulde keepe his soule. Certes it benimmeth also Goddes due lordship (and that is mannes soule) and the love of his neighbours; it reveth him the quiet of his herte, and subverteth his soule."

And farther on he continues: "After the sinne of wrath, now wolle I speke of the sinne of accidie, or slouth; for envie blindeth the herte of a man, and ire troubleth a man, and accidie maketh him hevy, thoughtful, and wrawe. Envie and ire maken bitternesse in herte, which bitternesse is mother of accidie, and benimmeth him the love of alle goodnesse; than is accidie the anguish of a trouble herte."

And Burton, *Anatomy of Melancholy,* I. 3. i. 3, speaking of that kind of melancholy which proceeds from "humors adust," says: "For example, if it proceeds from flegm (which is seldom, and not so frequent as the rest) it stirs up dull symptomes, and a kind of stupidity, or impassionate hurt; they are sleepy, saith Savonarola, dull, slow, cold, blockish, ass-like, *asininam melancholiam* Melancthon calls it, they are much given to weeping, and delight in waters, ponds, pools, rivers, fishing, fowling, &c. They are pale of color, slothful, apt to sleep, heavy, much troubled with the head-ache, continual meditation and muttering to themselves, they dream of waters, that they are in danger of drowning, and fear such things."

See also *Purg.* XVII. 85.

CANTO VIII

1. Boccaccio and some other commentators think the words "I say, continuing," are a confirmation of the theory that the first seven cantos of the *Inferno* were written before Dante's banishment from Florence. Others maintain that the words suggest only the continuation of the subject of the last canto in this.

4. These two signal fires announce the arrival of two persons to be ferried over the wash, and the other in the distance is on the watch-tower of the City of Dis, answering these.

19. Phlegyas was the father of Ixion and Coronis. He was king of the Lapithæ, and burned the temple of Apollo at Delphi to avenge the wrong done by the god to Coronis. His punishment in the infernal regions was to stand beneath a huge impending rock, always about to fall upon him. Virgil, *Æneid,* VI., says of him: "Phlegyas, most wretched, is a monitor to all and with loud voice proclaims through the shades, 'Being warned, learn righteousness, and not to contemn the gods.'"

27. Virgil, *Æneid,* VI.: "The boat of sewn hide groaned under the weight, and, being leaky, took in much water from the lake."

49. Mr. Wright here quotes Spenser, *Ruins of Time:* —

> How many great ones may remembered be,
> Who in their days most famously did flourish,
> Of whom no word we have, nor sign now see,
> But as things wiped out with a sponge do perish.

51. Chaucer's "sclandre of his diffame."

61. Of Philippo Argenti little is known, and nothing to his credit. Dante seems to have an especial personal hatred of him, as if in memory of some disagreeable passage between them in the streets of Florence. Boccaccio says of him in his *Comento:* "This Philippo Argenti, as Coppo di

Borghese Domenichi de' Cavicciuli was wont to say, was a very rich gentleman, so rich that he had the horse he used to ride shod with silver, and from this he had his surname; he was in person large, swarthy, muscular, of marvellous strength, and at the slightest provocation the most irascible of men; nor are any more known of his qualities than these two, each in itself very blameworthy." He was of the Adimari family, and of the Neri faction; while Dante was of the Bianchi party, and in banishment. Perhaps this fact may explain the bitterness of his invective.*

This is the same Philippo Argenti who figures in Boccaccio's tale. See *Inf.* VI., note 52. The *Ottimo Comento* says of him: "He was a man of great pomp, and great ostentation, and much expenditure, and little virtue and worth; and therefore the author says, 'Goodness is none that decks his memory.'"

And this is all that is known of the *"Fiorentino spirito bizzaro,"* forgotten by history, and immortalized in song. "What a barbarous strength and confusion of ideas," exclaims Leigh Hunt, *Italian Poets,* p. 60, "is there in this whole passage about him! Arrogance punished by arrogance, a Christian mother blessed for the unchristian disdainfulness of her son, revenge boasted of and enjoyed, passion arguing in a circle."

70. The word "mosques" paints at once to the imagination the City of Unbelief.

78. Virgil, *Æneid,* VI., Davidson's Translation: —

"Æneas on a sudden looks back, and under a rock on the left sees vast prisons inclosed with a triple wall, which Tartarean Phlegethon's rapid flood environs with torrents of flame, and whirls roaring rocks along. Fronting is a huge gate, with columns of solid adamant, that no strength of men, nor the gods themselves, can with steel demolish. An iron tower rises aloft; and there wakeful Tisiphone, with her bloody robe tucked up around her, sits to watch the vestibule both night and day."

124. This arrogance of theirs; *tracotanza, oltracotanza;* Brantome's *outrecuidance;* and Spenser's *surquedrie.*

125. The gate of the Inferno.

130. The coming of the Angel, whose approach is described in the next canto, beginning at line 64.

CANTO IX

1. The flush of anger passes from Virgil's cheek on seeing the pallor of Dante's, and he tries to encourage him with assurances of success; but betrays his own apprehensions in the broken phrase, "If not," which he immediately covers with words of cheer.

8. Such, or so great a one, is Beatrice, the "fair and saintly Lady" of Canto II. 53.

9. The Angel who will open the gates of the City of Dis.

16. Dante seems to think that he has already reached the bottom of the infernal conch, with its many convolutions.

41. Cerastes. Nicander in Elton's *Classic Poets.* I. 399.

52. Gower, *Confessio Amantis,* I.: —

> Cast nought thin eye upon Meduse
> That thou be turned into stone.

Hawthorne has beautifully told the story of "The Gorgon's Head," as well as many more of the classic fables, in his *Wonder-Book.*

54. The attempt which Theseus and Pirithous made to rescue Proserpine from the infernal regions.

62. The hidden doctrine seems to be, that Negation or Unbelief is the Gorgon's head which changes the heart to stone; after which there is "no more returning upward." The Furies display it from the walls of the City of Heretics.

112. At Arles lie buried, according to old tradition, the Peers of Charlemagne and their ten thousand men at arms. Archbishop Turpin, in his famous *History of Charles the Great,* XXX., Rodd's Translation, I. 52, says: —

"After this the King and his army proceeded by the way of Gascony and Thoulouse, and came to Arles, where we found the army of Burgundy, which had left us in the hostile valley, bringing their dead by the way of Morbihan and Thoulouse, to bury them in the plain of Arles. Here we performed the rites of Estolfo, Count of Champagne; of Solomon; Sampson, Duke of Burgundy; Arnold of Berlanda; Alberic of Burgundy; Gumard, Esturinite, Hato, Juonius, Berard, Berengaire, and Naaman, Duke of Bourbon, and of ten thousand of their soldiers."

Boccaccio comments upon these tombs as follows: —

"At Arles, somewhat out of the city, are many tombs of stone, made of old for sepulchres, and some are large, and some are small, and some are better sculptured, and some not so well, peradventure according to the means of those who had them made; and upon some of them appear inscriptions after the ancient custom, I suppose in indication of those who are buried within. The inhabitants of the country repeat a tradition of them, affirming that in that place there was once a great battle between William of Orange, or some other Christian prince, with his forces on one side, and infidel barbarians from Africa [on the other]; and that many

Christians were slain in it; and that on the following night, by divine miracle, those tombs were brought there for the burial of the Christians, and so on the following morning all the dead Christians were buried in them."

113. Pola is a city in Istria. "Near Pola," says Benvenuto da Imola, "are seen many tombs, about seven hundred, and of various forms."

Quarnaro is a gulf of the northern extremity of the Adriatic.

Canto X

1. In this Canto is described the punishment of Heretics. Brunetto Latini, *Tesoretto*, XIII.: —

> Or va mastro Brunetto
> Per lo cammino stretto.

14. Sir Thomas Browne, *Urn Burial*, Chap. IV., says: "They may sit in the orchestra and noblest seats of heaven who have held up shaking hands in the fire, and humanly contended for glory. Meanwhile Epicurus lies deep in Dante's hell, wherein we meet with tombs enclosing souls, which denied their immortalities. But whether the virtuous heathen, who lived better than he spake, or, erring in the principles of himself, yet lived above philosophers of more specious maxims, lie so deep as he is placed, at least so low as not to rise against Christians, who, believing or knowing that truth, have lastingly denied it in their practice and conversation,—were a query too sad to insist on."

Also Burton, *Anatomy of Melancholy*, Part II. Sec. 2. Mem. 6. Subs. 1, thus vindicates the memory of Epicurus: "A quiet mind is that *voluptas*, or *summum bonum* of Epicurus; *non dolere, curis vacare, animo tranquillo esse*, not to grieve, but to want cares, and have a quiet soul, is the only pleasure of the world, as Seneca truly recites his opinion, not that of eating and drinking, which injurious Aristotle maliciously puts upon him, and for which he is still mistaken, *mala audit et vapulat*, slandered without a cause, and lashed by all posterity."

32. Farinata degli Uberti was the most valiant and renowned leader of the Ghibellines in Florence. Boccaccio, *Comento*, says: "He was of the opinion of Epicurus, that the soul dies with the body, and consequently maintained that human happiness consisted in temporal pleasures; but he did not follow these in the way that Epicurus did, that is by making long fasts to have afterwards pleasure in eating dry bread; but was fond of good and delicate viands, and ate them without waiting to be hungry; and for this sin he is damned as a Heretic in this place."

Farinata led the Ghibellines at the famous battle of Monte Aperto in 1260, where the Guelfs were routed, and driven out of Florence. He died in 1264.

46. The ancestors of Dante, and Dante himself, were Guelfs. He did not become a Ghibelline till after his banishment. Boccaccio in his *Life of Dante* makes the following remarks upon his party spirit. I take the passage as given in Mrs. Bunbury's translation of Balbo's *Life and Times of Dante*, II. 227.

"He was," says Boccaccio, "a most excellent man, and most resolute in adversity. It was only on one subject that he showed himself, I do not know whether I ought to call it impatient, or spirited,—it was regarding anything relating to Party; since in his exile he was more violent in this respect than suited his circumstances, and more than he was willing that others should believe. And in order that it may be seen for what party he was thus violent and pertinacious, it appears to me I must go further back in my story. I believe that it was the just anger of God that permitted, it is a long time ago, almost all Tuscany and Lombardy to be divided into two parties; I do not know how they acquired those names, but one party was called Guelf and the other party Ghibelline. And these two names were so revered, and had such an effect on the folly of many minds, that, for the sake of defending the side any one had chosen for his own against the opposite party, it was not considered hard to lose property, and even life, if it were necessary. And under these names the Italian cities many times suffered serious grievances and changes; and among the rest our city, which was sometimes at the head of one party, and sometimes of the other, according to the citizens in power; so much so that Dante's ancestors, being Guelfs, were twice expelled by the Ghibellines from their home, and he likewise under the title of Guelf held the reins of the Florentine Republic, from which he was expelled, as we have shown, not by the Ghibellines, but by the Guelfs; and seeing that he could not return, he so much altered his mind that there never was a fiercer Ghibelline, or a bitterer enemy to the Guelfs, than he was. And that which I feel most ashamed at for the sake of his memory is, that it was a well-known thing in Romagna, that if any boy or girl, talking to him on party matters, condemned the Ghibelline side, he would become frantic, so that if they did not be silent he would have been induced to throw stones at them; and with this violence of party feeling he lived until his death. I am certainly ashamed to tarnish with any fault the fame of such a man; but the order of my subject in some degree demands it, because if I were silent in those things in which he was to blame, I should not be believed in those things I have already related in his praise. Therefore I excuse myself to himself, who perhaps looks down from heaven with a disdainful eye on me writing."

51. The following account of the Guelfs and Ghibellines is from the *Pecorone* of Giovanni Fiorentino, a writer of the fourteenth century. It forms the first Novella of the Eighth Day, and will be found in Roscoe's *Italian Novelists*, I. 322.

"There formerly resided in Germany two wealthy and well-born individuals, whose names were Guelfo and Ghibellino, very near neighbors, and greatly attached to each other. But returning together one day from the chase, there unfortunately arose some difference of opinion as to the merits of one of their hounds, which was maintained on both sides so very warmly, that, from being almost inseparable friends and companions, they became each other's deadliest enemies. This unlucky division between them still increasing, they on either side collected parties of their followers, in order more effectually to annoy each other. Soon extending its malignant influence among the neighboring lords and barons of Germany, who divided, according to their motives, either with the Guelf or the Ghibelline, it not only produced many serious affrays, but several persons fell victims to its rage. Ghibellino, finding himself hard pressed by his enemy, and unable longer to keep the field against him, resolved to apply for assistance to Frederick the First, the reigning Emperor. Upon this, Guelfo, perceiving that his adversary sought the alliance of this monarch, applied on his side to Pope Honorius II., who being at variance with the former, and hearing how the affair stood, immediately joined the cause of the Guelfs, the Emperor having already embraced that of the Ghibellines. It is thus that the apostolic see became connected with the former, and the empire with the latter faction; and it was thus that a vile hound became the origin of a deadly hatred between the two noble families. Now it happened that in the year of our dear Lord and Redeemer 1215, the same pestiferous spirit spread itself into parts of Italy, in the following manner. Messer Guido Orlando being at that time chief magistrate of Florence, there likewise resided in that city a noble and valiant cavalier of the family of Buondelmonti, one of the most distinguished houses in the state. Our young Buondelmonte having already plighted his troth to a lady of the Amidei family, the lovers were considered as betrothed, with all the solemnity usually observed on such occasions. But this unfortunate young man, chancing one day to pass by the house of the Donati, was stopped and accosted by a lady of the name of Lapaccia, who moved to him from her door as he went along, saying: 'I am surprised that a gentleman of your appearance, Signor, should think of taking for his wife a woman scarcely worthy of handing him his boots. There is a child of my own, whom, to speak sincerely, I have long intended for you, and whom I wish you would just venture to see.' And on this she called out for her daughter, whose name was Ciulla, one of the prettiest and most enchanting girls in all Florence. Introducing her to Messer Buondelmonte, she whispered, 'This is she whom I had reserved for you'; and the young Florentine, suddenly becoming enamored of her, thus replied to her mother, 'I am quite ready, Madonna, to meet your wishes'; and before stirring from the spot he placed a ring upon her finger, and, wedding her, received her there as his wife.

"The Amidei, hearing that young Buondelmonte had thus espoused another, immediately met together, and took counsel with other friends and relations how they might best avenge themselves for such an insult offered to their house. There were present among the rest Lambertuccio Amidei, Schiatta Ruberti, and Mosca Lamberti, one of whom proposed to give him a box on the ear, another to strike him in the face; yet they were none of them able to agree about it among themselves. On observing this, Mosca hastily rose, in a great passion, saying, 'Cosa fatta capo ha,' wishing it to be understood that a dead man will never strike again. It was therefore decided that he should be put to death, a sentence which they proceeded to execute in the following manner.

"M. Buondelmonte returning one Easter morning from a visit to the Casa Bardi, beyond the Arno, mounted upon a snow-white steed, and dressed in a mantle of the same color, had just reached the foot of the Ponte Vecchio, or old bridge, where formerly stood a statue of Mars, whom the Florentines in their Pagan state were accustomed to worship, when the whole party issued out upon him, and, dragging him in the scuffle from his horse, in spite of the gallant resistance he made, despatched him with a thousand wounds. The tidings of this affair seemed to throw all Florence into confusion; the chief personages and noblest families in the place everywhere meeting, and dividing themselves into parties in consequence; the one party embracing the cause of the Buondelmonti, who placed themselves at the head of the Guelfs; and the other taking part with the Amidei, who supported the Ghibellines.

"In the same fatal manner, nearly all the seigniories and cities of Italy were involved in the original quarrel between these two German families: the Guelfs still supporting the interest of the Holy Church, and the Ghibellines those of the Emperor. And thus I have made you acquainted with the origin of the Germanic faction, between two noble houses, for the sake of a vile cur, and have shown how it afterwards disturbed the peace of Italy for the sake of a beautiful woman."

For an account of the Bianchi and Neri factions by the same author, see Canto VI., Note 65.

53. Cavalcante de' Cavalcanti, father of Dante's friend, Guido Cavalcanti. He was of the Guelf party; so that here are Guelf and Ghibelline buried in the same tomb.

60. This question recalls the scene in the Odyssey, where the shade of Agamemnon appears to Ulysses and asks for Orestes. Book XI. in Chapman's translation, line 603: —

> Doth my son yet survive
> In Orchomen or Pylos? Or doth live
> In Sparta with his uncle? Yet I see
> Divine Orestes is not here with me.

63. Guido Cavalcanti, whom Benvenuto da Imola calls "the other eye of Florence,"—*alter oculus Florentiæ tempore Dantis.* It is to this Guido that Dante addresses the sonnet, which is like the breath of Spring, beginning: —

> Guido, I wish that Lapo, thou, and I
> Could be by spells conveyed, as it were now,
> Upon a barque, with all the winds that blow,
> Across all seas at our good will to hie.

He was a poet of decided mark, as may be seen by his *Song of Fortune*, quoted in Note 68, Canto VII., and the sonnet to Dante, Note 136, *Purg.* XXX. But he seems not to have shared Dante's admiration for Virgil, and to have been more given to the study of philosophy than of poetry. Like Lucentio in *The Taming of the Shrew* he is

> So devote to Aristotle's ethics
> As Ovid be an outcast quite abjured.

Boccaccio, *Decamerone,* VI. 9, praises him for his learning and other good qualities; "for over and beside his being one of the best Logitians, as those times not yielded a better," so runs the old translation, "he was also a most absolute Natural Philosopher, a very friendly Gentleman, singularly well spoken, and whatsoever else was commendable in any man was no way wanting in him." In the same Novella he tells this anecdote of him: —

"It chanced upon a day that Signior Guido, departing from the Church of Saint Michael d' Horta, and passing along by the Adamari, so far as to Saint John's Church, which evermore was his customary walk: many goodly Marble Tombs were then about the said Church, as nowadays are at Saint Reparata, and divers more beside. He entring among the Columns of Porphiry, and the other Sepulchers being there, because the door of the Church was shut: Signior Betto and his Company came riding from Saint Reparata, and espying Signior Guido among the Graves and Tombs, said, 'Come, let us go make some jests to anger him.' So putting the Spurs to their Horses they rode apace towards him; and being upon him before hee perceived them, one of them said, 'Guido, thou refusest to be one of our society, and seekest for that which never was: when thou hast found it, tell us, what wilt thou do with it?'

"Guido seeing himself round engirt with them, suddenly thus replyed: 'Gentlemen, you may use me in your own House as you please.' And setting his hand upon one of the Tombs (which was somewhat great) he took his rising, and leapt quite over it on the further side, as being of an agile and sprightly body, and being thus freed from them, he went away to his own lodging.

"They stood all like men amazed, strangely looking one upon another, and began afterward to murmur among themselves: That Guido was a man without any understanding, and the answer which he had made unto them was to no purpose, neither savoured of any discretion, but meerly came from an empty Brain, because they had no more to do in the place where now they were, than any of the other Citizens, and Signior Guido (himself) as little as any of them; whereto Signior Betto thus replyed: 'Alas, Gentlemen, it is you your selves that are void of understanding: for, if you had but observed the answer which he made unto us: he did honestly, and (in very few words) not only notably express his own wisdom, but also deservedly reprehend us. Because, if we observe things as we ought to do, Graves and Tombs are the Houses of the dead, ordained and prepared to be the latest dwellings. He told us moreover that although we have here (in this life) our habitations and abidings, yet these (or the like) must at last be our Houses. To let us know, and all other foolish, indiscreet, and unlearned men, that we are worse than dead men, in comparison of him, and other men equal to him in skill and learning. And therefore, while we are here among the Graves and Monuments, it may be well said, that we are not far from our own Houses, or how soon we shall be possessors of them, in regard of the frailty attending on us.' "

Napier, *Florentine History,* I. 368, speaks of Guido as "a bold, melancholy man, who loved solitude and literature; but generous, brave, and courteous, a poet and philosopher, and one that seems to have had the respect and admiration of his age." He then adds this singular picture of the times: —

"Corso Donati, by whom he was feared and hated, would have had him murdered while on a pilgrimage to Saint James of Galicia; on his return this became known and gained him many supporters amongst the Cerchi and other youth of Florence; he took no regular measures of vengeance, but, accidentally meeting Corso in the street, rode violently towards him, casting his javelin at the same time; it missed by the tripping of his horse and he escaped with a slight wound from one of Donati's attendants."

Sacchetti, Nov. 68, tells a pleasant story of Guido's having his cloak nailed to the bench by a roguish boy, while he was playing chess in one of the streets of Florence, which is also a curious picture of Italian life.

75. Farinata pays no attention to this outburst of paternal tenderness on the part of his Guelfic kinsman, but waits, in stern indifference, till it is ended, and then calmly resumes his discourse.

80. The moon, called in the heavens Diana, on earth Luna, and in the infernal regions Proserpina.

86. In the great battle of Monte Aperto. The river Arbia is a few miles south of Siena. The traveller crosses it on his way to Rome. In this battle the banished Ghibellines of Florence, joining the Sienese, gained a victory over the Guelfs, and retook the city of Florence. Before the battle Buonaguida, Syndic of Siena, presented the keys of the city to the Virgin Mary in the Cathedral, and made a gift to her of the city and the neighboring country. After the battle the standard of the vanquished Florentines, together with their battle-bell, the Martinella, was tied to the tail of a jackass and dragged in the dirt. See Ampère, *Voyage Dantesque*, 254.

94. After the battle of Monte Aperto a diet of the Ghibellines was held at Empoli, in which the deputies from Siena and Pisa, prompted no doubt by provincial hatred, urged the demolition of Florence. Farinata vehemently opposed the project in a speech, thus given in Napier, *Florentine History*, I. 257: —

" 'It would have been better,' he exclaimed, 'to have died on the Arbia, than survive only to hear such a proposition as that which they were then discussing. There is no happiness in victory itself, *that* must ever be sought for amongst the companions who helped us to gain the day, and the injury we receive from an enemy inflicts a far more trifling wound than the wrong that comes from the hand of a friend. If I now complain, it is not that I fear the destruction of my native city, for as long as I have life to wield a sword Florence shall never be destroyed; but I cannot suppress my indignation at the discourses I have just been listening to: we are here assembled to discuss the wisest means of maintaining our influence in Florence, not to debate on its destruction, and my country would indeed be unfortunate, and I and my companions miserable, mean-spirited creatures, if it were true that the fate of our city depended on the fiat of the present assembly. I did hope that all former hatred would have been banished from such a meeting, and that our mutual destruction would not have been treacherously aimed at from under the false colors of general safety; I did hope that all here were convinced that counsel dictated by jealousy could never be advantageous to the general good! But to what does your hatred attach itself? To the ground on which the city stands? To its houses and insensible walls? To the fugitives who have abandoned it? Or to ourselves that now possess it? Who is he that thus advises? Who is the bold bad man that dare thus give voice to the malice he hath engendered in his soul? Is it meet then that all *your* cities should exist unharmed, and ours alone be devoted to destruction? That *you* should return in triumph to your hearths, and we with whom you have conquered should have nothing in exchange but exile and the ruin of our country? Is there one of you who can believe that I could even hear such things with patience? Are you indeed ignorant that if I have carried arms, if I have persecuted my foes, I still have never ceased to love my country, and that I never will allow what even our enemies have respected to be violated by your hands, so that posterity may call *them* the saviours, *us* the destroyers of our country? Here then I declare, that, although I stand alone amongst the Florentines, I will never permit my native city to be destroyed, and if it be necessary for her sake to die a thousand deaths, I am ready to meet them all in her defence.'

"Farinata then rose, and with angry gestures quitted the assembly; but left such an impression on the mind of his audience that the project was instantly dropped, and the only question for the moment was how to regain a chief of such talent and influence."

119. Frederick II., son of the Emperor Henry VI., surnamed the Severe, and grandson of Barbarossa. He reigned from 1220 to 1250, not only as Emperor of Germany, but also as King of Naples and Sicily, where for the most part he held his court, one of the most brilliant of the Middle Ages. Villani, *Cronica,* V. 1, thus sketches his character: "This Frederick reigned thirty years as Emperor, and was a man of great mark and great worth, learned in letters and of natural ability, universal in all things; he knew the Latin language, the Italian, the German, French, Greek, and Arabic; was copiously endowed with all virtues, liberal and courteous in giving, valiant and skilled in arms, and was much feared. And he was dissolute and voluptuous in many ways, and had many concubines and mamelukes,

after the Saracenic fashion; he was addicted to all sensual delights, and led an Epicurean life, taking no account of any other; and this was one principal reason why he was an enemy to the clergy and the Holy Church."

Milman, *Lat. Christ.*, B. X., Chap. iii., says of him: "Frederick's predilection for his native kingdom, for the bright cities reflected in the blue Mediterranean, over the dark barbaric towns of Germany, of itself characterizes the man. The summer skies, the more polished manners, the more elegant luxuries, the knowledge, the arts, the poetry, the gayety, the beauty, the romance of the South, were throughout his life more congenial to his mind than the heavier and more chilly climate, the feudal barbarism, the ruder pomp, the coarser habits of his German liegemen. . . . And no doubt that delicious climate and lovely land, so highly appreciated by the gay sovereign, was not without influence on the state, and even the manners of his court, to which other circumstances contributed to give a peculiar and romantic character. It resembled probably (though its full splendor was of a later period) Grenada in its glory, more than any other in Europe, though more rich and picturesque from the variety of races, of manners, usages, even dresses, which prevailed within it."

Gibbon also, *Decline and Fall*, Chap. lix., gives this graphic picture: —

"Frederick the Second, the grandson of Barbarossa, was successively the pupil, the enemy, and the victim of the Church. At the age of twenty-one years, and in obedience to his guardian Innocent the Third, he assumed the cross; the same promise was repeated at his royal and imperial coronations; and his marriage with the heiress of Jerusalem forever bound him to defend the kingdom of his son Conrad. But as Frederick advanced in age and authority, he repented of the rash engagements of his youth: his liberal sense and knowledge taught him to despise the phantoms of superstition and the crowns of Asia: he no longer entertained the same reverence for the successors of Innocent; and his ambition was occupied by the restoration of the Italian monarchy, from Sicily to the Alps. But the success of this project would have reduced the Popes to their primitive simplicity; and, after the delays and excuses of twelve years, they urged the Emperor, with entreaties and threats, to fix the time and place of his departure for Palestine. In the harbors of Sicily and Apulia he prepared a fleet of one hundred galleys, and of one hundred vessels, that were framed to transport and land two thousand five hundred knights, with horses and attendants; his vassals of Naples and Germany formed a powerful army; and the number of English crusaders was magnified to sixty thousand by the report of fame. But the inevitable, or affected, slowness of these mighty preparations consumed the strength and provisions of the more indigent pilgrims; the multitude was thinned by sickness and desertion, and the sultry summer of Calabria anticipated the mischiefs of a Syrian campaign. At length the Emperor hoisted sail at Brundusium with a fleet and army of forty thousand men; but he kept the sea no more than three days; and his hasty retreat, which was ascribed by his friends to a grievous indisposition, was accused by his enemies as a voluntary and obstinate disobedience. For suspending his vow was Frederick excommunicated by Gregory the Ninth; for presuming, the next year, to accomplish his vow, he was again excommunicated by the same Pope. While he served under the banner of the cross, a crusade was preached against him in Italy; and after his return he was compelled to ask pardon for the injuries which he had suffered. The clergy and military orders of Palestine were previously instructed to renounce his communion and dispute his commands; and in his own kingdom the Emperor was forced to consent that the orders of the camp should be issued in the name of God and of the Christian republic. Frederick entered Jerusalem in triumph; and with his own hands (for no priest would perform the office) he took the crown from the altar of the holy sepulchre."

Matthew Paris, A.D. 1239, gives a long letter of Pope Gregory IX., in which he calls the Emperor some very hard names; "a beast, full of the words of blasphemy," "a wolf in sheep's clothing," "a son of lies," "a staff of the impious," and "hammer of the earth"; and finally accuses him of being the author of a work, *De Tribus Impostoribus,* which haunted the Middle Ages like a ghost. "There is one thing," he says in conclusion, "at which, although we ought to mourn for a lost man, you ought to rejoice greatly, and for which you ought to return thanks to God, namely, that this man, who delights in being called a forerunner of Antichrist, by God's will, no longer endures to be veiled in darkness; not expecting that his trial and disgrace are near, he with his own hands undermines the wall of his abominations, and, by the said letters of his, brings his works of darkness to the light, boldly setting forth in them, that he could not be excommunicated by us, although the Vicar of Christ; thus affirming that the Church had not the power of binding and loosing, which was given by our Lord to St. Peter and his successors. . . . But as it may not be easily believed by some people that he has ensnared himself by the words of his own mouth, proofs are ready, to the triumph of the faith; for this king of pestilence openly asserts that the whole world was deceived by three, namely, Christ Jesus, Moses, and Mahomet; that, two of them having died in glory, the said Jesus was suspended on the cross; and he, moreover, presumes plainly to affirm (or rather to lie), that all are foolish who believe that God, who created nature, and could do all things, was born of the Virgin."

120. This is Cardinal Ottaviano degli Ubaldini, who is accused of saying, "If there be any soul, I have lost mine for the Ghibellines." Dante takes him at his word.

CANTO XI

8. Some critics and commentators accuse Dante of confounding Pope Anastasius with the Emperor of that name. It is however highly probable that Dante knew best whom he meant. Both were accused of heresy, though the heresy of the Pope seems to have been of a mild type. A few years previous to his time, namely, in the year 484, Pope Felix III. and Acacius, Bishop of Constantinople, mutually excommunicated each other. When Anastasius II. became Pope in 496, "he dared," says Milman, *Hist. Lat. Christ.,* I. 349, "to doubt the damnation of a bishop excommunicated by the See of Rome: 'Felix and Acacius are now both before a higher tribunal; leave them to that unerring judgment.' He would have the name of Acacius passed over in silence, quietly dropped, rather than publicly expunged from the diptychs. This degenerate successor of St. Peter is not admitted to the rank of a saint. The Pontifical book (its authority on this point is indignantly repudiated) accuses Anastasius of having communicated with a deacon of Thessalonica, who had kept up communion with Acacius; and of having entertained secret designs of restoring the name of Acacius in the services of the Church."

9. Photinus is the Deacon of Thessalonica alluded to in the preceding note. His heresy was, that the Holy Ghost did not proceed from the Father, and that the Father was greater than the Son. The writers who endeavor to rescue the Pope at the expense of the Emperor say that Photinus died before the days of Pope Anastasius.

50. Cahors is the cathedral town of the Department of the Lot, in the south of France, and the birthplace of the poet Clément Marot and of the romance-writer Calprenède. In the Middle Ages it seems to have been a nest of usurers. Matthew Paris, in his *Historia Major,* under date of 1235, has a chapter entitled, *Of the Usury of the Caursines,* which in the translation of Rev. J. A. Giles runs as follows: —

"In these days prevailed the horrible nuisance of the Caursines to such a degree that there was hardly any one in all England, especially among the bishops, who was not caught in their net. Even the king himself was held indebted to them in an uncalculable sum of money. For they circumvented the needy in their necessities, cloaking their usury under the show of trade, and pretending not to know that whatever is added to the principal is usury, under whatever name it may be called. For it is manifest that their loans lie not in the path of charity, inasmuch as they do not hold out a helping hand to the poor to relieve them, but to deceive them; not to aid others in their starvation, but to gratify their own covetousness; seeing that the motive stamps our every deed."

70. *Those within the fat lagoon,* the Irascible, Canto VII., VIII.

71. *Whom the wind drives,* the Wanton, Canto V., *and whom the rain doth beat,* the Gluttonous, Canto VI.

72. *And who encounter with such bitter tongues,* the Prodigal and Avaricious, Canto VII.

80. The *Ethics* of Aristotle, VII. i. "After these things, making another beginning, it must be observed by us that there are three species of things which are to be avoided in manners, viz. Malice, Incontinence, and Bestiality."

99. Young, *Night Thoughts,* ix. 1269.

The course of Nature is the Art of God.

101. The *Physics* of Aristotle, Book II.

107. *Genesis* i. 28: "And God said unto them, Be fruitful, and multiply, and replenish the earth, and subdue it."

109. Gabriele Rossetti, in the *Comento Analitico* of his edition of the *Divina Commedia,* quotes here the lines of Florian: —

Nous ne recevons l'existence
Qu'afin de travailler pour nous, ou pour autrui:
De ce devoir sacré quiconque se dispense
Est puni par la Providence,
Par le besoin, ou par l'ennui.

110. The constellation Pisces precedes Aries, in which the sun now is. This indicates the time to be a little before sunrise. It is Saturday morning.

114. The Wain is the constellation Charles's Wain, or, Boötes; and Caurus is the Northwest, indicated by the Latin name of the northwest wind.

CANTO XII

1. With this Canto begins the Seventh Circle of the Inferno, in which the Violent are punished. In the first *Girone* or round are the Violent against their neighbors, plunged more or less deeply in the river of boiling blood.

2. Mr. Ruskin, *Modern Painters,* III. 242, has the following remarks upon Dante's idea of rocks and mountains: —

"At the top of the abyss of the seventh circle, appointed for the 'violent,' or souls who had done evil by force, we are told, first, that the edge of it was composed of 'great broken stones in a circle'; then, that the place was 'Alpine'; and, becoming hereupon attentive, in order to hear what an Alpine place is like, we find that it was 'like the place beyond Trent, where the rock, either by earthquake, or failure of support, has broken down to the plain, so that it gives any one at the top some means of getting down to the bottom.' This is not a very elevated or enthusiastic description of an Alpine scene; and it is far from mended by the following verses, in which we are told that Dante 'began to go down by this great *unloading* of stones,' and that they moved often under his feet by reason of the new weight. The fact is that Dante, by many expressions throughout the poem, shows himself to have been a notably bad climber; and being fond of sitting in the sun, looking at his fair Baptistery, or walking in a dignified manner on flat pavement in a long robe, it puts him seriously out of his way when he has to take to his hands and knees, or look to his feet; so that the first strong impression made upon him by any Alpine scene whatever is, clearly, that it is bad walking. When he is in a fright and hurry, and has a very steep place to go down, Virgil has to carry him altogether."

5. Speaking of the region to which Dante here alludes, Eustace, *Classical Tour,* I. 71, says: —

"The descent becomes more rapid between Roveredo and Ala; the river, which glided gently through the valley of Trent, assumes the roughness of a torrent; the defiles become narrower; and the mountains break into rocks and precipices, which occasionally approach the road, sometimes rise perpendicular from it and now and then hang over it in terrible majesty."

In a note he adds: —

"Amid these wilds the traveller cannot fail to notice a vast tract called the *Slavini di Marco,* covered with fragments of rock torn from the sides of the neighboring mountains by an earthquake, or perhaps by their own unsupported weight, and hurled down into the plains below. They spread over the whole valley, and in some places contract the road to a very narrow space. A few firs and cypresses scattered in the intervals, or sometimes rising out of the crevices of the rocks, cast a partial and melancholy shade amid the surrounding nakedness and desolation. This scene of ruin seems to have made a deep impression upon the wild imagination of Dante, as he has introduced it into the twelfth canto of the *Inferno,* in order to give the reader an adequate idea of one of his infernal ramparts."

9. [Editor's annotation: This later note of Longfellow's deals with a subsequent edition's change of "some" to "no" in line 9.]

In this passage I was at first inclined to give *alcuna* its usual meaning of "some"; but after seeing the spot alluded to, and the inaccessible precipice left by the land-slide, I am confident it should be rendered in a negative sense, as before in Canto III. 42.

12. The Minotaur, half bull, half man. See the infamous story in all the classical dictionaries.

18. The Duke of Athens is Theseus. Chaucer gives him the same title in *The Knightes Tale:* —

> Whilom, as olde stories tellen us,
> Ther was a duk that highte Theseus.
> Of Athenes he was lord and governour,
> That greter was ther non under the sonne.
> Ful many a rich contree had he wonne.
> What with his wisdom and his chevalrie,
> He conquerd all the regne of Feminie,
> That whilom was ycleped Scythia;
> And wedded the freshe quene Ipolita,
> And brought hire home with him to his contree
> With mochel glorie and great solempnitee,
> And eke hire yonge suster Emelie.
> And thus with victorie and with melodie
> Let I this worthy duk to Athenes ride
> And all his host, in armes him beside.

Shakespeare also, in the *Midsummer Night's Dream,* calls him the Duke of Athens.

20. Ariadne, who gave Theseus the silken thread to guide him back through the Cretan labyrinth after slaying the Minotaur. Hawthorne has beautifully told the old story in his *Tanglewood Tales.* "Ah, the bull-headed villain!" he says. "And O my good little people, you will perhaps see, one of these days, as I do now, that every human being who suffers anything evil to get into his nature, or to remain there, is a kind of Minotaur, an enemy of his fellow-creatures, and separated from all good companionship, as this poor monster was."

39. Christ's descent into Limbo, and the earthquake at the Crucifixion.

42. This is the doctrine of Empedocles and other old philosophers. See Rit-

ter, *History of Ancient Philosophy*, Book V., Chap. vi. The following passages are from Mr. Morrison's translation: —

"Empedocles proceeded from the Eleatic principle of the oneness of all truth. In its unity it resembles a ball; he calls it the sphere, wherein the ancients recognized the God of Empedocles. . . .

"Into the unity of the sphere all elementary things are combined by love, without difference or distinction: within it they lead a happy life, replete with holiness, and remote from discord: —

> They know no god of war nor the spirit of battles,
> Nor Zeus, the sovereign, nor Cronos, nor yet Poseidon,
> But Cypris the queen. . . .

"The actual separation of the elements one from another is produced by discord; for originally they were bound together in the sphere, and therein continued perfectly unmovable. Now in this Empedocles posits different periods and different conditions of the world; for, according to the above position, originally all is united in love, and then subsequently the elements and living essences are separated. . . .

"His assertion of certain mundane periods was taken by the ancients literally; for they tell us that, according to his theory, All was originally one by love, but afterwards many and at enmity with itself through discord."

56. The Centaurs are set to guard this Circle, as symbolizing violence, with some form of which the classic poets usually associate them.

68. Chaucer, *The Monkes Tale:* —

> A lemman had this noble champion,
> That highte Deianire, as fresh as May;
> And as thise clerkes maken mention,
> She hath him sent a sherte fresh and gay:
> Alas! this sherte, alas and wala wa!
> Envenimed was sotilly withalle,
> That or that he had wered it half a day,
> It made his flesh all from his bones falle.

Chiron was a son of Saturn; Pholus, of Silenus; and Nessus, of Ixion and the Cloud.

71. Homer, *Iliad,* XI. 832, "Whom Chiron instructed, the most just of the Centaurs." Hawthorne gives a humorous turn to the fable of Chiron, in the *Tanglewood Tales,* p. 273: —

"I have sometimes suspected that Master Chiron was not really very different from other people, but that, being a kind-hearted and merry old fellow, he was in the habit of making believe that he was a horse, and scrambling about the school-room on all fours, and letting the little boys ride upon his back. And so, when his scholars had grown up, and grown old, and were trotting their grandchildren on their knees, they told them about the sports of their school days; and these young folks took the idea that their grandfathers had been taught their letters by a Centaur, half man and half horse. . . .

"Be that as it may, it has always been told for a fact, (and always will be told, as long as the world lasts,) that Chiron, with the head of a school-master, had the body and legs of a horse. Just imagine the grave old gentleman clattering and stamping into the school-room on his four hoofs, perhaps treading on some little fellow's toes, flourishing his switch tail instead of a rod, and now and then trotting out of doors to eat a mouthful of grass!"

77. Mr. Ruskin refers to this line in confirmation of his theory that "all great art represents something that it sees or believes in; nothing unseen or uncredited." The passage is as follows, *Modern Painters,* III. 83: —

"And just because it is always something that it sees or believes in, there is the peculiar character above noted, almost unmistakable, in all high and true ideals, of having been as it were studied from the life, and involving pieces of sudden familiarity, and close *specific* painting which never would have been admitted or even thought of, had not the painter drawn either from the bodily life or from the life of faith. For instance, Dante's Centaur, Chiron, dividing his beard with his arrow before he can speak, is a thing that no mortal would ever have thought of, if he had not actually seen the Centaur do it. They might have composed handsome bodies of men and horses in all possible ways, through a whole life of pseudo-idealism, and yet never dreamed of any such thing. But the real living Centaur actually trotted across Dante's brain, and he saw him do it."

107. Alexander of Thessaly and Dionysius of Syracuse.

110. Azzolino, or Ezzolino di Romano, tyrant of Padua, nicknamed the Son of the Devil. Ariosto, *Orlando Furioso,* III. 33, describes him as

> Fierce Ezelin, that most inhuman lord,
> Who shall be deemed by men a child of hell.

His story may be found in Sismondi's *Histoire des Républiques Italiennes,* Chap. XIX. He so outraged the religious sense of the people by his cruelties, that a crusade was preached against him, and he died a prisoner in 1259, tearing the bandages from his wounds, and fierce and defiant to the last.

"Ezzolino was small of stature," says Sismondi, "but the whole aspect of his person, all his movements, indicated the soldier. His language was bitter, his countenance proud; and by a single look, he made the boldest tremble. His soul, so greedy of all crimes, felt no attraction for sensual pleasures. Never had Ezzolino loved women; and this perhaps is the reason why in his punishments he was as pitiless against them as against men. He was in his sixty-sixth year when he died; and his reign of blood had lasted thirty-four years."

Many glimpses of him are given in the *Cento Novelle Antiche,* as if his memory long haunted the minds of men. Here are two of them, from Novella 83.

"Once upon a time Messer Azzolino di Romano made proclamation, through his own territories and elsewhere, that he wished to do a great charity, and therefore that all the beggars, both men and women, should assemble in his meadow, on a certain day, and to each he would give a new gown, and abundance of food. The news spread among the servants on all hands. When the day of assembling came, his seneschals went among them with the gowns and the food, and made them strip naked one by one, and then clothed them with new clothes, and fed them. They asked for their old rags, but it was all in vain; for he put them into a heap and set fire to them. Afterwards he found there so much gold and silver melted, that it more than paid the expense, and then he dismissed them with his blessing....

"To tell you how much he was feared, would be a long story, and many people know it. But I will recall how he, being one day with the Emperor on horseback, with all their people, they laid a wager as to which of them had the most beautiful sword. The Emperor drew from its sheath his own, which was wonderfully garnished with gold and precious stones. Then said Messer Azzolino: 'It is very beautiful; but mine, without any great ornament, is far more beautiful'; —and he drew it forth. Then six hundred knights, who were with him, all drew theirs. When the Emperor beheld this cloud of swords, he said: 'Yours is the most beautiful.'"

111. Obizzo da Esti, Marquis of Ferrara. He was murdered by Azzo, "whom he thought to be his son," says Boccaccio, "though he was not." The *Ottimo* remarks: "Many call themselves sons, and are step-sons."

119. Guido di Monforte, who murdered Prince Henry of England "in the

bosom of God," that is, in the church, at Viterbo. The event is thus narrated by Napier, *Florentine History,* I. 283: —

"Another instance of this revengeful spirit occurred in the year 1271 at Viterbo, where the cardinals had assembled to elect a successor to Clement the Fourth, about whom they had been long disputing: Charles of Anjou and Philip of France, with Edward and Henry, sons of Richard, Duke of Cornwall, had repaired there, the two first to hasten the election, which they finally accomplished by the elevation of Gregory the Tenth. During these proceedings Prince Henry, while taking the sacrament in the church of San Silvestro at Viterbo, was stabbed to the heart by his own cousin, Guy de Montfort, in revenge for the Earl of Leicester's death, although Henry was then endeavoring to procure his pardon. This sacrilegious act threw Viterbo into confusion, but Montfort had many supporters, one of whom asked him what he had done. *'I have taken my revenge,'* said he. *'But your father's body was trailed!'* At this reproach, De Montfort instantly re-entered the church, walked straight to the altar, and, seizing Henry's body by the hair, dragged it through the aisle, and left it, still bleeding, in the open street: he then retired unmolested to the castle of his father-in-law, Count Rosso of the Maremma, and there remained in security!"

"The body of the Prince," says Barlow, *Study of the Divine Comedy,* p. 125, "was brought to England, and interred at Hayles, in Gloucestershire, in the Abbey which his father had there built for monks of the Cistercian order; but his heart was put into a golden vase, and placed on the tomb of Edward the Confessor, in Westminster Abbey; most probably, as stated by some writers, in the hands of a statue."

123. Violence in all its forms was common enough in Florence in the age of Dante.

134. Attila, the Scourge of God. Gibbon, *Decline and Fall,* Chap. 39, describes him thus: —

"Attila, the son of Mundzuk, deduced his noble, perhaps his regal, descent from the ancient Huns, who had formerly contended with the monarchs of China. His features, according to the observation of a Gothic historian, bore the stamp of his national origin; and the portrait of Attila exhibits the genuine deformity of a modern Calmuk; a large head, a swarthy complexion, small, deep-seated eyes, a flat nose, a few hairs in the place of a beard, broad shoulders, and a short, square body, of nervous strength, though of a disproportioned form. The haughty step and demeanor of the King of the Huns expressed the consciousness of his superiority above the rest of mankind; and he had a custom of fiercely rolling his eyes, as if he wished to enjoy the terror which he inspired."

135. Which Pyrrhus and which Sextus, the commentators cannot determine; but incline to Pyrrhus of Epirus, and Sextus Pompey, the corsair of the Mediterranean.

137. Nothing more is known of these highwaymen than that the first infested the Roman sea-shore, and that the second was of a noble family of Florence.

CANTO XIII

1. In this Canto is described the punishment of those who had laid violent hands on themselves or their property.

2. Chaucer, *Knightes Tale*, 1977: —

> First on the wall was peinted a forest,
> In which ther wonneth neyther man ne best,
> With knotty knarry barrein trees old
> Of stubbes sharpe and hidous to behold;
> In which there ran a romble and a swough
> As though a storme shuld bresten every bough.

9. The Cecina is a small river running into the Mediterranean not many miles south of Leghorn; Corneto, a village in the Papal States, north of Civita Vecchia. The country is wild and thinly peopled, and studded with thickets, the haunts of the deer and the wild boar. This region is the fatal Maremma, thus described by Forsyth, *Italy*, p. 156: —

"Farther south is the Maremma, a region which, though now worse than a desert, is supposed to have been anciently both fertile and healthy. The Maremma certainly formed part of that Etruria which was called from its harvests the *annonaria*. Old Roman cisterns may still be traced, and the ruins of Populonium are still visible in the worst part of this tract: yet both nature and man seem to have conspired against it.

"Sylla threw this maritime part of Tuscany into enormous *latifundia* for his disbanded soldiers. Similar distributions continued to lessen its population during the Empire. In the younger Pliny's time the climate was pestilential. The Lombards gave it a new aspect of misery. Wherever they found culture they built castles, and to each castle they allotted a 'bandita' or military fief. Hence baronial wars which have left so many picturesque ruins on the hills, and such desolation round them. Whenever a baron was conquered, his vassals escaped to the cities, and the vacant fief was annexed to the victorious. Thus stripped of men, the lands returned into a state of nature: some were flooded by the rivers, others grew into horrible forests, which enclose and concentrate the pestilence of the lakes and marshes.

"In some parts the water is brackish, and lies lower than the sea: in others it oozes full of tartar from beds of travertine. At the bottom or on the sides of hills are a multitude of hot springs, which form pools, called *Lagoni*. A few of these are said to produce borax: some, which are called *fumache*, exhale sulphur; others, called *bulicami*, boil with a mephitic gas. The very air above is only a pool of vapors, which sometimes undulate, but seldom flow off. It draws corruption from a rank, unshorn, rotting vegetation, from reptiles and fish both living and dead.

"All nature conspires to drive man away from this fatal region; but man will ever return to his bane, if it be well baited. The Casentine peasants still migrate hither in the winter to feed their cattle: and here they sow corn, make charcoal, saw wood, cut hoops, and peel cork. When summer returns they decamp, but often too late; for many leave their corpses on the road, or bring home the Maremmian disease."

11. *Æneid*, III., Davidson's Tr.: —

"The shores of the Strophades first receive me rescued from the waves. The Strophades, so called by a Greek name, are islands situated in the great Ionian Sea; which direful Celæno and the other Harpies inhabit, from what time Phineus' palace was closed against them, and they were frighted from his table, which they formerly haunted. No monster more fell than they, no plague and scourge of the gods more cruel, ever issued from the Stygian waves. They are fowls with virgin faces, most loathsome is their bodily discharge, hands hooked, and looks ever pale with famine. Hither conveyed, as soon as we entered the port, lo! we observe joyous herds of cattle roving up and down the plains and flocks of goats along the meadows without a keeper. We rush upon them with our swords, and invoke the gods and Jove himself to share the booty. Then along the winding shore we raise the couches, and feast on the rich repast. But suddenly, with direful swoop, the Harpies are upon us from the mountains, shake their wings with loud din, prey upon our banquet, and defile everything with their touch: at the same time, together with a rank smell, hideous screams arise."

21. His words in the *Æneid*, III., Davidson's Tr.: —

"Near at hand there chanced to be a rising ground, on whose top were young cornel-trees, and a myrtle rough with thick, spear-like branches. I came up to it, and attempting to tear from the earth the verdant wood, that I might cover the altars with the leafy boughs, I observe a dreadful prodigy, and wondrous to relate. For from that tree which first is torn from the soil, its rooted fibres being burst asunder, drops of black blood distil, and stain the ground with gore: cold terror shakes my limbs, and my chill blood is congealed with fear. I again essay to tear off a limber bough from another, and thoroughly explore the latent cause: and from the rind of that other the purple blood descends. Raising in my mind many an anxious thought, I with reverence besought the rural nymphs, and father Mars, who presides over the Thracian territories, kindly to prosper the vision and avert evil from the omen. But when I attempted the boughs a third time with a more vigorous effort, and on my knees struggled against the opposing mould, (shall I speak, or shall I forbear?) a piteous groan is heard from the bottom of the rising ground, and a voice sent forth reaches my ears: 'Æneas, why dost thou tear an unhappy wretch? Spare me, now that I am in my grave; forbear to pollute with guilt thy pious hands: Troy brought me forth no stranger to you; nor is it from the trunk this blood distils.'"

40. Chaucer, *Knightes Tale*, 2339: —

> And as it queinte, it made a whisteling
> As don these brondes wet in hir brenning,
> And at the brondes ende outran anon
> As it were blody dropes many on.

See also Spenser, *Faerie Queene*, I. ii. 30.

58. Pietro della Vigna, Chancellor of the Emperor Frederick II. Napier's account of him is as follows, *Florentine History*, I. 197: —

"The fate of his friend and minister, Piero delle Vigne of Capua, if truly told, would nevertheless impress us with an unfavorable idea of his mercy and magnanimity: Piero was sent with Taddeo di Sessa as Frederick's advocate and representative to the Council of Lyons, which was assembled by his friend Innocent the Fourth, nominally to reform the Church, but really to impart more force and solemnity to a fresh sentence of excommunication and deposition. There Taddeo spoke with force and boldness for his master; but Piero was silent; and hence he was accused of being, like several others, bribed by the Pope, not only to desert the Emperor, but to attempt his life; and whether he were really culpable, or the victim of court intrigue, is still doubtful. Frederick, on apparently good evidence, condemned him to have his eyes burned out, and the sentence was executed at San Miniato al Tedesco: being afterwards sent on horseback to Pisa, where he was hated, as an object for popular derision, he died, as is conjectured, from the effects of a fall while thus cruelly exposed, and not by his own hand, as Dante believed and sung."

Milman, *Latin Christianity*, V. 499, gives the story thus: —

"Peter de Vineâ had been raised by the wise choice of Frederick to the highest rank and influence. All the acts of Frederick were attributed to his Chancellor. De Vineâ, like his master, was a poet; he was one of the counsellors in his great scheme of legislation. Some rumors spread abroad that at the Council of Lyons, though Frederick had forbidden all his representatives from holding private intercourse with the Pope, De Vineâ had many secret conferences with Innocent, and was accused of betraying his master's interests. Yet there was no seeming diminution in the trust placed in De Vineâ. Still, to the end the Emperor's letters concerning the disaster at Parma are by the same hand. Over the cause of his disgrace and death, even in his own day, there was deep doubt and obscurity. The popular rumor ran that Frederick was ill; the physician of De Vineâ prescribed for him; the Emperor having received some warning, addressed De Vineâ: 'My friend, in thee I have full trust; art thou sure that this is medicine, not poison?' De Vineâ replied: 'How often has my physician ministered healthful medicines!—why are you now afraid?' Frederick took the cup, sternly commanded the physician to drink half of it. The physician threw himself at the King's feet, and, as he fell, overthrew the liquor. But what was left was administered to some criminals, who died in agony. The Emperor wrung his hands and wept bitterly: 'Whom can I now trust, betrayed by my own familiar friend? Never can I know security, never can I know joy more.' By one account Peter de Vineâ was led ignominiously on an ass through Pisa, and thrown into prison, where he dashed his brains out against the wall. Dante's immortal verse has saved the fame of De Vineâ: according to the poet he was the victim of wicked and calumnious jealousy."

See also Giuseppe de Blasiis, *Vita et Opere de Pietro della Vigna*.

64. Chaucer, *Legende of Goode Women*: —

> Envie ys lavendere of the court alway;
> For she ne parteth neither nyght ne day
> Out of the house of Cesar, thus saith Daunte.

112. *Iliad*, XII. 146: "Like two wild boars, which catch the coming tumult of men and dogs in the mountains, and, advancing obliquely to the attack, break down the wood about them, cutting it off at the roots."

120. "Lano," says Boccaccio, *Comento*, "was a young gentleman of Siena, who

had a large patrimony, and associating himself with a club of other young Sienese, called the Spend-thrift Club, they also being all rich, together with them, not spending but squandering, in a short time he consumed all that he had and became very poor." Joining some Florentine troops sent out against the Aretines, he was in a skirmish at the parish of Toppo, which Dante calls a joust; "and notwithstanding he might have saved himself," continues Boccaccio, "remembering his wretched condition, and it seeming to him a grievous thing to bear poverty, as he had been very rich, he rushed into the thick of the enemy and was slain, as perhaps he desired to be."

125. Some commentators interpret these dogs as poverty and despair, still pursuing their victims. The *Ottimo Comento* calls them "poor men who, to follow pleasure and the kitchens of other people, abandoned their homes and families, and are therefore transformed into hunting dogs, and pursue and devour their masters."

133. Jacopo da St. Andrea was a Paduan of like character and life as Lano. "Among his other squanderings," says the *Ottimo Comento*, "it is said that, wishing to see a grand and beautiful fire, he had one of his own villas burned."

143. Florence was first under the protection of the god Mars; afterwards under that of St. John the Baptist. But in Dante's time the statue of Mars was still standing on a column at the head of the Ponte Vecchio. It was overthrown by an inundation of the Arno in 1333. See Canto XV. Note 62.

149. Florence was destroyed by Totila in 450, and never by Attila. In Dante's time the two seem to have been pretty generally confounded. The *Ottimo Comento* remarks upon this point, "Some say that Totila was one person and Attila another; and some say that he was one and the same man."

150. Dante does not mention the name of this suicide; Boccaccio thinks, for one of two reasons; "either out of regard to his surviving relatives, who peradventure are honorable men, and therefore he did not wish to stain them with the infamy of so dishonest a death, or else (as in those times, as if by a malediction sent by God upon our city, many hanged themselves) that each one might apply it to either he pleased of these many."

CANTO XIV

1. In this third round of the seventh circle are punished the Violent against God,

> In heart denying and blaspheming him,
> And by disdaining Nature and her bounty.

15. When he retreated across the Libyan desert with the remnant of Pompey's army after the battle of Pharsalia. Lucan, *Pharsalia*, Book IX.: —

> Foremost, behold, I lead you to the toil,
> My feet shall foremost print the dusty soil.

31. Boccaccio confesses that he does not know where Dante found this tradition of Alexander. Benvenuto da Imola says it is in a letter which Alexander wrote to Aristotle. He quotes the passage as follows: "In India ignited vapors fell from heaven like snow. I commanded my soldiers to trample them under foot."

Dante perhaps took the incident from the old metrical *Romance of Alexander*, which in some form or other was current in his time. In the English version of it, published by the Roxburghe Club, we find the rain of fire, and a fall of snow; but it is the snow, and not the fire, that the soldiers trample down. So likewise in the French version. The English runs as follows, line 4164: —

> Than fandis he furth as I finde five and twenti days,
> Come to a velanus vale thare was a vile cheele,
> Quare flaggis of the fell snawe fell fra the heven,
> That was a brade, sais the buke, as battes ere of wolle.
> Than bett he many brigt fire and lest it bin nold,
> And made his folk with thaire feete as flores it to trede.
>
> . . . . .
>
> Than fell ther fra the firmament as it ware fell sparkes,
> Ropand doune o rede fire, than any rayne thikir.

45. Canto VIII. 83.

56. Mount Etna, under which, with his Cyclops, Vulcan forged the thunderbolts of Jove.

63. Capaneus was one of the seven kings who besieged Thebes. Euripides, *Phœnissœ*, line 1188, thus describes his death: —

> While o'er the battlements sprung Capaneus,
> Jove struck him with his thunder, and the earth
> Resounded with the crack; meanwhile mankind
> Stood all aghast; from off the ladder's height
> His limbs were far asunder hurled, his hair
> Flew to'ards Olympus, to the ground his blood,
> His hands and feet whirled like Ixion's wheel,
> And to the earth his flaming body fell.

Also Gower, *Confes. Amant.,* I.: —

> As he the cite wolde assaile,
> God toke him selfe the bataile
> Ayen his pride, and fro the sky
> A firy thonder sudeinly
> He sende and him to pouder smote.

72. Sophocles, *Œdipus Coloneus,* Franklin's Tr., Act I. sc. 11: —

> Remain perverse
> And obstinate, old man; but know hereafter
> Time will convince thee thou hast ever been
> Thy own worst foe; thy fiery temper still
> Must make thee wretched.

79. The Bulicame or Hot Springs of Viterbo. Villani, *Cronica,* Book I. ch. 51, gives the following brief account of these springs, and of the origin of the name of Viterbo: —

"The city of Viterbo was built by the Romans, and in old times was called Vigezia, and the citizens Vigentians. And the Romans sent the sick there on account of the baths which flow from the Bulicame, and therefore it was called *Vita Erbo,* that is, life of the sick, or city of life."

80. "The building thus appropriated," says Mr. Barlow, *Contributions to the Study of the Divine Comedy,* p. 129, "would appear to have been the large ruined edifice known as the Bagno di Ser Paolo Benigno, situated between the Bulicame and Viterbo. About half a mile beyond the Porta di Faule which leads to Toscanella, we come to a way called Riello, after which we arrive at the said ruined edifice, which received the water from the Bulicame by conduits, and has popularly been regarded as the Bagno delle Meretrici alluded to by Dante; there is no other building here found, which can dispute with it the claim to this distinction."

102. The shouts and cymbals of the Corybantes, drowning the cries of the infant Jove, lest Saturn should find him and devour him.

103. The statue of Time, turning its back upon the East and looking towards Rome. Compare *Daniel* ii. 31.

105. The Ages of Gold, Silver, Brass, and Iron. See Ovid, *Metamorph.* I.

See also Don Quixote's discourse to the goatherds, inspired by the acorns they gave him, Book II. Chap. 3; and Tasso's Ode to the Golden Age, in the *Aminta.*

113. The Tears of Time, forming the infernal rivers that flow into Cocytus.

116. Plato, *Phœdo,* Cary's Tr.: —

> "Now there are many other large and various streams, but among this great number there are four certain streams, of which the largest, and that which flows most outwardly round the earth, is called Ocean, but directly opposite this, and flowing in a contrary direction, is Acheron, which flows through other desert places, and moreover passing under the earth, reaches the Acherusian lake, where the souls of most who die arrive, and having remained there for certain destined periods, some longer and some shorter, are again sent forth into the generations of animals. A third river issues midway between these, and near its source falls into a vast region, burning with abundance of fire, and forms a lake larger than our sea, boiling with water and mud; from hence it proceeds in a circle, turbulent and muddy, and folding itself round it reaches both other places and the extremity of the Acherusian lake, but does not mingle with its water; but folding itself oftentimes beneath the earth, it discharges itself into the lower parts of Tartarus. And this is the river which they call Pyriphlegethon, whose burning streams emit dissevered fragments in whatever part of the earth they happen to be. Opposite to this again the fourth river first falls into a place dreadful and savage, as it is said, having its whole color like cyanus:[1] this they call Stygian, and the lake, which the river forms by its discharge, Styx. This river having fallen in here, and received awful power in the water, sinking beneath the earth, proceeds, folding itself round, in an opposite course to Pyriphlegethon, and meets it in the Acherusian lake from a contrary direction. Neither does the water of this river mingle with any other, but it too, having gone round in a circle, discharges itself into Tartarus, opposite to Pyriphlegethon. Its name, as the poets say, is Cocytus."

Milton, *Paradise Lost,* II. 577: —

> Abhorred Styx, the flood of deadly hate;
> Sad Acheron of sorrow, black and deep;
> Cocytus, named of lamentation loud
> Heard on the rueful stream; fierce Phlegeton,
> Whose waves of torrent fire inflame with rage.
> Far off from these a slow and silent stream,
> Lethè, the river of oblivion, rolls
> Her watery labyrinth, whereof who drinks

---

1. A metallic substance of a deep blue color, frequently mentioned by the earliest Grecian writers, but of which the nature is unknown.

> Forthwith his former state and being forgets,
> Forgets both joy and grief, pleasure and pain.

136. See *Purgatorio* XXVIII.

CANTO XV

1. In this Canto is described the punishment of the Violent against Nature; —

> And for this reason does the smallest round
> Seal with its signet Sodom and Cahors.

4. Guizzante is not Ghent, but Cadsand, an island opposite L'Ecluse, where the great canal of Bruges enters the sea. A canal thus flowing into the sea, the dikes on either margin uniting with the sea-dikes, gives a perfect image of this part of the Inferno.

Lodovico Guicciardini in his *Descrittione di tutti i Paesi Bassi* (1581), p. 416, speaking of Cadsand, says: "This is the very place of which our great poet Dante makes mention in the fifteenth chapter of the *Inferno,* calling it incorrectly, perhaps by error of the press, Guizzante; where still at the present day great repairs are continually made upon the dikes, because here, and in the environs towards Bruges, the flood, or I should rather say the tide, on account of the situation and lowness of the land, has very great power, particularly during a northwest wind."

5. These lines recall Goldsmith's description in the *Traveller:* —

> Methinks her patient sons before me stand,
> Where the broad ocean leans against the land,
> And, sedulous to stop the coming tide,
> Lift the tall rampire's artificial pride.
> Onward, methinks, and diligently slow
> The firm connected bulwark seems to grow;
> Spreads its long arms amidst the watery roar,
> Scoops out an empire and usurps the shore.

9. That part of the Alps in which the Brenta rises.

29. The reading *la mia* seems preferable to *la mano*, and is justified by line 45.

30. Brunetto Latini, Dante's friend and teacher. Villani thus speaks of him, *Cronica,* VIII. 10: "In this year 1294 died in Florence a worthy citizen, whose name was Ser Brunetto Latini, who was a great philosopher and perfect master of rhetoric, both in speaking and in writing. He com-

mented the Rhetoric of Tully, and made the good and useful book called the *Tesoro,* and the *Tesoretto,* and the *Keys of the Tesoro,* and many other books of philosophy, and of vices and of virtues, and he was Secretary of our Commune. He was a worldly man, but we have made mention of him because he was the first master in refining the Florentines, and in teaching them how to speak correctly, and how to guide and govern our Republic on political principles."

Boccaccio, *Comento,* speaks of him thus: "This Ser Brunetto Latini was a Florentine, and a very able man in some of the liberal arts, and in philosophy; but his principal calling was that of Notary; and he held himself and his calling in such great esteem, that, having made a mistake in a contract drawn up by him, and having been in consequence accused of fraud, he preferred to be condemned for it rather than to confess that he had made a mistake; and afterwards he quitted Florence in disdain, and leaving in memory of himself a book composed by him, called the *Tesoretto,* he went to Paris and lived there a long time, and composed a book there which is in French, and in which he treats of many matters regarding the liberal arts, and moral and natural philosophy, and metaphysics, which he called the *Tesoro;* and finally, I believe, he died in Paris."

He also wrote a short poem, called the *Favoletto,* and perhaps the *Pataffio,* a satirical poem in the Florentine dialect, "a jargon," says Nardini, "which cannot be understood even with a commentary." But his fame rests upon the *Tesoretto* and the *Tesoro,* and more than all upon the fact that he was Dante's teacher, and was put by him into a very disreputable place in the Inferno. He died in Florence, not in Paris, as Boccaccio supposes, and was buried in Santa Maria Novella, where his tomb still exists. It is strange that Boccaccio should not have known this, as it was in this church that the "seven young gentlewomen" of his *Decameron* met "on a Tuesday morning," and resolved to go together into the country, where they "might hear the birds sing, and see the verdure of the hills and plains, and the fields full of grain undulating like the sea."

The poem of the *Tesoretto,* written in a jingling metre, which reminds one of the *Vision of Piers Ploughman,* is itself a Vision, with the customary allegorical personages of the Virtues and Vices. Ser Brunetto, returning from an embassy to King Alphonso of Spain, meets on the plain of Roncesvalles a student of Bologna, riding on a bay mule, who informs him that the Guelfs have been banished from Florence. Whereupon Ser Brunetto, plunged in meditation and sorrow, loses the high-road and wanders in a wondrous forest. Here he discovers the august and gigantic figure of Nature, who relates to him the creation of the world, and gives him a banner to protect him on his pilgrimage through the forest, in which he meets with no adventures, but with the Virtues and Vices, Philosophy, Fortune, Ovid, and the God of Love, and sundry other characters, which are sung at large through eight or ten chapters. He then emerges from the forest, and confesses himself to the Monks of Montpellier; after which he goes back into the forest again, and suddenly finds himself on the summit of Olympus; and the poem abruptly leaves him discoursing about the elements with Ptolemy,

> Mastro di storlomia
> E di filosofia.

It has been supposed by some commentators that Dante was indebted to the *Tesoretto* for the first idea of the *Commedia*. "If any one is pleased to imagine this," says the Abbate Zannoni in the Preface to his edition of the *Tesoretto*, (Florence, 1824,) "he must confess that a slight and almost invisible spark served to kindle a vast conflagration."

The *Tesoro*, which is written in French, is a much more ponderous and pretentious volume. Hitherto it has been known only in manuscript, or in the Italian translation of Giamboni, but at length appears as one of the volumes of the *Collection de Documents Inédits sur l'Histoire de France*, under the title of *Li Livres dou Tresor*, edited by P. Chabaille, Paris, 1863; a stately quarto of some seven hundred pages, which it would assuage the fiery torment of Ser Brunetto to look upon, and justify him in saying

> Commended unto thee be my Tesoro,
> In which I still live, and no more I ask.

The work is quaint and curious, but mainly interesting as being written by Dante's schoolmaster, and showing what he knew and what he taught his pupil. I cannot better describe it than in the author's own words, Book I. ch. 1: —

"The smallest part of this Treasure is like unto ready money, to be expended daily in things needful; that is, it treats of the beginning of time, of the antiquity of old histories, of the creation of the world, and in fine of the nature of all things. . . .

"The second part, which treats of the vices and virtues, is of precious stones, which give unto man delight and virtue; that is to say, what things a man should do, and what he should not, and shows the reason why. . . .

"The third part of the Treasure is of fine gold; that is to say, it teaches a man to speak according to the rules of rhetoric, and how a ruler ought to govern those beneath him. . . .

"And I say not that this book is extracted from my own poor sense and my own naked knowledge, but, on the contrary, it is like a honeycomb gathered from diverse flowers; for this book is wholly compiled from the wonderful sayings of the authors who before our time have treated of philosophy, each one according to his knowledge. . . .

"And if any one should ask why this book is written in Romance, according to the language of the French, since we are Italian, I should say it is for two reasons; one, because we are in France, and the other, because this speech is more delectable, and more common to all people."

62. "Afterwards," says Brunetto Latini, *Tresor,* Book I. Pt. I. ch. 37, "the Romans besieged Fiesole, till at last they conquered it and brought it into subjection. Then they built upon the plain, which is at the foot of the high rocks on which that city stood, another city, that is now called Florence. And know that the spot of ground where Florence stands was formerly called the House of Mars, that is to say the House of War; for Mars, who is one of the seven planets, is called the God of War, and as such was worshipped of old. Therefore it is no wonder that the Florentines are always in war and in discord, for that planet reigns over them. Of this Master Brunez Latins ought to know the truth, for he was born there, and was in exile on account of war with the Florentines, when he composed this book."

See also Villani, I. 38, who assigns a different reason for the Florentine dissensions. "And observe, that if the Florentines are always in war and dissension among themselves it is not to be wondered at, they being descended from two nations so contrary and hostile and different in customs, as were the noble and virtuous Romans and the rude and war-like Fiesolans."

Again, IV. 7, he attributes the Florentine dissensions to both the above-mentioned causes.

63. *Macigno,* which I have rendered granite, is,—according to Ferber, *Travels through Italy in 1771–72;* Raspe's translation, p. 91,—"a micaceous stone, consisting of clay and some lime; appearing rather to be entirely composed of glimmer. In the uppermost strata it is shivery, but very compact and hard in a greater depth. Hence Petrarch's and other poets' *petti di macigno* of their unyielding cruel fair ones."

And further on, p. 269, "There remains at Fiesole a piece of an old Etruscan wall, consisting in large square-cut stones of *macigno,* which are put together without cement. The present quarries of *macigno* near Fiesole are situated on the hill called *Ceceri,* and in another over against to the southwest called *Settignano.* All the other hills hereabout consist likewise of *macigno,* bordering on calcareous hills, such as *Monte Morello* and others. I have noticed already in one of my former Letters that *macigno* is a species of slate, composed of an argillaceous earth, much mica, and some lime."

67. Villani, IV. 31, tells the story of certain columns of porphyry given by the Pisans to the Florentines for guarding their city while the Pisan army had gone to the conquest of Majorca. The columns were cracked by fire, but being covered with crimson cloth, the Florentines did not perceive it. Boccaccio repeats the story with variations, but does not think it a sufficient reason for calling the Florentines blind, and confesses that he does not know what reason there can be for so calling them.

89. The "other text" is the prediction of his banishment, Canto X. 81, and the Lady is Beatrice.

96. Boileau, *Épitre,* V.: —

> Qu'à son gré désormais la fortune me joue,
> On me verra dormir au branle de sa roue.

And Tennyson's Song of *Fortune and her Wheel:* —

> Turn, Fortune, turn thy wheel and lower the proud;
> Turn thy wild wheel thro' sunshine, storm, and cloud;
> Thy wheel and thee we neither love nor hate.
>
> Turn, Fortune, turn thy wheel with smile or frown;
> With that wild wheel we go not up or down;
> Our hoard is little, but our hearts are great.
>
> Smile and we smile, the lords of many lands;
> Frown and we smile, the lords of our own hands;
> For man is man and master of his fate.
>
> Turn, turn thy wheel above the staring crowd;
> Thy wheel and thou are shadows in the cloud;
> Thy wheel and thee we neither love nor hate.

109. Priscian, the grammarian of Constantinople in the sixth century.

110. Francesco d'Accorso, a distinguished jurist and Professor at Bologna in the thirteenth century, celebrated for his Commentary upon the Code Justinian.

113. Andrea de' Mozzi, Bishop of Florence, transferred by the Pope, the "Ser-

vant of Servants," to Vicenza; the two cities being here designated by the rivers on which they are respectively situated.

119. See Note 30.

122. The *Corsa del Pallio,* or foot-races, at Verona; in which a green mantle, or *Pallio,* was the prize. Buttura says that these foot-races are still continued (1823), and that he has seen them more than once; but certainly not in the nude state in which Boccaccio describes them, and which renders Dante's comparison more complete and striking.

CANTO XVI

1. In this Canto the subject of the preceding is continued.

4. Guidoguerra, Tegghiajo Aldobrandi, and Jacopo Rusticucci.

37. The good Gualdrada was a daughter of Bellincion Berti, the simple citizen of Florence in the olden time, who used to walk the streets "begirt with bone and leather," as mentioned in the *Paradiso,* XV. 112. Villani, I. 37, reports a story of her with all the brevity of a chronicler. Boccaccio tells the same story, as if he were writing a page of the *Decameron.* In his version it runs as follows.

"The Emperor Otho IV., being by chance in Florence and having gone to the festival of St. John, to make it more gay with his presence, it happened that to the church with the other city dames, as our custom is, came the wife of Messer Berto, and brought with her a daughter of hers called Gualdrada, who was still unmarried. And as they sat there with the others, the maiden being beautiful in face and figure, nearly all present turned round to look at her, and among the rest the Emperor. And having much commended her beauty and manners, he asked Messer Berto, who was near him, who she was. To which Messer Berto smiling answered: 'She is the daughter of one who, I dare say, would let you kiss her if you wished.' These words the young lady heard, being near the speaker; and somewhat troubled by the opinion her father seemed to have of her, that, if he wished it, she would suffer herself to be kissed by any one in this free way, rising, and looking a moment at her father, and blushing with shame, said: 'Father, do not make such courteous promises at the expense of my modesty, for certainly, unless by violence, no one shall ever kiss me, except him whom you shall give me as my husband.' The Emperor, on hearing this, much commended the words and the young lady. . . . And calling forward a noble youth named Guido Beisangue, who was afterwards called Guido the Elder, who as yet had no wife, he insisted upon his marrying her; and gave him as her dowry a large territory in Cassentino and the Alps, and made him Count thereof."

Ampère says in his *Voyage Dantesque,* page 242: "Near the battle-field of Campaldino stands the little town of Poppi, whose castle was built in 1230 by the father of the Arnolfo who built some years later the Palazzo Vecchio of Florence. In this castle is still shown the bedroom of the beautiful and modest Gualdrada."

Francesco Sansovino, an Italian novelist of the sixteenth century, has made Gualdrada the heroine of one of his tales, but has strangely perverted the old tradition. His story may be found in Roscoe's *Italian Novelists,* III. p. 107.

41. Tegghiajo Aldobrandi was a distinguished citizen of Florence, and opposed what Malaspina calls "the ill counsel of the people," that war should be declared against the Sienese, which war resulted in the battle of Monte Aperto and the defeat of the Florentines.

44. Jacopo Rusticucci was a rich Florentine gentleman, whose chief misfortune seems to have been an ill-assorted marriage. Whereupon the amiable Boccaccio in his usual Decameron style remarks: "Men ought not then to be over-hasty in getting married; on the contrary, they should come to it with much precaution." And then he indulges in five octavo pages against matrimony and woman in general.

45. See Macchiavelli's story of *Belfagor,* wherein Minos and Rhadamanthus, and the rest of the infernal judges, are greatly surprised to hear an infinite number of condemned souls "lament nothing so bitterly as their folly in having taken wives, attributing to them the whole of their misfortune."

70. Boccaccio, in his *Comento,* speaks of Guglielmo Borsiere as "a courteous gentleman of good breeding and excellent manners"; and in the *Decamerone,* Gior. I. Nov. 8, tells of a sharp rebuke administered by him to Messer Ermino de' Grimaldi, a miser of Genoa.

"It came to pass, that, whilst by spending nothing he went on accumulating wealth, there came to Genoa a well-bred and witty gentleman called Gulielmo Borsiere, one nothing like the courtiers of the present day; who, to the great reproach of the debauched dispositions of such as would now be reputed fine gentlemen, should more properly style themselves asses, brought up amidst the filthiness and sink of mankind, rather than in courts. . . .

"This Gulielmo, whom I before mentioned, was much visited and respected by the better sort of people at Genoa; when having made some stay here, and hearing much talk of Ermino's sordidness, he became desirous of seeing him. Now Ermino had been informed of Gulielmo's worthy character, and having, however covetous he was, some small sparks of gentility, he received him in a courteous manner, and, entering into discourse together, he took him, and some Genoese who came along with him, to see a fine house which he had lately built: and when he had showed every part of it, he said, 'Pray, sir, can you, who have heard and seen so much, tell me of something that was never yet seen, to have painted in my hall?' To whom Gulielmo, hearing him speak so simply, replied: 'Sir, I can tell you of nothing which has never yet been seen, that I know of; unless it be sneezing, or something of that sort; but if you please, I can tell you of a thing which, I believe, you never saw.' Said Ermino (little expecting such an answer as he received), 'I beg you would let me know what that is.' Gulielmo immediately replied, 'Paint Liberality.' When Ermino heard this, such a sudden shame seized him, as quite changed his temper from what it had hitherto been; and he said: 'Sir, I will have her painted in such a manner that neither you, nor any one else, shall be able to say, hereafter, that I am unacquainted with her.' And from that time such effect had Gulielmo's words upon him, he became the most liberal and courteous gentleman, and was the most respected, both by strangers and his own citizens, of any in Genoa."

95. Monte Veso is among the Alps, between Piedmont and Savoy, where the Po takes its rise. From this point eastward to the Adriatic, all the rivers on the left or northern slope of the Apennines are tributaries to the Po, until we come to the Montone, which above Forlì is called Acquacheta. This is the first which flows directly into the Adriatic, and not into the Po. At least it was so in Dante's time. Now, by some change in its course, the Lamone, farther north, has opened itself a new outlet, and is the first to make its own way to the Adriatic. See Barlow, *Study of the Divine Comedy*, p. 131. This comparison shows the delight which Dante took in the study of physical geography. To reach the waterfall of Acquacheta he traverses in thought the entire valley of the Po, stretching across the whole of Northern Italy.

102. Boccaccio's interpretation of this line, which has been adopted by most of the commentators since his time, is as follows: "I was for a long time in doubt concerning the author's meaning in this line; but being by chance at this monastery of San Benedetto, in company with the abbot, he told me that there had once been a discussion among the Counts who owned the mountain, about building a village near the waterfall, as a convenient place for a settlement, and bringing into it their vassals scattered on neighboring farms; but the leader of the project dying, it was not carried into effect; and that is what the author says, *Ove dovea per mille*, that is, for many, *esser ricetto*, that is, home and habitation."

Doubtless grammatically the words will bear this meaning. But evidently the idea in the author's mind, and which he wished to impress upon the reader's, was that of a waterfall plunging at a single leap down a high precipice. To this idea, the suggestion of buildings and inhabitants is wholly foreign, and adds neither force nor clearness. Whereas, to say that the river plunged at one bound over a precipice high enough for a thousand cascades, presents at once a vivid picture to the imagination, and I have interpreted the line accordingly, making the contrast between *una scesa* and *mille*. It should not be forgotten that, while some editions read *dovea*, others read *dovria*, and even *potria*.

106. This cord has puzzled the commentators exceedingly. Boccaccio, Volpi, and Venturi do not explain it. The anonymous author of the *Ottimo*, Benvenuto da Imola, Buti, Landino, Vellutello, and Daniello, all think it means fraud, which Dante had used in the pursuit of pleasure,—"the panther with the painted skin." Lombardi is of opinion that, "by girding himself with the Franciscan cord, he had endeavored to restrain his sensual appetites, indicated by the panther; and still wearing the cord as a Tertiary of the Order, he makes it serve here to deceive Geryon, and bring him up." Biagioli understands by it "the humility with which a man should approach Science, because it is she that humbles the proud." Fraticelli thinks it means vigilance; Tommaseo, "the good faith with which he hoped to win the Florentines, and now wishes to deal with their fraud, so that it may not harm him"; and Gabriele Rossetti says, "Dante flattered himself, acting as a sincere Ghibelline, that he should meet with good faith from his Guelf countrymen, and met instead with horrible fraud."

Dante elsewhere speaks of the cord in a good sense. In *Purgatorio*, VII. 114, Peter of Aragon is "girt with the cord of every virtue." In *Inferno*, XXVII. 92, it is mortification, "the cord that used to make those girt with it more meagre"; and in *Paradiso*, XI. 87, it is humility, "that family which had already girt the humble cord."

It will be remembered that St. Francis, the founder of the Cordeliers (the wearers of the cord), used to call his body *asino*, or ass, and to subdue it with the *capestro*, or halter. Thus the cord is made to symbolize the subjugation of the animal nature. This renders Lombardi's interpretation the most intelligible and satisfactory, though Virgil seems to have thrown the cord into the abyss simply because he had nothing else to throw, and not with the design of deceiving.

112. As a man does naturally in the act of throwing.

131. That Geryon, seeing the cord, ascends, expecting to find some *moine défroqué*, and carry him down, as Lombardi suggests, is hardly admissible; for that was not his office. The spirits were hurled down to their appointed places, as soon as Minos doomed them. *Inferno*, V. 15.

132. Even to a steadfast heart.

CANTO XVII

1. In this Canto is described the punishment of Usurers, as sinners against Nature and Art. See *Inferno*, XI. 109: —

> And since the usurer takes another way,
> Nature herself and in her follower
> Disdains he, for elsewhere he puts his hope.

The monster Geryon, here used as the symbol of Fraud, was born of Chrysaor and Callirrhoe, and is generally represented by the poets as having three bodies and three heads. He was in ancient times King of Hesperia or Spain, living on Erytheia, the Red Island of sunset, and was slain by Hercules, who drove away his beautiful oxen. The nimble fancy of Hawthorne thus depicts him in his *Wonder-Book*, p. 148: —

"But was it really and truly an old man? Certainly at first sight it looked very like one; but on closer inspection, it rather seemed to be some kind of a creature that lived in the sea. For on his legs and arms there were scales, such as fishes have; he was web-footed and web-fingered, after the fashion of a duck; and his long beard, being of a greenish tinge, had more the appearance of a tuft of sea-weed than of an ordinary beard. Have you never seen a stick of timber, that has been long tossed about by the waves, and has got all overgrown with barnacles, and at last, drifting ashore, seems to have been thrown up from the very deepest bottom of the sea? Well, the old man would have put you in mind of just such a wave-tost spar."

The three bodies and three heads, which old poetic fable has given to the monster Geryon, are interpreted by modern prose as meaning the three Balearic Islands, Majorca, Minorca, and Ivica, over which he reigned.

10. Ariosto, *Orlando Furioso*, XIV. 87, Rose's Tr., thus depicts Fraud: —

> With pleasing mien, grave walk, and decent vest,
> Fraud rolled her eyeballs humbly in her head;
> And such benign and modest speech possest,
> She might a Gabriel seem who *Ave* said.
> Foul was she and deformed in all the rest;
> But with a mantle, long and widely spread,
> Concealed her hideous parts; and evermore
> Beneath the stole a poisoned dagger wore.

The Gabriel saying *Ave* is from Dante, *Purgatory,* X. 40: —

> One would have sworn that he was saying *Ave*.

17. Tartars nor Turks, "who are most perfect masters therein," says Boccaccio, "as we can clearly see in Tartarian cloths, which truly are so skilfully woven, that no painter with his brush could equal, much less surpass them. The Tartars are . . ." And with this unfinished sentence close the Lectures upon Dante, begun by Giovanni Boccaccio on Sunday, August 9, 1373, in the church of San Stefano, in Florence. That there were some critics among his audience is apparent from this sonnet, which he addressed "to one who had censured his public Exposition of Dante." See D. G. Rossetti, *Early Italian Poets,* p. 447: —

> If Dante mourns, there wheresoe'er he be,
>> That such high fancies of a soul so proud
>> Should be laid open to the vulgar crowd,
>> (As, touching my Discourse, I'm told by thee,)
> This were my grievous pain; and certainly
>> My proper blame should not be disavowed;
>> Though hereof somewhat, I declare aloud,
>> Were due to others, not alone to me.
> False hopes, true poverty, and therewithal
>> The blinded judgment of a host of friends,
>> And their entreaties, made that I did thus.
> But of all this there is no gain at all
>> Unto the thankless souls with whose base ends
>> Nothing agrees that's great or generous.

18. Ovid, *Metamorph.* VI.: —

> One at the loom so excellently skilled,
> That to the Goddess she refused to yield.

57. Their love of gold still haunting them in the other world.
59. The arms of the Gianfigliacci of Florence.
63. The arms of the Ubbriachi of Florence.
64. The Scrovigni of Padua.
68. Vitaliano del Dente of Padua.
73. Giovanni Bujamonte, who seems to have had the ill-repute of being the greatest usurer of his day, called here in irony the "sovereign cavalier."

74. As the ass-driver did in the streets of Florence, when Dante beat him for singing his verses amiss. See Sacchetti, Nov. CXV.

78. Dante makes as short work with these usurers, as if he had been a curious traveller walking through the Ghetto of Rome, or the Judengasse of Frankfort.

107. Ovid, *Metamorph*. II., Addison's Tr.: —

> Half dead with sudden fear he dropt the reins;
> The horses felt 'em loose upon their manes,
> And, flying out through all the plains above,
> Ran uncontrolled where'er their fury drove;
> Rushed on the stars, and through a pathless way
> Of unknown regions hurried on the day.
> And now above, and now below they flew,
> And near the earth the burning chariot drew.
>
> .　　.　　.　　.　　.　　.
>
> At once from life and from the chariot driv'n,
> Th' ambitious boy fell thunder-struck from heav'n.
> The horses started with a sudden bound,
> And flung the reins and chariot to the ground:
> The studded harness from their necks they broke,
> Here fell a wheel, and here a silver spoke,
> Here were the beam and axle torn away;
> And, scattered o'er the earth, the shining fragments lay.
> The breathless Phaeton, with flaming hair,
> Shot from the chariot, like a falling star,
> That in a summer's ev'ning from the top
> Of heav'n drops down, or seems at least to drop;
> Till on the Po his blasted corpse was hurled,
> Far from his country, in the Western World.

108. The Milky Way. In Spanish *El camino de Santiago;* in the Northern Mythology the pathway of the ghosts going to Valhalla.

109. Ovid, *Metamorph*. VIII., Croxall's Tr.: —

> The soft'ning wax, that felt a nearer sun,
> Dissolv'd apace, and soon began to run.
> The youth in vain his melting pinions shakes,
> His feathers gone, no longer air he takes.
> O father, father, as he strove to cry,
> Down to the sea he tumbled from on high,
> And found his fate; yet still subsists by fame,

> Among those waters that retain his name.
> The father, now no more a father, cries,
> Ho, Icarus! where are you? as he flies:
> Where shall I seek my boy? he cries again,
> And saw his feathers scattered on the main.

127–131. Belamy, *Treatise upon Falconry,* p. 125. "Every hawk of the soar mounts by a circling course."

Sheridan Knowles, *Love,* Act I. Sc. 2.

> 'T is not by them he makes
> His ample wheels; mounts up, and up, and up
> In spiry rings, piercing the firmament,
> Till he o'ertops his prey, then gives his stoop,
> More fleet and sure than ever arrow sped.

136. Lucan, *Pharsal.* I.: —

> To him the Balearic sling is slow,
> And the shaft loiters from the Parthian bow.

CANTO XVIII

1. Here begins the third division of the *Inferno,* embracing the Eighth and Ninth Circles, in which the Fraudulent are punished.

> But because fraud is man's peculiar vice,
> More it displeases God; and so stand lowest
> The fraudulent, and greater dole assails them.

The Eighth Circle is called Malebolge, or Evil-budgets, and consists of ten concentric ditches, or *Bolge* of stone, with dikes between, and rough bridges running across them to the centre like the spokes of a wheel.

In the First Bolgia are punished Seducers, and in the Second, Flatterers.

2. Mr. Ruskin, *Modern Painters,* III. p. 237, says: —

"Our slates and granites are often of very lovely colors; but the Apennine limestone is so gray and toneless, that I know not any mountain district so utterly melancholy as those which are composed of this rock, when unwooded. Now, as far as I can discover from the internal evidence in his poem, nearly all Dante's mountain wanderings had been upon this ground. He had journeyed once or twice among the Alps, indeed, but seems to have been impressed chiefly by the road from Garda to Trent, and that along the Cornice, both of which are either upon those lime-stones, or a dark serpentine, which shows hardly any color till it is pol-ished. It is not ascertainable that he had ever seen rock scenery of the finely colored kind, aided by the Alpine mosses: I do not know the fall at Forlì (*Inferno,* XVI. 99), but every other scene to which he alludes is among these Apennine limestones; and when he wishes to give the idea of enormous mountain size, he names Tabernicch and Pietra-pana,— the one clearly chosen only for the sake of the last syllable of its name, in order to make a sound as of crackling ice, with the two sequent rhymes of the stanza,—and the other is an Apennine near Lucca.

"His idea, therefore, of rock color, founded on these experiences, is that of a dull or ashen gray, more or less stained by the brown of iron ochre, precisely as the Apennine limestones nearly always are; the gray being peculiarly cold and disagreeable. As we go down the very hill which stretches out from Pietra-pana towards Lucca, the stones laid by the roadside to mend it are of this ashen gray, with efflorescences of manganese and iron in the fissures. The whole of Malebolge is made of this rock, 'All wrought in stone of iron-colored grain.' "

29. The year of Jubilee 1300. Mr. Norton, in his *Notes of Travel and Study in Italy,* p. 255, thus describes it: —

"The beginning of the new century brought many pilgrims to the Papal city, and the Pope, seeing to what account the treasury of indul-gences possessed by the Church might now be turned, hit upon the plan of promising plenary indulgence to all who, during the year, should visit with fit dispositions the holy places of Rome. He accordingly, in the most solemn manner, proclaimed a year of Jubilee, to date from the Christmas of 1299, and appointed a similar celebration for each hundredth year thereafter. The report of the marvellous promise spread rapidly through Europe; and as the year advanced, pilgrims poured into Italy from re-mote as well as from neighboring lands. The roads leading to Rome were dusty with bands of travellers pressing forward to gain the unwonted in-dulgence. The Crusades had made travel familiar to men, and a journey to Rome seemed easy to those who had dreamed of the Farther East, of Constantinople, and Jerusalem. Giovanni Villani, who was among the pilgrims from Florence, declares that there were never less than two hundred thousand strangers at Rome during the year; and Guglielmo Ventura, the chronicler of Asti, reports the total number of pilgrims at not less than two millions. The picture which he draws of Rome during the Jubilee is a curious one. '*Mirandum est quod passim ibant viri et mulieres, qui anno illo Romœ fuerunt quo ego ibi fui et per dies* XV. *steti. De pance, vino, carnibus, piscibus, et avena, bonum mercatum ibi erat; fœnum carissimum ibi fuit; hospitia carissima; taliter quod lectus meus et equi mei super fœno et avena constabat mihi tornesium unum grossum. Exiens de Roma in Vigilia Nativitatis Christi, vidi turbam magnam, quam dinumerare nemo poterat; et fama erat inter Romanos, quod ibi fuerant plusquam vigenti centum millia virorum et mulierum. Pluries ego vidi ibi tam viros quam mulieres conculcatos sub pedibus aliorum; et etiam egomet in eodem periculo plures vices evasi. Papa innumerabilem pecuniam ab eisdem recepit, quia die ac nocte duo clerici stabant ad altare Sancti Pauli tenentes in eorum manibus rastellos, rastellantes pecuniam infinitam.'* To accommodate the throng of pilgrims, and to protect them as far as possible from the danger which Ventura feelingly describes, a barrier was erected along the middle of the bridge under the castle of Sant' Angelo, so that those going to St. Peter's and those coming from the church, passing on opposite sides, might not interfere with each other. It seems not unlikely that Dante himself was one of the crowd who thus crossed the old bridge, over whose arches, during this year, a flood of men was flowing almost as constantly as the river's flood ran through below."

31. The castle is the Castle of St. Angelo, and the mountain Monte Gianicolo. See Barlow, *Study of the Divine Comedy,* p. 126. Others say Monte Giordano.

50. "This Caccianimico," says Benvenuto da Imola, "was a Bolognese; a liberal, noble, pleasant, and very powerful man." Nevertheless he was so utterly corrupt as to sell his sister, the fair Ghisola, to the Marquis of Este.

51. In the original the word is *salse.* "In Bologna," says Benvenuto da Imola, "the name of *Salse* is given to a certain valley outside the city, and near to Santa Maria in Monte, into which the mortal remains of desperadoes, usurers, and other infamous persons are wont to be thrown. Hence I have sometimes heard boys in Bologna say to each other, by way of insult, 'Your father was thrown into the *Salse.*'"

    There is also a region in the Apennines between Modena and Lucca called the Salsa. Ferber in his *Travels in Italy,* Raspe's translation, p. 287, thus describes it: "The *Salsa di Modena* is a remarkable swamp in the hills near Sassuolo, where the new road is making over the Apennines to Massa di Carrara. It seems to be the exterior or upper covering of a volcano, which is said to sometimes throw out earth, pyrites, and large stones. A pole may be driven or forced into it to the depth of a fathom; being taken out, the water springs with violence from the hole which it had produced."

61. The two rivers between which Bologna is situated. In the Bolognese dialect *sipa* is used for *sì.*

72. They cease going round the circles as heretofore, and now go straight forward to the centre of the abyss.

86. For the story of Jason, Medea, and the Golden Fleece, see Ovid, *Metamorph.* VII. Also Chaucer, *Legende of Goode Women:* —

> Thou roote of fals loveres, duke Jason!
> Thou slye devourer and confusyon
> Of gentil wommen, gentil creatures!

92. When the women of Lemnos put to death all the male inhabitants of the island, Hypsipyle concealed her father Thoas, and spared his life. Apollonius Rhodius, *Argonautics,* II., Fawkes's Tr.: —

> Hypsipyle alone, illustrious maid,
> Spared her sire Thoas, who the sceptre swayed.

122. "Allessio Interminelli," says Benvenuto da Imola, "a soldier, a nobleman, and of gentle manners, was of Lucca, and from him descended that tyrant Castruccio who filled all Tuscany with fear, and was lord of Pisa, Lucca, and Pistoja, of whom Dante makes no mention, because he became illustrious after the author's death. Allessio took such delight in flattery, that he could not open his mouth without flattering. He besmeared everybody, even the lowest menials."

The *Ottimo* says, that in the dialect of Lucca the head "was facetiously called a pumpkin."

133. Thaïs, the famous courtesan of Athens. Terence, *The Eunuch,* Act III. Sc. 1: —

> "*Thraso.* Did Thaïs really return me many thanks?
>
> "*Gnatho.* Exceeding thanks.
>
> "*Thraso.* Was she delighted, say you?
>
> "*Gnatho.* Not so much, indeed, at the present itself, as because it was given by you; really, in right earnest, she does exult at that."

136. "The filthiness of some passages," exclaims Landor, *Pentameron,* p. 15, "would disgrace the drunkenest horse-dealer; and the names of such criminals are recorded by the poet, as would be forgotten by the hangman in six months."

Canto XIX

1. The Third Bolgia is devoted to the Simoniacs, so called from Simon Magus, the Sorcerer mentioned in *Acts* viii. 9, 18. See *Par.* XXX. Note 147.

Brunetto Latini touches lightly upon them in the *Tesoretto,* XXI. 259, on account of their high ecclesiastical dignity. His pupil is less reverential in this particular.

> Altri per simonia
> > Si getta in mala via,
> E Dio e' Santi offende
> > E vende le prebende,
> E Sante Sagramente,
> > E mette 'nfra la gente
> Assempri di mal fare.
> > Ma questo lascio stare,
> Chè tocca a ta' persone,
> > Che non è mia ragione
> Di dirne lungamente.

Chaucer, *Persones Tale,* speaks thus of Simony: —

"Certes simonie is cleped of Simon Magus, that wold have bought for temporel catel the yefte that God had yeven by the holy gost to Seint Peter, and to the Apostles: and therefore understood ye, that both he that selleth and he that byeth thinges spirituel ben called Simoniackes, be it by catel, be it by procuring, or by fleshly praier of his frendes, fleshly frendes, or spirituel frendes, fleshly in two manners, as by kinrede or other frendes, sothly, if they pray for him that is not worthy and able, it is simonie, if he take the benefice: and if he be worthy and able, ther is non."

5. Gower, *Confes. Amant.* I.: —

> A trompe with a sterne breth,
> Which was cleped the trompe of deth.
> . . . .
> He shall this dredfull trompe blowe
> To-fore his gate and make it knowe,
> How that the jugement is yive
> Of deth, which shall nought be foryive.

19. Lami, in his *Deliciæ Eruditorum,* makes a strange blunder in reference to this passage. He says: "Not long ago the baptismal font, which stood in the middle of Saint John's at Florence, was removed; and in the pavement may still be seen the octagonal shape of its ample outline. Dante says, that, when a boy, he fell into it and was near drowning; or rather he fell into one of the circular basins of water, which surrounded the principal

font." Upon this Arrivabeni, *Comento Storico*, p. 588, where I find this extract, remarks: "Not Dante, but Lami, staring at the moon, fell into the hole."

20. Dante's enemies had accused him of committing this act through impiety. He takes this occasion to vindicate himself.

33. Probably an allusion to the red stockings worn by the Popes.

50. Burying alive with the head downward and the feet in the air was the inhuman punishment of hired assassins, "according to justice and the municipal law in Florence," says the *Ottimo.* It was called *Propagginare,* to plant in the manner of vine-stocks.

Dante stood bowed down like the confessor called back by the criminal in order to delay the moment of his death.

52. *Isaiah* xiv. 9, 10: "Hell from beneath is moved for thee to meet thee at thy coming: it stirreth up the dead for thee, even all the chief ones of the earth; it hath raised up from their thrones all the kings of the nations. All they shall speak, and say unto thee, Art thou also become weak as we? art thou become like unto us?"

53. Benedetto Gaetani, Pope Boniface VIII. Gower, *Confes. Amant.* II., calls him

> Thou Boneface, thou proude clerke,
> Misleder of the papacie.

This is the Boniface who frightened Celestine from the papacy, and persecuted him to death after his resignation.

"The lovely Lady" is the Church. The fraud was his collusion with Charles II. of Naples. "He went to King Charles by night, secretly, and with few attendants," says Villani, VIII. ch. 6, "and said to him: 'King, thy Pope Celestine had the will and the power to serve thee in thy Sicilian wars, but did not know how: but if thou wilt contrive with thy friends the cardinals to have me elected Pope, I shall know how, and shall have the will and the power'; promising upon his faith and oath to aid him with all the power of the Church." Farther on he continues: "He was very magnanimous and lordly, and demanded great honor, and knew well how to maintain and advance the cause of the Church, and on account of his knowledge and power was much dreaded and feared. He was avaricious exceedingly in order to aggrandize the Church and his relations, not being over-scrupulous about gains, for he said that all things were lawful which were of the Church."

He was chosen Pope in 1294. "The inauguration of Boniface," says

Milman, *Latin Christ.*, Book IX. ch. 7, "was the most magnificent which Rome had ever beheld. In his procession to St. Peter's and back to the Lateran palace, where he was entertained, he rode not a humble ass, but a noble white horse, richly caparisoned: he had a crown on his head; the King of Naples held the bridle on one side, his son, the King of Hungary, on the other. The nobility of Rome, the Orsinis, the Colonnas, the Savellis, the Stefanesechi, the Annibaldi, who had not only welcomed him to Rome, but conferred on him the Senatorial dignity, followed in a body: the procession could hardly force its way through the masses of the kneeling people. In the midst, a furious hurricane burst over the city, and extinguished every lamp and torch in the church. A darker omen followed: a riot broke out among the populace, in which forty lives were lost. The day after, the Pope dined in public in the Lateran; the two Kings waited behind his chair."

Dante indulges towards him a fierce Ghibelline hatred, and assigns him his place of torment before he is dead. In Canto XXVII. 85, he calls him "the Prince of the new Pharisees"; and, after many other bitter allusions in various parts of the poem, puts into the mouth of St. Peter, *Par.* XXVII. 22, the terrible invective that makes the whole heavens red with anger.

> He who usurps upon the earth my place,
>> My place, my place, which vacant has become
>> Now in the presence of the Son of God,
> Has of my cemetery made a sewer
>> Of blood and fetor, whereat the Perverse,
>> Who fell from here, below there is appeased.

He died in 1303. See *Purg.* XX. Note 87.

70. Nicholas III., of the Orsini (the Bears) of Rome, chosen Pope in 1277. "He was the first Pope or one of the first," says Villani, VII. ch. 54, "in whose court simony was openly practised." On account of his many accomplishments he was surnamed *Il Compiuto.* Milman, *Lat. Christ.*, Book XI. ch. 4, says of him: "At length the election fell on John Gaetano, of the noble Roman house, the Orsini, a man of remarkable beauty of person and demeanor. His name, 'the Accomplished,' implied that in him met all the graces of the handsomest clerks in the world, but he was a man likewise of irreproachable morals, of vast ambition, and of great ability." He died in 1280.

83. The French Pope Clement V., elected in 1305, by the influence of Philip

the Fair of France, with sundry humiliating conditions. He transferred the Papal See from Rome to Avignon, where it remained for seventy-one years in what Italian writers call its "Babylonian captivity." He died in 1314, on his way to Bordeaux. "He had hardly crossed the Rhone," says Milman, *Lat. Christ.,* Book XII. ch. 5, "when he was seized with mortal sickness at Roquemaure. The Papal treasure was seized by his followers, especially his nephew; his remains were treated with such utter neglect, that the torches set fire to the catafalque under which he lay, not in state. His body, covered only with a single sheet, all that his rapacious retinue had left to shroud their forgotten master, was half burned . . . before alarm was raised. His ashes were borne back to Carpentras, and solemnly interred."

85. Jason, to whom Antiochus Epiphanes granted a "license to set him up a place for exercise, and for the training up of youth in the fashions of the heathen."

2 *Maccabees* iv. 13: "Now such was the height of Greek fashions, and increase of the heathenish manners, through the exceeding profaneness of Jason, that ungodly wretch, and not high priest, that the priests had no courage to serve any more at the altar, but, despising the temple, and neglecting the sacrifices, hastened to be partakers of the unlawful allowance in the place of exercise, after the game of Discus called them forth."

87. Philip the Fair of France. See Note 82. "He was one of the handsomest men in the world," says Villani, IX. 66, "and one of the largest in person, and well proportioned in every limb,—a wise and good man for a layman."

94. Matthias, chosen as an Apostle in the place of Judas.

99. According to Villani, VII. 54, Pope Nicholas III. wished to marry his niece to a nephew of Charles of Anjou, King of Sicily. To this alliance the King would not consent, saying: "Although he wears the red stockings, his lineage is not worthy to mingle with ours, and his power is not hereditary." This made the Pope indignant, and together with the bribes of John of Procida, led him to encourage the rebellion in Sicily, which broke out a year after the Pope's death in the "Sicilian Vespers," 1282.

107. The Church of Rome under Nicholas, Boniface, and Clement. *Revelation* xvii. 1–3: —

"And there came one of the seven angels which had the seven vials, and talked with me, saying unto me, Come hither; I will show unto thee the judgment of the great whore that sitteth upon many waters; with whom the kings of the earth have committed fornication, and the inhabitants of the earth have been made drunk with the wine of her fornication. So he carried me away in the Spirit into the wilderness; and I saw a woman sit upon a scarlet-colored beast, full of names of blasphemy, having seven heads and ten horns."

The seven heads are interpreted to mean the Seven Virtues, and the ten horns the Ten Commandments.

110. *Revelation* xvii. 12, 13: —

"And the ten horns which thou sawest are ten kings, . . . and shall give their power and strength unto the beast."

117. Gower, *Confes. Amant., Prologus:* —

> The patrimonie and the richesse
> Which to Silvester in pure almesse
> The firste Constantinus lefte.

Upon this supposed donation of immense domains by Constantine to the Pope, called the "Patrimony of St. Peter," Milman, *Lat. Christ.,* Book I. ch. 2, remarks: —

"Silvester has become a kind of hero of religious fable. But it was not so much the genuine mythical spirit which unconsciously transmutes history into legend; it was rather deliberate invention, with a specific aim and design, which, in direct defiance of history, accelerated the baptism of Constantine, and sanctified a porphyry vessel as appropriated to, or connected with, that holy use: and at a later period produced the monstrous fable of the Donation.

"But that with which Constantine actually did invest the Church, the right of holding landed property, and receiving it by bequest, was far more valuable to the Christian hierarchy, and not least to the Bishop of Rome, than a premature and prodigal endowment."

Canto XX

1. In the Fourth Bolgia are punished the Soothsayers: —

> Because they wished to see too far before them,
> Backward they look, and backward make their way.

9. Processions chanting prayers and supplications.

13. Ignaro in Spenser's *Faerie Queene,* I. viii. 31: —

> But very uncouth sight was to behold
> How he did fashion his untoward pace;

> For as he forward moved his footing old,
> So backward still was turned his wrinkled face.

29. In the Rubaijat of Omar Khayyám are these lines: —

> O Thou who burn'st in Heart for those who burn
> In Hell, whose fires thyself shall feed in turn,
> How long be crying, "Mercy on them, God!"
> Why, who art Thou to teach, and He to learn?

34. Amphiaraus was one of the seven kings against Thebes. Foreseeing his own fate, he concealed himself, to avoid going to the war; but his wife Eriphyle, bribed by a diamond necklace (as famous in ancient story as the Cardinal de Rohan's in modern), revealed his hiding-place, and he went to his doom with the others.

Æschylus, *The Seven against Thebes:* "I will tell of the sixth, a man most prudent and in valor the best, the seer, the mighty Amphiaraus. . . . And through his mouth he gives utterance to this speech. . . . 'I, for my part, in very truth shall fatten this soil, seer as I am, buried beneath a hostile earth.'"

Statius, *Thebaid,* VIII. 47, Lewis's Tr.: —

> Bought of my treacherous wife for cursed gold,
> And in the list of Argive chiefs enrolled,
> Resigned to fate I sought the Theban plain;
> Whence flock the shades that scarce thy realm contain;
> When, how my soul yet dreads! an earthquake came,
> Big with destruction, and my trembling frame,
> Rapt from the midst of gaping thousands, hurled
> To night eternal in thy nether world.

40. The Theban soothsayer. Ovid, *Met.,* III., Addison's Tr.: —

> It happen'd once, within a shady wood,
> Two twisted snakes he in conjunction view'd.
> When with his staff their slimy folds he broke,
> And lost his manhood at the fatal stroke.
> But, after seven revolving years, he view'd
> The self-same serpents in the self-same wood:
> "And if," says he, "such virtue in you lie,

That he who dares your slimy folds untie
Must change his kind, a second stroke I'll try."
Again he struck the snakes, and stood again
New-sex'd, and straight recovered into man.

· · · · · ·

                              When Juno fired,
More than so trivial an affair required,
Deprived him, in her fury, of his sight,
And left him groping round in sudden night.
But Jove (for so it is in heav'n decreed
That no one god repeal another's deed)
Irradiates all his soul with inward light,
And with the prophet's art relieves the want of sight.

45. His beard. The word "plumes" is used by old English writers in this
sense. Ford, *Lady's Trial:* —

                              Now the down
              Of softness is exchanged for plumes of age.

See also *Purg.* I. 42.

46. An Etrurian soothsayer. Lucan, *Pharsalia,* I., Rowe's Tr.: —

              Of these the chief, for learning famed and age,
              Aruns by name, a venerable sage,
              At Luna lived.

Ruskin, *Modern Painters,* III. p. 246, says: —
"But in no part of the poem do we find allusion to mountains in any
other than a stern light; nor the slightest evidence that Dante cared to
look at them. From that hill of San Miniato, whose steps he knew so well,
the eye commands, at the farther extremity of the Val d' Arno, the whole
purple range of the mountains of Carrara, peaked and mighty, seen al-
ways against the sunset light in silent outline, the chief forms that rule
the scene as twilight fades away. By this vision Dante seems to have been
wholly unmoved, and, but for Lucan's mention of Aruns at Luna, would
seemingly not have spoken of the Carrara hills in the whole course of his
poem: when he does allude to them, he speaks of their white marble, and
their command of stars and sea, but has evidently no regard for the hills
themselves. There is not a single phrase or syllable throughout the poem
which indicates such a regard. Ugolino, in his dream, seemed to himself
to be in the mountains, 'by cause of which the Pisan cannot see Lucca';

and it is impossible to look up from Pisa to that hoary slope without re-
membering the awe that there is in the passage; nevertheless it was as a
hunting-ground only that he remembered these hills. Adam of Brescia,
tormented with eternal thirst, remembers the hills of Romena, but only
for the sake of their sweet waters."

55. Manto, daughter of Tiresias, who fled from Thebes, the "City of Bac-
chus," when it became subject to the tyranny of Cleon.

63. Lake Benacus is now called the Lago di Garda. It is pleasantly alluded to
by Claudian in his *Old Man of Verona*, who has seen "the grove grow old
coeval with himself."

> Verona seems
> To him remoter than the swarthy Ind;
> He deems the Lake Benacus as the shore
> Of the Red Sea.

65. The Pennine Alps, or *Alpes Pœnæ*, watered by the brooklets flowing
into the Sarca, which is the principal tributary of Benaco.

69. The place where the three dioceses of Trent, Brescia, and Verona meet.

70. At the outlet of the lake.

77. *Æneid*, X.: —

> Mincius crowned with sea-green reeds.

Milton, *Lycidas:* —

> Smooth-sliding Mincius, crowned with vocal reeds.

82. Manto. Benvenuto da Imola says: "Virgin should here be rendered Vi-
rago."

93. *Æneid*, X.: "Ocnus, . . . son of the prophetic Manto, and of the Tuscan
river, who gave walls and the name of his mother to thee, O Mantua!"

95. Pinamonte dei Buonacossi, a bold, ambitious man, persuaded Alberto,
Count of Casalodi and Lord of Mantua, to banish to their estates the
chief nobles of the city, and then, stirring up a popular tumult, fell upon
the rest, laying waste their houses, and sending them into exile or to
prison, and thus greatly depopulating the city.

110. *Iliad*, I. 69: "And Calchas, the son of Thestor, arose, the best of augurs, a
man who knew the present, the future, and the past, and who had guided
the ships of the Achæans to Ilium, by that power of prophecy which
Phœbus Apollo gave him."

112. *Æneid*, II. 114: "In suspense we send Eurypylus to consult the oracle of

Apollo, and he brings back from the shrine these mournful words: 'O Greeks, ye appeased the winds with blood and a virgin slain, when first ye came to the Trojan shores; your return is to be sought by blood, and atonement made by a Grecian life.' "

Dante calls Virgil's poem a Tragedy, to mark its sustained and lofty style, in contrast with that of his own Comedy, of which he has already spoken once, Canto XVI. 138, and speaks again, Canto XXI. 2; as if he wished the reader to bear in mind that he is wearing the sock, and not the buskin.

116. "Michael Scott, the Magician," says Benvenuto da Imola, "practised divination at the court of Frederick II., and dedicated to him a book on natural history, which I have seen, and in which among other things he treats of Astrology, then deemed infallible. . . . It is said, moreover, that he foresaw his own death, but could not escape it. He had prognosticated that he should be killed by the falling of a small stone upon his head, and always wore an iron skull-cap under his hood, to prevent this disaster. But entering a church on the festival of Corpus Domini, he lowered his hood in sign of veneration, not of Christ, in whom he did not believe, but to deceive the common people, and a small stone fell from aloft on his bare head."

The reader will recall the midnight scene of the monk of St. Mary's and William of Deloraine in Scott's *Lay of the Last Minstrel,* Canto II.: —

> In these far climes it was my lot
> To meet the wondrous Michael Scott;
>   A wizard of such dreaded fame
> That when, in Salamanca's cave,
> Him listed his magic wand to wave,
>   The bells would ring in Notre Dame!
> Some of his skill he taught to me;
> And, warrior, I could say to thee
> The words that cleft Eildon hills in three,
> And bridled the Tweed with a curb of stone;
> But to speak them were a deadly sin;
> And for having but thought them my heart within,
> A treble penance must be done.

And the opening of the tomb to recover the Magic Book: —

> Before their eyes the wizard lay,
> As if he had not been dead a day.

His hoary beard in silver rolled,
He seemed some seventy winters old;
A palmer's amice wrapped him round,
With a wrought Spanish baldric bound,
　　Like a pilgrim from beyond the sea;
His left hand held his book of might;
A silver cross was in his right;
　　The lamp was placed beside his knee:
High and majestic was his look,
At which the fellest fiends had shook,
And all unruffled was his face: —
　　They trusted his soul had gotten grace.

　　　　See also *Appendix to the Lay of the Last Minstrel.*

118. Guido Bonatti, a tiler and astrologer of Forlì, who accompanied Guido di Montefeltro when he marched out of Forlì to attack the French "under the great oak." Villani, VII. 81, in a passage in which the *he* and *him* get a little entangled, says: "It is said that the Count of Montefeltro was guided by divination and the advice of Guido Bonatti (a tiler who had become an astrologer), or some other strategy, and he gave the orders; and in this enterprise he gave him the gonfalon and said, 'So long as a rag of it remains, wherever thou bearest it, thou shalt be victorious'; but I rather think his victories were owing to his own wits and his mastery in war."

Benvenuto da Imola reports the following anecdote of the same personages. "As the Count was standing one day in the large and beautiful square of Forlì, there came a rustic mountaineer and gave him a basket of pears. And when the Count said, 'Stay and sup with me,' the rustic answered, 'My Lord, I wish to go home before it rains; for infallibly there will be much rain to-day.' The Count, wondering at him, sent for Guido Bonatti, as a great astrologer, and said to him, 'Dost thou hear what this man says?' Guido answered, 'He does not know what he is saying; but wait a little.' Guido went to his study, and, having taken his astrolabe, observed the aspect of the heavens. And on returning he said that it was impossible it should rain that day. But the rustic obstinately affirming what he had said, Guido asked him, 'How dost thou know?' The rustic answered, 'Because to-day my ass, in coming out of the stable, shook his head and pricked up his ears, and whenever he does this, it is a certain sign that the weather will soon change.' Then Guido replied, 'Supposing this to be so, how dost thou know there will be much rain?' 'Because,' said he, 'my ass, with his ears pricked up, turned his head aside, and wheeled about more than usual.' Then, with the Count's leave, the rustic departed in haste, much fearing the rain, though the weather was very clear. And an hour afterwards, lo, it began to thunder, and there was a great downpouring of waters, like a deluge. Then Guido began to cry out, with great indignation and derision, 'Who has deluded me? Who has put me to shame?' And for a long time this was a great source of merriment among the people."

Asdente, a cobbler of Parma. "I think," says Benvenuto, "he must have had acuteness of mind, although illiterate; some having the gift of prophecy by the inspiration of Heaven." Dante mentions him in the *Convito*, IV. 16, where he says that, if nobility consisted in being known and talked about, "Asdente the shoemaker of Parma would be more noble than any of his fellow-citizens."

126. The moon setting in the sea west of Seville. In the Italian popular tradition to which Dante again alludes, *Par.* II. 51, the Man in the Moon is Cain with his Thorns. This belief seems to have been current too in England, *Midsummer Night's Dream*, III. 1: "Or else one must come in with a bush of thorns and a lantern, and say he comes to disfigure, or to present, the person of moon-shine." And again, V. 2: "The man should be put into the lantern. How is it else the man i' the moon? . . . All that I have to say is to tell you, that the lantern is the moon; I, the man in the moon; this thorn-bush, my thorn-bush; and this dog, my dog."

The time here indicated is an hour after sunrise on Saturday morning. See also Chaucer. *Testament of Creseide*. And again in *The Tempest*, II. 2: —

"*Stephano*. I was the man in the moon when time was."

"*Caliban*. I have seen thee in her, and I do adore thee: my mistress showed me thee, and thy dog, and thy bush."

In an old German popular tale given in Thorpe's *Yule-Tide Stories*, the legend is thus told: —

"Very, very long ago there was a man who went into the forest one Sunday to cut wood. Having chopped a large quantity of brushwood, he tied it together, thrust a stick through the bundle, threw it over his shoulder, and was on his way home, when there met him on the road a comely man, dressed in his Sunday clothes, who was going to church. He stopped, and, accosting the wood-cutter, said: 'Dost thou not know that on earth this is Sunday, the day on which God rested from his works, after he had created the world, with all the beasts of the field, and also man? Dost thou not know what is written in the fourth commandment, "Thou shalt keep holy the Sabbath day"?' The questioner was our Lord himself. The wood-cutter was hardened, and answered: 'Whether it is Sunday on earth or Monday (Moonday) in heaven, what does it concern thee or me?'

"'For this thou shalt ever bear thy bundle of wood,' said the Lord; 'and because the Sunday on earth is profaned by thee, thou shalt have an everlasting Monday, and stand in the moon,—a warning to all such as break the Sunday by work.'

"From that time the man stands in the moon, with his fagot of brushwood, and will stand there to all eternity."

CANTO XXI

1. The Fifth Bolgia, and the punishment of Barrators, or "Judges who take bribes for giving judgment."

2. Having spoken in the preceding Canto of Virgil's "lofty Tragedy," Dante here speaks of his own Comedy, as if to prepare the reader for the scenes which are to follow, and for which he apologizes in Canto XXII. 14, by repeating the proverb,

> In the church
> With saints, and in the tavern with the gluttons.

7. Of the Arsenal of Venice, Mr. Hillard thus speaks in his *Six Months in Italy*, I. 63: —

"No reader of Dante will fail to pay a visit to the Arsenal, from which, in order to illustrate the terrors of his Inferno, the great poet drew one of these striking and picturesque images, characteristic alike of the boldness and the power of his genius, which never hesitated to look for its materials among the homely details and familiar incidents of life. In his hands, the boiling of pitch and the calking of seams ascend to the dignity of poetry. Besides, it is the most impressive and characteristic spot in Venice. The Ducal Palace and the Church of St. Mark's are symbols of pride and power, but the strength of Venice resided here. Her whole history, for six hundred years, was here epitomized, and as she rose and sunk, the hum of labor here swelled and subsided. Here was the index-hand which marked the culmination and decline of her greatness. Built upon several small islands, which are united by a wall of two miles in circuit, its extent and completeness, decayed as it is, show what the naval power of Venice once was, as the disused armor of a giant enables us to measure his stature and strength. Near the entrance are four marble lions, brought by Morosini from the Peloponnesus in 1685, two of which are striking works of art. Of these two, one is by far the oldest thing in Venice, being not much younger than the battle of Marathon; and thus, from the height of twenty-three centuries, entitled to look down upon St. Mark's as the growth of yesterday. The other two are nondescript animals, of the class commonly called heraldic, and can be styled lions only by courtesy. In the armory are some very interesting objects, and none more so than the great standard of the Turkish admiral, made of crimson silk, taken at the battle of Lepanto, and which Cervantes may have grasped with his unwounded hand. A few fragments of some of the very galleys that were engaged in that memorable fight are also preserved here."

37. Malebranche, Evil-claws, a general name for the devils.

38. Santa Zita, the Patron Saint of Lucca, where the magistrates were called Elders, or Aldermen. In Florence they bore the name of Priors.

41. A Barrator, in Dante's use of the word, is to the State what a Simoniac is to the Church; one who sells justice, office, or employment.

Benvenuto says that Dante includes Bontura with the rest, "because he is speaking ironically, as who should say, 'Bontura is the greatest barrator of all.' For Bontura was an arch-barrator, who sagaciously led and managed the whole commune, and gave offices to whom he wished. He likewise excluded whom he wished."

46. Bent down in the attitude of one in prayer; therefore the demons mock him with the allusion to the *Santo Volto.*

48. The *Santo Volto,* or Holy Face, is a crucifix still preserved in the Cathedral of Lucca, and held in great veneration by the people. The tradition is that it is the work of Nicodemus, who sculptured it from memory.

See also Sacchetti, Nov. 73, in which a preacher mocks at the *Santo Volto* in the church of Santa Croce at Florence.

49. The Serchio flows near Lucca. Shelley, in a poem called *The Boat, on the Serchio,* describes it as a "torrent fierce,"

> Which fervid from its mountain source,
> Shallow, smooth, and strong, doth come;
> Swift as fire, tempestuously
> It sweeps into the affrighted sea.
> In morning's smile its eddies coil,
> Its billows sparkle, toss, and boil,
> Torturing all its quiet light
> Into columns fierce and bright.

63. Canto IX. 22: —

> True is it once before I here below
>   Was conjured by that pitiless Erictho,
>   Who summoned back the shades unto their bodies.

95. A fortified town on the Arno, in the Pisan territory. It was besieged by the troops of Florence and Lucca in 1289, and capitulated. As the garrison marched out under safeguard, they were terrified by the shouts of the crowd, crying: "Hang them! hang them!" In this crowd was Dante, "a youth of twenty-five," says Benvenuto da Imola.

110. Along the circular dike that separates one Bolgia from another.

111. This is a falsehood, as all the bridges over the next Bolgia are broken. See Canto XXIII. 140.

112. At the close of the preceding Canto the time is indicated as being an hour after sunrise. Five hours later would be noon, or the scriptural sixth hour, the hour of the Crucifixion. Dante understands St. Luke to say that Christ died at this hour. *Convito,* IV. 23: "Luke says that it was about the sixth hour when he died; that is, the culmination of the day." Add to the "one thousand and two hundred sixty-six years" the thirty-four of Christ's life on earth, and it gives the year 1300, the date of the Infernal Pilgrimage.

114. Broken by the earthquake at the time of the Crucifixion as the rock leading to the Circle of the Violent, Canto XII. 45: —

> And at that moment this primeval rock
> Both here and elsewhere made such overthrow.

As in the next Bolgia Hypocrites are punished, Dante couples them with the Violent, by making the shock of the earthquake more felt near them than elsewhere.

125. The next crag or bridge, traversing the dikes and ditches.

137. See Canto XVII. 75.

Canto XXII

1. The subject of the preceding Canto is continued in this.

5. Aretino, *Vita di Dante,* says that Dante in his youth was present at the "great and memorable battle, which befell at Campaldino, fighting valiantly on horseback in the front rank." It was there he saw the vaunt-couriers of the Aretines, who began the battle with such a vigorous charge, that they routed the Florentine cavalry, and drove them back upon the infantry.

7. Napier, *Florentine Hist.,* I. 214–217, gives this description of the *Carroccio* and the *Martinella* of the Florentines: —

"In order to give more dignity to the national army and form a rallying point for the troops, there had been established a great car, called the *Carroccio,* drawn by two beautiful oxen, which, carrying the Florentine standard, generally accompanied them into the field. This car was painted vermilion, the bullocks were covered with scarlet cloth, and the driver, a man of some consequence, was dressed in crimson, was exempt from taxation, and served without pay; these oxen were maintained at the public charge in a public hospital, and the white and red banner of the city was spread above the car between two lofty spars. Those taken at the battle of Monteapetro are still exhibited in Siena Cathedral as trophies of that fatal day.

"Macchiavelli erroneously places the adoption of the *Carroccio* by the Florentines at this epoch, but it was long before in use, and probably was copied from the Milanese, as soon as Florence became strong and independent enough to equip a national army. Eribert, Archbishop of Milan, seems to have been its author, for in the war between Conrad I. and that city, besides other arrangements for military organization, he is said to have finished by the invention of the *Carroccio*: it was a pious and not impolitic imitation of the ark as it was carried before the Israelites. This vehicle is described, and also represented in ancient paintings, as a four-wheeled oblong car, drawn by two, four, or six bullocks: the car was always red, and the bullocks, even to their hoofs, covered as above described, but with red or white according to the faction; the ensign staff was red, lofty, and tapering, and surmounted by a cross or golden bull: on this, between two white fringed veils, hung the national standard, and half-way down the mast, a crucifix. A platform ran out in front of the car, spacious enough for a few chosen men to defend it, while behind, on a corresponding space, the musicians with their military instruments gave spirit to the combat: mass was said on the *Carroccio* ere it quitted the city, the surgeons were stationed near it, and not unfrequently a chaplain also attended it to the field. The loss of the *Carroccio* was a great disgrace, and betokened utter discomfiture; it was given to the most distinguished knight, who had a public salary and wore conspicuous armor and a golden belt: the best troops were stationed round it, and there was frequently the hottest of the fight. . . .

"Besides the *Carroccio*, the Florentine army was accompanied by a great bell, called *Martinella*, or *Campana degli Asini*, which, for thirty days before hostilities began, tolled continually day and night from the arch of *Porta Santa Maria*, as a public declaration of war, and, as the ancient chronicle hath it, 'for greatness of mind, that the enemy might have full time to prepare himself.' At the same time also, the *Carroccio* was drawn from its place in the offices of San Giovanni by the most distinguished knights and noble vassals of the republic, and conducted in state to the

Mercato Nuovo, where it was placed upon the circular stone still existing, and remained there until the army took the field. Then also the *Martinella* was removed from its station to a wooden tower placed on another car, and with the *Carroccio* served to guide the troops by night and day. 'And with these two pomps, of the Carroccio and Campana,' says Malaspina, 'the pride of the old citizens, our ancestors, was ruled.'"

15. Equivalent to the proverb, "Do in Rome as the Romans do."

48. Giampolo, or Ciampolo, say all the commentators; but nothing more is known of him than his name, and what he tells us here of his history.

52. It is not very clear which King Tybalt is here meant, but it is probably King Tybalt IV., the crusader and poet, born 1201, died 1253. His poems have been published by Lévêque de la Ravallière, under the title of *Les Poésies du Roi de Navarre;* and in one of his songs (Chanson 53) he makes a clerk address him as the *Bons Rois Thiebaut.* Dante cites him two or three times in his *Volg. Eloq.,* and may have taken this expression from his song, as he does afterwards, Canto XXVIII. 135, *lo Re joves,* the *Re Giovane,* or Young King, from the songs of Bertrand de Born.

65. A Latian, that is to say, an Italian.

82. This Frate Gomita was a Sardinian in the employ of Nino de' Visconti, judge in the jurisdiction of Gallura, the "gentle Judge Nino" of *Purg.* VIII. 53. The frauds and peculations of the Friar brought him finally to the gallows. Gallura is the northeastern jurisdiction of the island.

88. Don Michael Zanche was Seneschal of King Enzo of Sardinia, a natural son of the Emperor Frederick II. Dante gives him the title of *Don,* still used in Sardinia for *Signore.* After the death of Enzo in prison at Bologna, in 1271, Don Michael won by fraud and flattery his widow Adelasia, and became himself Lord of Logodoro, the northwestern jurisdiction, adjoining that of Gallura.

The gossip between the Friar and the Seneschal, which is here described by Ciampolo, recalls the *Vision* of the Sardinian poet Araolla, a dialogue between himself and Gavino Sambigucci, written in the soft dialect of Logodoro, a mixture of Italian, Spanish, and Latin, and beginning: —

> Dulche, amara memoria de giornadas
> Fuggitivas cun doppia pena mia,
> Qui quanto plus l' istringo sunt passadas.

See Valery, *Voyages en Corse et en Sardaigne,* II. 410.

Canto XXIII

1. In this Sixth Bolgia the Hypocrites are punished.

> A painted people there below we found,
> Who went about with footsteps very slow,
> Weeping in their looks subdued and weary.

Chaucer, *Knightes Tale,* 2780: —

> In his colde grave
> Alone, withouten any compagnie.

And Gower, *Confes. Amant.:* —

> To muse in his philosophie
> Sole withouten compaignie.

4. The *Fables of Æsop,* by Sir Roger L'Estrange. IV.: "There fell out a bloody quarrel once betwixt the Frogs and the Mice, about the sovereignty of the Fenns; and whilst two of their champions were disputing it at swords point, down comes a kite powdering upon them in the interim, and gobbles up both together, to part the fray."

7. Both words signifying "now"; *mo,* from the Latin *modo;* and *issa,* from the Latin *ipsa;* meaning *ipsa hora.* "The Tuscans say *mo,*" remarks Benvenuto, "the Lombards *issa.*"

37. "When he is in a fright and hurry, and has a very steep place to go down, Virgil has to carry him altogether," says Mr. Ruskin. See Canto XII. Note 2.

63. Benvenuto speaks of the cloaks of the German monks as "ill-fitting and shapeless."

66. The leaden cloaks which Frederick put upon malefactors were straw in comparison. The Emperor Frederick II. is said to have punished traitors by wrapping them in lead, and throwing them into a heated caldron. I can find no historic authority for this. It rests only on tradition; and on the same authority the same punishment is said to have been inflicted in Scotland, and is thus described in the ballad of "Lord Soulis," Scott's *Minstrelsy of the Scottish Border,* IV. 256: —

> On a circle of stones they placed the pot,
> On a circle of stones but barely nine;

They heated it red and fiery hot,
  Till the burnished brass did glimmer and shine.

They roll'd him up in a sheet of lead,
  A sheet of lead for a funeral pall,
And plunged him into the caldron red,
  And melted him,—lead, and bones, and all.

We get also a glimpse of this punishment in Ducange, *Glos. Capa Plumbea,* where he cites the case in which one man tells another: "If our Holy Father the Pope knew the life you are leading, he would have you put to death in a cloak of lead."

67. *Comedy of Errors,* IV. 2: —

A devil in an everlasting garment hath him.

91. Bologna was renowned for its University; and the speaker, who was a Bolognese, is still mindful of his college.

95. Florence, the *bellissima e famosissima figlia di Roma,* as Dante calls it, *Convito,* I. 3.

103. An order of knighthood, established by Pope Urban IV. in 1261, under the title of "Knights of Santa Maria." The name *Frati Gaudenti,* or "Jovial Friars," was a nickname, because they lived in their own homes and were not bound by strict monastic rules. Napier, *Flor. Hist.* I. 269, says: —

"A short time before this a new order of religious knighthood under the name of *Frati Gaudenti* began in Italy: it was not bound by vows of celibacy, or any very severe regulations, but took the usual oaths to defend widows and orphans and make peace between man and man: the founder was a Bolognese gentleman, called Loderingo di Liandolo, who enjoyed a good reputation, and along with a brother of the same order, named Gatalano di Malavolti, one a Guelph and the other a Ghibelline, was now invited to Florence by Count Guido to execute conjointly the office of Podestà. It was intended by thus dividing the supreme authority between two magistrates of different politics, that one should correct the other, and justice be equally administered; more especially as, in conjunction with the people, they were allowed to elect a deliberative council of thirty-six citizens, belonging to the principal trades without distinction of party."

Farther on he says that these two *Frati Gaudenti* "forfeited all public confidence by their peculation and hypocrisy." And Villani, VII. 13: "Although they were of different parties, under cover of a false hypocrisy, they were of accord in seeking rather their own private gains than the common good."

108. A street in Florence, laid waste by the Guelfs.

113. *Hamlet*, I. 2: —

> Nor windy suspiration of forced breath.

115. Caiaphas, the High-Priest, who thought "expediency" the best thing.

121. Annas, father-in-law of Caiaphas.

134. The great outer circle surrounding this division of the Inferno.

142. He may have heard in the lectures of the University an exposition of *John* viii. 44: "Ye are of your father the devil, said the lusts of your father ye will do: he was a murderer from the beginning, and abode not in the truth, because there is no truth in him. When he speaketh a lie, he speaketh of his own; for he is a liar, and the father of it."

Canto XXIV

1. The Seventh Bolgia, in which Thieves are punished.

2. The sun enters Aquarius during the last half of January, when the Equinox is near, and the hoar-frost in the morning looks like snow on the fields, but soon evaporates. If Dante had been a monk of Monte Casino, illuminating a manuscript, he could not have made a more clerkly and scholastic flourish with his pen than this, nor have painted a more beautiful picture than that which follows. The mediæval poets are full of lovely descriptions of Spring, which seems to blossom and sing through all their verses; but none is more beautiful or suggestive than this, though serving only as an illustration.

21. In Canto I.

43. See what Mr. Ruskin says of Dante as "a notably bad climber," Canto XII. Note 2.

55. The ascent of the Mount of Purgatory.

73. The next circular dike, dividing the fosses.

86. This list of serpents is from Lucan, *Phars.* IX. 711, Rowe's Tr.: —

> Slimy Chelyders the parched earth distain
> And trace a reeking furrow on the plain.
> The spotted Cenchris, rich in various dyes,
> Shoots in a line, and forth directly flies.
>
> . . . .
>
> The Swimmer there the crystal stream pollutes,
> And swift thro' air the flying Javelin shoots.

· · · · ·

The Amphisbæna doubly armed appears,
At either end a threatening head she rears;
Raised on his active tail Pareas stands,
And as he passes, furrows up the sands.

Milton, *Parad. Lost,* X. 521: —

Dreadful was the din
Of hissing through the hall, thick-swarming snow
With complicated monsters head and tail,
Scorpion, and asp, and amphisbæna dire,
Cerastes horned, hydrus, and elops drear,
And dipsas.

Of the Phareas, Peter Comestor, *Hist. Scholast.,* Gloss of *Genesis* iii. 1, says: "And this he (Lucifer) did by means of the serpent; for then it was erect like man; being afterwards made prostrate by the curse; and it is said the *Phareas* walks erect even to this day."

Of the Amphisbæna, Brunetto Latini, *Tresor,* I. v. 140, says: "The Amphimenie is a kind of serpent which has two heads; one in its right place, and the other in the tail; and with each she can bite; and she runs swiftly, and her eyes shine like candles."

93. Without a hiding-place, or the heliotrope, a precious stone of great virtue against poisons, and supposed to render the wearer invisible. Upon this latter vulgar error is founded Boccaccio's comical story of Calandrino and his friends Bruno and Buffulmacco, *Decamerone,* Gior. VIII., Nov. 3.

107. Saint Clement of Rome, *Epist. ad Corinth.* § 25, Harwood's Tr., says of the phœnix: —

"Let us contemplate that wonderful phenomenon in the eastern countries, namely, about Arabia. There is a certain bird called a Phœnix. There is never but one of the species, and it lives five hundred years. When the time of its dissolution approaches, it forms a nest of frankincense, myrrh, and other aromatics. Into this, when its time is completed, it enters and dies. Its flesh, putrefying, generates a worm, which feeds on the carcass of its deceased parent until it puts forth wings; becoming then robust and vigorous, it takes the nest, where the bones of its predecessor lie, and carries it through the air from Arabia to Egypt, into a city called Heliopolis; and there, in open day, in the sight of all the inhabitants, it lays them upon the altar of the sun, and then returns. When the priests examine the records, they find that this phenomenon hath made its appearance precisely at the consummation of a period of five hundred years."

Stehelin, *Traditions of the Jews,* London, 1742, i. 219, gives the following legend of the phœnix: —

"The generation of the Bird Phœnix was preserved from him [the Angel of Death], because when Eve had eaten of the Fruit of the Tree of Knowledge, and given thereof to the Man, she envied the Rest of the Creatures and gave thereof to every one to eat: And seeing the Bird Phœnix, she said to him, Eat of This, whereof all other Birds have eaten. But he (the Phœnix) said to her, It sufficeth not that you have sinned against the holy and blessed God, and betray'd others to a Necessity of Dying; You must likewise come to tempt me. Wouldst thou, Eve, also beguile and delude me to break the Commandment of the holy and blessed God, and to eat and die? But I will not hearken to Thee. Then he rebuked Eve and all the Creatures. And presently a Voice was heard from Heaven, which said to Adam and Eve, You have not kept my Commandment, but have sinned. You have been with the bird Phœnix, to draw him to Sin likewise; but he consented not, but feared me, and regarded my Commandment, tho' I had not given it him. Wherefore I have decreed, that neither he nor his Seed shall taste of Death."

Sylvester's Du Bartas, *Weeks and Days.* Week 1, Day 5.

> Perchéd, therefore, upon a branch of palm,
> With incense, cassia, spikenard, myrrh, and balm,
> By break of day she builds, in narrow room,
> Her urn, her nest, her cradle, and her tomb.

See Salgues. *Des Erreurs et des Préjugés.* I. 242.

Brunetto Latini, *Tresor,* I. v. 164, says of the Phœnix: "He goeth to a good tree, savory and of good odor, and maketh a pile thereof, to which he setteth fire, and entereth straightway into it toward the rising of the sun."

And Milton, *Samson Agonistes,* 1697: —

> So Virtue, given for lost,
> Depressed and overthrown, as seemed,
> Like that self-begotten bird
> In the Arabian woods embost,
> That no second knows nor third,
> And lay erewhile a holocaust,

> From out her ashy womb now teemed,
> Revives, reflourishes, then vigorous most
> When most unactive deemed;
> And, though her body die, her fame survives
> A secular bird ages of lives.

114. Any obstruction, "such as the epilepsy," says Benvenuto. "Gouts and dropsies, catarrhs and oppilations," says Jeremy Taylor.

125. Vanni Fucci, who calls himself a mule, was a bastard son of Fuccio de' Lazzari. All the commentators paint him in the darkest colors. Dante had known him as "a man of blood and wrath," and seems to wonder he is here, and not in the circle of the Violent, or of the Irascible. But his great crime was the robbery of a sacristy. Benvenuto da Imola relates the story in detail. He speaks of him as a man of depraved life, many of whose misdeeds went unpunished, because he was of noble family. Being banished from Pistoia for his crimes, he returned to the city one night of the Carnival, and was in company with eighteen other revellers, among whom was Vanni della Nona, a notary; when, not content with their insipid diversions, he stole away with two companions to the church of San Giacomo, and, finding its custodians absent, or asleep with feasting and drinking, he entered the sacristy and robbed it of all its precious jewels. These he secreted in the house of the notary, which was close at hand, thinking that on account of his honest repute no suspicion would fall upon him. A certain Rampino was arrested for the theft, and put to the torture; when Vanni Fucci, having escaped to Monte Carelli, beyond the Florentine jurisdiction, sent a messenger to Rampino's father, confessing all the circumstances of the crime. Hereupon the notary was seized "on the first Monday in Lent, as he was going to a sermon in the church of the Minorite Friars," and was hanged for the theft, and Rampino set at liberty.

No one has a good word to say for Vanni Fucci, except the Canonico Crescimbeni, who, in the *Comentarj* to the *Istoria della Volg. Poesia*, II. ii. p. 99, counts him among the Italian Poets, and speaks of him as a man of great courage and gallantry, and a leader of the Neri party of Pistoia, in 1300. He smooths over Dante's invectives by remarking that Dante "makes not too honorable mention of him in the Comedy"; and quotes a sonnet of his, which is pathetic from its utter despair and self-reproach. The whole of this sonnet of Vanni Fucci runs as follows: —

> Shine not for me henceforth or Moon or Sun,
> Nor let the Earth bring forth its fruits for me;

> Let air, and fire, and water hostile be
> Forever more, and me let fortune shun!
> Let every star and planet, one by one,
>> Blast me, and brutify each sense! for see,
>> Ruined I cannot be more utterly,
> Nor suffer greater pain than I have done!
> Now will I live even as a savage wight,
>> Barefoot and naked, dwelling in desert place,
> And he who will may do me wrong and spite;
>> I cannot suffer any worse disgrace.
> April or May can bring me no delight,
>> Nor anything my sense of shame efface;
> Since I have lost the good I might have still,
> Through little wit, and not of my own will.

It is like the wail of a lost soul, and the same in tone as the words which Dante here puts into his mouth. Dante may have heard him utter similar self-accusations while living, and seen on his face the blush of shame, which covers it here.

143. The Neri were banished from Pistoia in 1301; the Bianchi, from Florence in 1302.

145. This vapor or lightning flash from Val di Magra is the Marquis Malaspina, and the "turbid clouds" are the banished Neri of Pistoia, whom he is to gather about him to defeat the Bianchi at Campo Piceno, the old battlefield of Catiline. As Dante was of the Bianchi party, this prophecy of impending disaster and overthrow could only give him pain. See Canto VI. Note 65.

Canto XXV

1. The subject of the preceding Canto is continued in this.

2. This vulgar gesture of contempt consists in thrusting the thumb between the first and middle fingers. It is the same that the ass-driver made at Dante in the street; Sacchetti, Nov. CXV.: "When he was a little way off, he turned round to Dante, and, thrusting out his tongue and making a fig at him with his hand, said, 'Take that.'"

   Villani, VI. 5, says: "On the Rock of Carmignano there was a tower seventy yards high, and upon it two marble arms, the hands of which were making the figs at Florence." Others say these hands were on a finger-post by the roadside.

   In the *Merry Wives of Windsor*, I. 3, Pistol says: —

> Convey, the wise it call;
> Steal, foh; a fico for the phrase!

And Martino, in Beaumont and Fletcher's *Widow,* V. 1: —

> The fig of everlasting obloquy
> Go with him.

10. Pistoia is supposed to have been founded by the soldiers of Catiline. Brunetto Latini, *Tresor,* I. i. 37, says: "They found Catiline at the foot of the mountains, and he had his army and his people in that place where is now the city of Pestoire. There was Catiline conquered in battle, and he and his were slain; also a great part of the Romans were killed. And on account of the pestilence of that great slaughter the city was called Pestoire."

   The Italian proverb says, *Pistoia la ferrigna,* iron Pistoia, or Pistoia the pitiless.

15. Capaneus, Canto XIV. 44.

19. See Canto XIII. Note 9.

25. Cacus was the classic Giant Despair, who had his cave in Mount Aventine, and stole a part of the herd of Geryon, which Hercules had brought to Italy. Virgil, *Æneid,* VIII., Dryden's Tr.: —

> See yon huge cavern, yawning wide around,
> Where still the shattered mountain spreads the ground:
> That spacious hold grim Cacus once possessed,
> Tremendous fiend! half human, half a beast:
> Deep, deep as hell, the dismal dungeon lay,
> Dark and impervious to the beams of day.
> With copious slaughter smoked the purple floor,
> Pale heads hung horrid on the lofty door,
> Dreadful to view! and dropped with crimson gore.

28. Dante makes a Centaur of Cacus, and separates him from the others because he was fraudulent as well as violent. Virgil calls him only a monster, a half-man, *Semihominis Caci facies.*

35. Agnello Brunelleschi, Buoso degli Abati, and Puccio Sciancato.

38. The story of Cacus, which Virgil was telling.

43. Cianfa Donati, a Florentine nobleman. He appears immediately as a serpent with six feet, and fastens upon Agnello Brunelleschi.

65. Some commentators contend that in this line *papiro* does not mean paper,

but a lamp-wick made of papyrus. This destroys the beauty and aptness of the image, and rather degrades

> The leaf of the reed,
> Which has grown through the clefts in the ruins of ages.

73. These four lists, or hands, are the fore feet of the serpent and the arms of Agnello.

76. Shakespeare, in the *Additional Poems to Chester's Love's Martyrs*, Knight's Shakespeare, VII. 193, speaks of "Two distincts, division none"; and continues: —

> Property was thus appalled
> That the self was not the same,
> Single nature's double name
> Neither two nor one was called.
>
> Reason, in itself confounded,
> Saw division grow together;
> To themselves yet either neither,
> Simple were so well compounded.

83. This black serpent is Guercio Cavalcanti, who changes form with Buoso degli Abati.

95. Lucan, *Phars.* IX., Rowe's Tr.: —

> But soon a fate more sad with new surprise
> From the first object turns their wondering eyes.
> Wretched Sabellus by a Seps was stung:
> Fixed on his leg with deadly teeth it hung.
> Sudden the soldier shook it from the wound,
> Transfixed and nailed it to the barren ground.
> Of all the dire, destructive serpent race,
> None have so much of death, though none are less.
> For straight around the part the skin withdrew,
> The flesh and shrinking sinews backward flew,
> And left the naked bones exposed to view.
> The spreading poisons all the parts confound,
> And the whole body sinks within the wound.
>
> . . . .
>
> Small relics of the mouldering mass were left,
> At once of substance as of form bereft;

Dissolved, the whole in liquid poison ran,
And to a nauseous puddle shrunk the man.

.   .   .   .   .

So snows dissolved by southern breezes run,
So melts the wax before the noonday sun.
Nor ends the wonder here; though flames are known
To waste the flesh, yet still they spare the bone:
Here none were left, no least remains were seen,
No marks to show that once the man had been.

.   .   .   .   .

A fate of different kind Nasidius found,—
A burning Prester gave the deadly wound,
And straight a sudden flame began to spread,
And paint his visage with a glowing red.
With swift expansion swells the bloated skin,—
Naught but an undistinguished mass is seen,
While the fair human form lies lost within;
The puffy poison spreads and heaves around,
Till all the man is in the monster drowned.
No more the steely plate his breast can stay,
But yields, and gives the bursting poison way.
Not waters so, when fire the rage supplies,
Bubbling on heaps, in boiling caldrons rise;
Nor swells the stretching canvas half so fast,
When the sails gather all the driving blast,
Strain the tough yards, and bow the lofty mast.
The various parts no longer now are known,
One headless, formless heap remains alone.

97. Ovid, *Metamorph.* IV., Eusden's Tr.: —

"Come, my Harmonia, come, thy face recline
Down to my face: still touch what still is mine.
O let these hands, while hands, be gently pressed,
While yet the serpent has not all possessed."
More he had spoke, but strove to speak in vain,—
The forky tongue refused to tell his pain,
And learned in hissings only to complain.

Then shrieked Harmonia, "Stay, my Cadmus, stay:
Glide not in such a monstrous shape away!
Destruction, like impetuous waves, rolls on.
Where are thy feet, thy legs, thy shoulders, gone?

> Changed is thy visage, changed is all thy frame,—
> Cadmus is only Cadmus now in name.
> Ye Gods! my Cadmus to himself restore,
> Or me like him transform,—I ask no more."

And V., Maynwaring's Tr.: —

> The God so near, a chilly sweet possessed
> My fainting limbs, at every pore expressed;
> My strength distilled in drops, my hair in dew,
> My form was changed, and all my substance new;
> Each motion was a stream, and my whole frame
> Turned to a fount, which still preserves my name.

See also Shelley's *Arethusa:* —

> Arethusa arose
> From her couch of snows
> In the Acroceraunian mountains,—
> From cloud and from crag
> With many a jag
> Shepherding her bright fountains.
> She leapt down the rocks,
> With her rainbow locks
> Streaming among the streams;
> Her steps paved with green
> The downward ravine
> Which slopes to the western gleams;
> And gliding and springing,
> She went, ever singing,
> In murmurs as soft as sleep.
> The Earth seemed to love her,
> And Heaven smiled above her,
> As she lingered towards the deep.

134. Some editions read *la penna*, the pen, instead of *la lingua*, the tongue.
151. Gaville was a village in the Valdarno, where Guercio Cavalcanti was murdered. The family took vengeance upon the inhabitants in the old Italian style, thus causing Gaville to lament the murder.

CANTO XXVI

1. The Eighth Bolgia, in which Fraudulent Counsellors are punished.

4. Of these five Florentine nobles, Cianfa Donati, Agnello Brunelleschi, Buoso degli Abati, Puccio Sciancato, and Guercio Cavalcanti, nothing is known but what Dante tells us. Perhaps that is enough.

7. See *Purg.* IX. 13: —

> Just at the hour when her sad lay begins
>> The little swallow, near unto the morning,
>> Perchance in memory of her former woes,
> And when the mind of man, a wanderer
>> More from the flesh, and less by thought imprisoned,
>> Almost prophetic in its visions is.

9. The disasters soon to befall Florence, and in which even the neighboring town of Prato would rejoice, to mention no others. These disasters were the fall of the wooden bridge of Carraia, with a crowd upon it, witnessing a Miracle Play on the Arno; the strife of the Bianchi and Neri; and the great fire of 1304. See Villani, VIII. 70, 71. Napier, *Florentine History,* I. 394, gives this account: —

"Battles first began between the Cerchi and Giugni at their houses in the Via del Garbo; they fought day and night, and with the aid of the Cavalcanti and Antellesi the former subdued all that quarter: a thousand rural adherents strengthened their bands, and that day might have seen the Neri's destruction if an unforeseen disaster had not turned the scale. A certain dissolute priest, called Neri Abati, prior of San Piero Scheraggio, false to his family and in concert with the Black chiefs, consented to set fire to the dwellings of his own kinsmen in Orto-san-Michele; the flames, assisted by faction, spread rapidly over the richest and most crowded part of Florence: shops, warehouses, towers, private dwellings and palaces, from the old to the new market-place, from *Vacchereccia* to *Porta Santa Maria* and the *Ponte Vecchio,* all was one broad sheet of fire: more than nineteen hundred houses were consumed; plunder and devastation revelled unchecked amongst the flames, whole races were reduced in one moment to beggary, and vast magazines of the richest merchandise were destroyed. The Cavalcanti, one of the most opulent families in Florence, beheld their whole property consumed, and lost all courage; they made no attempt to save it, and, after almost gaining possession of the city, were finally overcome by the opposite faction."

10. *Macbeth*, I. 7: —

> If it were done when 't is done, then 't were well
> It were done quickly.

23. See *Parad.* XII. 112: —

> O glorious stars! O light impregnated
> With mighty virtue, from which I acknowledge
> All of my genius, whatsoe'er it be.

24. I may not balk or deprive myself of this good.

34. The Prophet Elisha, 2 *Kings* ii. 23: —

"And he went up from thence unto Bethel; and as he was going up by the way, there came forth little children out of the city, and mocked him, and said unto him, Go up, thou bald head; go up, thou bald head. And he turned back, and looked on them, and cursed them in the name of the Lord: and there came forth two she-bears out of the wood, and tare forty and two children of them."

35. 2 *Kings* ii. 11: —

"And it came to pass, as they still went on and talked, that, behold, there appeared a chariot of fire, and horses of fire, and parted them both asunder; and Elijah went up by a whirlwind into heaven."

54. These two sons of Œdipus, Eteocles and Polynices, were so hostile to each other, that, when after death their bodies were burned on the same funeral pile, the flames swayed apart, and the ashes separated. Statius, *Thebaid*, XII. 430, Lewis's Tr.: —

> Again behold the brothers! When the fire
> Pervades their limbs in many a curling spire,
> The vast hill trembles, and the intruder's corse
> Is driven from the pile with sudden force.
> The flames, dividing at the point, ascend,
> And at each other adverse rays extend.
> Thus when the ruler of the infernal state,
> Pale-visaged Dis, commits to stern debate
> The sister-fiends, their brands, held forth to fight,
> Now clash, then part, and shed a transient light.

56. The most cunning of the Greeks at the siege of Troy, now united in their punishment, as before in warlike wrath.

59. As Troy was overcome by the fraud of the wooden horse, it was in a poetic sense the gateway by which Æneas went forth to establish the Roman empire in Italy.

62. Deidamia was a daughter of Lycomedes of Scyros, at whose court Ulysses found Achilles, disguised in woman's attire, and enticed him away to the siege of Troy, telling him that, according to the oracle, the city could not be taken without him, but not telling him that, according to the same oracle, he would lose his life there.

63. Ulysses and Diomed together stole the Palladium, or statue of Pallas, at Troy, the safeguard and protection of the city.

75. The Greeks scorned all other nations as "outside barbarians." Even Virgil, a Latin, has to plead with Ulysses the merit of having praised him in the Æneid.

108. The Pillars of Hercules at the straits of Gibraltar; Abyla on the African shore, and Gibraltar on the Spanish; in which the popular mind has lost its faith, except as symbolized in the columns on the Spanish dollar, with the legend, *Plus ultra.*

Brunetto Latini, *Tesor.* IX. 119: —

> Appresso questo mare,
> Vidi diritto stare
> Gran colonne, le quali
> Vi mise per segnali
> Ercules il potente,
> Per mostrare alla gente
> Che loco sia finata
> La terra e terminata.

125. *Odyssey,* XI. 155: "Well-fitted oars, which are also wings to ships."

127. Humboldt, *Personal Narrative,* II. 19, Miss Williams's Tr., has this passage: "From the time we entered the torrid zone, we were never wearied with admiring, every night, the beauty of the Southern sky, which, as we advanced toward the south, opened new constellations to our view. We feel an indescribable sensation, when, on approaching the equator, and particularly on passing from one hemisphere to the other, we see those stars, which we have contemplated from our infancy, progressively sink, and finally disappear. Nothing awakens in the traveller a livelier remembrance of the immense distance by which he is separated from his country, than the aspect of an unknown firmament. The grouping of the stars of the first magnitude, some scattered nebulæ, rivalling in splendor the milky way, and tracks of space remarkable for their extreme blackness, give a

particular physiognomy to the Southern sky. This sight fills with admiration even those who, uninstructed in the branches of accurate science, feel the same emotion of delight in the contemplation of the heavenly vault, as in the view of a beautiful landscape, or a majestic site. A traveller has no need of being a botanist, to recognize the torrid zone on the mere aspect of its vegetation; and without having acquired any notions of astronomy, without any acquaintance with the celestial charts of Flamstead and De la Caille, he feels he is not in Europe, when he sees the immense constellation of the Ship, or the phosphorescent clouds of Magellan, arise on the horizon."

142. Compare Tennyson's *Ulysses:* ——

> There lies the port; the vessel puffs her sail:
> There gloom the dark broad seas. My mariners,
> Souls that have toiled, and wrought, and thought with me,——
> That ever with a frolic welcome took
> The thunder and the sunshine, and opposed
> Free hearts, free foreheads,——you and I are old;
> Old age hath yet his honor and his toil;
> Death closes all: but something ere the end,
> Some work of noble note, may yet be done,
> Not unbecoming men that strove with Gods.
> The lights begin to twinkle from the rocks:
> The long day wanes: the slow moon climbs: the deep
> Moans round with many voices. Come, my friends,
> 'Tis not too late to seek a newer world.
> Push off, and, sitting well in order, smite
> The sounding furrows; for my purpose holds
> To sail beyond the sunset, and the baths
> Of all the western stars, until I die.
> It may be that the gulfs will wash us down:
> It may be we shall touch the Happy Isles,
> And see the great Achilles, whom we knew.
> Though much is taken, much abides; and though
> We are not now that strength which in old days
> Moved earth and heaven, that which we are, we are;
> One equal temper of heroic hearts,
> Made weak by time and fate, but strong in will
> To strive, to seek, to find, and not to yield.

CANTO XXVII

1. The subject of the preceding Canto is continued in this.

7. The story of the Brazen Bull of Perillus is thus told in the *Gesta Romanorum,* Tale 48, Swan's Tr.: —

"Dionysius records, that when Perillus desired to become an artificer of Phalaris, a cruel and tyrannical king who depopulated the kingdom, and was guilty of many dreadful excesses, he presented to him, already too well skilled in cruelty, a brazen bull, which he had just constructed. In one of its sides there was a secret door, by which those who were sentenced should enter and be burnt to death. The idea was, that the sounds produced by the agony of the sufferer confined within should resemble the roaring of a bull; and thus, while nothing human struck the ear, the mind should be unimpressed by a feeling of mercy. The king highly applauded the invention, and said, 'Friend, the value of thy industry is yet untried: more cruel even than the people account me, thou thyself shalt be the first victim.'"

Also in Gower, *Confes. Amant.,* VII.: —

> He had of counseil many one,
> Among the whiche there was one,
> By name which Berillus hight.
> And he bethought him how he might
> Unto the tirant do liking.
> And of his own ymagining
> Let forge and make a bulle of bras,
> And on the side cast there was
> A dore, where a man may inne,
> Whan he his peine shall beginne
> Through fire, which that men put under
> And all this did he for a wonder,
> That when a man for peine cride,
> The bull of bras, which gapeth wide,
> It shulde seme, as though it were
> A bellewing in a mannes ere
> And nought the crieng of a man.
> But he, which alle sleightes can,
> The devil, that lith in helle fast,
> Him that it cast hath overcast,
> That for a trespas, which he dede,
> He was put in the same stede.

> And was himself the first of alle,
> Which was into that peine falle
> That he for other men ordeigneth.

21. Virgil being a Lombard, Dante suggests that, in giving Ulysses and Diomed license to depart, he had used the Lombard dialect, saying, *"Issa t' en va."* See Canto XXIII. Note 7.
28. The inhabitants of the province of Romagna, of which Ravenna is the capital.
29. It is the spirit of Guido da Montefeltro that speaks. The city of Montefeltro lies between Urbino and that part of the Apennines in which the Tiber rises. Count Guido was a famous warrior, and one of the Great Ghibelline leaders. He tells his own story sufficiently in detail in what follows.
40. Lord Byron, *Don Juan,* III. 105, gives this description of Ravenna, with an allusion to Boccaccio's Tale, versified by Dryden under the title of *Theodore and Honoria:* —

> Sweet hour of twilight!—in the solitude
>   Of the pine forest, and the silent shore
> Which bounds Ravenna's immemorial wood,
>   Rooted where once the Adrian wave flow'd o'er,
> To where the last Cæsarean fortress stood.
>   Ever-green forest! which Boccaccio's lore
> And Dryden's lay made haunted ground to me,
> How have I loved the twilight hour and thee!
>
> The shrill cicalas, people of the pine,
>   Making their summer lives one ceaseless song,
> Were the sole echoes, save my steed's and mine,
>   And vesper-bells that rose the boughs along;
> The spectre huntsman of Onesti's line,
>   His hell-dogs, and their chase, and the fair throng
> Which learned from this example not to fly
> From a true lover, shadowed my mind's eye.

Dryden's *Theodore and Honoria* begins with these words: —

> Of all the cities in Romanian lands,
> The chief, and most renowned, Ravenna stands,
> Adorned in ancient times with arms and arts,
> And rich inhabitants, with generous hearts.

It was at Ravenna that Dante passed the last years of his life, and there he died and was buried.

41. The arms of Guido da Polenta, Lord of Ravenna, Dante's friend, and father (or nephew) of Francesca da Rimini, were an eagle half white in a field of azure, and half red in a field of gold. Cervia is a small town some twelve miles from Ravenna.

43. The city of Forlì, where Guido da Montefeltro defeated and slaughtered the French in 1282. See Canto XX. Note 118.

45. A Green Lion was the coat of arms of the Ordelaffi, then Lords of Forlì.

46. Malatesta, father and son, tyrants of Rimini, who murdered Montagna, a Ghibelline leader. Verrucchio was their castle, near the city. Of this family were the husband and lover of Francesca. Dante calls them mastiffs, because of their fierceness, making "wimbles of their teeth" in tearing and devouring.

49. The cities of Faenza on the Lamone, and Imola on the Santerno. They were ruled by Mainardo, surnamed "the Devil," whose coat of arms was a lion azure in a white field.

52. The city of Cesena.

67. Milton, *Parad. Lost*, III. 479: —

> Dying put on the weeds of Dominic,
> Or in Franciscan think to pass disguised.

70. Boniface VIII., who in line 85 is called "the Prince of the new Pharisees."

81. Dante, *Convito*, IV. 28, quoting Cicero, says: "Natural death is as it were a haven and rest to us after long navigation. And the noble soul is like a good mariner; for he, when he draws near the port, lowers his sails, and enters it softly with feeble steerage."

86. This Papal war, which was waged against Christians, and not against pagan Saracens, nor unbelieving Jews, nor against the renegades who had helped them at the siege of Acre, or given them aid and comfort by traffic, is thus described by Mr. Norton, *Travel and Study in Italy*, p. 263: —

"This 'war near the Lateran' was a war with the great family of Colonna. Two of the house were Cardinals. They had been deceived in the election, and were rebellious under the rule of Boniface. The Cardinals of the great Ghibelline house took no pains to conceal their ill-will toward the Guelf Pope. Boniface, indeed, accused them of plotting with his enemies for his overthrow. The Colonnas, finding Rome unsafe, had withdrawn to their strong town of Palestrina, whence they could issue forth at will for plunder, and where they could give shelter to those who shared in their hostility toward the Pope. On the other hand, Boniface, not trusting himself in Rome, withdrew to the secure height of Orvieto, and thence, on the 14th of December, 1297, issued a terrible bull for a crusade against them, granting plenary indulgence to all, (such was the Christian temper of the times, and so literally were the violent seizing upon the kingdom of Heaven,) granting plenary indulgence to all who would take up arms against these rebellious sons of the Church and march against their chief stronghold, their *'alto seggio'* of Palestrina. They and their adherents had already been excommunicated and put under the ban of the Church; they had been stripped of all dignities and privileges; their property had been confiscated; and they were now by this bull placed in the position of enemies, not of the Pope alone, but of the Church Universal. Troops gathered against them from all quarters of Papal Italy. Their lands were ravaged, and they themselves shut up within their stronghold; but for a long time they held out in their ancient high-walled mountain town. It was to gain Palestrina that Boniface 'had war near the Lateran.' The great church and palace of the Lateran, standing on the summit of the Cœlian Hill, close to the city wall, overlooks the Campagna, which, in broken levels of brown and green and purple fields, reaches to the base of the encircling mountains. Twenty miles away, crowning the top and clinging to the side of one of the last heights of the Sabine range, are the gray walls and roofs of Palestrina. It was a far more conspicuous place at the close of the thirteenth century than it is now; for the great columns of the famous temple of Fortune still rose above the town, and the ancient citadel kept watch over it from its high rock. At length, in September, 1298, the Colonnas, reduced to the hardest extremities, became ready for peace. Boniface promised largely. The two Cardinals presented themselves before him at Rieti, in coarse brown dresses, and with ropes around their necks, in token of their repentance and submission. The Pope gave them not only pardon and absolution, but hope of being restored to their titles and possessions. This was the *'lunga promessa con l'attender corto';* for, while the Colonnas were retained near him, and these deceptive hopes held out to them, Boniface sent the Bishop of Orvieto to take possession of Palestrina, and to destroy it utterly, leaving only the church to stand as a monument above its ruins. The work was done thoroughly; —a plough was drawn across the site of the unhappy town, and salt scattered in the furrow, that the land might thenceforth be desolate. The inhabitants were removed from the mountain to the plain, and there forced to build new homes for themselves, which, in their turn, two years afterwards, were thrown down and burned by order of the implacable Pope. This last piece of malignity was accomplished in 1300, the year of the Jubilee, the year in which Dante was in Rome, and in which he saw Guy of Montefeltro, the counsellor of Boniface in deceit, burning in Hell."

94. The story of Sylvester and Constantine is one of the legends of the *Legenda Aurea*. The part of it relating to the Emperor's baptism is thus condensed by Mrs. Jameson in her *Sacred and Legendary Art*, II. 313: —

"Sylvester was born at Rome of virtuous parents; and at a time when Constantine was still in the darkness of idolatry and persecuted the Christians, Sylvester, who had been elected Bishop of Rome, fled from the persecution, and dwelt for some time in a cavern, near the summit of Monte Calvo. While he lay there concealed, the Emperor was attacked by a horrible leprosy: and having called to him the priests of his false gods, they advised that he should bathe himself in a bath of children's blood, and three thousand children were collected for this purpose. And as he proceeded in his chariot to the place where the bath was to be prepared, the mothers of these children threw themselves in his way with dishevelled hair, weeping, and crying aloud for mercy. Then Constantine was moved to tears, and he ordered his chariot to stop, and he said to his nobles and to his attendants who were around him, 'Far better is it that I should die, than cause the death of these innocents!' And then he commanded that the children should be restored to their mothers with great gifts, in recompense of what they had suffered; so they went away full of joy and gratitude, and the Emperor returned to his palace.

"On that same night, as he lay asleep, St. Peter and St. Paul appeared at his bedside: and they stretched their hands over him and said, 'Because thou hast feared to spill the innocent blood, Jesus Christ has sent us to bring thee good counsel. Send to Sylvester, who lies hidden among the mountains, and he shall show thee the pool in which, having washed three times, thou shalt be clean from thy leprosy; and henceforth thou shalt adore the God of the Christians, and thou shalt cease to persecute and to oppress them.' Then Constantine, awaking from this vision, sent his soldiers in search of Sylvester. And when they took him, he supposed that it was to lead him to death; nevertheless he went cheerfully: and when he appeared before the Emperor, Constantine arose and saluted him, and said, 'I would know of thee who are those two gods who appeared to me in the visions of the night?' And Sylvester replied, 'They were not gods, but the apostles of the Lord Jesus Christ.' Then Constantine desired that he would show him the effigies of these two apostles; and Sylvester sent for two pictures of St. Peter and St. Paul, which were in the possession of certain pious Christians. Constantine, having beheld them, saw that they were the same who had appeared to him in his dream. Then Sylvester baptized him, and he came out of the font cured of his malady."

Gower also, *Confes. Amantis*, II., tells the story at length:

> And in the while it was begunne
> A light, as though it were a sunne,
> Fro heven into the place come
> Where that he toke his christendome,
> And ever amonge the holy tales
> Lich as they weren fisches scales
> They fellen from him now and efte,
> Till that there was nothing belefte
> Of all this grete maladie.

96. Montefeltro was in the Franciscan monastery at Assisi.
102. See Note 86 of this Canto. Dante calls the town Penestrino from its Latin name Præneste.
105. Pope Celestine V., who made "the great refusal," or abdication of the papacy. See Canto III. Note 59.
118. Gower, *Confes. Amantis*, II.: —

> For shrifte stant of no value
> To him, that woll him nought vertue,
> To leve of vice the folie,
> For worde is wind, but the maistrie
> Is, that a man himself defende
> Of thing whiche is nought to commende,
> Whereof ben fewe now a day.

CANTO XXVIII

1. The Ninth Bolgia, in which are punished the Schismatics, and

> Where is paid the fee
> By those who sowing discord win their burden;

a burden difficult to describe even with untrammelled words, or in plain prose, free from the fetters of rhyme.

9. Apulia, or La Puglia, is in the southeastern part of Italy, "between the spur and the heel of the boot."

10. The people slain in the conquest of Apulia by the Romans. Of the battle of Maleventum, Livy, X. 15, says: —

"Here likewise there was more of flight than of bloodshed. Two thousand of the Apulians were slain, and Decius, despising such an enemy, led his legions into Samnium."

11. Hannibal's famous battle at Cannæ, in the second Punic war. According to Livy, XXII. 49, "The number of the slain is computed at forty thousand foot, and two thousand seven hundred horse."

He continues, XXII. 51, Baker's Tr.: "On the day following, as soon as light appeared, his troops applied themselves to the collecting of the spoils, and viewing the carnage made, which was such as shocked even enemies; so many thousand Romans, horsemen and footmen, lay promiscuously on the field, as chance had thrown them together, either in the battle, or flight. Some, whom their wounds, being pinched by the morning cold, had roused from their posture, were put to death by the enemy, as they were rising up, all covered with blood, from the midst of the heaps of carcasses. Some they found lying alive, with their thighs and hams cut, who, stripping their necks and throats, desired them to spill what remained of their blood. Some were found, with their heads buried in the earth, in holes which it appeared they had made for themselves, and covering their faces with earth thrown over them, had thus been suffocated. The attention of all was particularly attracted by a living Numidian with his nose and ears mangled, stretched under a dead Roman, who lay over him, and who, when his hands had been rendered unable to hold a weapon, his rage being exasperated to madness, had expired in the act of tearing his antagonist with his teeth."

When Mago, son of Hamilcar, carried the news of the victory to Carthage, "in confirmation of his joyful intelligence," says the same historian, XXIII. 12, "he ordered the gold rings taken from the Romans to be poured down in the porch of the senate-house, and of these there was so great a heap that, according to some writers, on being measured, they filled three pecks and a half; but the more general account, and likewise the more probable is, that they amounted to no more than one peck. He also explained to them, in order to show the greater extent of the slaughter, that none but those of equestrian rank, and of these only the principal, wore this ornament."

14. Robert Guiscard, the renowned Norman conqueror of southern Italy. Dante places him in the Fifth Heaven of Paradise, in the planet Mars. For an account of his character and achievements see Gibbon, Ch. LVI. See also *Parad.* XVIII. Note 20.

Matthew Paris, Giles's Tr., I. 171, A.D. 1239, gives the following account of the manner in which he captured the monastery of Monte Cassino: —

"In the same year, the monks of Monte Cassino (where St. Benedict had planted a monastery), to the number of thirteen, came to the Pope in old and torn garments, with dishevelled hair and unshorn beards, and with tears in their eyes; and on being introduced to the presence of his Holiness, they fell at his feet, and laid a complaint that the Emperor had ejected them from their house at Monte Cassino. This mountain was impregnable, and indeed inaccessible to any one unless at the will of the monks and others who dwelt on it; however, R. Guiscard, by a device, pretending that he was dead and being carried thither on a bier, thus took possession of the monks' castle. When the Pope heard this, he concealed his grief, and asked the reason; to which the monks replied, 'Because, in obedience to you, we excommunicated the Emperor.' The Pope then said, 'Your obedience shall save you'; on which the monks went away without receiving anything more from the Pope."

16. The battle of Ceperano, near Monte Cassino, was fought in 1265, between Charles of Anjou and Manfred, king of Apulia and Sicily. The Apulians, seeing the battle going against them, deserted their king and passed over to the enemy.

17. The battle of Tagliacozzo in Abruzzo was fought in 1268, between Charles of Anjou and Curradino or Conradin, nephew of Manfred. Charles gained the victory by the strategy of Count Alardo di Valleri, who,

> Weaponless himself,
> Made arms ridiculous.

This valiant but wary crusader persuaded the king to keep a third of his forces in reserve; and when the soldiers of Curradino, thinking they had won the day, were scattered over the field in pursuit of plunder, Charles fell upon them, and routed them.

Alardo is mentioned in the *Cento Novelle Antiche*, Nov. LVII., as "celebrated for his wonderful prowess even among the chief nobles, and no less esteemed for his singular virtues than for his courage."

31. Gibbon, Ch. L., says: "At the conclusion of the Life of Mahomet, it may perhaps be expected that I should balance his faults and virtues, that I should decide whether the title of enthusiast or impostor more properly belongs to that extraordinary man. Had I been intimately conversant with the son of Abdallah, the task would still be difficult, and the success

uncertain; at the distance of twelve centuries, I darkly contemplate his shade through a cloud of religious incense; and could I truly delineate the portrait of an hour, the fleeting resemblance would not equally apply to the solitary of Mount Hera, to the preacher of Mecca, and to the conqueror of Arabia. . . . From enthusiasm to imposture the step is perilous and slippery; the dæmon of Socrates affords a memorable instance how a wise man may deceive himself, how a good man may deceive others, how the conscience may slumber in a mixed and middle state between self-illusion and voluntary fraud."

Of Ali, the son-in-law and faithful follower of Mahomet, he goes on to say: "He united the qualifications of a poet, a soldier, and a saint; his wisdom still breathes in a collection of moral and religious sayings; and every antagonist, in the combats of the tongue or of the sword, was subdued by his eloquence and valor. From the first hour of his mission to the last rites of his funeral, the apostle was never forsaken by a generous friend, whom he delighted to name his brother, his vicegerent, and the faithful Aaron of a second Moses."

55. Fra Dolcino was one of the early social and religious reformers in the North of Italy. His sect bore the name of "Apostles," and its chief, if not only, heresy was a desire to bring back the Church to the simplicity of the apostolic times. In 1305 he withdrew with his followers to the mountains overlooking the Val Sesia in Piedmont, where he was pursued and besieged by the Church party, and, after various fortunes of victory and defeat, being reduced by "stress of snow" and famine, was taken prisoner, together with his companion, the beautiful Margaret of Trent. Both were burned at Vercelli on the first of June, 1307. This "last act of the tragedy" is thus described by Mr. Mariotti, *Historical Memoir of Fra Dolcino and his Times,* p. 290: —

"Margaret of Trent enjoyed the precedence due to her sex. She was first led out into a spot near Vercelli, bearing the name of 'Arena Servi,' or more properly 'Arena Cervi,' in the sands, that is, of the torrent Cervo, which has its confluent with the Sesia at about one mile above the city. A high stake had been erected in a conspicuous part of the place. To this she was fastened, and a pile of wood was reared at her feet. The eyes of the inhabitants of town and country were upon her. On her also were the eyes of Dolcino. She was burnt alive with slow fire.

"Next came the turn of Dolcino: he was seated high on a car drawn by oxen, and thus paraded from street to street all over Vercelli. His tormentors were all around him. Beside the car, iron pots were carried, filled with burning charcoals; deep in the charcoals were iron pincers, glowing at white heat. These pincers were continually applied to the various parts of Dolcino's naked body, all along his progress, till all his flesh was torn piecemeal from his limbs; when every bone was bare and the whole town was perambulated, they drove the still living carcass back to the same arena, and threw it on the burning mass in which Margaret had been consumed."

Farther on he adds: —

"Divested of all fables which ignorance, prejudice, or open calumny involved it in, Dolcino's scheme amounted to nothing more than a reformation, not of religion, but of the Church; his aim was merely the destruction of the temporal power of the clergy, and he died for his country no less than for his God. The wealth, arrogance, and corruption of the Papal See appeared to him, as it appeared to Dante, as it appeared to a thousand other patriots before and after him, an eternal hindrance to the union, peace, and welfare of Italy, as it was a perpetual check upon the progress of the human race, and a source of infinite scandal to the piety of earnest believers. . . .

"To this clear mission of Italian protestantism Dolcino was true throughout. If we bring the light of even the clumsiest criticism to bear on his creed, even such as it has been summed up by the ignorance or malignity of men who never utter his name without an imprecation, we have reason to be astonished at the little we find in it that may be construed into a wilful deviation from the strictest orthodoxy. Luther and Calvin would equally have repudiated him. He was neither a Presbyterian nor an Episcopalian, but an uncompromising, stanch Papist. His was, most eminently, the heresy of those whom we have designated as 'literal Christians.' He would have the Gospel strictly—perhaps blindly—adhered to. Neither was that, in the abstract, an unpardonable offence in the eyes of the Romanism of those times—witness St. Francis and his early flock—provided he had limited himself to make Gospel-law binding upon himself and his followers only. But Dolcino must needs enforce it upon the whole Christian community, enforce it especially on those who set up as teachers of the Gospel, on those who laid claim to Apostolical succession. That was the error that damned him."

Of Margaret he still farther says, referring to some old manuscript as authority: —

"She was known by the emphatic appellation of Margaret the Beautiful. It is added, that she was an orphan, heiress of noble parents, and had been placed for her education in a monastery of St. Catherine in Trent; that there Dolcino—who had also been a monk, or at least a novice, in a convent of the Order of the Humiliati, in the same town, and had been expelled in consequence either of his heretic tenets, or of immoral conduct—succeeded nevertheless in becoming domesticated in the nunnery of St. Catherine, as a steward or agent to the nuns, and there accomplished the fascination and abduction of the wealthy heiress."

59. Val Sesia, among whose mountains Fra Dolcino was taken prisoner, is in the diocese of Novara.

73. A Bolognese, who stirred up dissensions among the citizens.

74. The plain of Lombardy sloping down two hundred miles and more, from Vercelli in Piedmont to Marcabo, a village near Ravenna.

76. Guido del Cassero and Angiolello da Cagnano, two honorable citizens of Fano, going to Rimini by invitation of Malatestino, were by his order thrown into the sea and drowned, as here prophesied or narrated, near the village of Cattolica on the Adriatic.

85. Malatestino had lost one eye.

86. Rimini.

89. Focara is a headland near Cattolica, famous for dangerous winds, to be preserved from which mariners offered up vows and prayers. These men will not need to do it; they will not reach that cape.

102. Curio, the banished Tribune, who, fleeing to Cæsar's camp on the Rubicon, urged him to advance upon Rome. Lucan, *Pharsalia,* I., Rowe's Tr.: —

> To Cæsar's camp the busy Curio fled;
> Curio, a speaker turbulent and bold,
> Of venal eloquence, that served for gold,
> And principles that might be bought and sold.
>
> . . . .
>
> To Cæsar thus, while thousand cares infest,
> Revolving round the warrior's anxious breast,
> His speech the ready orator addressed.
>
> . . . .
>
> "Haste, then, thy towering eagles on their way;
> When fair occasion calls, 't is fatal to delay."

106. Mosca degl' Uberti, or dei Lamberti, who, by advising the murder of Buondelmonte, gave rise to the parties of Guelf and Ghibelline, which so long divided Florence. See Canto X. Note 51.

117. Shakespeare, Second Part of *King Henry VI.* Act III. Sc. 2: —

> What stronger breastplate than a heart untainted?
> Thrice is he armed that hath his quarrel just.

Sir Henry Wotton, *The Character of a Happy Life:* —

> How happy is he born or taught
>> Who serveth not another's will;
> Whose armour is his honest thought,
>> And simple truth his utmost skill.

Horace, *Epist.* Lib. i. I. 60, Francis Tr.: —

> Be this thy brazen bulwark of defense
> Still to preserve thy conscious innocence
> Nor e'er turn pale with guilt.

134. Bertrand de Born, the turbulent Troubadour of the last half of the twelfth century, was alike skilful with his pen and his sword, and passed his life in alternately singing and fighting, and in stirring up dissension and strife among his neighbors. He is the author of that spirited war-song, well known to all readers of Troubadour verse, beginning

> The beautiful spring delights me well,
>> When flowers and leaves are growing;
> And it pleases my heart to hear the swell
>> Of the birds' sweet chorus flowing
>>> In the echoing wood;
> And I love to see, all scattered around,
> Pavilions and tents on the martial ground;
>>> And my spirit finds it good,
> To see, on the level plains beyond,
> Gay knights and steeds caparison'd: —

and ending with a challenge to Richard Cœur de Lion, telling his minstrel Papiol to go

> And tell the Lord of 'Yes and No'
> That peace already too long has been.

"Bertrand de Born," says the old Provençal biography published by Raynouard, *Choix de Poésies Originales des Troubadours,* V. 76, "was a chatelain of the bishopric of Périgueux, Viscount of Hautefort, a castle with nearly a thousand retainers. He had a brother, and would have dispossessed him of his inheritance, had it not been for the king of England. He was always at war with all his neighbors, with the Count of Périgueux, and with the Viscount of Limoges, and with his brother Constantine, and with Richard, when he was Count of Poitou. He was a good cavalier, and a good warrior, and a good lover, and a good troubadour; and well informed and well spoken; and knew well how to bear good and evil fortune. Whenever he wished, he was master of King Henry of England and of his son; but always desired that father and son should be at war with each other, and one brother with the other. And he always wished that the king of France and the king of England should be at variance; and if there were either peace or truce, straightway he sought and endeavored by his satires to undo the peace, and to show how each was dishonored by it. And he had great advantages and great misfortunes by thus exciting feuds between them. He wrote many satires, but only two songs. The king of Aragon called the songs of Giraud de Borneil the wives of Bertrand de Born's satires. And he who sang for him bore the name of Papiol. And he was handsome and courteous; and called the Count of Britany, Rassa; and the king of England, Yes and No; and his son, the young king, Marinier. And he set his whole heart on fomenting war; and embroiled the father and son of England, until the young king was killed by an arrow in a castle of Bertrand de Born.

"And Bertrand used to boast that he had more wits than he needed. And when the king took him prisoner, he asked him, 'Have you all your wits, for you will need them now?' And he answered, 'I lost them all when the young king died.' Then the king wept, and pardoned him, and gave him robes, and lands, and honors. And he lived long and became a Cistercian monk."

Fauriel, *Histoire de la Poésie Provençale*, Adler's Tr., p. 483, quoting part of this passage, adds: —

"In this notice the old biographer indicates the dominant trait of Bertrand's character very distinctly; it was an unbridled passion for war. He loved it not only as the occasion for exhibiting proofs of valor, for acquiring power, and for winning glory, but also, and even more on account of its hazards, on account of the exaltation of courage and of life which it produced, nay, even for the sake of the tumult, the disorders, and the evils which are accustomed to follow in its train. Bertrand de Born is the ideal of the undisciplined and adventuresome warrior of the Middle Age, rather than that of the chevalier in the proper sense of the term."

See also Millot, *Hist. Litt. des Troubadours*, I. 210, and *Hist. Litt. de la France par les Bénédictins de St. Maur*, continuation, XVII. 425.

Bertrand de Born, if not the best of the Troubadours, is the most prominent and striking character among them. His life is a drama full of romantic interest; beginning with the old castle in Gascony, "the dames, the cavaliers, the arms, the loves, the courtesy, the bold emprise"; and ending in a Cistercian convent, among friars and fastings and penitence and prayers.

135. A vast majority of manuscripts and printed editions read in this line, *Re Giovanni*, King John, instead of *Re Giovane*, the Young King. Even Boccaccio's copy, which he wrote out with his own hand for Petrarca, has *Re Giovanni*. Out of seventy-nine Codici examined by Barlow, he says, *Study of the Divina Commedia*, p. 153, "Only five were found with the correct reading—*re giovane*. . . . The reading *re giovane* is not found in any of the early editions, nor is it noticed by any of the early commentators." See also Ginguené, *Hist. Litt. de l'Italie*, II. 586, where the subject is elaborately discussed, and the note of Biagioli, who takes the opposite side of the question.

Henry II. of England had four sons, all of whom were more or less rebellious against him. They were, Henry, surnamed Curt-Mantle, and called by the Troubadours and novelists of his time "The Young King," because he was crowned during his father's life; Richard Cœur-de-Lion, Count of Guienne and Poitou; Geoffroy, Duke of Brittany; and John Lackland. Henry was the only one of these who bore the title of king at the time in question. Bertrand de Born was on terms of intimacy with him, and speaks of him in his poems as *lo Reys joves*, sometimes lauding, and sometimes reproving him. One of the best of these poems is his *Complainte*, on the death of Henry, which took place in 1183, from disease, say some accounts, from the bolt of a crossbow say others. He complains that he has lost "the best king that was ever born of mother"; and goes on to say, "King of the courteous, and emperor of the valiant, you would have been Seigneur if you had lived longer; for you bore the name of the Young King, and were the chief and peer of youth. Ay! hauberk and sword, and beautiful buckler, helmet and gonfalon, and purpoint and sark, and joy and love, there is none to maintain them!" See Raynouard, *Choix de Poésies*, IV. 49.

In the *Bible Guiot de Provins*, Barbazan, *Fabliaux et Contes*, II. 518, he is spoken of as

> Li jones Rois,
> Li proux, li saiges, li cortois.

In the *Cento Novelle Antiche*, XVIII., XIX., XXXV., he is called *il Re Giovane*; and in Roger de Wendover's *Flowers of History*, A.D. 1179–1183, "Henry the Young King."

It was to him that Bertrand de Born "gave the evil counsels," embroiling him with his father and his brothers. Therefore, when the commentators challenge us as Pistol does Shallow, "Under which king, Bezonian?

speak or die!" I think we must answer as Shallow does, "Under King Harry."

37. See 2 *Samuel* xvii. 1, 2: —

"Moreover, Ahithophel said unto Absalom, Let me now choose out twelve thousand men, and I will arise and pursue after David this night. And I will come upon him while he is weary and weak-handed, and I will make him afraid; and all the people that are with him shall flee; and I will smite the king only."

Dryden, in his poem of *Absalom and Achitophel,* gives this portrait of the latter: —

> Of these the false Achitophel was first;
> A name to all succeeding ages curst;
> For close designs and crooked counsels fit;
> Sagacious, bold, and turbulent of wit;
> Restless, unfix'd in principles and place;
> In power unpleas'd, impatient of disgrace:
> A fiery soul, which, working out its way,
> Fretted the pigmy body to decay,
> And o'er inform'd the tenement of clay.

Then he puts into the mouth of Achitophel the following description of Absalom: —

> Auspicious prince, at whose nativity
> Some royal planet rul'd the southern sky;
> Thy longing country's darling and desire;
> Their cloudy pillar and their guardian fire;
> Their second Moses, whose extended wand,
> Divides the seas, and shows the promised land;
> Whose dawning day, in every distant age,
> Has exercised the sacred prophet's rage;
> The people's prayer, the glad diviner's theme,
> The young men's vision, and the old men's dream.

CANTO XXIX

1. The Tenth and last "cloister of Malebolge," where

> Justice infallible
> Punishes forgers,

and falsifiers of all kinds. This Canto is devoted to the alchemists.

27. Geri del Bello was a disreputable member of the Alighieri family, and was murdered by one of the Sacchetti. His death was afterwards avenged by his brother, who in turn slew one of the Sacchetti at the door of his house.

29. Bertrand de Born.

35. Like the ghost of Ajax in the *Odyssey,* XI. "He answered me not at all, but went to Erebus amongst the other souls of the dead."

36. Dante seems to share the feeling of the Italian *vendetta,* which required retaliation from some member of the injured family.

"Among the Italians of this age," says Napier, *Florentine Hist.,* I. Ch. VII., "and for centuries after, private offence was never forgotten until revenged, and generally involved a succession of mutual injuries; vengeance was not only considered lawful and just, but a positive duty, dishonorable to omit; and, as may be learned from ancient private journals, it was sometimes allowed to sleep for five-and-thirty years, and then suddenly struck a victim who perhaps had not yet seen the light when the original injury was inflicted."

46. The Val di Chiana, near Arezzo, was in Dante's time marshy and pestilential. Now, by the effect of drainage, it is one of the most beautiful and fruitful of the Tuscan valleys. The Maremma was and is notoriously unhealthy; see Canto XIII. Note 9, and Sardinia would seem to have shared its ill repute.

57. Forgers or falsifiers in a general sense. The "fals semblaunt" of Gower, *Confes. Amant.,* II.: —

> Of fals semblaunt if I shall telle,
> Above all other it is the welle
> Out of the which deceipte floweth.

They are registered here on earth to be punished hereafter.

59. The plague of Ægina is described by Ovid, *Metamorph.* VII., Stonestreet's Tr.: —

> Their black dry tongues are swelled, and scarce can move,
> And short thick sighs from panting lungs are drove.
> They gape for air, with flatt'ring hopes t' abate
> Their raging flames, but that augments their heat.
> No bed, no cov'ring can the wretches bear,
> But on the ground, exposed to open air,
> They lie, and hope to find a pleading coolness there.

The suff'ring earth, with that oppression curst,
Returns the heat which they imparted first.

. . . . . .

Here one, with fainting steps, does slowly creep
O'er heaps of dead, and straight augments the heap;
Another, while his strength and tongue prevailed,
Bewails his friend, and falls himself bewailed;
This with imploring looks surveys the skies,
The last dear office of his closing eyes,
But finds the Heav'ns implacable, and dies.

The birth of the Myrmidons, "who still retain the thrift of ants, though now transformed to men," is thus given in the same book: —

As many ants the num'rous branches bear,
The same their labor, and their frugal care;
The branches too alike commotion found,
And shook th' industrious creatures on the ground,
Who by degrees (what's scarce to be believed)
A nobler form and larger bulk received,
And on the earth walked an unusual pace,
With manly strides, and an erected face;
Their num'rous legs, and former color lost,
The insects could a human figure boast.

88. Latian, or Italian; any one of the Latin race.
109. The speaker is a certain Griffolino, an alchemist of Arezzo, who practised upon the credulity of Albert, a natural son of the Bishop of Siena. For this he was burned; but was "condemned to the last Bolgia of the ten for alchemy."
116. The inventor of the Cretan labyrinth. Ovid, *Metamorph.* VIII.: —

Great Dædalus of Athens was the man
Who made the draught, and formed the wondrous plan.

Not being able to find his way out of the labyrinth, he made wings for himself and his son Icarus, and escaped by flight.
122. Speaking of the people of Siena, Forsyth, *Italy,* 532, says: "Vain, flighty, fanciful, they want the judgment and penetration of their Florentine neighbors; who, nationally severe, call a nail without a head *chiodo Sanese.*

The accomplished Signora Rinieri told me, that her father, while Governor of Siena, was once stopped in his carriage by a crowd at Florence, where the mob, recognizing him, called out: '*Lasciate passare il Governatore de' matti.*' A native of Siena is presently known at Florence; for his very walk, being formed to a hilly town, detects him on the plain."

125. The persons here mentioned gain a kind of immortality from Dante's verse. The Stricca, or Baldastricca, was a lawyer of Siena; and Niccolò dei Salimbeni, or Bonsignori, introduced the fashion of stuffing pheasants with cloves, or, as Benvenuto says, of roasting them at a fire of cloves. Though Dante mentions them apart, they seem, like the two others named afterwards, to have been members of the *Brigata Spendereccia*, or Spendthrift Club, of Siena, whose extravagances are recorded by Benvenuto da Imola. This club consisted of "twelve very rich young gentlemen, who took it into their heads to do things that would make a great part of the world wonder." Accordingly each contributed eighteen thousand golden florins to a common fund, amounting in all to two hundred and sixteen thousand florins. They built a palace, in which each member had a splendid chamber, and they gave sumptuous dinners and suppers; ending their banquets sometimes by throwing all the dishes, table-ornaments, and knives of gold and silver out of the window. "This silly institution," continues Benvenuto, "lasted only ten months, the treasury being exhausted, and the wretched members became the fable and laughing-stock of all the world."

In honor of this club, Folgore da San Geminiano, a clever poet of the day (1260), wrote a series of twelve convivial sonnets, one for each month of the year, with Dedication and Conclusion. A translation of these sonnets may be found in D. G. Rosetti's *Early Italian Poets*. The Dedication runs as follows: —

> Unto the blithe and lordly Fellowship,
> (I know not where, but wheresoe'er, I know,
> Lordly and blithe,) be greeting; and thereto,
> Dogs, hawks, and a full purse wherein to dip;
> Quails struck i' the flight; nags mottled to the whip;
>   Hart-hounds, hare-hounds, and blood-hounds even so;
>   And o'er that realm, a crown for Niccolò,
>   Whose praise in Siena springs from lip to lip.
> Tingoccio, Atuin di Togno, and Ancaiàn,
>   Bartolo, and Murgaro, and Faënot,
>   Who well might pass for children of King Ban,
> Courteous and valiant more than Lancelot,—

> To each, God speed! How worthy every man
> To hold high tournament in Camelot.

136. "This Capocchio," says the *Ottimo,* "was a very subtle alchemist; and because he was burned for practising alchemy in Siena, he exhibits his hatred to the Sienese, and gives us to understand that the author knew him."

CANTO XXX

1. In this Canto the same Bolgia is continued, with different kinds of Falsifiers.

4. Athamas, king of Thebes and husband of Ino, daughter of Cadmus. His madness is thus described by Ovid, *Metamorph.* IV., Eusden's Tr.: —

> Now Athamas cries out, his reason fled,
> "Here, fellow-hunters, let the toils be spread.
> I saw a lioness, in quest of food,
> With her two young, run roaring in this wood."
> Again the fancied savages were seen,
> As through his palace still he chased his queen;
> Then tore Learchus from her breast: the child
> Stretched little arms, and on its father smiled,—
> A father now no more,—who now begun
> Around his head to whirl his giddy son,
> And, quite insensible to nature's call,
> The helpless infant flung against the wall.
> The same mad poison in the mother wrought;
> Young Melicerta in her arms she caught,
> And with disordered tresses, howling, flies,
> "O Bacchus, Evôe, Bacchus!" loud she cries.
> The name of Bacchus Juno laughed to hear,
> And said, "Thy foster-god has cost thee dear."
> A rock there stood, whose side the beating waves
> Had long consumed, and hollowed into caves.
> The head shot forwards in a bending steep,
> And cast a dreadful covert o'er the deep.
> The wretched Ino, on destruction bent,
> Climbed up the cliff,—such strength her fury lent:
> Thence with her guiltless boy, who wept in vain,
> At one bold spring she plunged into the main.

16. Hecuba, wife of Priam of Troy, and mother of Polyxena and Polydorus. Ovid, XIII., Stanyan's Tr.: —

When on the banks her son in ghastly hue
Transfixed with Thracian arrow strikes her view,
The matron shrieked; her big swoln grief surpassed
The power of utterance; she stood aghast;
She had nor speech, nor tears to give relief:
Excess of woe suppressed the rising grief.
Lifeless as stone, on earth she fix'd her eyes;
And then look'd up to Heav'n with wild surprise.
Now she contemplates o'er with sad delight
Her son's pale visage; then her aking sight
Dwells on his wounds: she varies thus by turns,
Till with collected rage at length she burns,
Wild as the mother-lion, when among
The haunts of prey she seeks her ravished young:
Swift flies the ravisher; she marks his trace,
And by the print directs her anxious chase.
So Hecuba with mingled grief and rage
Pursues the king, regardless of her age.

. . . .

Fastens her forky fingers in his eyes;
Tears out the rooted balls; her rage pursues,
And in the hollow orbs her hand imbrues.

   The Thracians, fired at this inhuman scene,
With darts and stones assail the frantic queen.
She snarls and growls, nor in an human tone;
Then bites impatient at the bounding stone;
Extends her jaws, as she her voice would raise
To keen invectives in her wonted phrase;
But barks, and thence the yelping brute betrays.

31. Griffolino d' Arezzo, mentioned in Canto XXIX. 109.

42. The same "mad sprite," Gianni Schicchi, mentioned in line 32. "Buosco Donati of Florence," says Benvenuto, "although a nobleman and of an illustrious house, was nevertheless like other noblemen of his time, and by means of thefts had greatly increased his patrimony. When the hour of death drew near, the sting of conscience caused him to make a will in which he gave fat legacies to many people; whereupon his son Simon, (the *Ottimo* says his nephew,) thinking himself enormously aggrieved, suborned Vanni Schicchi dei Cavalcanti, who got into Buoso's bed, and made a will in opposition to the other. Gianni much resembled Buoso." In this will Gianni Schicchi did not forget himself, while making Simon heir; for, according to the *Ottimo*, he put this clause into it: "To Gianni

Schicchi I bequeath my mare." This was the "lady of the herd," and Benvenuto adds, "none more beautiful was to be found in Tuscany; and it was valued at a thousand florins."

61. Messer Adamo, a false-coiner of Brescia, who at the instigation of the Counts Guido, Alessandro, and Aghinolfo of Romena, counterfeited the golden florin of Florence, which bore on one side a lily, and on the other the figure of John the Baptist.

64. Tasso, *Gerusalemme Liberata,* XIII. 60, Fairfax's Tr.: —

> He that the gliding rivers erst had seen
> Adown their verdant channels gently rolled,
> Or falling streams, which to the valleys green,
> Distilled from tops of Alpine mountains cold,
> Those he desired in vain, new torments been
> Augmented thus with wish of comforts old;
> Those waters cool he drank in vain conceit,
> Which more increased his thirst, increased his heat.

65. The upper valley of the Arno is in the province of Cassentino. Quoting these three lines, Ampère, *Voyage Dantesque,* 246, says: "In these untranslatable verses, there is a feeling of humid freshness, which almost makes one shudder. I owe it to truth to say, that the Cassentine was a great deal less fresh and less verdant in reality than in the poetry of Dante, and that in the midst of the aridity which surrounded me, this poetry, by its very perfection, made one feel something of the punishment of Master Adam."

73. Forsyth, *Italy,* 116, says: "The castle of Romena, mentioned in these verses, now stands in ruins on a precipice about a mile from our inn, and not far off is a spring which the peasants call Fonte Branda. Might I presume to differ from his commentators, Dante, in my opinion, does not mean the great fountain of Siena, but rather this obscure spring; which, though less known to the world, was an object more familiar to the poet himself, who took refuge here from proscription, and an image more natural to the coiner who was burnt on the spot."

Ampère is of the same opinion, *Voyage Dantesque,* 246: "The Fonte Branda, mentioned by Master Adam, is assuredly the fountain thus named, which still flows not far from the tower of Romena, between the place of the crime and that of its punishment."

On the other hand, Mr. Barlow, *Contributions,* remarks: "This little fount was known only to so few, that Dante, who wrote for the Italian people generally, can scarcely be thought to have meant this, when the famous Fonte Branda at Siena was, at least by name, familiar to them all, and formed an image more in character with the insatiable thirst of Master Adam."

Poetically the question is of slight importance; for, as Fluellen says, "There is a river in Macedon, and there is also moreover a river at Monmouth, . . . and there is salmons in both."

86. This line and line 11 of Canto XXIX. are cited by Gabriele Rossetti in confirmation of his theory of the "Principal Allegory of the Inferno," that the city of Dis is Rome. He says, *Spirito Antipapale,* I. 62, Miss Ward's Tr.: —

"This well is surrounded by a high wall, and the wall by a vast trench; the circuit of the trench is twenty-two miles, and that of the wall eleven miles. Now the outward trench of the walls of Rome (whether real or imaginary we say not) was reckoned by Dante's contemporaries to be exactly twenty-two miles; and the walls of the city were then, and still are, eleven miles round. Hence it is clear, that the *wicked time* which looks into Rome, as into a mirror, sees there the corrupt place which is the final goal to its waters or people, that is, the figurative Rome, 'dread seat of Dis.' "

The trench here spoken of is the last trench of Malebolge. Dante mentions no wall about the well; only giants standing round it like towers.

97. Potiphar's wife.

98. Virgil's "perjured Sinon," the Greek who persuaded the Trojans to accept the wooden horse, telling them it was meant to protect the city, in lieu of the statue of Pallas, stolen by Diomed and Ulysses.

Chaucer, *Nonnes Preestes Tale:* —

> O false dissimilour, O Greek Sinon,
> That broughtest Troye at utterly to sorwe.

103. The disease of *tympanites* is so called "because the abdomen is distended with wind, and sounds like a drum when struck."

128. Ovid, *Metamorph.* III.: —

> A fountain in a darksome wood,
> Nor stained with falling leaves nor rising mud.

CANTO XXXI

1. This Canto describes the Plain of the Giants, between Malebolge and the mouth of the Infernal Pit.

4. *Iliad,* XVI.: "A Pelion ash, which Chiron gave to his (Achilles') father, cut from the top of Mount Pelion, to be the death of heroes."

Chaucer, *Squieres Tale:* —

> And of Achilles for his queinte spere,
> For he coude with it bothe hele and drere.

And Shakespeare, in Second Part of *King Henry the Sixth,* V. i.: —

> Whose smile and frown, like to Achilles' spear,
> Is able with the change to kill and cure.

16. The battle of Roncesvalles,

> When Charlemain with all his peerage fell
> By Fontarabia.

18. Archbishop Turpin, *Chronicle,* XXIII., Rodd's Tr., thus describes the blowing of Orlando's horn: —

"He now blew a loud blast with his horn, to summon any Christian concealed in the adjacent woods to his assistance, or to recall his friends beyond the pass. This horn was endued with such power, that all other horns were split by its sound; and it is said that Orlando at that time blew it with such vehemence, that he burst the veins and nerves of his neck. The sound reached the king's ears, who lay encamped in the valley still called by his name, about eight miles from Ronceval, towards Gascony, being carried so far by supernatural power. Charles would have flown to his succor, but was prevented by Ganalon, who, conscious of Orlando's sufferings, insinuated it was usual with him to sound his horn on light occasions. 'He is, perhaps,' said he, 'pursuing some wild beast, and the sound echoes through the woods; it will be fruitless, therefore, to seek him.' O wicked traitor, deceitful as Judas! What dost thou merit?"

Walter Scott in *Marmion,* VI. 33, makes allusion to Orlando's horn: —

> O for a blast of that dread horn,
> On Fontarabian echoes borne,
>   That to King Charles did come,
> When Rowland brave, and Olivier.
> And every paladin and peer,
>   On Roncesvalles died!

Orlando's horn is one of the favorite fictions of old romance, and is surpassed in power only by that of Alexander, which took sixty men to blow it, and could be heard at a distance of sixty miles!

41. Montereggione is a picturesque old castle on an eminence near Siena. Ampère, *Voyage Dantesque,* 251, remarks: "This fortress, as the commentators say, was furnished with towers all round about, and had none in the centre. In its present state it is still very faithfully described by the verse,

Montereggion di torri si corona."

59. This pine-cone of bronze, which is now in the gardens of the Vatican, was found in the mausoleum of Hadrian, and is supposed to have crowned its summit. "I have looked daily," says Mrs. Kemble, *Year of Consolation,* 152, "over the lonely, sunny gardens, open like the palace halls to me, where the wide-sweeping orange-walks end in some distant view of the sad and noble Campagna, where silver fountains call to each other through the silent, overarching cloisters of dark and fragrant green, and where the huge bronze pine, by which Dante measured his great giant, yet stands in the midst of graceful vases and bass-reliefs wrought in former ages, and the more graceful blossoms blown within the very hour."

And Ampère, *Voyage Dantesque,* 277, remarks: "Here Dante takes as a point of comparison an object of determinate size; the *pigna* is eleven feet high, the giant then must be seventy; it performs, in the description, the office of those figures which are placed near monuments to render it easier for the eye to measure their height."

Mr. Norton, *Travel and Study in Italy,* 253, thus speaks of the same object: —

"This pine-cone of bronze was set originally upon the summit of the Mausoleum of Hadrian. After this imperial sepulchre had undergone many evil fates, and as its ornaments were stripped one by one from it, the cone was in the sixth century taken down, and carried off to adorn a fountain, which had been constructed for the use of dusty and thirsty pilgrims, in a pillared enclosure called the *Paradiso,* in front of the old basilica of St. Peter. Here it remained for centuries; and when the old church gave way to the new, it was put where it now stands, useless and out of place, in the trim and formal gardens of the Papal palace."

And adds in a note: —

"At the present day it serves the bronze-workers of Rome as a model for an inkstand, such as is seen in the shop-windows every winter, and is sold to travellers, few of whom know the history and the poetry belonging to its original."

John Evelyn in his *Diary*, Rome, Jan. 18, 1645, describing the Vatican Gardens, says: "We were likewise showed the relics of the Hadrian Moles; viz., the Pine, a vast piece of metal which stood on the summit of that mausoleum."

67. "The gaping monotony of this jargon," says Leigh Hunt, "full of the vowel *a*, is admirably suited to the mouth of the vast half-stupid speaker. It is like a babble of the gigantic infancy of the world."

77. Nimrod, the "mighty hunter before the Lord," who built the tower of Babel, which, according to the Italian popular tradition, was so high that whoever mounted to the top of it could hear the angels sing.

Cory, *Ancient Fragments*, 51, gives this extract from the *Sibylline Oracles:*—

> But when the judgments of the Almighty God
> Were ripe for execution; when the Tower
> Rose to the skies upon Assyria's plain
> And all mankind one language only knew;
> A dread commission from on high was given
> To the fell whirlwinds, which with dire alarms
> Beat on the Tower, and to its lowest base
> Shook it convulsed. And now all intercourse,
> By some occult and overruling power,
> Ceased among men: by utterance they strove
> Perplexed and anxious to disclose their mind;
> But their lip failed them, and in lieu of words
> Produced a painful babbling sound: the place
> Was thence called Babel; by th' apostate crew
> Named from the event. Then severed far away
> They sped uncertain into realms unknown;
> Thus kingdoms rose, and the glad world was filled.

94. *Odyssey*, XI., Buckley's Tr.: "God-like Otus and far-famed Ephialtes; whom the faithful earth nourished, the tallest and far the most beautiful, at least after illustrious Orion. For at nine years old they were also nine cubits in width, and in height they were nine fathoms. Who even threatened the immortals that they would set up a strife of impetuous war in Olympus. They attempted to place Ossa upon Olympus, and upon Ossa leafy Pelion, that heaven might be accessible. And they would have accomplished it, if they had reached the measure of youth; but the son of Jove, whom fair-haired Latona bore, destroyed them both, before the down flowered under their temples and thickened upon their cheeks with a flowering beard."

98. The giant with a hundred hands. *Æneid*, X.: "Ægæon, who, they say, had a hundred arms and a hundred hands, and flashed fire from fifty mouths and breasts; when against the thunderbolts of Jove he on so many equal bucklers clashed; unsheathed so many swords."

     He is supposed to have been a famous pirate, and the fable of the hundred hands arose from the hundred sailors that manned his ship.

100. The giant Antæus is here unbound, because he had not been at "the mighty war" against the gods.

115. The valley of the Bagrada, one of whose branches flows by Zama, the scene of Scipio's great victory over Hannibal, by which he gained his greatest renown and his title of Africanus.

     Among the neighboring hills, according to Lucan, *Pharsalia*, IV., the giant Antæus had his cave. Speaking of Curio's voyage, he says: —

> To Afric's coast he cuts the foamy way,
> Where low the once victorious Carthage lay.
> There landing, to the well-known camp he hies,
> Where from afar the distant seas he spies;
> Where Bagrada's dull waves the sands divide,
> And slowly downward roll their sluggish tide.
> From thence he seeks the heights renowned by fame,
> And hallowed by the great Cornelian name:
> Th rocks and hills which long, traditions say,
> Were held by huge Antæus' horrid sway.
>
> .   .   .   .   .   .
>
> But greater deeds this rising mountain grace,
> And Scipio's name ennobles much the place,
> While, fixing here his famous camp, he calls
> Fierce Hannibal from Rome's devoted walls.
> As yet the mouldering works remain in view,
> Where dreadful once the Latian eagles flew.

124. *Æneid*, VI.: "Here too you might have seen Tityus, the foster-child of all-bearing earth, whose body is extended over nine whole acres; and a huge vulture, with her hooked beak, pecking at his immortal liver." Also *Odyssey*, XI., in similar words.

     Typhœus was a giant with a hundred heads, like a dragon's, who made war upon the gods as soon as he was born. He was the father of Geryon and Cerberus.

132. The battle between Hercules and Antæus is described by Lucan, *Pharsalia*, IV.: —

> Bright in Olympic oil Alcides shone,
> Antæus with his mother's dust is strown,
> And seeks her friendly force to aid his own.

136. One of the leaning towers of Bologna, which Eustace, *Classical Tour*, I. 167, thinks are "remarkable only for their unmeaning elevation and dangerous deviation from the perpendicular."

CANTO XXXII

1. In this Canto begins the Ninth and last Circle of the Inferno, where Traitors are punished.

> Hence in the smallest circle, where the point is
> Of the Universe, upon which Dis is seated,
> Whoe'er betrays forever is consumed.

3. The word *thrust* is here used in its architectural sense, as the thrust of a bridge against its abutments, and the like.

9. Still using the babble of childhood.

11. The Muses; the poetic tradition being that Amphion built the walls of Thebes by the sound of his lyre; and the prosaic interpretation, that he did it by his persuasive eloquence.

15. *Matthew* xxvi. 24: "Woe unto that man by whom the Son of man is betrayed! it had been good for that man if he had not been born."

28. Tambernich is a mountain of Sclavonia, and Pietrapana another near Lucca.

55. These two "miserable brothers" are Alessandro and Napoleone, sons of Alberto degli Alberti, lord of Falterona in the valley of the Bisenzio. After their father's death they quarrelled, and one treacherously slew the other.

58. Caïna is the first of the four divisions of this Circle, and takes its name from the first fratricide.

62. Sir Mordred, son of King Arthur. See *La Mort d'Arthure*, III. ch. 167: "And there King Arthur smote Sir Mordred under the shield with a foine of his speare throughout the body more than a fadom."

    Nothing is said here of the sun's shining through the wound, so as to break the shadow on the ground, but that incident is mentioned in the Italian version of the Romance of Launcelot of the Lake, *L' illustre e famosa istoria di Lancillotto del Lago*, III. ch. 162: "Behind the opening made by the lance there passed through the wound a ray of the sun so manifestly, that Girflet saw it."

63. Focaccia was one of the Cancellieri Bianchi, of Pistoia, and was engaged in the affair of cutting off the hand of his half-brother. See Note 65, Canto VI. He is said also to have killed his uncle.

65. Sassol Mascheroni, according to Benvenuto, was one of the Toschi family of Florence. He murdered his nephew in order to get possession of his property; for which crime he was carried through the streets of Florence nailed up in a cask, and then beheaded.

68. Camicion de' Pazzi of Valdarno, who murdered his kinsman Ubertino. But his crime will seem small and excusable when compared with that of another kinsman, Carlino de' Pazzi, who treacherously surrendered the castle of Piano in Valdarno, wherein many Florentine exiles were taken and put to death.

81. The speaker is Bocca degli Abati, whose treason caused the defeat of the Guelfs at the famous battle of Montaperti, in 1260. See Note 86, Canto X.

"Messer Bocca degli Abati, the traitor," says Malaspina, *Storia,* ch. 171, "with his sword in hand, smote and cut off the hand of Messer Jacopo de' Pazzi of Florence, who bore the standard of the cavalry of the Commune of Florence. And the knights and the people, seeing the standard down, and the treachery, were put to rout."

88. The second division of the Circle, called Antenora, from Antenor, the Trojan prince, who betrayed his country by keeping up a secret correspondence with the Greeks. Virgil, *Æneid,* I. 242, makes him founder of Padua.

106. See Note 81 of this Canto.

116. Buoso da Duera of Cremona, being bribed, suffered the French cavalry under Guido da Monforte to pass through Lombardy on their way to Apulia, without opposing them as he had been commanded.

117. There is a double meaning in the Italian expression *sta fresco,* which is well rendered by the vulgarism, *left out in the cold,* so familiar in American politics.

119. Beccaria of Pavia, Abbot of Vallombrosa, and Papal Legate at Florence, where he was beheaded in 1258 for plotting against the Guelfs.

121. Gianni de' Soldanieri, of Florence, a Ghibelline, who betrayed his party. Villani, VII. 14, says: "Messer Gianni de' Soldanieri put himself at the head of the populace from motives of ambition, regardless of consequences which were injurious to the Ghibelline party, and to his own detriment, which seems always to have been the case in Florence with those who became popular leaders."

122. The traitor Ganellon, or Ganalon, who betrayed the Christian cause at

Roncesvalles, persuading Charlemagne not to go to the assistance of Orlando. See Canto XXXI. Note 18.

Tebaldello de' Manfredi treacherously opened the gates of Faenza to the French in the night.

130. Tydeus, son of the king of Calydon, slew Menalippus at the siege of Thebes and was himself mortally wounded. Statius, *Thebaid,* VIII., thus describes what followed: —

> O'ercome with joy and anger, Tydeus tries
> To raise himself, and meets with eager eyes
> The deathful object, pleased as he surveyed
> His own condition in his foe's portrayed.
> The severed head impatient he demands,
> And grasps with fervor in his trembling hands,
> While he remarks the restless balls of sight
> That sought and shunned alternately the light.
> Contented now, his wrath began to cease,
> And the fierce warrior had expired in peace;
> But the fell fiend a thought of vengeance bred,
> Unworthy of himself and of the dead.
> Meanwhile, her sire unmoved, Tritonia came,
> To crown her hero with immortal fame;
> But when she saw his jaw besprinkled o'er
> With spattered brains, and tinged with living gore,
> Whilst his imploring friends attempt in vain,
> To calm his fury, and his rage restrain,
> Again, recoiling from the loathsome view,
> The sculptur'd target o'er her face she threw.

CANTO XXXIII

1. In this Canto the subject of the preceding is continued.
13. Count Ugolino della Gherradesca was Podestà of Pisa. "Raised to the highest offices of the republic for ten years," says Napier, *Florentine History,* I. 318, "he would soon have become absolute, had not his own nephew, Nino Visconte, Judge of Gallura, contested this supremacy and forced himself into conjoint and equal authority; this could not continue, and a sort of compromise was for the moment effected, by which Visconte retired to the absolute government of Sardinia. But Ugolino, still dissatisfied, sent his son to disturb the island; a deadly feud was the consequence, Guelph against Guelph, while the latent spirit of Ghibellinism, which filled the breasts of the citizens and was encouraged by

priest and friar, felt its advantage; the Archbishop Ruggiero Rubaldino was its real head, but he worked with hidden caution as the apparent friend of either chieftain. In 1287, after some sharp contests, both of them abdicated, for the sake, as it was alleged, of public tranquillity; but, soon perceiving their error, again united, and scouring the streets with all their followers, forcibly re-established their authority. Ruggieri seemed to assent quietly to this new outrage, even looked without emotion on the bloody corpse of his favorite nephew, who had been stabbed by Ugolino; and so deep was his dissimulation, that he not only refused to believe the murdered body to be his kinsman's, but zealously assisted the Count to establish himself alone in the government, and accomplish Visconte's ruin. The design was successful; Nino was overcome and driven from the town, and in 1288 Ugolino entered Pisa in triumph from his villa, where he had retired to await the catastrophe. The Archbishop had neglected nothing, and Ugolino found himself associated with this prelate in the public government; events now began to thicken; the Count could not brook a competitor, much less a Ghibelline priest: in the month of July both parties flew to arms, and the Archbishop was victorious. After a feeble attempt to rally in the public palace, Count Ugolino, his two sons, Uguccione and Gaddo, and two young grandsons, Anselmuccio and Brigata, surrendered at discretion, and were immediately imprisoned in a tower, afterwards called the *Torre della fame,* and there perished by starvation. Count Ugolino della Gherradesca, whose tragic story after five hundred years still sounds in awful numbers from the lyre of Dante, was stained with the ambition and darker vices of the age; like other potent chiefs, he sought to enslave his country, and checked at nothing in his impetuous career; he was accused of many crimes; of poisoning his own nephew, of failing in war, making a disgraceful peace, of flying shamefully, perhaps traitorously, at Meloria, and of obstructing all negotiations with Genoa for the return of his imprisoned countrymen. Like most others of his rank in those frenzied times he belonged more to faction than his country, and made the former subservient to his own ambition; but all these accusations, even if well founded, would not draw him from the general standard; they would only prove that he shared the ambition, the cruelty, the ferocity, the recklessness of human life and suffering, and the relentless pursuit of power in common with other chieftains of his age and country. Ugolino was overcome, and suffered a cruel death; his family was dispersed, and his memory has perhaps been blackened with a darker coloring to excuse the severity of his punishment; but his sons, who naturally followed their parent's fortune, were scarcely implicated in his crimes, although they shared his fate; and his grandsons, though not children, were still less guilty, though one of these was not unstained with blood. The Archbishop had public and private wrongs to revenge, and had he fallen, his sacred character alone would probably have procured for him a milder destiny."

Villani, VII. 128, gives this account of the imprisonment: —

"The Pisans, who had imprisoned Count Ugolino and his two sons and two grandsons, children of Count Guelfo, as we have before mentioned, in a tower on the Piazza degli Anziani, ordered the door of the tower to be locked, and the keys to be thrown into the Arno, and forbade any food should be given to the prisoners, who in a few days died of hunger. And the five dead bodies, being taken together out of the tower, were ignominiously buried; and from that day forth the tower was called the Tower of Famine, and shall be forever more. For this cruelty the Pisans were much blamed through all the world where it was known; not so much for the Count's sake, as on account of his crimes and treasons he perhaps deserved such a death, but for the sake of his children and grandchildren, who were young and innocent boys; and this sin, committed by the Pisans, did not remain unpunished."

Chaucer's version of the story in the *Monkes Tale* is as follows: —

> Of the erl Hugelin of Pise the langour
> There may no tonge tellen for pitee.
> But litel out of Pise stant a tour,
> In whiche tour in prison yput was he,
> And with him ben his litel children three,
> The eldest scarsely five yere was of age:
> Alas! fortune, it was gret crueltee
> Swiche briddes for to put in swiche a cage.
>
> Dampned was he to die in that prison,
> For Roger, which that bishop of Pise,
> Had on him made a false suggestion,
> Thurgh which the peple gan upon him rise,
> And put him in prison, in swiche a wise,
> As ye han herd; and mete and drinke he had
> So smale, that wel unnethe it may suffise,
> And therewithal it was ful poure and bad.
>
> And on a day befell, that in that houre,
> Whan that his mete wont was to be brought,
> The gailer shette the dores of the toure;
> He hered it wel, but he spake right nought.

And in his herte anon there fell a thought,
That they for hunger wolden do him dien;
Alas! I quod he, alas that I was wrought!
Therwith the teres fellen fro his eyen.

His yonge sone, that three yere was of age,
Unto him said, fader, why do ye wepe?
Whan will the gailer bringen our potage?
Is ther no morsel bred that ye do kepe?
I am so hungry, that I may not slepe.
Now wolde God that I might slepen ever,
Than shuld not hunger in my wombe crepe;
Ther n'is no thing, sauf bred, that me were lever.

Thus day by day this childe began to crie,
Til in his fadres barme adoun it lay,
And saide, farewel, fader, I mote die;
And kist his fader, and dide the same day.
And whan the woful fader did it sey,
For wo his armes two he gan to bite,
And saide, alas! fortune, and wala wa!
Thy false whele my wo all may I wite.

His children wenden, that for hunger it was
That he his armes gnowe, and not for wo,
And sayden: fader, do not so, alas!
But rather ete the flesh upon us two.
Our flesh thou yaf us, take our flesh us fro,
And ete ynough: right thus they to him seide,
And after that within a day or two,
They laide hem in his lappe adoun, and deide.

Himself dispeired eke for hunger starf.
Thus ended is this mighty Erl of Pise:
From high estat fortune away him carf.
Of this tragedie it ought ynough suffice;
Who so wol here it in a longer wise,
Redeth the grete poete of Itaille,
That highte Dante, for he can it devise
Fro point to point, not o word wol he faille.

Buti, *Commento,* says: "After eight days they were removed from prison and carried wrapped in matting to the church of the Minor Friars at San Francesco, and buried in the monument, which is on the side of the steps leading into the church near the gate of the cloister, with irons on their legs, which irons I myself saw taken out of the monument."

22. "The remains of this tower," says Napier, *Florentine History,* I. 319, note, "still exist in the Piazza de' Cavalieri, on the right of the archway as the spectator looks toward the clock." According to Buti it was called the Mew, "because the eagles of the Commune were kept there to moult."

Shelley thus sings of it, *Poems,* III. 91: —

> Amid the desolation of a city,
> Which was the cradle, and is now the grave
> Of an extinguished people, so that pity
> Weeps o'er the shipwrecks of oblivion's wave,
> There stands the Tower of Famine. It is built
> Upon some prison-homes, whose dwellers rave
> For bread, and gold, and blood: pain, linked to guilt,
> Agitates the light flame of their hours,
> Until its vital oil is spent or spilt;
> There stands the pile, a tower amid the towers
> And sacred domes; each marble-ribbed roof,
> The brazen-gated temples, and the bowers
> Of solitary wealth! The tempest-proof
> Pavilions of the dark Italian air
> Are by its presence dimmed,—they stand aloof,
> And are withdrawn,—so that the world is bare,
> As if a spectre, wrapt in shapeless terror,
> Amid a company of ladies fair
> Should glide and glow, till it became a mirror
> Of all their beauty, and their hair and hue,
> The life of their sweet eyes, with all its error,
> Should be absorbed till they to marble grew.

30. Monte San Giuliano, between Pisa and Lucca.
Shelley, *Poems,* III. 166: —

> It was that hill whose intervening brow
> Screens Lucca from the Pisan's envious eye,
> Which the circumfluous plain waving below
> Like a wide lake of green fertility,
> With streams and fields and marshes bare,
> Divides from the far Apennine, which lie
> Islanded in the immeasurable air.

31. The hounds are the Pisan mob; the hunters, the Pisan noblemen here mentioned; the wolf and whelps, Ugolino and his sons.

46. It is a question whether in this line *chiavar* is to be rendered *nailed up* or *locked*. Villani and Benvenuto say the tower was locked, and the keys thrown into the Arno; and I believe most of the commentators interpret the line in this way. But the locking of a prison door, which must have been a daily occurrence, could hardly have caused the dismay here portrayed, unless it can be shown that the lower door of the tower was usually left unlocked.

   "The thirty lines from *Ed io senti'* are unequalled," says Landor, *Pentameron*, 40, "by any other continuous thirty in the whole dominions of poetry."

80. Italy; it being an old custom to call countries by the affirmative particle of the language.

82. Capraia and Gorgona are two islands opposite the mouth of the Arno. Ampère, *Voyage Dantesque*, 217, remarks: "This imagination may appear grotesque and forced if one looks at the map, for the isle of Gorgona is at some distance from the mouth of the Arno, and I had always thought so, until the day when, having ascended the tower of Pisa, I was struck with the aspect which the Gorgona presented from that point. It seemed to shut up the Arno. I then understood how Dante might naturally have had this idea, which had seemed strange to me, and his imagination was justified in my eyes. He had not seen the Gorgona from the Leaning Tower, which did not exist in his time, but from some one of the numerous towers which protected the ramparts of Pisa. This fact alone would be sufficient to show what an excellent interpretation of a poet travelling is."

86. Napier, *Florentine History*, I. 313: "He without hesitation surrendered Santa Maria a Monte, Fuccechio, Santa Croce, and Monte Calvole to Florence; exiled the most zealous Ghibellines from Pisa, and reduced it to a purely Guelphic republic; he was accused of treachery, and certainly his own objects were admirably forwarded by the continued captivity of so many of his countrymen, by the banishment of the adverse faction, and by the friendship and support of Florence."

87. Thebes was renowned for its misfortunes and grim tragedies, from the days of the sowing of the dragon's teeth by Cadmus, down to the destruction of the city by Alexander, who commanded it to be utterly demolished, excepting only the house in which the poet Pindar was born. Moreover, the tradition runs that Pisa was founded by Pelops, son of King Tantalus of Thebes, although it derived its name from "the Olympic Pisa on the banks of the Alpheus."

118. Friar Alberigo, of the family of the Manfredi, Lords of Faenza, was one

of the *Frati Gaudenti*, or Jovial Friars, mentioned in Canto XXIII. 103. The account which the *Ottimo* gives of his treason is as follows: "Having made peace with certain hostile fellow-citizens, he betrayed them in this wise. One evening he invited them to supper, and had armed retainers in the chambers round the supper-room. It was in summer-time, and he gave orders to his servants that, when after the meats he should order the fruit, the chambers should be opened, and the armed men should come forth and should murder all the guests. And so it was done. And he did the like the year before at Castello delle Mura at Pistoia. These are the fruits of the Garden of Treason, of which he speaks." Benvenuto says that his guests were his brother Manfred and his (Manfred's) son. Other commentators say they were certain members of the Order of *Frati Gaudenti*. In 1300, the date of the poem, Alberigo was still living.

120. A Rowland for an Oliver.

124. This division of Cocytus, the Lake of Lamentation, is called Ptolomæa from Ptolomeus, 1 *Maccabees* xvi. 11, where "the captain of Jericho inviteth Simon and two of his sons into his castle, and there treacherously murdereth them"; for "when Simon and his sons had drunk largely, Ptolomee and his men rose up, and took their weapons, and came upon Simon into the banqueting-place, and slew him, and his two sons, and certain of his servants."

Or perhaps from Ptolemy, who murdered Pompey after the battle of Pharsalia.

126. Of the three Fates, Clotho held the distaff, Lachesis spun the thread, and Atropos cut it.

Odyssey, XI.: "After him I perceived the might of Hercules, an image; for he himself amongst the immortal gods is delighted with banquets, and has the fair-legged Hebe, daughter of the mighty Jove, and golden-sandalled Juno."

137. Ser Branca d' Oria was a Genoese, and a member of the celebrated Doria family of that city. Nevertheless he murdered at table his father-in-law, Michel Zanche, who is mentioned Canto XXII. 88.

151. This vituperation of the Genoese reminds one of the bitter Tuscan proverb against them: "Sea without fish; mountains without trees; men without faith; and women without shame."

There is also a Spanish proverb that says: —

> Al Andaluz
> Hazle la cruz;
> Y al Genoes
> Hazle tres.

154. Friar Alberigo.

155. Chaucer, *The Man of Lawes Tale.*

> Fy feendly spirit, for I dar wel telle,
> Though thou here walke, thy spirit is in helle.

CANTO XXXIV

1. The fourth and last division of the Ninth Circle, the Judecca.

   The first line, "The banners of the king of Hell come forth," is a parody of the first line of a Latin hymn of the sixth century, sung in the churches during Passion week, and written by Fortunatus, an Italian by birth, but who died Bishop of Poitiers in 600. The first stanza of this hymn is,—

> Vexilla regis prodeunt,
> Fulget crucis mysterium,
> Quo carne carnis conditor,
> Suspensus est patibulo.

   See Königsfeld, *Lateinische Hymnen und Gesänge aus dem Mittelalter,* 64.

18. Milton, *Parad. Lost,* V. 708: —

> His countenance as the morning star, that guides
> The starry flock.

28. Compare Milton's descriptions of Satan, *Parad. Lost,* I. 192, 589, II. 636, IV. 985: —

> Thus Satan, talking to his nearest mate,
> With head uplift above the wave, and eyes
> That sparkling blazed; his other parts besides
> Prone on the flood, extended long and large,
> Lay floating many a rood, in bulk as huge
> As whom the fables name of monstrous size,
> Titanian, or Earth-born, that warred on Jove,
> Briareus, or Typhon, whom the den
> By ancient Tarsus held, or that sea-beast
> Leviathan, which God of all his works
> Created hugest that swim the ocean stream:
> Him, haply, slumbering on the Norway foam,
> The pilot of some small night-foundered skiff,
> Deeming some island, oft, as seamen tell,

With fixed anchor in his scaly rind
Moors by his side under the lee, while night
Invests the sea, and wished morn delays.
So stretched out huge in length the Arch-fiend lay
Chained on the burning lake.

He, above the rest
In shape and gesture proudly eminent,
Stood like a tower: his form had yet not lost
All her original brightness, nor appeared
Less than archangel ruined, and the excess
Of glory obscured: as when the sun new-risen
Looks through the horizontal misty air,
Shorn of his beams; or from behind the moon,
In dim eclipse, disastrous twilight sheds
On half the nations, and with fear of change
Perplexes monarchs: darkened so, yet shone
Above them all the Archangel.

As when far off at sea a fleet descried
Hangs in the clouds, by equinoctial winds
Close sailing from Bengala or the isles
Of Ternate and Tidore, whence merchants bring
Their spicy drugs: they on the trading flood
Through the wide Æthiopian to the Cape
Ply, stemming nightly toward the pole: so seemed
Far off the flying fiend.

On the other side, Satan, alarmed,
Collecting all his might, dilated stood,
Like Teneriff or Atlas, unremoved:
His stature reached the sky, and on his crest
Sat horror plumed; nor wanted in his grasp
What seemed both spear and shield.

38. The *Ottimo* and Benvenuto both interpret the three faces as symbolizing Ignorance, Hatred, and Impotence. Others interpret them as signifying the three quarters of the then known world, Europe, Asia, and Africa.
45. Æthiopia; the region about the Cataracts of the Nile.
48. Milton, *Parad. Lost*, II. 527: —

At last his sail-broad vans
He spreads for flight, and in the surging smoke
Uplifted spurns the ground.

55. Landro in his *Pentameron,* 527, makes Petrarca say: "This is atrocious, not terrific nor grand. Alighieri is grand by his lights, not by his shadows; by his human affections, not by his infernal. As the minutest sands are the labors of some profound sea, or the spoils of some vast mountain, in like manner his horrid wastes and wearying minutenesses are the chafings of a turbulent spirit, grasping the loftiest things, and penetrating the deepest, and moving and moaning on the earth in loneliness and sadness."

62. Gabriele Rossetti, *Spirito Antipapale,* I. 75, Miss Ward's Tr., says: "The three spirits, who hang from the mouths of his Satan, are Judas, Brutus, and Cassius. The poet's reason for selecting those names has never yet been satisfactorily accounted for; but we have no hesitation in pronouncing it to have been this,—he considered the Pope not only a betrayer and seller of Christ,—'Where gainful merchandise is made of Christ throughout the livelong day,' (*Parad.* XVII.,) and for that reason put Judas into his centre mouth; but a traitor and rebel to Cæsar, and therefore placed Brutus and Cassius in the other two mouths; for the Pope, who was originally no more than Cæsar's vicar, became his enemy, and usurped the capital of his empire, and the supreme authority. His treason to Christ was not discovered by the world in general; hence the face of Judas is hidden,—'He that hath his head within, and plies the feet without' (*Inf.* XXXIV.); his treason to Cæesar was open and manifest, therefore Brutus and Cassius show their faces."

   He adds in a note: "The situation of Judas is the same as that of the Popes who were guilty of simony."

68. The evening of Holy Saturday.

77. *Iliad,* V. 305: "With this he struck the hip of Æneas, where the thigh turns on the hip."

95. The canonical day, from sunrise to sunset, was divided into four equal parts, called in Italian *Terza, Sesta, Nona,* and *Vespro,* and varying in length with the change of season. "These hours," says Dante, *Convito,* III. 6, "are short or long . . . according as day and night increase or diminish." *Terza* was the first division after sunrise; and at the equinox would be from six till nine. Consequently *mezza terza,* or middle tierce, would be half past seven.

114. Jerusalem.

125. The Mountain of Purgatory, rising out of the sea at a point directly opposite Jerusalem, upon the other side of the globe. It is an island in the South Pacific Ocean.

130. This brooklet is Lethe, whose source is on the summit of the Mountain of Purgatory, flowing down to mingle with Acheron, Styx, and Phlegethon, and form Cocytus. See Canto XIV. 136.

138. It will be observed that each of the three divisions of the Divine Comedy ends with the word "Stars," suggesting and symbolizing endless aspiration. At the end of the *Inferno* Dante "re-beholds the stars"; at the end of the *Purgatorio* he is "ready to ascend to the stars"; at the end of the *Paradiso* he feels the power of "that Love which moves the sun and other stars." He is now looking upon the morning stars of Easter Sunday.

ILLUSTRATIONS

L' OTTIMO COMENTO
Inferno, X. 85

I, THE writer, heard Dante say that never a rhyme had led him to say other than he would, but that many a time and oft he had made words say in his rhymes what they were not wont to express for other poets.

VILLANI'S NOTICE OF DANTE
Cronica, Lib. IX. cap. 136. Tr. in Napier's Florentine History, Book I. ch. 16

IN the month of July, 1321, died the Poet Dante Alighieri of Florence, in the city of Ravenna in Romagna, after his return from an embassy to Venice for the Lords of Polenta with whom he resided; and in Ravenna before the door of the principal church he was interred with high honor, in the habit of a poet and great philosopher. He died in banishment from the community of Florence, at the age of about fifty-six. This Dante was an honorable and ancient citizen of Porta San Piero at Florence, and our neighbor; and his exile from Florence was on the occasion of Charles of Valois, of the house of France, coming to Florence in 1301, and the expulsion of the White party, as has already in its place been mentioned. The said Dante was of the supreme governors of our city, and of that party although a Guelf; and therefore without any other crime was with the said White party expelled and banished from Florence; and he went to the University of Bologna, and into many parts of the world. This was a great and learned person in almost every science, although a layman; he was a consummate poet and philosopher and rhetorician; as perfect in prose and verse as he was in public speaking a most noble orator; in rhyming excellent, with the most polished and beautiful style that ever appeared in our language up to his time or since. He wrote in his youth the book of *The Early Life of Love,* and afterwards when in exile made twenty moral and amorous canzonets very excellent, and amongst other things three noble epistles: one he sent to the Florentine government, complaining of his undeserved exile; another to the Emperor Henry when he was at the siege of Brescia, reprehending him for his delay, and almost prophesying; the third to the Italian cardinals during the vacancy after the death of Pope Clement, urging them to agree in electing an Italian Pope; all in Latin, with noble precepts and excellent sentences and authorities, which were much commended by the wise and learned. And he wrote the *Commedia,* where, in polished verse and with great and subtile arguments, moral, natural, astrological, philosophical, and theological, with new and beautiful figures, similes, and poetical graces, he composed and treated in a hundred chapters or cantos of the existence of hell, purgatory, and paradise; so loftily as may be said of it, that whoever is of subtile intellect may by his said treatise perceive and understand. He was well pleased in this poem to blame and cry out, in the manner of poets, in some places perhaps more than he ought to have done; but it may be that his exile made him do so. He also wrote the *Monarchia,* where he treats of the office of popes and emperors. And he began a comment on fourteen of the above-named moral canzonets in the vulgar tongue, which in consequence of his death is found imperfect except on three, which to judge from what is seen would have proved a lofty, beautiful, subtile, and most important work; because it is equally ornamented with noble opinions and fine philosophical and astrological reasoning. Besides these he composed a little book which he entitled *De Vulgari Eloquentia,* of which he promised to make four books, but only two are to be found, perhaps in consequence of his early death; where, in powerful and elegant Latin and good reasoning, he rejects all the vulgar tongues of Italy. This Dante, from his knowledge, was somewhat presumptuous, harsh, and disdainful, like an ungracious philosopher; he scarcely deigned to converse with laymen; but for his other virtues, science, and worth as a citizen, it seems but reasonable to give him perpetual remembrance in this our chronicle; nevertheless, his noble works, left to us in writing, bear true testimony of him, and honorable fame to our city.

LETTER OF FRATE ILARIO

Arrivabene, Comento Storico, p. 379

... HITHER he came, passing through the diocese of Luni, moved either by the religion of the place, or by some other feeling. And seeing him, as yet unknown to me and to all my brethren, I questioned him of his wishings and his seekings there. He moved not; but stood silently contemplating the columns and arches of the cloister. And again I asked him what he wished, and whom he sought. Then, slowly turning his head, and looking at the friars and at me, he answered: "Peace!" Thence kindling more and more the wish to know him and who he might be, I led him aside somewhat, and, having spoken a few words with him, I knew him; for although I had never seen him till that hour, his fame had long since reached me. And when he saw that I hung upon his countenance, and listened to him with strange affection, he drew from his bosom a book, did gently open it, and offered it to me, saying: "Sir Friar, here is a portion of my work, which peradventure thou hast not seen. This remembrance I leave with thee. Forget me not." And when he had given me the book, I pressed it gratefully to my bosom, and in his presence fixed my eyes upon it with great love. But I beholding there the vulgar tongue, and showing by the fashion of my countenance my wonderment thereat, he asked the reason of the same. I answered, that I marvelled he should sing in that language; for it seemed a difficult thing, nay, incredible, that those most high conceptions could be expressed in common language; nor did it seem to me right that such and so worthy a science should be clothed in such plebeian garments. "You think aright," he said, "and I myself have thought so. And when at first the seeds of these matters, perhaps inspired by Heaven, began to bud, I chose that language which was most worthy of them: and not alone chose it, but began forthwith to poetize therein, after this wise:

> Ultima regna canam fluido contermina mundo,
> Spiritibus quæ lata patent; quæ præmia solvunt
> Pro meritis cuicumque suis.

But when I recalled the condition of the present age, and saw the songs of the illustrious poets esteemed almost as naught, and knew that the generous men, for whom in better days these things were written, had abandoned, ah me! the liberal arts unto vulgar hands, I threw aside the delicate lyre, which had armed my flank, and attuned another more befitting the ear of moderns;—for the food that is hard we hold in vain to the mouths of sucklings."

Having said this, he added with emotion, that, if the occasion served, I should make some brief annotations upon the work, and, thus apparailed, should forward it to you. Which task in truth, although I may not have extracted all the marrow of his words, I have nevertheless performed with fidelity; and the work required of me I frankly send you, as was enjoined upon me by that most friendly man; in which work, if it appear that any ambiguity still remains, you must impute it to my insufficiency, for there is no doubt that the text is perfect in all points. . . .

PASSAGE FROM THE CONVITO, I. III

Leigh Hunt, Stories from the Italian Poets, p. 12

AH! would it had pleased the Dispenser of all things that this excuse had never been needed; that neither others had done me wrong, nor myself undergone penalty undeservedly,—the penalty, I say, of exile and of poverty. For it pleased the citizens of the fairest and most renowned daughter of Rome—Florence—to cast me out of her most sweet bosom, where I was born, and bred, and passed half of the life of man, and in which, with her good leave, I still desire with all my heart to repose my weary spirit, and finish the days allotted me; and so I have wandered in almost every place to which our language extends, a stranger, almost a beggar, exposing against my will the wounds given me by fortune, too often unjustly imputed to the sufferer's fault. Truly I have been a vessel without sail and without rudder, driven about upon different ports and shores by the dry wind that springs out of dolorous poverty; and hence have I appeared vile in the eyes of many, who, perhaps, by some better report had conceived of me a different impression, and in whose sight not only has my person become thus debased, but an unworthy opinion created of everything which I did, or which I had to do.

DANTE'S LETTER TO A FRIEND

Leigh Hunt, Stories from the Italian Poets, p. 13

FROM your letter, which I received with due respect and affection, I observe how much you have at heart my restoration to my country. I am bound to you the more gratefully, inasmuch as an exile rarely finds a friend. But after mature consideration I must, by my answer, disappoint the wishes of some little minds; and I confide in the judgment to which your impartiality and prudence will lead you. Your nephew and mine has written to me, what indeed had been mentioned by many other friends, that by a decree concerning the exiles I am allowed to return to Florence, provided I pay a certain sum of money, and submit to the humiliation of asking and receiving absolution: wherein, my father, I see two propositions that are ridiculous and impertinent. I speak of the impertinence of those who mention such conditions to me; for in your letter, dictated by judgment and discretion, there is no such thing. Is such an invitation, then, to return to his country glorious to Dante Alighieri, after suffering in exile almost fifteen years? Is it thus they would recompense innocence which all the world knows, and the labor and fatigue of unremitting study? Far from the man who is familiar with philosophy be the senseless baseness of a heart of earth, that could act like a little sciolist, and imitate the infamy of some others, by offering himself up as it were in chains: far from the man who cries aloud for justice, this compromise by his money with his persecutors. No, my father, this is not the way that shall lead me back to my country. I will return with hasty steps, if you or any other can open to me a way that shall not derogate from the fame and honor of Dante; but if by no such way Florence can be entered, then Florence I shall never enter. What! shall I not everywhere enjoy the light of the sun and stars? and may I not seek and contemplate, in every corner of the earth, under the canopy of heaven, consoling and delightful truth, without first rendering myself inglorious, nay infamous, to the people and republic of Florence? Bread, I hope, will not fail me.

PORTRAITS OF DANTE

By Charles E. Norton

IN his *Life of Dante*, Boccaccio, the earliest of the biographers of the poet, describes him in these words: "Our poet was of middle height, and after reaching mature years he went somewhat stooping; his gait was grave and sedate; always clothed in most becoming garments, his dress was suited to the ripeness of his years; his face was long, his nose aquiline, his eyes rather large than small, his jaw heavy, and his under lip prominent; his complexion was dark, and his hair and beard thick, black, and crisp, and his countenance was always sad and thoughtful.... His manners, whether in public or at home, were wonderfully composed and restrained, and in all his ways he was more courteous and civil than any one else."

Such was Dante as he appeared in his later years to those from whose recollections of him Boccaccio drew this description.

But Boccaccio, had he chosen so to do, might have drawn another portrait of Dante, not the author of the *Divine Comedy*, but the author of the *New Life*. The likeness of the youthful Dante was familiar to those Florentines who had never looked on the living presence of their greatest citizen.

On the altar-wall of the chapel of the Palace of the Podestà (now the Bargello) Giotto had painted a grand religious composition, in which, after the fashion of the times, he exalted the glory of Florence by the introduction of some of her most famous citizens into the assembly of the blessed in Paradise. "The head of Christ, full of dignity, appears above, and lower down, the escutcheon of Florence, supported by angels, with two rows of saints, male and female, attendant to the right and left, in front of whom stand a company of the *magnates* of the city, headed by two crowned personages, close to one of whom, to the right, stands Dante, a pomegranate in his hand, and wearing the graceful falling cap of the day."[1] The date when this picture was painted is uncertain, but Giotto represented his friend in it as a youth, such as he may have been in the first flush of early fame, at the season of the beginning of their memorable friendship.

Of all the portraits of the revival of Art, there is none comparable in interest to this likeness of the supreme poet by the supreme artist of mediæval Europe. It was due to no accident of fortune that these men were contemporaries, and of the same country; but it was a fortunate and delightful incident, that they were so brought together by sympathy of genius and by favoring circumstance as to become friends, to love and honor each other in life, and to celebrate each other through all time in their respective works. The story of

---

1. Lord Lindsay's *History of Christian Art*, Vol. II. p. 174.

their friendship is known only in its outline, but that it began when they were young is certain, and that it lasted till death divided them is a tradition which finds ready acceptance.

It was probably between 1290 and 1300, when Giotto was just rising to unrivalled fame, that this painting was executed. There is no contemporary record of it, the earliest known reference to it being that by Filippo Villani, who died about 1404. Gianozzo Manetti, who died in 1459, also mentions it, and Vasari, in his *Life of Giotto*, published in 1550, says, that Giotto "became so good an imitator of nature, that he altogether discarded the stiff Greek manner, and revived the modern and good art of painting, introducing exact drawing from nature of living persons, which for more than two hundred years had not been practised, or if indeed any one had tried it, he had not succeeded very happily, nor anything like so well as Giotto. And he portrayed among other persons, as may even now be seen, in the chapel of the Palace of the Podestà in Florence, Dante Alighieri, his contemporary and greatest friend, who was not less famous a poet than Giotto was painter in those days. . . . In the same chapel is the portrait by the same hand of Ser Brunetto Latini, the master of Dante, and of Messer Corso Donati, a great citizen of those times."

One might have supposed that such a picture as this would have been among the most carefully protected and jealously prized treasures of Florence. But such was not the case. The shameful neglect of many of the best and most interesting works of the earlier period of Art, which accompanied and was one of the symptoms of the moral and political decline of Italy during the sixteenth and seventeenth centuries, extended to this as to other of the noblest paintings of Giotto. Florence, in losing consciousness of present worth, lost care for the memorials of her past honor, dignity, and distinction. The Palace of the Podestà, no longer needed for the dwelling of the chief magistrate of a free city, was turned into a jail for common criminals, and what had once been its beautiful and sacred chapel was occupied as a larder or storeroom. The walls, adorned with paintings more precious than gold, were covered with whitewash, and the fresco of Giotto was swept over by the brush of the plasterer. It was not only thus hidden from the sight of those unworthy indeed to behold it, but it almost disappeared from memory also; and from the time of Vasari down to that of Moreni, a Florentine antiquary, in the early part of the present century, hardly a mention of it occurs. In a note found among his papers, Moreni laments that he had spent two years of his life in unavailing efforts to recover the portrait of Dante, and the other portions of the fresco of Giotto in the Bargello, mentioned by Vasari; that others before him had made a like effort, and had failed in like manner; and that he hoped that better times would come, in which this painting, of such historic and artistic interest, would again be sought for, and at length recovered. Stimulated by these words, three gentlemen, one an American, Mr. Richard Henry Wilde, one an Englishman, Mr. Seymour Kirkup, and one an Italian, Signor C. Aubrey Bezzi, all scholars devoted to the study of Dante, undertook new researches, in 1840, and, after many hindrances on the part of the government, which were at length successfully overcome, the work of removing the crust of plaster from the walls of the ancient chapel was intrusted to the Florentine painter, Marini. This new and well-directed search did not fail. After some months' labor the fresco was found, almost uninjured, under the whitewash that had protected while concealing it, and at length the likeness of Dante was uncovered.

"But," says Mr. Kirkup, in a letter published in the *Spectator* (London), May 11, 1850, "the eye of the beautiful profile was wanting. There was a hole an inch deep, or an inch and a half. Marini said it was a nail. It did seem precisely the damage of a nail drawn out. Afterwards . . . Marini filled the hole, and made a new eye, too little and ill designed, and then he retouched the whole face and clothes, to the great damage of the expression and character. The likeness of the face, and the three colors in which Dante was dressed, the same with those of Beatrice, those of young Italy, white, green, and red, stand no more; the green is turned to chocolate-color; moreover, the form of the cap is lost and confounded.

"I desired to make a drawing. . . . It was denied to me. . . . But I obtained the means to be shut up in the prison for a morning; and not only did I make a drawing, but a tracing also, and with the two I then made a fac-simile sufficiently careful. Luckily it was before the *rifacimento*."

This fac-simile afterwards passed into the hands of Lord Vernon, well known for his interest in all Dantesque studies, and by his permission it had been admirably reproduced in chromo-lithography under the auspices of the Arundel Society. The reproduction is entirely satisfactory as a presentation of the authentic portrait of the youthful Dante, in the state in which it was when Mr. Kirkup was so fortunate as to gain admission to it. . . .

This portrait by Giotto is the only likeness of Dante known to have been made of the poet during his life, and is of inestimable value on this account. But there exists also a mask, concerning which there is a tradition that it was taken from the face of the dead poet, and which, if its genuineness could be established, would not be of inferior interest to the early portrait. But there is no trustworthy historic testimony concerning it, and its authority as a likeness depends upon the evidence of truth which its own character affords. On the very threshold of the inquiry concerning it, we are met with the doubt whether the art of taking casts was practised at the time of Dante's death. In his *Life of Andrea de Verrocchio*, Vasari says that this art began to come into use in his time, that is, about the middle of the fifteenth century; and Bottari refers to the likeness of Brunelleschi, who died in 1446, which was taken in this manner, and was preserved in the office of the Works of the Cathedral at Florence. It is not impossible that so simple an art may have been sometimes practised at an earlier period; and if so, there is no inherent improbability in the supposition that Guido Novello, the friend and protector of Dante at Ravenna, may, at the time of the poet's death, have had a mask taken to serve as a model for the head of a statue intended to form part of the monument which he proposed to erect in honor of Dante. And it may further be supposed, that, this design failing, owing to the fall of Guido from power before its accomplishment, the mask may have been preserved at Ravenna, till we first catch a trace of it nearly three centuries later.

There is in the Magliabecchiana Library at Florence an autograph manuscript by Giovanni Cinelli, a Florentine antiquary who died in 1706, entitled *La Toscana letterata, ovvero Istoria degli Scrittori Fiorentini*, which contains a life of Dante. In the course of the biography Cinelli states that the Archbishop of Ravenna caused the head of the poet which had adorned his sepulchre to be taken therefrom, and that it came into the possession of the famous sculptor, Gian Bologna, who left it at his death, in 1606, to his pupil Pietro Tacca. "One day Tacca showed it, with other curiosities, to the Duchess Sforza, who, having wrapped it in a scarf of green cloth, carried it away, and God knows into whose hands the precious object has fallen, or where it is to be found. . . . On account of its singular beauty, it had often been drawn by the scholars of Tacca." It has been supposed that this head was the original mask from which the casts now existing are derived. Mr. Seymour Kirkup, in a note on this passage from Cinelli, says that "there are three masks of Dante at Florence, all of which have been judged by the first Roman and Florentine sculptors to have been taken from life, [that is, from the face after death,]—the slight differences noticeable between them being such as might occur in casts made from the original mask." One of these casts was given to Mr. Kirkup by the sculptor Bartolini, another belonged to the late sculptor Professor Ricci, and the third is in the possession of the Marchese Torrigiani. . . .

In the absence of historical evidence in regard to this mask, some support is given to the belief in its genuineness by the fact that it appears to be the type of the greater number of the portraits of Dante executed from the fourteenth to the sixteenth century, and was adopted by Raffaelle as the original from which he drew the likeness which has done most to make the features of the poet familiar to the world.

The character of the mask itself affords, however, the only really satisfactory ground for confidence in the truth of the tradition concerning it. It was plainly taken as a cast from a face after death. It has none of the characteristics which a fictitious and imaginative representation of the sort would be likely to present. It bears no trace of being a work of skilful and deceptive art. The difference in the fall of the two half-closed eyelids, the difference between the sides of the face, the slight deflection in the line of the nose, the droop of the corners of the mouth, and other delicate, but none the less convincing indications, combine to show that it was in all probability taken directly from nature. The countenance, moreover, and expression, are worthy of Dante; no ideal forms could so answer to the face of him who had led a life apart from the world in which he dwelt, and had been conducted by love and faith along hard, painful, and solitary ways to behold

L' alto trionfo del regno verace.

The mask conforms entirely to the description by Boccaccio of the poet's countenance, save that it is beardless, and this difference is to be accounted for by the fact that to obtain the cast the beard must have been removed.

The face is one of the most pathetic upon which human eyes ever looked, for it exhibits in its expression the conflict between the strong nature of the man and the hard dealings of fortune,—between the idea of his life and its practical experience. Strength is the most striking attribute of the countenance, displayed alike in the broad forehead, the masculine nose, the firm lips, the heavy jaw and wide chin; and this strength, resulting from the main forms of the features, is enforced by the strength of the lines of expression. The look is grave and stern almost to grimness; there is a scornful lift to the eyebrow, and a contraction of the forehead as from painful thought; but obscured under this look, yet not lost, are the marks of tenderness, refinement, and self-mastery, which, in combination with the more obvious characteristics, give to the countenance of the dead poet an ineffable dignity and melancholy. There is neither weakness nor failure here. It is the image of the strong fortress of a strong soul "buttressed on conscience and impregnable will," battered by the blows of enemies without and within, bearing upon its walls the dints of many a siege, but standing firm and unshaken against all attacks until the warfare was at end.

The intrinsic evidence for the truth of this likeness, from its correspondence, not only with the description of the poet, but with the imagination that we form of him from his life and works, is strongly confirmed by a comparison of the mask with the portrait by Giotto. So far as I am aware, this comparison has not hitherto been made in a manner to exhibit effectively the resemblance between the two. A direct comparison between the painting and the mask, owing to the difficulty of reducing the forms of the latter to a plain surface of light and shade, is unsatisfactory. But by taking a photograph from the mask, in the same position as that in which the face is painted by Giotto, and placing it alongside of the fac-simile from the painting, a very remarkable similarity becomes at once apparent.... The differences are only such as must exist between the portrait of a man in the freshness of a happy youth, and the portrait of him in his age, after much experience and many trials. Dante was fifty-six years old at the time of his death, when the mask was taken; the portrait by Giotto represents him as not much past twenty. There is an interval of at least thirty years between the two. And what years they had been for him!

The interest of this comparison lies not only in the mutual support which the portraits afford each other, in the assurance each gives that the other is genuine, but also in their joint illustration of the life and character of Dante. As Giotto painted him, he is the lover of Beatrice, the gay companion of princes, the friend of poets, and himself already the most famous writer of love verses in Italy. There is an almost feminine softness in the lines of the face, with a sweet and serious tenderness well befitting the lover, and the author of the sonnets and canzoni which were in a few years to be gathered into the incomparable record of his *New Life*. It is the face of Dante in the Maytime of youthful hope, in that serene season of promise and of joy, which was so soon to reach its foreordained close in the death of her who had made life new and beautiful for him, and to the love and honor of whom he dedicated his soul and gave all his future years. It is the same face with that of the mask; but the one is the face of a youth, "with all triumphant splendor on his brow," the other of a man, burdened with "the dust and injury of age." The forms and features are alike, but as to the later face,

> That time of year thou mayst in it behold
> When yellow leaves, or none, or few, do hang
> Upon those boughs which shake against the cold,
> Bare ruined choirs, where late the sweet birds sang.

The face of the youth is grave, as with the shadow of distant sorrow; the face of the man is solemn, as of one who had gone

> Per tutti i cerchj del dolente regno.

The one is the young poet of Florence, the other the supreme poet of the world,—

> Che al divino dall' umano,
> All' eterno dal tempo era venuto.

BOCCACCIO'S ACCOUNT OF THE COMMEDIA

Balbo, Life of Dante. Tr. by Mrs. Bunbury, II. 61, 269, 290

IT should be known that Dante had a sister who was married to one of our citizens, called Leon Poggi, by whom she had several children. Among these was one called Andrew, who wonderfully resembled Dante in the outline of his features, and in his height and figure; and he also walked rather stooping, as Dante is said to have done. He was a weak man, but with naturally good feelings, and his language and conduct were regular and praiseworthy. And I having become intimate with him, he often spoke to me of Dante's habits and ways; but among those things which I delight most in recollecting, is what he told me relating to that of which we are now speaking. He said then, that Dante belonged to the party of Messer Vieri de' Cerchi, and was one of its great leaders; and when Messer Vieri and many of his followers left Florence, Dante left that city also and went to Verona. And on account of this departure, through the solicitation of the opposite party, Messer Vieri, and all who had left Florence, especially the principal persons, were considered as rebels, and had their persons condemned and their property confiscated. When the people heard this, they ran to the houses of those proscribed, and plundered all that was within them. It is true that Dante's wife, Madonna Gemma, fearing this, and by the advice of some of her friends and relations, had withdrawn from his house some chests containing certain precious things, and Dante's writings along with them, and had put them in a place of safety. And not satisfied with having plundered the houses of the proscribed, the most powerful partisans of the opposite faction occupied their possessions,—some taking one and some another,—and thus Dante's house was occupied.

But after five years or more had elapsed, and the city was more rationally governed, it is said, than it was when Dante was sentenced, persons began to question their rights, on different grounds, to what had been the property of the exiles, and they were heard. Therefore Madonna Gemma was advised to demand back Dante's property, on the ground that it was her dowry. She, to prepare this business, required certain writings and documents which were in one of the chests, which, in the violent plunder of the effects, she had sent away, nor had she ever since removed them from the place where she had deposited them. For this purpose, this Andrew said, she had sent for him, and as Dante's nephew had intrusted him with the keys of these chests, and had sent him with a lawyer to search for the required papers; while the lawyer searched for these, he, Andrew, among other of Dante's writings, found many sonnets, canzoni, and such similar pieces. But among them what pleased him the most was a sheet in which, in Dante's handwriting, the seven preceding cantos were written; and therefore he took it and carried it off with him, and read it over and over again; and although he understood but little of it, still it appeared to him a very fine thing; and therefore he determined, in order to know what it was, to carry it to an esteemed man of our city, who in those times was a much celebrated reciter of verses, whose name was Dino, the son of Messer Lambertuccio Frescobaldi.

It pleased Dino marvellously; and having made copies of it for several of his friends, and knowing that the composition was merely begun, and not completed, he thought that it would be best to send it to Dante, and at the same time to beg him to follow up his design, and to finish it; and having inquired, and ascertained that Dante was at this time in the Lunigiana, with a noble man of the family of Malaspina, called the Marquis Moroello, who was a man of understanding, and who had a singular friendship for him, he thought of sending it, not to Dante himself, but to the Marquis, in order that he should show it to him: and so Dino did, begging him that, as far as it lay in his power, he would exert his good offices to induce Dante to continue and finish his work.

The seven aforesaid cantos having reached the Marquis's hands, and having marvellously pleased him, he showed them to Dante; and having heard from him that they were his composition, he entreated him to continue the work. To this it is said that Dante answered: "I really supposed that these, along with many of my other writings and effects, were lost when my house was plundered, and therefore I had given up all thoughts of them. But since it has pleased God that they should not be lost, and he has thus restored them to me, I shall endeavor, as far as I am able, to proceed with them according to my first design." And recalling his old thoughts, and resuming his interrupted work, he speaks thus in the beginning of the eighth canto: "My wondrous history I here renew."

Now precisely the same story, almost without any alteration, has been related to me by a Ser Dino Perino, one of our citizens and an intelligent man, who, according to his own account, had been on the most friendly and familiar terms with Dante; but he so far alters the story, that he says, "It was not Andrea Leoni, but I myself, who was sent by the lady to the chests for the papers, and that found these seven cantos and took them to Dino, the son of Messer Lambertuccio." I do not know to which of these I ought to give most credit, but whichever of them spoke the truth, still a doubt occurs to me in what they say, which I cannot in any manner solve to my satisfaction; and my doubt is this. The poet introduces Ciacco into the sixth canto, and makes him prophesy, that before three years had elapsed from the moment he was speaking, the party to which Dante belonged should fall, and so it happened. But we know the removal of the Bianchi from office, and their departure from Florence, all happened at once; and therefore, if the author departed at that time, how could he have written this,—and not only this, but another canto after it? . . .

And those friends he left behind him, his sons and his disciples, having searched at many times and for several months everything of his writing, to see whether he had left any conclusion to his work, could find in nowise any of the remaining cantos; his friends generally being much mortified that God had not at least lent him so long to the world, that he might have been able to complete the small remaining part of his work; and having sought so long and never found it; they remained in despair. Jacopo and Piero were sons of Dante, and each of them being rhymers, they were induced by the persuasions of their friends to endeavor to complete, as far as they were able, their father's work, in order that it should not remain imperfect; when to Jacopo, who was more eager about it than his brother, there appeared a wonderful vision, which not only induced him to abandon such presumptuous folly, but showed him where the thirteen cantos were which were wanting to the *Divina Commedia,* and which they had not been able to find. . . .

A worthy man of Ravenna, whose name was Pier Giardino, and who had long been Dante's disciple, grave in his manner and worthy of credit, relates that, after the eighth month from the day of his master's death, there came to his house before dawn Jacopo di Dante, who told him that that night, while he was asleep, his father Dante had appeared to him, clothed in the whitest garments, and his face resplendent with an extraordinary light; that he, Jacopo, asked him if he lived, and that Dante replied: "Yes, but in the true life, not our life." Then he, Jacopo, asked him if he had completed his work before passing into the true life and, if he had done so, what had become of that part of it which was missing, which they none of them had been able to find. To this Dante seemed to answer, "Yes, I finished it"; and then took him, Jacopo, by the hand, and led him into that chamber in which he, Dante, had been accustomed to sleep when he lived in this life, and, touching one of the walls, he said, "What you have sought for so much, is here"; and at these words both Dante and sleep fled from Jacopo at once. For which reason Jacopo said he could not rest without coming to explain what he had seen to Pier Giardino, in order that they should go together and search out the place thus pointed out to him, which he had retained excellently in his memory, and to see whether this had been pointed out by a true spirit, or a false delusion. For which purpose, although it was still far in the night, they set off together, and went to the house in which Dante resided at the time of his death. Having called up its present owner, he admitted them, and they went to the place thus pointed out; there they found a blind fixed to the wall, as they had always been used to see it in past days; they lifted it gently up, when they found a little window in the wall, never before seen by any of them, nor did they even know it was there. In it they found several writings, all mouldy from the dampness of the walls, and had they remained there longer, in a little while they would have crumbled away. Having thoroughly cleared away the mould, they found them to be the thirteen cantos that had been wanting to complete the *Commedia*.

THE POSTHUMOUS DANTE

By J. R. Lowell in the American Cyclopædia, Art. Dante

LOOKED at outwardly, the life of Dante seems to have been an utter and disastrous failure. What its inward satisfaction must have been, we, with the *Paradiso* open before us, can form some faint conception. To him, longing with an intensity which only the word *Dantesque* will express to realize an ideal upon earth, and continually baffled and misunderstood, the far greater part of his mature life must have been labor and sorrow. We can see how essential all that sad experience was to him, can understand why all the fairy stories hide the luck in the ugly black casket; but to him, then and there, how seemed it?

> Thou shalt relinquish everything of thee
> Beloved most dearly; this that arrow is
> Shot from the bow of exile first of all;
> And thou shalt prove how salt a savor hath
> The bread of others, and how hard a path
> To climb and to descend the stranger's stairs!
> *Parad.* xvii.

Come sa di sale! Who never wet his bread with tears, says Goethe, knows ye not, ye heavenly powers! Our nineteenth century made an idol of the noble lord who broke his heart in verse once every six months, but the fourteenth was lucky enough to produce and not to make an idol of that rarest earthly phenomenon, a man of genius who could hold heartbreak at bay for twenty years, and would not let himself die till he had done his task. At the end of the *Vita Nuova*, his first work, Dante wrote down that remarkable aspiration that God would take him to himself after he had written of Beatrice such things as were never yet written of woman. It was literally fulfilled when the *Commedia* was finished, twenty-five years later. Scarce was Dante at rest in his grave when Italy felt instinctively that this was her great man. Boccaccio tells us that in 1329 Cardinal Poggetto (du Poiet) caused Dante's treatise *De Monarchiâ* to be publicly burned at Bologna, and proposed further to dig up and burn the bones of the poet at Ravenna, as having been a heretic; but so much opposition was roused that he thought better of it. Yet this was during the pontificate of the Frenchman, John XXII., the reproof of whose simony Dante puts in the mouth of St. Peter, who declares his seat vacant (*Parad.* XXVII.), whose damnation the poet himself seems to prophesy (*Inf.* XI.), and against whose election he had endeavored to persuade the cardinals, in a vehement letter. In 1350 the republic of Florence voted the sum of ten golden florins to be paid by the hands of Messer Giovanni Boccaccio to Dante's daughter Beatrice, a nun in the convent of Santa Chiara at Ravenna. In 1396 Florence voted a monument, and begged in vain for the metaphorical ashes of the man of whom she had threatened to make literal cinders if she could catch him alive. In 1429 she begged again, but Ravenna, a dead city, was tenacious of the dead poet. In 1519 Michael Angelo would have built the monument, but Leo X. refused to allow the sacred dust to be removed. Finally, in 1829, five hundred and eight years after the death of Dante, Florence got a cenotaph fairly built in Santa Croce (by Ricci), ugly beyond even the usual lot of such, with three colossal figures on it, Dante in the middle, with Italy on one side and Poesy on the other. The tomb at Ravenna, built originally in 1483, by Cardinal Bembo, was restored by Cardinal Conri in 1692, and finally rebuilt in its present form by Cardinal Gonzaga, in 1780, all three of whom commemorated themselves in Latin inscriptions. It is a little shrine covered with a dome, not unlike the tomb of a Mohammedan saint, and is now the chief magnet which draws foreigners and their gold to Ravenna. The *valet de place* says that Dante is not buried under it, but beneath the pavement of the street in front of it, where also, he says, he saw my Lord Byron kneel and weep. Like everything in Ravenna, it is dirty and neglected. In 1373 (Aug. 9) Florence instituted a chair of the *Divina Commedia,* and Boccaccio was named first professor. He accordingly began his lectures on Sunday, Oct. 3, following, but his comment was broken off abruptly at the seventeenth verse of the seventeenth canto of the *Inferno,* by the illness which ended in his death, Dec. 21, 1375. Among his successors was Filippo Villani and Filelfo. Bologna was the first to follow the example of Florence, Benvenuto da Imola having begun his lectures, according to Tiraboschi, as early as 1375. Chairs were established also at Pisa, Venice, Piacenza, and Milan before the close of the century. The lectures were delivered in the churches and on feast days, which shows their popular character. Balbo reckons (but that is guesswork) that the manuscript copies of the *Divina Commedia* made during the fourteenth century, and now existing in the libraries of Europe, are more numerous than those of all other works, ancient and modern, made during the same period. Between the invention of printing and the year 1500, more than twenty editions were published in Italy, the earliest in 1472. During the sixteenth century there were forty editions; during the seventeenth, a period, for Italy, of sceptical dilettantism, only three; during the eighteenth, thirty-four; and already, during the first half of the nineteenth, at least eighty. The first translation was into Spanish, in 1428.

M. St. René Taillandier says that the *Commedia* was condemned by the Inquisition in Spain, but this seems too general a statement, for, according to Foscolo (*Dante*, Vol. IV. p. 116), it was the commentary of Landino and Vellutello, and a few verses in the *Inferno* and *Paradiso*, which were condemned. The first French translation was that of Grangier, 1596, but the study of Dante struck no root there till the present century. Rivarol, who translated the *Inferno* in 1783, was the first Frenchman who divined the wonderful force and vitality of the *Commedia*. The expressions of Voltaire represent very well the average opinion of cultivated persons in respect of Dante in the middle of the eighteenth century. He says: "The Italians call him divine; but it is a hidden divinity; few people understand his oracles. He has commentators, which, perhaps, is another reason for his not being understood. His reputation will go on increasing, because scarce anybody reads him." (*Dict. Phil.*, art. "Dante.") To Father Bettinelli he writes: "I estimate highly the courage with which you have dared to say that Dante was a madman and his work a monster." But he adds, what shows that Dante had his admirers even in that flippant century: "There are found among us, and in the eighteenth century, people who strive to admire imaginations so stupidly extravagant and barbarous." (*Corresp. gén., Œuvres*, Tom. LVII. pp. 80, 81.) Elsewhere he says that the *Commedia* was "an odd poem, but gleaming with natural beauties, a work in which the author rose in parts above the bad taste of his age and his subject, and full of passages written as purely as if they had been of the time of Ariosto and Tasso." (*Essai sur les Mœurs, Œuvres*, Tom. XVII. pp. 371, 372.) It is curious to see this antipathetic fascination which Dante exercised over a nature so opposite to his own. At the beginning of this century Châteaubriand speaks of Dante with vague commendation, evidently from a very superficial acquaintance, and that only with the *Inferno*, probably from Rivarol's version. Since then there have been four or five French versions in prose or verse, including one by Lamennais. But the austerity of Dante will not condescend to the conventional elegance which makes the charm of French, and the most virile of poets cannot be adequately rendered in the most feminine of languages. Yet in the works of Fauriel, Ozanam, Ampère, and Villemain, France has given a greater impulse to the study of Dante than any other country except Germany. Into Germany the *Commedia* penetrated later. How utterly Dante was unknown there in the sixteenth century is plain from a passage in the *Vanity of the Arts and Sciences* of Cornelius Agrippa, where he is spoken of among the authors of lascivious stories: "There have been many of these historical pandars, of which some of obscure fame, as Æneas Sylvius, Dantes, and Petrarch, Boccace, Pontanus," &c. The first German translation was that of Kannegiesser (1809). Versions by Streckfuss, Kopisch, and Prince John (now king) of Saxony followed. Goethe seems never to have given that attention to Dante which his ever-alert intelli-

gence might have been expected to bestow on so imposing a moral and æs-
thetic phenomenon. Unless the conclusion of the second part of *Faust* be
an inspiration of the *Paradiso,* we remember no adequate word from him
on this theme. His remarks on one of the German translations are brief,
dry, and without that breadth which comes only of thorough knowledge and
sympathy. But German scholarship and constructive criticism, through Witte,
Kopisch, Wegele, Ruth, and others, have been of pre-eminent service in deep-
ening the understanding and facilitating the study of the poet. In England, the
first recognition of Dante is by Chaucer in the *Hugelin of Pisa* of the *Monkes
Tale,* and an imitation of the opening verses of the third canto of the *Inferno*
(*Assembly of Foules*). In 1417, Giovanni da Serravalle, Bishop of Fermo, com-
pleted a Latin prose translation of the *Commedia,* a copy of which, as he made
it at the request of two English bishops whom he met at the Council of
Constance, was doubtless sent to England. Later we find Dante now and
then mentioned, but evidently from hearsay only, till the time of Mil-
ton, who shows that he has read his works closely. Thenceforward for
more than a century Dante became a mere name, used without meaning
by literary sciolists. Lord Chesterfield echoes Voltaire, and Dr. Drake in
his *Literary Hours* could speak of Darwin's *Botanic Garden* as showing the
"wild and terrible sublimity of Dante"! The first complete English transla-
tion was by Boyd, of the *Inferno,* 1785, of the whole poem, 1802. There
have been six other complete translations, beginning with Cary's in 1814,
four since 1850, beside several of the *Inferno* singly. It is only within the
last twenty years, however, that the study of Dante, in any true sense, became
at all general. Even Coleridge seems to have been familiar only with the *In-
ferno.*

THE SCHOLASTIC PHILOSOPHY

From Milman's History of Latin Christianity, Book XIV. Ch. III

Now came the great age of the Schoolmen. Latin Christianity raised up
those vast monuments of Theology which amaze and appall the mind with
the enormous accumulation of intellectual industry, ingenuity, and toil; but of
which the sole result to posterity is this barren amazement. The tomes of
Scholastic Divinity may be compared with the Pyramids of Egypt, which
stand in that rude majesty which is commanding from the display of immense
human power, yet oppressive from the sense of the waste of that power for no
discoverable use. Whoever penetrates within finds himself bewildered and
lost in a labyrinth of small, dark, intricate passages and chambers, devoid of
grandeur, devoid of solemnity: he may wander without end, and find nothing!
It was not indeed the enforced labor of a slave population: it was rather vol-
untary slavery, submitting in its intellectual ambition and its religious pa-

tience to monastic discipline: it was the work of a small intellectual oligarchy, monks, of necessity, in mind and habits; for it imperiously required absolute seclusion either in the monastery or in the university, a long life under monastic rule. No Schoolman could be a great man but as a Schoolman. William of Ockham alone was a powerful demagogue,—scholastic even in his political writings, but still a demagogue. It is singular to see every kingdom in Latin Christendom, every order in the social state, furnishing the great men, not merely to the successive lines of Doctors, who assumed the splendid titles of the Angelical, the Seraphic, the Irrefragable, the most Profound, the most Subtile, the Invincible, even the Perspicuous, but to what may be called the supreme Pentarchy of Scholasticism. Italy sent Thomas of Aquino and Bonaventura; Germany, Albert the Great; the British Isles (they boasted also of Alexander Hales and Bradwardine) Duns Scotus and William of Ockham; France alone must content herself with names somewhat inferior (she had already given Abélard, Gilbert de la Porée, Amauri de Bene, and other famous or suspected names), now William of Auvergne, at a later time Durandus. Albert and Aquinas were of noble houses, the Counts of Bollstadt and Aquino; Bonaventura of good parentage at Fidenza; of Scotus the birth was so obscure as to be untraceable; Ockham was of humble parents in the village of that name in Surrey. But France may boast that the University of Paris was the great scene of their studies, their labors, their instruction: the University of Paris was the acknowledged awarder of the fame and authority obtained by the highest Schoolmen. It is no less remarkable that the new Mendicant Orders sent forth these five Patriarchs, in dignity, of the science. Albert and Aquinas were Dominicans; Bonaventura, Duns Scotus, Ockham, Franciscans. It might have been supposed that the popularizing of religious teaching, which was the express and avowed object of the Friar Preachers and of the Minorites, would have left the higher places of abstruse and learned Theology to the older Orders, or to the more dignified secular ecclesiastics. Content with being the vigorous antagonists of heresy in all quarters, they would not aspire also to become the aristocracy of theologic erudition. But the dominant religious impulse of the times could not but seize on all the fervent and powerful minds which sought satisfaction for their devout yearnings. No one who had strong religious ambition could be anything but a Dominican or a Franciscan; to be less was to be below the highest standard. Hence on one hand the Orders aspired to rule the Universities, contested the supremacy with all the great established authorities in the schools; and having already drawn into their vortex almost all who united powerful abilities with a devotional temperament, never wanted men who could enter into this dreary but highly rewarding service,—men who could rule the schools, as others of their brethren had begun to rule the Councils and the minds of kings. It may be strange to contrast the popular simple preaching—for such must have been that of St. Dominic and St. Francis, such that of their followers, in order to contend with success against the plain and austere sermons of the heretics—with the Sum of Theology of Aquinas, which of itself (and it is but one volume in the works of Thomas) would, as it might seem, occupy a whole life of the most secluded study to write, almost to read. The unlearned, unreasoning, only profoundly passionately loving and dreaming St. Francis, is still more oppugnant to the intensely subtle and dry Duns Scotus, at one time carried by his severe logic into Pelagianism: or to William of Ockham, perhaps the hardest and severest intellectualist of all,—a political fanatic, not like his visionary brethren, who brooded over the Apocalypse and their own prophets, but for the Imperial against the Papal sovereignty.

As then in these five men culminates the age of genuine Scholasticism, the rest may be left to be designated and described to posterity by the names assigned to them by their own wondering disciples.

We would change, according to our notion, the titles which discriminated this distinguished pentarchy. Albert the Great would be the Philosopher, Aquinas the Theologian, Bonaventura the Mystic, Duns Scotus the Dialectician, Ockham the Politician. It may be said of Scholasticism, as a whole, that whoever takes delight in what may be called gymnastic exercises of the reason or the reasoning powers, efforts which never had, and hardly cared to have, any bearing on the life, or even on the sentiments and opinions of mankind, may study these works, the crowning effort of Latin, of Sacerdotal, and Monastic Christianity, and may acquire something like respect for these forgotten athletes in the intellectual games of antiquity. They are not of so much moment in the history of religion, for their theology was long before rooted in the veneration and awe of Christendom; nor in that of philosophy, for except what may be called mythological subtilties, questions relating to the world of angels and spirits, of which, according to them, we might suppose the revelation to man as full and perfect as that of God or of the Redeemer, there is hardly a question which has not been examined in other language and in less dry and syllogistic form. There is no acute observation on the workings of the human mind, no bringing to bear extraordinary facts on the mental, or mingled mental and corporeal, constitution of our being. With all their researches into the unfathomable, they have fathomed nothing; with all their vast logical apparatus, they have proved nothing to the satisfaction of the inquisitive mind. Not only have they not solved any of the insoluble problems of our mental being, our primary conceptions, our relations to God, to the Infinite, neither have they (a more possible task) shown them to be insoluble.

HOMER'S ODYSSEY

Book XI. Buckley's Translation

BUT when we were come down to the ship and the sea, we first of all drew the ship into the divine sea; and we placed a mast and sails in the black ship. And taking the sheep we put them on board; and we ourselves also embarked grieving, shedding the warm tear. And fair-haired Circe, an awful goddess, possessing human speech, sent behind our dark-blue-prowed ship a moist wind that filled the sails, an excellent companion. And we sat down, making use of each of the instruments in the ship; and the wind and the pilot directed it. And the sails of it passing over the sea were stretched out the whole day; and the sun set, and all the ways were overshadowed. And it reached the extreme boundaries of the deep-flowing ocean; where are the people and city of the Cimmerians, covered with shadow and vapor, nor does the shining sun behold them with his beams neither when he goes towards the starry heaven, nor when he turns back again from heaven to earth; but pernicious night is spread over hapless mortals. Having come there, we drew up our ship; and we took out the sheep; and we ourselves went again to the stream of the ocean, until we came to the place which Circe mentioned. There Perimedes and Eurylochus made sacred offerings; but I, drawing my sharp sword from my thigh, dug a trench, the width of a cubit each way; and around it we poured libations to all the dead, first with mixed honey, then with sweet wine, again a third time with water; and I sprinkled white meal over it. And I much besought the unsubstantial heads of the dead, promising that, when I came to Ithaca, I would offer up in my palace a barren heifer, whichever is the best, and would fill a pyre with excellent things; and that I would sacrifice separately to Tiresias alone a sheep all black, which excels amongst our sheep.

But when I had besought them, the nations of the dead, with vows and prayers, then taking the sheep, I cut off their heads into the trench, and the black blood flowed: and the souls of the perished dead were assembled forth from Erebus, betrothed girls and youths, and much-enduring old men, and tender virgins, having a newly-grieved mind, and many Mars-renowned men wounded with brass-tipped spears, possessing gore-smeared arms, who, in great numbers, were wandering about the trench on different sides with a divine clamor: and pale fear seized upon me. Then at length exhorting my companions, I commanded them, having skinned the sheep which lay there, slain with the cruel brass, to burn them, and to invoke the gods, both Pluto and dread Proserpine. But I, having drawn my sharp sword from my thigh, sat down, nor did I suffer the powerless heads of the dead to draw nigh the blood, before I inquired of Tiresias. And first the soul of my companion Elpenor came; for he was not yet buried beneath the wide-wayed earth; for we left his body in the palace of Circe unwept for and unburied, since another toil then urged us. Beholding him, I wept, and pitied him in my mind, and addressing him, spoke winged words: "O Elpenor, how didst thou come under the dark west? Thou hast come sooner, being on foot, than I with a black ship."

Thus I spoke; but he, groaning, answered me in discourse, "O Jove-born son of Laertes, much-contriving Ulysses, the evil destiny of the deity and the abundant wine hurt me. Lying down in the palace of Circe, I did not think to go down backwards, having come to the long ladder, but I fell downwards from the roof; and my neck was broken from the vertebræ, and my soul descended to Hades. Now, I entreat thee by those who are left behind, and not present, by thy wife and father, who nurtured thee when little, and Telemachus, whom thou didst leave alone in thy palace; for I know that, going hence from the house of Pluto, thou wilt moor thy well-wrought ship at the island of Æǣa: there then, O king, I exhort thee to be mindful of me, nor, when thou departest, leave me behind, unwept for, unburied, going at a distance, lest I should become some cause to thee of the wrath of the gods: but burn me with whatever arms are mine, and build on the shore of the hoary sea a monument for me, a wretched man, to be heard of even by posterity; perform these things for me, and fix upon the tomb the oar with which I rowed whilst alive, being with my companions."

Thus he spoke; but I, answering, addressed him: "O wretched one, I will perform and do these things for thee."

Thus we sat answering one another with bitter words; I indeed holding my sword off over the blood, but the image of my companion on the other side spoke many things. And afterwards there came on the soul of my deceased mother, Anticlea, daughter of magnanimous Autolycus, whom I left alive, on going to sacred Ilium. I indeed wept beholding her, and pitied her in my mind; but not even thus, although grieving very much, did I suffer her to go forward near to the blood, before I inquired of Tiresias. But at length the soul of Theban Tiresias came on, holding a golden sceptre, but me he knew and addressed: "O Jove-born son of Laertes, why, O wretched one, leaving the light of the sun, hast thou come, that thou mayest see the dead and this joyless region? but go back from the trench, and hold off thy sharp sword, that I may drink the blood and tell thee what is unerring."

Thus he spoke; but I, retiring back, fixed my silver-hilted sword in the sheath; but when he had drunk the black blood, then at length the blameless prophet addressed me with words: "Thou seekest a pleasant return, O illustrious Ulysses; but the deity will render it difficult for thee; for I do not think that thou wilt escape the notice of Neptune, who has set wrath in his mind against thee, enraged because thou hast blinded his dear son. But still, even so, although suffering ills, thou mayest come, if thou art willing to restrain thy longing, and that of thy companions, when thou shalt first drive thy well-wrought ship to the Trinacrian island, escaping from the azure main, and find the beeves pasturing, and the fat cattle of the sun, who beholds all things, and hears all things; if indeed thou shalt leave these unharmed, and art careful of thy return, even then thou mayest come to Ithaca, although suffering ills: but if thou harmest them, then I foretell to thee destruction for thy ship and thy companions; but even if thou shouldst thyself escape, thou wilt return late, in calamity, having lost all thy companions, in a foreign ship; and thou wilt find troubles in thine house, overbearing men, who consume thy livelihood, wooing thy goddess-like wife, and offering thyself for her dowry gifts. But certainly when thou comest thou wilt revenge their violence; but when thou slayest the suitors in thy palace, either by deceit, or openly with sharp brass, then go, taking a well-fitted oar, until thou comest to those men, who are not acquainted with the sea, nor eat food mixed with salt, nor indeed are acquainted with crimson-cheeked ships, nor well-fitted oars, which also are wings to ships. But I will tell thee a very manifest sign, nor will it escape thee: when another traveller, now meeting thee, shall say that thou hast a winnowing-fan on thine illustrious shoulder, then at length having fixed thy well-fitted oar in the earth, and having offered beautiful sacrifices to King Neptune, a ram, and bull, and boar, the mate of swine, return home, and offer up sacred hecatombs to the immortal gods, who possess the wide heaven, to all in order: but death will come upon thee away from the sea, gentle, very much such a one, as will kill thee, taken with gentle old age; and the people around thee will be happy: these things I tell thee true."

Thus he spoke: but I, answering, addressed him: "O Tiresias, the gods themselves have surely decreed these things. But come, tell me this, and relate it truly. I behold this the soul of my deceased mother; she sits near the blood in silence, nor does she dare to look openly at her son, nor to speak to him. Tell me, O king, how she can know me, being such a one."

Thus I spoke; but he, immediately answering, addressed me: "I will tell thee an easy word, and will place it in thy mind; whomever of the deceased dead thou sufferest to come near the blood, he will tell thee the truth; but whomsoever thou grudgest it, he will go back again."

Thus having spoke, the soul of King Tiresias went within the house of Pluto, when he had spoken the oracles: but I remained there firmly, until my mother came and drank of the blood; but she immediately knew me, and, lamenting, addressed to me winged words: "My son, how didst thou come under the shadowy darkness, being alive? but it is difficult for the living to behold these things; for in the midst there are mighty rivers and terrible streams, first indeed the ocean, which it is not possible to pass, being on foot, except any one having a well-built ship. Dost thou now come here wandering from

Troy, with thy ship and companions, after a long time? nor hast thou yet reached Ithaca? nor hast thou seen thy wife in thy palace?"

Thus she spoke; but I, answering, addressed her: "O my mother, necessity led me to Hades, to consult the soul of Theban Tiresias. For I have not yet come near Achaia, nor have I ever stept upon my own land, but I still wander about, having grief, since first I followed divine Agamemnon to steed-excelling Ilium, that I might fight with the Trojans. But come, tell me this, and relate it truly, what fate of long-sleeping death subdued thee? Whether a long disease? or did shaft-rejoicing Diana, coming upon thee with her mild weapons, slay thee? And tell me of my father and my son, whom I left, whether my property is still with them, or does some other of men now possess it, and do they think that I shall not any more return? And tell me the counsel and mind of my wooed wife, whether does she remain with her son, and guard all things safe? or now has one of the Grecians, whoever is the best, wedded her?"

Thus I spoke; but my venerable mother immediately answered me: "She by all means remains with an enduring mind in thy palace: and her miserable nights and days are continually spent in tears. But no one as yet possesses thy noble property: but Telemachus manages thy estates in quiet, and feasts upon equal feasts, which it is fit for a man who is a prince to prepare; for all invite him: but thy father remains there in the country, nor does he come to the city; nor has he beds, and couches, and clothes, and variegated rugs. But he sleeps indeed, during the winter, where the servants sleep, in the house, in the dust, near the fire, and he puts sad garments about his body: but when summer arrives, and flourishing autumn, his bed is strewn on the ground, of the leaves that fall on every side of his wine-producing vineyard. Here he lies sorrowing, and he cherishes great grief in his mind, lamenting thy fate; and severe old age comes upon him: for so I also perished and drew on my fate. Nor did the well-aiming, shaft-delighting goddess, coming upon me with her mild weapons, slay me in the palace. Nor did any disease come upon me, which especially takes away the mind from the limbs with hateful consumption. But regret for thee, and cares for thee, O illustrious Ulysses, and kindness for thee, deprived me of my sweet life."

Thus she spoke; but I, meditating in my mind, wished to lay hold of the soul of my departed mother. Thrice indeed I essayed it, and my mind urged me to lay hold of it, but thrice it flew from my hands, like unto a shadow, or even to a dream: but sharp grief arose in my heart still more; and addressing her, I spoke winged words: "Mother mine, why dost thou not remain for me, desirous to take hold of thee, that even in Hades, throwing around our dear hands, we may both be satiated with sad grief? Has illustrious Proserpine sent forth this an image for me, that I may lament still more, mourning?"

Thus I spoke; my venerable mother immediately answered me: "Alas! my son, unhappy above all mortals, Proserpine, the daughter of Jove, by no means deceives thee, but this is the condition of mortals, when they are dead. For their nerves no longer have flesh and bones, but the strong force of burning fire subdues them, when first the mind leaves the white bones, but the soul, like as a dream, flittering, flies away. But hasten as quick as possible to the light; and know all these things, that even hereafter thou mayest tell them to thy wife."

Thus we twain answered each other with words; but the women came,— for illustrious Proserpine excited them,—as many as were the wives and daughters of chiefs. And they were assembled together around the black blood. And I took counsel how I might inquire of each; and this plan in my mind appeared to me to be the best: having drawn my long sword from my stout thigh, I did not suffer them all to drink the black blood at the same time. But they came one after another, and each related her race; but I inquired of all. There then I saw Tyro first, born of a noble father, who said that she was the offspring of blameless Salmoneus. And she said that she was the wife of Cretheus, son of Æolus. She loved the divine river Enipeus, which flows far the fairest of rivers upon the earth; and she was constantly walking near the beautiful streams of the Enipeus. Earth-shaking Neptune, therefore, likened unto him, lay with her at the mouth of the eddying river: and the purple wave surrounded them, like unto a mountain, arched, and concealed the god, and the mortal woman; and he loosed her virgin zone, and shed sleep over her. But when the god had accomplished the deeds of love, he laid hold of her hand, and spoke and addressed her: "Rejoice, O woman, on account of our love; for when a year has rolled round, thou shalt bring forth illustrious children; since the beds of the immortals are not in vain; but do thou take care of them, and bring them up, but now go to thine house, and restrain thyself, nor mention it; but I am Earth-shaking Neptune."

Thus having spoke, he dived beneath the billowy sea; but she, having conceived, brought forth Pelias and Neleus, who both became noble servants of Jove. Pelias, indeed, abounding in cattle, dwelt in spacious Iolcus; but the other in sandy Pylos. And the queen of women brought forth the others to Cretheus, Æson, and Pheres, and steed-rejoicing Amithaon.

After her I beheld Antiope, the daughter of Asopus, who also boasted to have slept in the arms of Jove; and she brought forth two sons, Amphion and Zethus, who first laid the foundations of seven-gated Thebes, and surrounded it with turrets; since they were not able, although they were strong, to dwell in spacious Thebes without turrets.

After her I beheld Alcmene, the wife of Amphitryon, who, mingled in the arms of great Jove, brought forth bold, lion-hearted Hercules. And Megara, daughter of high-minded Creon, whom the son of Amphitryon, ever un-wasted in strength, wedded.

And I beheld the mother of Œdipus, beautiful Epicaste, who committed a dreadful deed in the ignorance of her mind, having married her own son; and he, having slain his father, married her: but the gods immediately made it public amongst men. Then he, suffering grief in delightful Thebes, ruled over the Cadmeians, through the pernicious counsels of the gods; but she went to the dwellings of strong-gated Hades, suspending the cord on high from the lofty house, held fast by her own sorrow; but she left behind for him very many griefs, as many as the Furies of a mother accomplish.

And I saw the very beautiful Chloris, whom Neleus once married, on account of her beauty, when he had given her countless dowries, the youngest daughter of Amphion, son of Iasus: who once ruled strongly in Minyean Orchomenus; and he reigned over Pylos; and she bore to him noble children, Nestor, and Chromius, and proud Periclymenus; and besides these she brought forth strong Pero, a marvel to mortals, whom all the neighboring inhabitants wooed; nor did Neleus at all offer her to any one, who could not drive away from Phylace the crumple-horned oxen of mighty Iphicles, with wide foreheads, and troublesome; a blameless seer alone promised that he would drive these away; but the severe Fate of the gods hindered him, and difficult fetters, and rustic herdsmen. But when the months and days were now completed, a year having again gone round, and the hours came on, then at length the mighty Iphicles loosed him, having told all the oracles; and the counsel of Jove was fulfilled.

And I beheld Leda, the wife of Tyndareus, who brought forth two noble-minded sons from Tyndareus, steed-subduing Castor, and Pollux who excelled in pugilism; both of these the fruitful earth detains alive; who, even beneath the earth, having honor from Jove, sometimes live on alternate days, and sometimes again are dead, and they have obtained by lot honor equally with the gods.

After her I beheld Iphimedia, wife of Aloëus, who said that she had been united to Neptune: and bore two sons, but they were short-lived, god-like Otus, and far-famed Ephialtes; whom the fruitful earth nourished, the tallest, and far the most beautiful, at least after illustrious Orion. For at nine years old they were also nine cubits in width, but in height they were nine fathoms. Who even threatened the immortals that they would set up a strife of impetuous war in Olympus: they attempted to place Ossa upon Olympus, and upon Ossa leafy Pelion, that heaven might be accessible. And they would have accomplished it, if they had reached the measure of youth: but the son of Jove, whom fair-haired Latona bore, destroyed them both, before the down flowered under their temples, and thickened upon their cheek with a flowering beard.

And I beheld Phædra and Procris, and fair Ariadne, the daughter of wise Minos, whom Theseus once led from Crete to the soil of sacred Athens, but he did not enjoy her; for Diana first slew her in the island Dia, on account of the testimony of Bacchus.

And I beheld Mæra and Clymene, and hateful Eriphyle, who received precious gold for her dear husband. But I cannot relate nor name all, how many wives and daughters of heroes I beheld: for even the immortal night would first waste away.

.   .   .   .

When chaste Proserpine had dispersed the souls of women in different places, the soul of Agamemnon, son of Atreus, came up, sorrowing: and the rest were assembled around him, as many as died, and drew on their fate in the house of Ægisthus together with him; and he immediately knew me, when he had drunk the black blood; and he wept shrilly, shedding the warm tear, holding out his hands to me, desiring to lay hold of me. But he had no longer firm strength, nor power at all, such as was before in his bending limbs. I wept indeed, beholding him, and pitied him in my mind, and addressing him I spoke winged words: "O most glorious son of Atreus, Agamemnon, king of men, what fate of long-sleeping death subdued thee? Did Neptune subdue thee in thy ships, raising an immense blast of cruel winds? Or did unjust men injure thee on land, while thou wert cutting off their oxen, and beautiful flocks of sheep, or contending for a city, or for women?"

Thus I spoke; but he immediately addressed me, answering: "O Jove-born son of Laertes, much-planning Ulysses, neither did Neptune subdue me in my ships, raising an immense blast of cruel winds, nor did unjust men injure me on land; but Ægisthus, having contrived death and Fate for me, slew me, conspiring with my pernicious wife, having invited me to his house, entertaining me at a feast, as any one has slain an ox at the stall. Thus I died by a most piteous death; and my other companions were cruelly slain around me, as swine with white tusks, which are slain either at the marriage or collation, or splendid banquet of a wealthy, very powerful man. Thou hast already been present at the slaughter of many men, slain separately, and in hard battle; but if thou hadst seen those things, thou wouldst have especially lamented in thy mind, how we lay in the palace about the cups and full tables; and the whole ground reeked with blood. And I heard the most piteous voice of the daughter of Priam, Cassandra, whom deceitful Clytemnestra slew near me; but I, raising my hands from the earth, dying, laid them on my sword; but she, impudent one, went away, nor did she endure to close my eyes with her hands, and shut my mouth, although I was going to Hades. So there is nothing else more terrible and impudent than a woman, who indeed casts about such deeds in her mind: what an unseemly deed has she indeed contrived, having prepared murder for her husband, whom she lawfully married! I thought indeed that I should return home welcome to my children and my servants; but she, above all acquainted with wicked things, has shed disgrace over herself, and female women about to be hereafter, even upon one who is a worker of good."

Thus he spoke; but I addressed him, answering: "O gods! of a truth wide-thundering Jove most terribly hates the race of Atreus, on account of women's plans, from the beginning: many of us indeed perished for the sake of Helen; and Clytemnestra has contrived a stratagem for thee when thou wast at a distance."

Thus I spoke; but he immediately addressed me in answer: "Now therefore do not thou ever be mild to thy wife, nor inform her of everything with which thou art well acquainted: but tell one thing, and let another be concealed. But for thee indeed there will not be murder at the hands of thy wife, O Ulysses: for prudent Penelope, the daughter of Icarus, is very wise, and is well acquainted with counsels in her mind. We left indeed her, when we came to the war, a young bride; and she had an infant boy at her breast, who now probably sits amongst the number of men, happy one; for his dear father will surely behold him, when returning, and he will embrace his sire, as is right; but she my wife did not suffer me to be satiated in mine eyes with my son, for she first slew even me myself. But I will tell thee something else, and do thou lay it up in thy mind; hold thy ship towards thy dear paternal land secretly, not openly; since confidence is no longer to be placed upon women. But come, tell me this and relate it truly; if thou hearest of my son anywhere yet alive, either somewhere in Orchomenus, or in sandy Pylos, or somewhere near Menelaus in wide Sparta? for divine Orestes has not yet died upon the earth."

Thus he spoke; but I addressed him in answer: "O son of Atreus, why dost thou inquire these things of me? I do not know at all whether he is alive or dead; and it is wrong to utter vain words."

We twain stood thus mourning, answering one another with sad words, shedding the warm tear. And the soul of Achilles, son of Peleus, came on, and of Patroclus, and spotless Antilochus and Ajax, who was the most excellent as to his form and person of all the Danaans after the blameless son of Peleus. And the soul of the swift-footed descendant of Æacus knew me, and, lamenting, addressed me in winged words: "O Jove-born son of Laertes, much-contriving Ulysses, wretched one, why dost thou meditate a still greater work in thy mind? how didst thou dare to descend to Orcus, where dwell the witless dead, the images of deceased mortals?"

Thus he spoke; but I addressed him in answer: "Achilles, son of Peleus, by far the most excellent of the Grecians, I came for the advice of Tiresias, if he could tell me how by any plan I may come to craggy Ithaca. For I have not yet come anywhere near Greece, nor have I ever gone on my land anywhere, but I still have troubles; but there was no man before more blessed than thou, O Achilles, nor will there be hereafter. For formerly we Argives honored thee when alive equally with the gods, and now again, when thou art here, thou hast great power amongst the deceased; do not therefore when dead be sad, O Achilles."

Thus I spoke; but he immediately addressed me in answer: "Do not, O illustrious Ulysses, speak to me of death; I would wish, being on earth, to serve for hire with another man of no estate, who had not much livelihood, rather than rule over all the departed dead. But come, tell me an account of my noble son; did he follow to the war so as to be a chief or not? and tell me if thou hast heard anything of blameless Peleus; whether has he still honor amongst the many Myrmidonians? or do they dishonor him in Greece and Phthia, because old age possesses his hands and feet? for I am not assistant to him under the beams of the sun, being such a one as when I slew the best of the people in wide Troy, fighting for the Grecians. If I should come as such a one even for a short time to the house of my father, so I would make my strength and unconquerable hands terrible to any who treat him with violence and keep him from honor."

Thus he spoke; but I, answering, addressed him: "I have not indeed heard anything of blameless Peleus. But I will tell thee the whole truth, as thou biddest me, about thy dear son Neoptolemus; for I myself led him in an equal hollow ship from Scyros to the well-greaved Grecians. Of a truth, when we were taking counsels concerning the city Troy, he always spoke first, and did not err in his words; and godlike Nestor and myself alone contended with him. But when we were fighting about the city of the Trojans, he never remained in the number of men, nor in the crowd, but ran on much before, yielding to no one in his might; and many men he slew in the terrible contest: but I could not tell nor name all, how great a people he slew, defending the Greeks. But I will relate how he slew the hero Eurypylus, son of Telephus, with the brass, and many Cetean companions were slain around him, on account of gifts to a woman: him certainly I beheld as the most beautiful, after divine Memnon. But when we, the chieftains of the Grecians, ascended into the horse which Epeus made, and all things were committed to me, both to open the thick ambush and to shut it, there the other leaders and rulers of the Greeks both wiped away their tears, and the limbs of each trembled under them; but him I never saw at all with my eyes, either turning pale as to his beauteous complexion, or wiping away the tears from his cheeks; but he implored me very much to go out of the horse; and grasped the hilt of his sword, and his brass-heavy spear, and he meditated evil against the Trojans. But when we had sacked the lofty city of Priam, having his share and excellent reward, he embarked unhurt on a ship, neither stricken with the sharp brass, nor wounded in fighting hand to hand, as oftentimes happens in war; for Mars confusedly raves."

Thus I spoke; but the soul of the swift-footed son of Æacus went away, taking mighty steps through the meadow of asphodel, in joyfulness, because I had said that his son was very illustrious. But the other souls of the deceased dead stood sorrowing, and each related their griefs. But the soul of Ajax, son of Telamon, stood afar off, angry on account of the victory in which I conquered him, contending in trial at the ships concerning the arms of Achilles; for his venerable mother proposed them: but the sons of the Trojans and Pallas Minerva adjudged them. How I wish that I had not conquered in such a contest; for the earth contained such a person on account of them, Ajax, who excelled in form and in deeds the other Greeks, after the blameless son of Peleus; him indeed I addressed with mild words: "O Ajax, son of blameless Telamon, art thou not about, even when dead, to forget thine anger towards me, on account of the destructive arms? for the gods made them a harm unto the Grecians. For thou, who was such a fortress to them, didst perish; for thee, when dead, we Greeks altogether mourned, equally as for the person of Achilles, the son of Peleus; nor was any one else the cause; but Jupiter vehemently hated the army of the warrior Greeks; and he laid fate upon you. But come hither, O king, that thou mayst hear our word and speech; and subdue thy strength and haughty mind."

Thus I spoke; but he answered me not at all, but went to Erebus amongst the other souls of the deceased dead. There however, although angry, he would have spoken to me, or I to him, but my mind in my breast wished to behold the souls of the other dead.

There then I beheld Minos, the illustrious son of Jove, having a golden sceptre, giving laws to the dead, sitting down; but the others around him, the king, pleaded their causes, sitting and standing through the wide-gated house of Pluto.

After him I beheld vast Orion, hunting beasts at the same time, in the meadow of asphodel, which he had himself killed in the desert mountains, having an all-brazen club in his hands, forever unbroken.

And I beheld Tityus, the son of the very renowned earth, lying on the ground; and he lay stretched over nine acres; and two vultures sitting on each side of him were tearing his liver, diving into the caul; but he did not ward them off with his hands; for he had dragged Latona, the celebrated wife of Jove, as she was going to Pythos, through the delightful Panopeus.

And I beheld Tantalus suffering severe griefs, standing in a lake; and it approached his chin. But he stood thirsting, and he could not get anything to drink; for as often as the old man stooped, desiring to drink, so often the water, being sucked up, was lost to him; and the black earth appeared around his feet, and the deity dried it up. And lofty trees shed down fruit from the top, pear-trees, and apples, and pomegranates producing glorious fruit, and sweet figs, and flourishing olives: of which, when the old man raised himself up to pluck some with his hands, the wind kept casting them away to the dark clouds.

And I beheld Sisyphus, having violent griefs, bearing an enormous stone with both his hands: he indeed leaning with his hands and feet kept thrusting the stone up to the top; but when it was about to pass over the summit, then strong force began to drive it back again, then the impudent stone rolled to the plain; but he, striving, kept thrusting it back, and the sweat flowed down from his limbs, and a dirt arose from his head.

After him I perceived the might of Hercules, an image; for he himself amongst the immortal gods is delighted with banquets, and has the fair-legged Hebe, daughter of mighty Jove and golden-sandalled Juno. And around him there was a clang of the dead, as of birds, frighted on all sides; but he, like unto dark night, having a naked bow, and an arrow at the string, looking about terribly, was always like unto one about to let fly a shaft. And there was a fearful belt around his breast, the thong was golden: on which wondrous forms were wrought, bears, and wild boars, and terrible lions, and contests, and battles, and slaughters, and slayings of men; he who devised that thong with his art, never having wrought such a one before, could not work any other such. But he immediately knew me, when he saw me with his eyes, and, pitying me, addressed winged words: "O Jove-born son of Laertes, much-contriving Ulysses, ah! wretched one, thou too art certainly pursuing some evil fate, which I also endured under the beams of the sun. I was indeed the son of Jove, the son of Saturn, but I had infinite labor; for I was subjected to a much inferior man, who enjoined upon me difficult contests: and once he sent me hither to bring the dog, for he did not think that there was any contest more difficult than this. I indeed brought it up and led it from Pluto, but Mercury and blue-eyed Minerva escorted me."

Thus having spoken, he went again within the house of Pluto. But I remained there firmly, if by chance any one of the heroes, who perished in former times, would still come; and I should now still have seen former men, whom I wished, Theseus, and Pirithous, glorious children of the gods; but first myriads of nations of the dead were assembled around me with a fine clamor; and pale fear seized me, lest to me illustrious Proserpine should send a Gorgon head of a terrific monster from Orcus. Going then immediately to my ship, I ordered my companions to go on board themselves, and to loose the halsers. But they quickly embarked, and sat down on the benches. And the wave of the stream carried it through the ocean river, first the rowing and afterwards a fair wind.

VIRGIL'S ÆNEID

Book VI. Davidson's Tr., revised by Buckley

... YE gods, to whom the empire of ghosts belongs, and ye silent shades, and Chaos, and Phlegethon, places where silence reigns around in night! permit me to utter the secrets I have heard; may I by your divine will disclose things buried in deep earth and darkness. They moved along amid the gloom under the solitary night through the shade, and through the desolate halls and empty realms of Pluto; such as is a journey in woods beneath the unsteady moon, under a faint, glimmering light, when Jupiter hath wrapped the heavens in shade, and sable night had stripped objects of color.

Before the vestibule itself, and in the first jaws of hell, Grief and vengeful Cares have placed their couches, and pale Diseases dwell, and disconsolate Old Age, and Fear, and the evil counsellor Famine, and vile, deformed Indigence, forms ghastly to the sight! and Death, and Toil; then Sleep, akin to Death, and criminal Joys of the mind; and in the opposite threshold murderous War, and the iron bedchambers of the Furies, and frantic Discord, having her viperous locks bound with bloody fillets.

In the midst a gloomy elm displays its boughs and aged arms, which seat vain Dreams are commonly said to haunt, and under every leaf they dwell. Many monstrous savages, moreover, of various forms, stable in the gates, the Centaurs and double-formed Scyllas, and Briareus with his hundred hands, and the enormous snake of Lerma hissing dreadful, and Chimæra armed with flames; Gorgons, Harpies, and the form of Geryon's three-bodied ghost. Here Æneas, disconcerted with sudden fear, grasps his sword, and presents the naked point to each approaching shade: and had not his skilful guide put him in mind that they were airy unbodied phantoms, fluttering about under an empty form, he had rushed in and with his sword struck at the ghosts in vain.

Hence is a path which leads to the floods of Tartarean Acheron: here a gulf turbid and impure boils up with mire and vast whirlpools, and disgorges all its sand into Cocytus. A grim ferryman guards these floods and rivers, Charon, of frightful slovenliness; on whose chin a load of gray hair neglected lies; his eyes are flame: his vestments hang from his shoulders by a knot, with filth overgrown. Himself thrusts on the barge with a pole, and tends the sails, and wafts over the bodies in his iron-colored boat, now in years: but the god is of fresh and green old age. Hither the whole tribe in swarms come pouring to the banks, matrons and men, the souls of magnanimous heroes who had gone through life, boys and unmarried maids, and young men who had been stretched on the funeral pile before the eyes of their parents; as numerous as withered leaves fall in the woods with the first cold of autumn, or as numerous as birds flock to the land from the deep ocean, when the chilling year drives them beyond sea, and sends them to sunny climes. They stood praying to cross the flood the first, and were stretching forth their hands with fond desire to gain the farther bank: but the sullen boatman admits sometimes these, sometimes those; while others to a great distance removed, he debars from the banks.

Æneas (for he was amazed and moved with the tumult) thus speaks: O virgin, say, what means that flocking to the river? what do the ghosts desire? or by what distinction must these recede from the banks, those sweep with oars the livid flood? To him the aged priestess thus briefly replied: Son of Anchises, undoubted offspring of the gods, you see the deep pools of Cocytus, and the Stygian lake, by whose divinity the gods dread to swear and violate their oath. All that crowd which you see consists of naked and unburied persons: that ferryman is Charon: these, whom the stream carries, are interred; for it is not permitted to transport them over the horrid banks, and hoarse waves, before their bones are quietly lodged in a final abode. They wander a hundred years, and flutter about these shores: then, at length admitted, they visit the wished-for lakes.

The offspring of Anchises paused and repressed his steps, deeply musing, and pitying from his soul their unkind lot. There he espies Leucaspis, and Orontes, the commander of the Lycian fleet, mournful, and bereaved of the honors of the dead: whom as they sailed from Troy, over the stormy seas, the south wind sunk together, whelming both ship and crew in the waves. Lo! the pilot Palinurus slowly advanced, who lately in his Libyan voyage, while he was observing the stars, had fallen from the stern, plunged in the midst of the waves. When with difficulty, by reason of the thick shade, Æneas knew him in this mournful mood, he thus first accosts him: What god, O Palinurus, snatched you from us, and overwhelmed you in the middle of the ocean? Come, tell me. For Apollo, whom I never before found false, in this one response deceived my mind, declaring that you should be safe on the sea, and arrive at the Ausonian coasts. Is this the amount of his plighted faith?

But he answers: Neither the oracle of Phœbus beguiled you, prince of the line of Anchises, nor a god plunged me in the sea; for, falling headlong, I drew along with me the helm, which I chanced with great violence to tear away, as I clung to it and steered our course, being appointed pilot. By the rough seas I swear that I was not so seriously apprehensive for myself, as that thy ship, despoiled of her rudder, dispossessed of her pilot, might sink while such high billows were rising. The south wind drove me violently on the water over the spacious sea, three wintry nights: on the fourth day I descried Italy from the high ridge of a wave whereon I was raised aloft. I was swimming gradually toward land, and should have been out of danger, had not the cruel people fallen upon me with the sword (encumbered with my wet garment, and grasping with crooked hands the rugged tops of a mountain), and ignorantly taking me for a rich prey. Now the waves possess me, and the winds toss me about the shore. But by the pleasant light of heaven, and by the vital air, by him who gave thee birth, by the hope of rising Iülus, I thee implore, invincible one, release me from these woes: either throw on me some earth (for thou canst do so), and seek out the Veline port; or, if there be any means, if thy goddess mother point out any, (for thou dost not, I presume, without the will of the gods, attempt to cross such mighty rivers and the Stygian lake,) lend your hand to an unhappy wretch, and bear me with you over the waves, that in death at least I may rest in peaceful seats.

Thus he spoke, when thus the prophetess began: Whence, O Palinurus, rises in thee this so impious desire? Shall you unburied behold the Stygian floods, and the grim river of the Furies, or reach the bank against the command of heaven? Cease to hope that the decrees of the gods are to be altered by prayers; but mindful take these predictions as the solace of your hard fate. For the neighboring people, compelled by portentous plagues from heaven, shall through their several cities far and wide offer atonement to thy ashes, erect a tomb, and stated anniversary offerings on that tomb present; and the place shall forever retain the name of Palinurus. By these words his cares were removed, and grief was for a time banished from his disconsolate heart: he rejoices in the land that is to bear his name.

They therefore accomplish their journey begun, and approach the river: whom when the boatman soon from the Stygian wave beheld advancing through the silent grove, and stepping forward to the bank, thus he first accosts them in words, and chides them unprovoked: Whoever thou mayest be, who art now advancing armed to our rivers, say quick for what end thou comest; and from that very spot repress thy step. This is the region of Ghosts, of Sleep, and drowsy Night: to waft over the bodies of the living in my Stygian boat is not permitted. Nor indeed was it joy to me that I received Alcides on the lake when he came, or Theseus and Pirithous, though they were the offspring of the gods, and invincible in might. One with his hand put the keeper of Tartarus in chains, and dragged him trembling from the throne of our king himself; the others attempted to carry off our queen from Pluto's bedchamber.

In answer to which the Amphrysian prophetess spoke: No such plots are here, be not disturbed; nor do these weapons bring violence: the huge porter may bay in his den forever, terrifying the incorporeal shades: chaste Proserpine may remain in her uncle's palace. Trojan Æneas, illustrious for piety and arms, descends to the deep shades of Erebus to his sire. If the image of such piety makes no impression on you, own a regard at least to this branch (she shows the branch that was concealed under her robe). Then his heart from swelling rage is stilled: nor passed more words than these. He, with wonder gazing on the hallowed present of the fatal branch, beheld after a long season, turns toward them his lead-colored barge, and approaches the bank. Thence he dislodges the other souls that sat on the long benches, and clears the hatches; at the same time receives into the hold the mighty Æneas. The boat of sewn hide groaned under the weight, and, being leaky, took in much water from the lake. At length he lands the hero and the prophetess safe on the other side of the river, on the foul, slimy strand and sea-green weed. Huge Cerberus makes these realms to resound with barking from his triple jaws, stretched at his enormous length in a den that fronts the gate. To whom the prophetess, seeing his neck now bristle with horrid snakes, flings a soporific cake of honey and medicated grain. He, in the mad rage of hunger, opening his three mouths, snatches the offered morsel, and, spread on the ground, relaxes his monstrous limbs, and is extended at vast length over all the cave. Æneas, now that the keeper of hell is buried in sleep, seizes the passage, and swift overpasses the bank of that flood whence there is no return.

Forthwith are heard voices, loud wailings, and weeping ghosts of infants, in the first opening of the gate: whom, bereaved of sweet life out of the course of nature, and snatched from the breast, a black day cut off, and buried in an untimely grave.

Next to those are such as had been condemned to death by false accusations. Nor yet were those seats assigned them without a trial, without a judge. Minos, as inquisitor, shakes the urn: he convokes the council of the silent, and examines their lives and crimes.

The next places in order those mournful ones possess who, though free from crime, procured death to themselves with their own hands, and, sick of the light, threw away their lives. How gladly would they now endure poverty and painful toils in the upper regions! Fate opposes, and the hateful lake imprisons them with its dreary waves, and Styx, nine times rolling between, confines them.

Not far from this part, extended on every side, are shown the fields of mourning: so they call them by name. Here by-paths remote conceal, and myrtle-groves cover those around, whom unrelenting love, with his cruel venom, consumed away. Their cares leave them not in death itself. In these places he sees Phædra and Procris, and disconsolate Eriphyle pointing to the wounds she had received from her cruel son; Evadne also, and Pasiphae: these Laodamia accompanies, and Cæneus, once a youth, then a woman, and again by fate transformed into his pristine shape. Among whom Phœnician Dido, fresh from her wound, was wandering in a spacious wood; whom as soon as the

Trojan hero approached, and discovered faintly through the shades, (in like manner as one sees, or thinks he sees, the moon rising through the clouds in the beginning of her monthly course,) he dropped tears, and addressed her in love's sweet accents: Hapless Dido, was it then a true report I had of your being dead, and that you had finished your own destiny by the sword? Was I, alas! the cause of your death? I swear by the stars, by the powers above, and by whatever faith may be under the deep earth, that against my will, O queen, I departed from your coast. But the mandates of the gods, which now compel me to travel through these shades, through noisome dreary regions and deep night, drove me from you by their authority; nor could I believe that I should bring upon you such deep anguish by my departure. Stay your steps, and withdraw not yourself from my sight. Whom do you fly? This is the last time fate allows me to address you. With these words Æneas thought to soothe her soul inflamed, and eyeing him with stern regard, and provoked his tears to flow. She, turned away, kept her eyes fixed on the ground; nor alters her looks more, in consequence of the conversation he had begun, than if she were fixed immovable like a stubborn flint or rock of Parian marble. At length she abruptly retired, and in detestation fled into a shady grove, where Sichæus, her first lord, answers her with amorous cares, and returns her love for love. Æneas, nevertheless, in commotion for her disastrous fate, with weeping eyes, pursues her far, and pities her as she goes.

Hence he holds on his destined way; and now they had reached the last fields, which by themselves apart renowned warriors frequent. Here Tydeus appears to him, here Parthenopœus illustrious in arms, and the ghost of pale Adrastus. Here appear those Trojans who had died in the field of battle, much lamented in the upper world: whom when he beheld all together in a numerous body, he inwardly groaned; Glaucus, Medon, Thersilochus, the three sons of Antenor, and Polybætes devoted to Ceres, and Idæus still handling his chariot, still his armor. The ghosts in crowds around him stand on the right and left: nor are they satisfied with seeing him once; they wish to detain him long, to come into close conference with him, and learn the reasons of his visit. But as soon as the Grecian chiefs and Agamemnon's battalions saw the hero, and his arms gleaming through the shades, they quaked with dire dismay: some turned their backs, as when they fled once to their ships; some raise their slender voices; the scream begun dies in their gasping throats.

And here he espies Deiphobus, the son of Priam, mangled in every limb, his face and both his hands cruelly torn, his temples bereft of the ears cropped off, and his nostrils slit with a hideously deformed wound. Thus he hardly knew him, quaking for agitation, and seeking to hide the marks of his dreadful punishment; and he first accosts him with well-known accents: Deiphobus, great in arms, sprung from Teucer's noble blood, who could choose to inflict such cruelties? Or who was allowed to exercise such power over you? To me, in that last night, a report was brought that you, tired with the vast slaughter of the Greeks, had fallen at last on a heap of mingled carcasses. Then, with my own hands, I raised to you an empty tomb on the Rhœtean shore, and thrice with loud voice I invoked your manes. Your name and arms possess the place. Your body, my friend, I could not find, or, at my departure, deposit in your native land. And upon this the son of Priam said: Nothing, my friend, has been omitted by you; you have discharged every duty to Deiphobus, and to the shadow of a corpse. But my own fate, and the cursed wickedness of Helen, plunged me in these woes: she hath left me these monuments of her love. For how we passed that last night amid ill-grounded joys you know, and must remember but too well, when the fatal horse came bounding over our lofty walls, and pregnant brought armed infantry in its womb. She, pretending a dance, led her train of Phrygian matrons yelling around the orgies: herself in the midst held a large flaming torch, and called to the Greeks from the lofty tower. I, being at that time oppressed with care, and overpowered with sleep, was lodged in my unfortunate bedchamber: rest, balmy, profound, and the perfect image of a calm, peaceful death, pressed me as I lay. Meanwhile my incomparable spouse removes all arms from my palace, and had withdrawn my trusty sword from my head: she calls Menelaus into the palace, and throws open the gates; hoping, no doubt, that would be a mighty favor to her amorous husband, and that thus the infamy of her former wicked deeds might be extinguished. In short, they burst into my bedchamber: that traitor of the race of Æolus, the promoter of villany, is joined in company with them. Ye gods, requite these cruelties to the Greeks, if I supplicate vengeance with pious lips! But come now, in your turn, say what adventure hath brought you hither alive. Do you come driven by the casualties of the main, or by the direction of the gods? or what fortune compels you to visit these dreary mansions, troubled regions where the sun never shines?

In this conversation the sun in his rosy chariot had now passed the meridian in his ethereal course; and they perhaps would in this manner have passed the whole time assigned them; but the Sibyl, his companion, put him in mind, and thus briefly spoke: Æneas, the night comes on apace, while we waste the hours in lamentations. This is the place where the path divides itself in two: the right is what leads beneath great Pluto's walls; by this our way to Elysium lies: but the left carries on the punishments of the wicked, and conveys to cursed Tartarus. On the other hand, Deiphobus said: Be not incensed, great priestess; I shall be gone; I will fill up the number of the ghosts and be rendered back to darkness. Go, go, thou glory of our nation: mayest thou find fates more kind! This only he spoke, and at the word turned his steps.

Æneas on a sudden looks back, and under a rock on the left sees vast prisons enclosed with a triple wall, which Tartarean Phlegethon's rapid flood environs with torrents of flame, and whirls roaring rocks along. Fronting is a huge gate, with columns of solid adamant, that no strength of men, nor the gods themselves, can with steel demolish. An iron tower rises aloft; and there wakeful Tisiphone, with her bloody robe tucked up around her, sits to watch the vestibule both night and day. Hence groans are heard; the cruel lashes resound; the grating too of iron, and clank of dragging chains. Æneas stopped short, and, starting, listened to the din. What scenes of guilt are these? O virgin, say; or with what pains are they chastised? what hideous yelling ascends to the skies! Then thus the prophetess began: Renowned leader of the Trojans, no holy person is allowed to tread the accursed threshold; but Hecate, when she sent me over the groves of Avernus, herself taught me the punishments appointed by the gods, and led me through every part. Cretan Rhadamanthus possesses these most ruthless realms; examines and punishes frauds; and forces every one to confess what crimes committed in the upper world he had left unatoned till the late hour of death, hugging himself in secret crime of no avail. Forthwith avenging Tisiphone, armed with her whip, scourges the guilty with cruel insult, and in her left hand shaking over them her grim snakes, calls the fierce troops of her sister Furies.

Then at length the accursed gates, grating on their dreadful-sounding hinges, are thrown open. See you what kind of watch sits in the entry? what figure guards the gate? An overgrown Hydra, more fell than any Fury, with fifty black gaping mouths, has her seat within. Then Tartarus itself sinks deep down, and extends toward the shades twice as far as is the prospect upward to the ethereal throne of Heaven. Here Earth's ancient progeny, the Titanian youth, hurled down with thunderbolts, welter in the profound abyss. Here too I saw the two sons of Aloeus, gigantic bodies, who attempted with their might to overturn the spacious heavens, and thrust down Jove from his exalted kingdom. Salmoneus likewise I beheld suffering severe punishment, for having imitated Jove's flaming bolts, and the sounds of heaven. He, drawn in his chariot by four horses, and brandishing a torch, rode triumphant among the nations of Greece, and in the midst of the city Elis, and claimed to himself the honor of the gods: infatuate! who, with brazen car, and the prancing of his horn-hoofed steeds, would needs counterfeit the storms and inimitable thunder. But the almighty Sire amid the thick clouds threw a bolt (not firebrands he, nor smoky light from torches), and hurled him down headlong in a vast whirlwind. Here too you might have seen Tityus, the foster-child of all-bearing Earth: whose body is extended over nine whole acres; and a huge vulture, with her hooked beak, pecking at his immortal liver, and his bowels, the fruitful source of punishment, both searches them for her banquet, and dwells in the deep recesses of his breast; nor is any respite given to his fibres still springing up afresh. Why should I mention that Lapithæ, Ixion, and Pirithous, over whom hangs a black flinty rock, every moment threatening to tumble down, and seeming to be actually falling? Golden pillars supporting lofty genial couches shine, and full in their view are banquets furnished out with regal magnificence; the chief of the Furies sits by them, and debars them from touching the provisions with their hands; and starts up, lifting her torch on high, and thunders over them with her voice. Here are those who, while life remained, had been at enmity with their brothers, had beaten a parent, or wrought deceit against a client; or who alone brooded over their acquired wealth, nor assigned a portion to their own, which class is the most numerous: those too who were slain for adultery, who joined in impious wars, and did not scruple to violate the faith they had plighted to their masters: shut up, they await their punishment. But what kind of punishment seek not to be informed, in what shape of misery, or in what state they are involved. Some roll a huge stone, and hang fast bound to the spokes of wheels. There sits, and to eternity shall sit, the unhappy Theseus: and Phlegyas most wretched is a monitor to all, and with loud voice proclaims through the shades: "Warned by example, learn righteousness, and not to contemn the gods." One sold his country for gold, and imposed on it a domineering tyrant; made and unmade laws for money. Another invaded his daughter's bed, and an unlawful wedlock: all of them dared some heinous crime, and accomplished what they dared. Had I a hundred tongues, and a hundred mouths, a voice of iron, I could not comprehend all the species of their crimes, nor enumerate the names of all their punishments.

When the aged priestess of Phœbus had uttered these words, she adds, But come now, set forward, and finish the task you have undertaken; let us haste on: I see the walls of Pluto, wrought in the forges of the Cyclops, and the gates with their arch full in our view, where our instructions enjoin us to deposit this our offering. She said; and, with equal pace advancing through the gloomy path, they speedily traverse the intermediate space, and approach the gates. Æneas springs forward to the entry, sprinkles his body with fresh water, and fixes the bough in the fronting portal.

Having finished these rites, and performed the offering to the goddess, they came at length to the regions of joy, delightful green retreats, and blessed abodes in groves, where happiness abounds. A freer and purer sky here clothes the fields with sheeny light: they know their own sun, their own stars. Some exercise their limbs on the grassy green, in sports contend, and wrestle on the tawny sand: some strike the ground with their feet in the distance, and sing hymns. Orpheus, too, the Thracian priest, in his long robe, replies in melodious numbers to the seven distinguished notes; and now strikes the same with his fingers, now with his ivory quill. Here may be seen Teucer's ancient race, a most illustrious line, magnanimous heroes, born in happier times,—Ilus, Assaracus, and Dardanus, the founder of Troy. From afar, Æneas views with wonder the arms and empty chariots of the chiefs. Their spears stand fixed in the ground, and up and down their horses feed at large through the plain. The same fondness they had when alive for chariots and arms, the same concern for training up shining steeds, follows them when deposited beneath the earth.

Lo! he beholds others on the right and left feasting upon the grass, and singing the joyful pæan to Apollo in concert, amid a fragrant grove of laurel; whence from on high the river Eridanus rolls in copious streams through the wood. Here is a band of those who sustained wounds in fighting for their country; priests who preserved themselves pure and holy, while life remained; pious poets, who sang in strains worthy of Apollo; those who improved life by the invention of arts, and who by their worthy deeds made others remember them: all these have their temples crowned with a snow-white fillet. Whom, gathered around, the Sibyl thus addressed, Musæus chiefly; for a numerous crowd had him in their centre, and looked up with reverence to him, raised above them by the height of his shoulders: Say, blessed souls, and thou, best of poets, what region, what place contains Anchises? on his account we have come, and crossed the greatest rivers of hell. And thus the hero briefly returned her answer: None of us have a fixed abode; in shady groves we dwell, or lie on couches all along the banks and on meadows fresh with rivulets; but do you, if so your heart's inclination leads, overpass this eminence, and I will set you in the easy path. He said, and advances his steps on before, and shows them from a rising ground the shining plains; then they descend from the summit of the mountain. But Father Anchises, deep in a verdant dale, was surveying with studious care the souls there enclosed, who were to revisit the light above; and happened to be reviewing the whole number of his race, his dear descendants, their fates and fortunes, their manners and achievements. As soon as he beheld Æneas advancing toward him across the meads, he joyfully stretched out both his hands, and tears poured down his cheeks, and these words dropped from his mouth: Are you come at length, and has that piety, experienced by your sire, surmounted the arduous journey? Am I permitted, my son, to see your face, to hear and return the well-known accents? So indeed I concluded in my mind, and reckoned it would happen, computing the time; nor have my anxious hopes deceived me. Over what lands, O son, and over what immense seas have you, I hear, been tossed! with what dangers harassed! how I dreaded lest you had sustained harm from Libya's realms! But he said: Your ghost, your sorrowing ghost, my sire, oftentimes appearing, compelled me to set forward to these thresholds. My fleet rides in the Tyrrhene Sea. Permit me, father, to join my right hand with yours; and withdraw not yourself from my embrace. So saying, he at the same time bedewed his cheeks with a flood of tears. There thrice he attempted to throw his arms around his neck; thrice the phantom, grasped in vain, escaped his hold, like the fleet gales, or resembling most a fugitive dream.

Meanwhile Æneas sees in the retired vale a grove situate by itself, shrubs rustling in the woods, and the river Lethe, which glides by those peaceful dwellings. Around this, unnumbered tribes and nations of ghosts were fluttering; as in meadows on a serene summer's day, when the bees sit on the various blossoms, and swarm around the snow-white lilies, all the plain buzzes with their humming noise. Æneas, confounded, shudders at the unexpected sight, and asks the causes,—what are those rivers in the distance, or what ghosts have in such crowds filled the banks? Then Father Anchises said: Those souls, for whom other bodies are destined by fate, at the stream of Lethe's flood quaff care-expelling draughts and lasting oblivion. Long indeed have I wished to give you a detail of these, and to point them out before you, and enumerate this my future race, that you may rejoice the more with me in the discovery of Italy. O father, is it to be imagined that any souls of an exalted nature will go hence to the world above, and enter again into inactive bodies? What direful love of the light possesses the miserable beings? I, indeed, replies Anchises, will inform you, my son, nor hold you longer in suspense: and thus he unfolds each particular in order.

In the first place, the spirit within nourishes the heavens, the earth, and watery plains, the moon's enlightened orb, and the Titanian stars; and the mind, diffused through all the members, actuates the whole frame, and mingles with the vast body of the universe. Thence the race of men and beasts, the vital principles of the flying kind, and the monsters which the ocean breeds under its smooth plain. These principles have the active force of fire, and are of a heavenly original, so far as they are not clogged by noxious bodies, blunted by earth-born limbs and dying members. Hence they fear and desire, grieve and rejoice; and, shut up in darkness and a gloomy prison, lose sight of their native skies. Even when with the last beams of light their life is gone, yet not every ill, nor all corporeal stains, are quite removed from the unhappy beings; and it is absolutely necessary that many imperfections which have long been joined to the soul should be in marvellous ways increased and riveted therein. Therefore are they afflicted with punishments, and pay the penalties of their former ills. Some, hung on high, are spread out to the empty winds; in others, the guilt not done away is washed out in a vast watery abyss, or burned away in fire. We each endure his own manes, thence are we conveyed along the spacious Elysium, and we, the happy few, possess the fields of bliss; till length of time, after the fixed period is elapsed, hath done away the inherent stain, and hath left the pure celestial reason, and the fiery energy of the simple spirit. All these, after they have rolled away a thousand years, are summoned forth by the god in a great body to the river Lethe; to the intent that, losing memory of the past, they may revisit the vaulted realms above, and again become willing to return into bodies. Anchises thus spoke, and leads his son, together with the Sibyl, into the midst of the assembly and noisy throng; thence chooses a rising ground, whence he may survey them all as they stand opposite to him in a long row, and discern their looks as they approach.

Now come, I will explain to you what glory shall henceforth attend the Trojan race, what descendants await them of the Italian nation, distinguished souls, and who shall succeed to our name; yourself too I will instruct in your particular fate. See you that youth who leans on his pointless spear? He by destiny holds a station nearest to the light; he shall ascend to the upper world the first of your race who shall have a mixture of Italian blood in his veins, Silvius, an Alban name, your last issue; whom late your consort Lavinia shall in the woods bring forth to you in your advanced age, himself a king, and the father of kings; in whom our line shall reign over Alba Longa. The next is Procas, the glory of the Trojan nation; then Capys and Numitor follow, and Æneas Silvius, who shall represent thee in name, equally distinguished for piety and arms, if ever he receive the crown of Alba. See what youths are these, what manly force they show! and bear their temples shaded with civic oak; these to thy honor shall build Nomentum, Gabii, and the city Fidena; these on the mountains shall raise the Collatine towers, Pometia, the fort of Inuus, Bola, and Cora. These shall then be famous names; now they are lands without names. Further, martial Romulus, whom Ilia of the line Assaracus shall bear, shall add himself as companion to his grandsire Numitor. See you now how the double plumes stand on his head erect, and how the father of the gods himself already marks him out with his distinguished honors! Lo, my son, under his auspicious influence, Rome, that city of renown, shall measure her dominion by the earth, and her valor by the skies, and that one city shall for herself wall around seven strong hills, happy in a race of heroes; like Mother Berecynthia, when crowned with turrets she rides in her chariot through the Phrygian towns, joyful in a progeny of gods, embracing a hundred grandchildren, all inhabitants of heaven, all seated in the high celestial abodes. This way now bend both your eyes; view this lineage, and your own Romans. This is Cæsar, and these are the whole race of Iülus, who shall one day rise to the spacious axle of the sky. This, this is the man whom you have often heard promised to you, Augustus Cæsar, the offspring of a god; who once more shall establish the golden age in Latium, through those lands where Saturn reigned of old, and shall extend his empire over the Garamantes and Indians: their land lies without the signs of the zodiac, beyond the sun's annual course, where Atlas, supporting heaven on his shoulders, turns the axle studded with flaming stars. Against his approach, even now both the Caspian realms and the land about the Palus Mæotis are dreadfully dismayed at the responses of the gods, and the quaking mouths of seven-fold Nile hurry on their troubled waves. Even Hercules did not run over so many countries, though he transfixed the brazen-footed hind, quelled the forests of Erymanthus, and made Lerna tremble with his bow: nor Bacchus, who in triumph drives his car with reins wrapped about with vine-leaves, driving the tigers from Nyssa's lofty top. And doubt we yet to extend our glory by our deeds? or is fear a bar to our settling in the Ausonian land?

But who is he at a distance, distinguished by the olive boughs, bearing the sacred utensils? I know the locks and hoary beard of the Roman king, who first shall establish this city by laws, sent from little Cures and a poor estate to vast empire. Whom Tullus shall next succeed, who shall break the peace of his country, and rouse to arms his inactive subjects, and troops now unused to triumphs. Whom follows next vainglorious Ancus, even now too much rejoicing in the breath of popular applause. Will you also see the Tarquin kings, and the haughty soul of Brutus, the avenger of his country's wrongs, and the recovered fasces? He first shall receive the consular power, and the axe of justice inflexibly severe; and the sire shall, for the sake of glorious liberty, summon to death his own sons, raising an unknown kind of war. Unhappy he! however posterity shall interpret that action, love to his country, and the unbounded desire of praise, will prevail over paternal affection. See besides at some distance the Decii, Drusi, Torquatus, inflexibly severe with the axe, and Camillus recovering the standards. But those two ghosts whom you observe to shine in equal arms, in perfect friendship now, and while they remain shut up in night, ah! what war, what battles and havoc, will they between them raise, if once they have attained to the light of life! the father-in-law descending from the Alpine hills, and the tower of Monœcus; the son-in-law furnished with the troops of the East to oppose him. Make not, my sons, make not such unnatural wars familiar to your minds; nor turn the powerful strength of your country against its bowels. And thou, Cæsar, first forbear, thou who derivest thy origin from heaven; fling those arms out of thy hand, O thou, my own blood! That one, having triumphed over Corinth, shall drive his chariot victorious to the lofty Capitol, illustrious from the slaughter of Greeks. The other shall overthrow Argus, and Mycenæ, Agamemnon's seat, and Eacides himself, the descendant of valorous Achilles; avenging his Trojan ancestors, and the violated temple of Minerva. Who can in silence pass over thee, great Cato, or thee, Cossus? who the family of Gracchus, or both the Scipios, those two thunderbolts of war, the bane of Africa, and Fabricius in low fortune exalted? or thee, Serranus, sowing in the furrow which thy own hands had made? Whither, ye Fabii, do you hurry me tired? Thou art that Fabius justly styled the Greatest, who alone shall repair our state by delay. Others, I grant indeed, shall with more delicacy mould the breathing brass; from marble draw the features to the life; plead causes better; describe with the rod the courses of the heavens, and explain the rising stars: to rule the nations with imperial sway be your care, O Romans; these shall be your arts; to impose terms of peace, to spare the humbled, and crush the proud.

Thus Father Anchises, and, as they are wondering, subjoins: Behold how adorned with triumphal spoils Marcellus stalks along, and shines victor above the heroes all? He, mounted on his steed, shall prop the Roman state in the rage of a formidable insurrection; the Carthaginians he shall humble, and the rebellious Gaul, and dedicate to Father Quirinus the third spoils. And upon this Æneas says; for he beheld marching with him a youth distinguished by his beauty and shining arms, but his countenance of little joy, and his eyes sunk and dejected: What youth is he, O father, who thus accompanies the hero as he walks? is he a son, or one of the illustrious line of his descendants? What bustling noise of attendants round him! How great resemblance in him to the other! but sable Night with her dreary shade hovers around his head. Then Father Anchises, while tears gushed forth, began: Seek not, my son, to know the deep disaster of thy kindred; him the Fates shall just show on earth, nor suffer long to exist. Ye gods, Rome's sons had seemed too powerful in your eyes, had these gifts been permanent. What groans of heroes shall that field near the imperial city of Mars send forth! what funeral pomp shall you, O Tiberinus, see, when you glide by his recent tomb! Neither shall any youth of the Trojan line in hope exalt the Latin fathers so high; nor shall the Land of Romulus ever glory so much in any of her sons. Ah piety! ah that faith of ancient times! and that right hand invincible in war! none with impunity had encountered him in arms, either when one foot he rushed upon the foe, or when he pierced with his spur his foaming courser's flanks. Ah youth, meet subject for pity! if by any means thou canst burst rigorous fate, thou shalt be a Marcellus. Give me lilies in handfuls; let me strew the blooming flowers; these offerings at least let me heap upon my descendant's shade, and discharge this unavailing duty. Thus up and down they roam through all the Elysian regions in spacious airy fields, and survey every object; through each of which when Anchises had conducted his son, and fired his soul with the love of coming fame, he next recounts to the hero what wars he must hereafter wage, informs him of the Laurentine people, and of the city of Latinus, and by what means he may shun or surmount every toil.

Two gates there are of Sleep, whereof the one is said to be of horn; by which an easy egress is given to true visions; the other shining, wrought of white ivory; but through it the infernal gods send up false dreams to the upper world. When Anchises had addressed this discourse to his son and the Sibyl together, and dismissed them by the ivory gate, the hero speeds his way to the ships, and revisits his friends; then steers directly along the coast for the port of Caïeta: where, when he had arrived, the anchor is thrown out from the fore-castle, the sterns rest upon the shore.

CICERO'S VISION OF SCIPIO

Translated by Cyrus R. Edmonds

WHEN I had arrived in Africa as military tribune of the fourth legion, as you know, under the Consul Lucius Manlius, nothing was more delightful to me than having an interview with Massinissa, a prince who, for good reasons, was most friendly to our family. When I arrived, the old man shed tears as he embraced me. Soon after, he raised his eyes up to heaven, and said, I thank thee, most glorious sun, and ye the other inhabitants of heaven, that before I depart from this life I see in my kingdom, and under this roof, Publius Cornelius Scipio, by whose very name I am refreshed, for never does the memory of that greatest, that most invincible of men vanish from my mind. After this I informed myself from him about his kingdom, and he from me about our government; and that day was consumed in much conversation on both sides.

Afterward, having been entertained with royal magnificence, we prolonged our conversation to a late hour of the night; while the old man talked of nothing but of Africanus, and remembered not only all his actions, but all his sayings. Then, when we departed to bed, owing to my journey and my sitting up to a late hour, a sleep sounder than ordinary came over me. In this, (I suppose from the subject on which we had been talking, for it commonly happens that our thoughts and conversations beget something analogous in our sleep, just as Ennius writes about Homer, of whom assuredly he was accustomed most frequently to think and talk when awake,) Africanus presented himself to me in that form which was more known from his statue than from his own person.

No sooner did I know him than I shuddered. "Draw near," said he, "with confidence, lay aside your dread, and commit what I say to your memory. You see that city, which by me was forced to submit to the people of Rome, but is now renewing its former wars, and cannot remain at peace," (he spoke these words pointing to Carthage from an eminence that was full of stars, bright and glorious,) "which you are now come, before you are a complete soldier, to attack. Within two years you shall be Consul, and shall overthrow it; and you shall acquire for yourself that surname that you now wear, as bequeathed by me. After you have destroyed Carthage, performed a triumph, and been censor; after, in the capacity of legate, you have visited Egypt, Syria, Asia, and Greece, you shall, in your absence, be chosen a second time Consul; then you shall finish a most dreadful war, and utterly destroy Numantia. But when you shall be borne into the capitol in your triumphal chariot, you shall find the government thrown into confusion by the machinations of my grandson; and here, my Africanus, you must display to your country the lustre of your spirit, genius, and wisdom.

"But at this period I perceive that the path of your destiny is a doubtful one; for when your life has passed through seven times eight oblique journeys and returns of the sun, and when these two numbers (each of which is regarded as a complete one—one on one account and the other on another) shall, in their natural circuit, have brought you to the crisis of your fate, then will the whole state turn itself toward you and your glory; the Senate, all virtuous men, our allies, and the Latins, shall look up to you. Upon your single person the preservation of your country will depend; and, in short, it is your part, as dictator, to settle the government, if you can but escape the impious hands of your kinsmen." (Here, when Lælius uttered an exclamation, and the rest groaned with great excitement, Scipio said, with a gentle smile, "I beg that you will not waken me out of my dream, give a little time and listen to the sequel.")

"But that you may be more earnest in the defence of your country, know from me, that a certain place in heaven is assigned to all who have preserved, or assisted, or improved their country, where they are to enjoy an endless duration of happiness. For there is nothing which takes place on earth more acceptable to that Supreme Deity who governs all this world, than those councils and assemblies of men bound together by law, which are termed states; the governors and preservers of these go from hence, and hither do they return." Here, frightened as I was, not so much from the dread of death as of the treachery of my friends, I nevertheless asked him whether my father Paulus, and others, whom we thought to be dead, were yet alive? "To be sure they are alive," replied Africanus, "for they have escaped from the fetters of the body as from a prison; that which is called your life is really death. But behold your father Paulus approaching you." No sooner did I see him, than I poured forth a flood of tears; but he, embracing and kissing me, forbade me to weep. And when, having suppressed my tears, I began first to be able to speak, "Why," said I, "thou most sacred and excellent father, since this is life, as I hear Africanus affirm, why do I tarry on earth, and not hasten to come to you?"

"Not so, my son," he replied; "unless that God, whose temple is all this which you behold, shall free you from this imprisonment in the body, you can have no admission to this place; for men have been created under this condition, that they should keep that globe which you see in the middle of this temple, and which is called the earth. And a soul has been supplied to them from those eternal fires which you call constellations and stars, and which, being globular and round, are animated with divine spirit, and complete their cycles and revolutions with amazing rapidity. Therefore you, my Publius, and all good men, must preserve your souls in the keeping of your bodies; nor are you, without the order of that Being who bestowed them upon you, to depart from mundane life, lest you seem to desert the duty of a man, which has been assigned you by God. Therefore, Scipio, like your grandfather here, and me who begot you, cultivate justice and piety; which, while it should be great toward your parents and relations, should be greatest toward your country. Such a life is the path to heaven and the assembly of those who have lived before, and who, having been released from their bodies, inhabit that place which thou beholdest."

Now the place my father spoke of was a radiant circle of dazzling brightness amid the flaming bodies, which you, as you have learned from the Greeks, term the Milky Way; from which position all other objects seemed to me, as I surveyed them, marvellous and glorious. There were stars which we never saw from this place, and their magnitudes were such as we never imagined; the smallest of which was that which, placed upon the extremity of the heavens, but nearest to the earth, shone with borrowed light. But the globular bodies of the stars greatly exceeded the magnitude of the earth, which now to me appeared so small, that I was grieved to see our empire contracted, as it were, into a very point.

Which, while I was too eagerly gazing on, Africanus said, "How long will your attention be fixed upon the earth? Do you see not into what temples you have entered? All things are connected by nine circles, or rather spheres; one of which (which is the outermost) is heaven, and comprehends all the rest, inhabited by that all-powerful God, who bounds and controls the others; and in this sphere reside the original principles of those endless revolutions which the planets perform. Within this are contained seven other spheres, that turn round backward, that is, in a contrary direction to that of the heaven. Of these, that planet which on earth you call Saturn occupies one sphere. That shining body which you see next is called Jupiter, and is friendly and salutary to mankind. Next the lucid one, terrible to the earth, which you call Mars. The Sun holds the next place, almost under the middle region; he is the chief, the leader, and the director of the other luminaries; he is the soul and guide of the world, and of such immense bulk, that he illuminates and fills all other objects with his light. He is followed by the orbit of Venus, and that of Mercury, as attendants; and the Moon rolls in the lowest sphere, enlightened by the rays of the Sun. Below this there is nothing but what is mortal and transitory, excepting those souls which are given to the human race by the goodness of the gods. Whatever lies above the Moon is eternal. For the earth, which is the ninth sphere, and is placed in the centre of the whole system, is immovable and below all the rest; and all bodies, by their natural gravitation, tend toward it."

Which as I was gazing at in amazement I said, as I recovered myself, From whence proceed these sounds, so strong and yet so sweet, that fill my ears?

"The melody," replies he, "which you hear, and which, though composed in unequal time, is nevertheless divided into regular harmony, is effected by the impulse and motion of the spheres themselves, which, by a happy temper of sharp and grave notes, regularly produces various harmonic effects. Now it is impossible that such prodigious movements should pass in silence; and nature teaches that the sounds which the spheres at one extremity utter must be sharp, and those on the other extremity must be grave; on which account, that highest revolution of the star-studded heaven, whose motion is more rapid, is carried on with a sharp and quick sound; whereas this of the moon, which is situated the lowest, and at the other extremity, moves with the gravest sound. For the earth, the ninth sphere, remaining motionless, abides invariably in the innermost position, occupying the central spot in the universe.

"Now these eight directions, two of which have the same powers, effect seven sounds, differing in their modulations, which number is the connecting principle of almost all things. Some learned men, by imitating this harmony with strings and vocal melodies, have opened a way for their return to this place; as all others have done, who, endued with pre-eminent qualities, have cultivated in their mortal life the pursuits of heaven.

"The ears of mankind, filled with these sounds, have become deaf, for of all your senses it is the most blunted. Thus, the people who live near the place where the Nile rushes down from very high mountains to the parts which are called Catadupa, are destitute of the sense of hearing, by reason of the greatness of the noise. Now this sound, which is effected by the rapid rotation of the whole system of nature, is so powerful that human hearing cannot comprehend it, just as you cannot look directly upon the sun, because your sight and sense are overcome by his beams."

Though admiring these scenes, yet I still continued directing my eyes in the same direction toward the earth. On this Africanus said, "I perceive that even now you are contemplating the abode and home of the human race. And as this appears to you diminutive, as it really is, fix your regard upon these celestial scenes, and despise those abodes of men. What celebrity are you able to attain to in the discourse of men, or what glory that ought to be desired? You perceive that men dwell on but few and scanty portions of the earth, and that amid these spots, as it were, vast solitudes are interposed. As to those who inhabit the earth, not only are they so separated that no communication can circulate among them from the one to the other, but part lie upon one side, part upon another, and part are diametrically opposite to you, from whom you assuredly can expect no glory.

"You are now to observe that the same earth is encircled and encompassed as it were by certain zones, of which the two that are most distant from one another, and lie as it were toward the vortexes of the heavens in both directions, are rigid as you see with frost, while the middle and the largest zone is burned up with the heat of the sun. Two of these are habitable; of which the southern, whose inhabitants imprint their footsteps in an opposite direction to you, have no relation to your race. As to this other, lying toward the north, which you inhabit, observe what a small portion of it falls to your share; for all that part of the earth which is inhabited by you, which narrows toward the south and north, but widens from east to west, is no other than a little island surrounded by that sea which on earth you call the Atlantic, sometimes the great sea, and sometimes the ocean; and yet, with so grand a name, you see how diminutive it is! Now do you think it possible for your renown, or that of any one of us, to move from those cultivated and inhabited spots of ground, and pass beyond that Caucasus, or swim across yonder Ganges? What inhabitant of the other parts of the east, or of the extreme regions of the setting sun, of those tracts that run toward the south or toward the north, shall ever hear of your name? Now, supposing them cut off, you see at once within what narrow limits your glory would fain expand itself. As to those who speak of you, how long will they speak?

"Let me even suppose that a future race of men shall be desirous of transmitting to their posterity your renown or mine, as they received it from their fathers; yet when we consider the convulsions and conflagrations that must necessarily happen at some definite period, we are unable to attain not only to an eternal, but even to a lasting fame. Now of what consequence is it to you to be talked of by those who are born after you, and not by those who were born before you, who certainly were as numerous and more virtuous,—especially as among the very men who are thus to celebrate our renown not a single one can preserve the recollections of a single year? For mankind ordinarily measure their year by the revolution of the sun, that is, of a single heavenly body. But when all the planets shall return to the same position which they once had, and bring back after a long rotation the same aspect of the entire heavens, then the year may be said to be truly completed; in which I do not venture to say how many ages of mankind will be contained. For, as of old, when the spirit of Romulus entered these temples, the sun disappeared to mortals and seemed to be extinguished; so whenever the sun be eclipsed at the same time with all the stars and constellations, brought back to the same starting-point, shall again disappear, then you are to reckon the year to be complete. But be assured that the twentieth part of such a year is not yet elapsed.

"If, therefore, you hope to return to this place, toward which all the aspirations of great and good men are tending, what must be the value of that human fame that endures for but a little part of a single year? If, then, you would fain direct your regards on high, and aspire to this mansion and eternal abode, you neither will devote yourself to the rumors of the vulgar, nor will you rest your hopes and your interest on human rewards. Virtue herself ought to attract you by her own charms to true glory; what others may talk of you, for talk they will, let themselves consider. But all such talk is confined to the narrow limits of those regions which you see. None respecting any man was everlasting. It is both extinguished by the death of the individual, and perishes altogether in the oblivion of posterity."

Which, when he had said, I replied, "Truly, O Africanus, since the path to heaven lies open to those who have deserved well of their country, though from my childhood I have ever trod in your and my father's footsteps without disgracing your glory, yet now, with so noble a prize set before me, I shall strive with much more diligence."

"Do so strive," replied he, "and do not consider yourself, but your body, to be mortal. For you are not the being which this corporeal figure evinces; but the mind of every man is the man, and not that form which may be delineated with a finger. Know therefore that you are a divine person. Since it is divinity that has consciousness, sensation, memory, and foresight,—that governs, regulates, and moves that body over which it has been appointed, just as the Supreme Deity rules this world; and in like manner as an eternal God guides this world, which in some respect is perishable, so an eternal spirit animates your frail body.

"For that which is ever moving is eternal; now that which communicates to another object a motion which it received elsewhere, must necessarily cease to live as soon as its motion is at an end. Thus the being which is self-motive is the only being that is eternal, because it never is abandoned by its own properties, neither is this self-motion ever at an end; nay, this is the fountain, this is the beginning of motion to all things that are thus subjects of motion. Now there can be no commencement of what is aboriginal, for all things proceed from a beginning; therefore a beginning can rise from no other cause, for if it proceeded from another cause it would not be aboriginal, which, if it have no commencement, certainly never has an end; for the primeval principle, if extinct, can neither be reproduced from any other source, nor produce anything else from itself, because it is necessary that all things should spring from some original source."

HELL, PURGATORY, AND HEAVEN

Milman's History of Latin Christianity. Book XIV. ch. 2

THROUGHOUT the Middle Ages the world after death continued to reveal more and more fully its awful secrets. Hell, Purgatory, Heaven became more distinct, if it may be so said, more visible. Their site, their topography, their torments, their trials, their enjoyments, became more conceivable, almost more palpable to sense: till Dante summed up the whole of this traditional lore, or at least, with a Poet's intuitive sagacity, seized on all which was most imposing, effective, real, and condensed it in his three co-ordinate poems. That Hell had a local existence, that immaterial spirits suffered bodily and material torments, none, or scarcely one hardy speculative mind, presumed to doubt. Hell had admitted, according to legend, more than one visitant from this upper world, who returned to relate his fearful journey to wondering man: St. Farcy, St. Vettin, a layman Bernilo. But all these early descents interest us only as they may be supposed or appear to have been faint types of the great Italian Poet. Dante is the one authorized topographer of the mediæval Hell. His originality is no more called in question by these mere signs and manifestations of the popular belief, than by the existence and reality of those objects or scenes in external nature which he describes with such unrivalled truth. In Dante meet unreconciled (who thought of or cared for their reconciliation?) those strange contradictions, immaterial souls subject to material torments: spirits which had put off the mortal body, cognizable by the corporeal sense. The mediæval Hell had gathered from all ages, all lands, all races, its imagery, its denizens, its site, its access, its commingling horrors; from the old Jewish traditions, perhaps from the regions beyond the sphere of the Old Testament; from the Pagan poets, with their black rivers, their Cerberus, their boatman and his crazy vessel; perhaps from the Teutonic Hela, through some of the earlier visions. Then came the great Poet, and reduced all this wild chaos to a kind of order, moulded it up with the cosmical notions of the times, and made it, as it were, one with the prevalent mundane system. Above all, he brought it to the very borders of our world; he made the life beyond the grave one with our present life; he mingled in close and intimate relation the present and the future. Hell, Purgatory, Heaven, were but an immediate expansion and extension of the present world. And this is among the wonderful causes of Dante's power, the realizing the unreal by the admixture of the real: even as in his imagery the actual, homely, everyday language or similitude mingles with and heightens the fantastic, the vague, the transmundane. What effect had Hell produced, if peopled by ancient, almost immemorial objects of human detestation, Nimrod or Iscariot, or Julian or Mohammed? It was when Popes all but living, Kings but now on their thrones, Guelfs who had hardly ceased to walk the streets of Florence, Ghibellines almost yet in exile, revealed their awful doom,—this it was which, as it expressed the passions and the fears of mankind of an instant, immediate, actual, bodily, comprehensible place of torment; so wherever it was read, it deepened that notion, and made it more distinct and natural. This was the Hell, conterminous to the earth, but separate, as it were, by a gulf passed by almost instantaneous transition, of which the Priesthood held the keys. These keys the audacious Poet had wrenched from their hands, and dared to turn on many of themselves, speaking even against Popes the sentence of condemnation. Of that which Hell, Purgatory, Heaven, were in popular opinion during the Middle Ages, Dante was but the full, deep, concentrated expression; what he embodied in verse, all men believed, feared, hoped.

Purgatory had now its intermediate place between Heaven and Hell, as unquestioned, as undisturbed by doubt; its existence was as much an article of uncontested popular belief as Heaven or Hell. It were as unjust and unphilosophical to attribute all the legendary lore which realized Purgatory to the sordid invention of the Churchman or the Monk, as it would be unhistorical to deny the use which was made of this superstition to exact tribute from the fears or the fondness of mankind. But the abuse grew out of the belief; the belief was not slowly, subtly, deliberately instilled into the mind for the sake of the abuse. Purgatory, possible with St. Augustine, probable with Gregory the Great, grew up, I am persuaded, (its growth is singularly indistinct and untraceable,) out of the mercy and modesty of the Priesthood. To the eternity of Hell torments there is and ever must be—notwithstanding the peremptory decrees of dogmatic theology and the reverential dread in so many religious minds of tampering with what seems the language of the New Testament—a tacit repugnance. But when the doom of every man rested on the lips of the Priest, on his absolution or refusal of absolution, that Priest might well tremble with some natural awe—awe not confessed to himself—at dismissing the soul to an irrevocable, unrepealable, unchangeable destiny. He would not be averse to pronounce a more mitigated, a reversible sentence. The keys of Heaven and of Hell were a fearful trust, a terrible responsibility; the key of Purgatory might be used with far less presumption, with less trembling confidence. Then came naturally, as it might seem, the strengthening and exaltation of the efficacy of prayer, of the efficacy of the religious ceremonials, of the efficacy of the sacrifice of the altar, and the efficacy of the intercession of the Saints: and these all within the province, within the power, of the Sacerdotal Order. Their authority, their influence, their intervention, closed not with the grave. The departed soul was still to a certain degree dependent upon the Priest. They had yet a mission, it might be of mercy; they had still some power of saving the soul after it had departed from the body. Their faithful love, their inexhaustible interest, might yet rescue the sinner; for he had not reached those gates—over which alone was written, "There is no Hope"—the gates of Hell. That which was a mercy, a consolation, became a trade, an inexhaustible source of wealth. Praying souls out of Purgatory by masses said on their behalf became an ordinary office, an office which deserved, which could demand, which did demand, the most prodigal remuneration. It was later that the Indulgence, originally the remission of so much penance, of so many days, weeks, months, years, or of that which was the commutation for penance, so much almsgiving or munificence to churches or churchmen, in sound at least extended (and mankind, the high and low vulgar of mankind, are governed by sound) its significance: it was literally understood as the remission of so many years, sometimes centuries, of Purgatory.

If there were living men to whom it had been vouchsafed to visit and to return and to reveal the secrets of remote and terrible Hell, there were those too who were admitted in vision, or in actual life to more accessible Purgatory, and brought back intelligence of its real local existence, and of the state of souls within its penitential circles. There is a legend of St. Paul himself; of the French monk St. Farcy; of Drithelm, related by Bede; of the Emperor Charles the Fat, by William of Malmesbury. Matthew Paris relates two or three journeys of the Monk of Evesham, of Thurkill, an Essex peasant, very wild and fantastic. The Purgatory of St. Patrick, the Purgatory of Owen Miles, the vision of Alberic of Monte Casino, were among the most popular and widespread legends of the ages preceding Dante; and as in Hell, so in Purgatory, Dante sums up in his noble verses the whole theory, the whole popular belief as to this intermediate sphere.

If Hell and Purgatory thus dimly divulged their gloomy mysteries, if they had been visited by those who returned to actual life, Heaven was unapproached, unapproachable. To be wrapt to the higher Heaven remained the privilege of the Apostle; the popular conception was content to rest in modest ignorance. Though the Saints might descend on beneficent missions to the world of man; of the site of their beatitude, of the state of the blessed, of the joys of the supernal world, they brought but vague and indefinite tidings. In truth, the notion of Heaven was inextricably mingled up with the astronomical and cosmogonical as well as with the theological notions of the age. Dante's Paradise blends the Ptolemaic system with the nine angelic circles of the Pseudo Dionysius; the material heavens in their nine circles; above and beyond them, in the invisible heavens, the nine Hierarchies; and yet higher than the highest heavens the dwelling of the Ineffable Trinity. The Beatific Vision, whether immediate or to await the Last Day, had been eluded rather than determined, till the rash and presumptuous theology of Pope John XXII. compelled a declaration from the Church. But yet this ascent to the Heaven of Heavens would seem from Dante, the best interpreter of the dominant conceptions, to have been an especial privilege, if it may be so said, of the most Blessed of the Blessed, the Saint of Saints. There is a manifest gradation in Beatitude and Sanctity. According to the universal cosmical theory, the Earth, the round and level earth, was the centre of the whole system. It was usually supposed to be encircled by the vast, circumambient, endless ocean; but beyond that ocean (with a dim reminiscence, it should seem, of the Elysian Fields of the poets) was placed a Paradise, where the souls of men hereafter to be blest awaited the final resurrection. Dante takes the other theory: he peoples the nine material heavens—that is, the cycle of the Moon, Venus, Mercury, the sun, Mars, Jupiter, Saturn, the fixed stars, and the firmament above, or the Primum Mobile—with those who are admitted to a progressively advancing state of glory and blessedness. All this, it should seem, is below the ascending circles of the Celestial Hierarchies, that immediate vestibule or fore-court of the Holy of Holies, the Heaven of Heavens, into which the most perfect of the Saints are admitted. They are commingled with, yet unabsorbed by, the Redeemer, in mystic union; yet the mysticism still reverently endeavors to maintain some distinction in regard to this Light, which, as it has descended upon earth, is drawn up again to the highest Heavens, and has a kind of communion with the yet Incommunicable Deity. That in all the Paradise of Dante there should be a dazzling sameness, a mystic indistinctness, an inseparable blending of the real and the unreal, is not wonderful, if we consider the nature of the subject, and the still more incoherent and incongruous popular conceptions which he had to represent and to harmonize. It is more wonderful that, with these few elements, Light, Music, and Mysticism, he should, by his singular talent of embodying the purely abstract and metaphysical thought in the liveliest imagery, represent such things with the most objective truth, yet without disturbing their fine spiritualism. The subtilest scholasticism is not more subtile than Dante. It is perhaps a bold assertion, but what is there on these transcendent subjects in the vast theology of Aquinas, of which the essence and sum is not in the Paradise of Dante? Dante, perhaps, though expressing to a great extent the popular conception of Heaven, is as much by his innate sublimity above it, as St. Thomas himself.

THE VISION OF FRATE ALBERICO

Wright, St. Patrick's Purgatory, p. 118

ALBERIC, when he wrote his vision, was a monk of Monte Cassino. His father was a baron, lord of the castle de' Sette Fratelli, in the Campagna of Rome. In his tenth year, the child Alberic was seized with a languor, and lay nine days and nine nights in a trance, to all appearance dead. As soon as he had fallen into this condition, a white bird, like a dove, came and put its bill into his mouth, and seemed to lift him up, and then he saw St. Peter and two angels, who carried him to the lower regions. St. Peter told him that he would see the least torments first, and afterwards, successively, the more terrible punishments of the other world. They came first to a place filled with red-hot burning cinders and boiling vapor, in which little children were purged; those of one year old being subjected to this torment during seven days; those of two years, fourteen days; and so on, in proportion to their age. Then they entered a terrible valley, in which Alberic saw a great number of persons plunged to different depths, according to their different degrees of criminality, in frost, and cold, and ice, which consumed them like fire; these were adulterers, and people who had led impure lives. Then they approached a still more fearful valley, filled with trees, the branches of which were long spikes, on which hung women transfixed through their breasts, while venomous serpents were sucking them; these were women who had refused pity to orphans. Other women, who had been faithless to the marriage bed, were suspended by the hair over raging fires. Next he saw an iron ladder, three hundred and sixty cubits long, red hot, and under it a great boiler of melted oil, pitch, and resin; married persons who had not been continent on sabbaths and holy days were compelled to mount this ladder, and ever as they were obliged to quit their hold by the heat, they dropped into the boiler below. Then they beheld vast fires in which were burnt the souls of tyrannical and cruel lords, and of women who had destroyed their offspring. Next was a great space full of fire like blood, in which homicides were thrown; and after this there stood an immense vessel filled with boiling brass, tin, lead, sulphur, and resin, in which were immersed during three years those who had encouraged wicked priests. They next came to the mouth of the infernal pit, (*os infernalis baratri,*) a vast gulf, dark, and emitting an intolerable stench, and full of screaming and howling. By the pit was a serpent of infinite magnitude, bound by a great chain, the one end of which seemed to be fastened in the pit; before the mouth of this serpent stood a multitude of souls, which he sucked in like flies at each breath, and then, with the return of respiration, blew them out scorched to sparks; and this process continued till the souls were purged of their sins. The pit was so dark that Alberic could not see what was going on in hell. After quitting this spot, Alberic was conducted first to a valley in which persons who had committed sacrilege were burnt in a sea of flames; then to a pit of fire in which simonists were punished; next to a place filled with flames, and with serpents and dragons, in which were tormented those who, having embraced the monastic profession, had quitted it and returned to a secular life; and afterwards to a great black lake of sulphureous water, full of serpents and scorpions, in which the souls of detractors and false witnesses were immersed to the chin, and their faces continually flogged with serpents by demons who hovered over them. On the borders of hell, Alberic saw two "malignant spirits" in the form of a dog and a lion, which he was told blew out from their fiery mouths all the torments that were outside of hell, and at every breath the souls before them were wafted each into the peculiar punishment appropriated to him. The visitor was here left for a moment by his conductors; and the demons seized upon him, and would have thrown him into the fire, had not St. Peter suddenly arrived to rescue him. He was carried thence to a fair plain, where he saw thieves carrying heavy collars of iron, red hot, about their necks, hands, and feet. He saw here a great burning pitchy river, issuing from hell, and an iron bridge over it, which appeared very broad and easy for the virtuous to pass; but when sinners attempted it, it became narrow as a thread, and they fell over into the river, and afterwards attempted it again, but were not allowed to pass until they had been sufficiently boiled to purge them of their sins. After this the Apostle showed Alberic an extensive plain, three days' and three nights' journey in breadth, covered with thorns and brambles, in which souls were hunted and tormented by a demon mounted on a great and swift dragon, and their clothing and limbs torn to pieces by the thorns as they endeavored to escape from him; by degrees they were purged of their sins, and became lighter, so that they could run faster, until at last they escaped into a very pleasant plain, filled with purified souls, where their torn members and garments were immediately restored; and here Alberic saw monks and martyrs, and good people, in great joy. He then proceeded through the habitations of the blessed. In the midst of a beautiful plain, covered with flowers, rose the mountain of paradise, with the tree at the top. After having conducted the visitor through the seven heavens, the last of which was held by Saturn, they brought him to a wall, and let him look over, but he was forbidden to tell what he had seen on the other side. They subsequently carried him through the different regions of the world, and showed him many extraordinary things, and, among the rest, some persons subjected to purgatorial punishments in different places on the earth.

THE VISION OF WALKELIN

Odericus Vitalis, Ecclesiastical History, Book VIII. ch. 17. Tr. by Thomas Forester

I CONSIDER that I ought not to suppress and pass over in silence what happened to a certain priest of the diocese of Lisieux in the beginning of January. In a village called Bonneval there was a priest named Walkelin who served the church of St. Aubin of Anjou, who from a monk became bishop and confessor. At the commencement of the month of January, 1091, this priest was summoned in the night-time, as the occasion required, to visit a sick man who lived at the farthest extremity of his parish. As he was pursuing his solitary road homewards, far from any habitation of man, he heard a great noise like the tramp of a numerous body of troops, and thought within himself that the sounds proceeded from the army of Robert de Belèsme on their march to lay siege to the castle of Courci. The moon, being in her eighth day in the constellation of the Ram, shed a clear light, so that it was easy to find the way. Now the priest was young, undaunted, and bold, and of a powerful and active frame of body. However, he hesitated when the sounds, which seemed to proceed from troops on the march, first reached his ears, and began to consider whether he should take to flight to avoid being laid hold of and discourteously stripped by the worthless camp followers, or manfully stand on his defence if any one molested him. Just then he espied four medlar-trees in a field at a good distance from the path, and determined to seek shelter behind them, as fast as he could, until the cavalry had passed. But as he was running he was stopped by a man of enormous stature, armed with a massive club, who, raising his weapon above his head, shouted to him, "Stand! Take not a step farther!" The priest, frozen with terror, stood motionless, leaning on his staff. The gigantic club-bearer also stood close to him, and, without offering to do him any injury, quietly waited for the passage of the troop. And now, behold, a great crowd of people came by on foot, carrying on their heads and shoulders sheep, clothes, furniture, and movables of all descriptions, such as robbers are in the habit of pillaging. All were making great lamentations, and urging one another to hasten their steps. Among them the priest recognized a number of his neighbors who had lately died, and heard them bewailing the excruciating sufferings with which they were tormented for their evil deeds. They were followed by a troop of corpse-bearers, who were joined by the giant already mentioned. These carried as many as fifty biers, each of which was borne by two bearers. On these were seated a number of men of the size of dwarfs, but whose heads were as large as barrels. Two Ethiopians also carried an immense trunk of a tree, to which a poor wretch was rudely bound, who, in his tortures, filled the air with fearful cries of anguish; for a horrible demon sat on the same trunk and goaded his loins and back with red-hot spurs until the blood streamed from them. Walkelin distinctly recognized in this wretch the assassin of Stephen the priest, and was witness to the intolerable tortures he suffered for the innocent blood he shed two years before, since which he had died without penance for so foul a crime.

Then followed a crowd of women who seemed to the priest to be innumerable. They were mounted on horseback, riding in female fashion, with women's saddles which were stuck with red-hot nails. The wind often lifted them a cubit from their saddles, and then let them drop again on the sharp points. Their haunches thus punctured with the burning nails, and suffering horrible torments from the wounds and the scorching heat, the women pitiably ejaculated, Woe! woe! and made open confession of the sins for which they were punished, undergoing in this manner fire and stench and unutterable tortures for the obscene allurements and filthy delights to which they had abandoned themselves when living among men. In this company the priest recognized several noble ladies, and beheld the palfreys and mules with the women's litters of others who were still alive.

The priest stood fixed to the spot at this spectacle, his thoughts deeply engaged in the reflections it suggested. Presently, however, he saw pass before him a numerous company of clergy and monks, with their rulers and judges, the bishops and abbots carrying croziers in their hands. The clergy and bishops wore black copes, and the abbots and monks cowls of the same hue. They all groaned and wailed, and some of them called to Walkelin, and implored him, in the name of their former friendship, to pray for them. The priest reported that he saw among them many who were highly esteemed, and who, in human estimation, were now associated with the saints in heaven. He recognized in the number Hugh, Bishop of Lisieux, and those eminent abbots, Manier of Evroult and Gerbert of Fontenelles, with many others whose names I either forget, or have no desire to publish. Human judgment is often fallible, but the eye of God seeth the inmost thoughts; for man looks only to outward appearances, God searcheth the heart. In the realms of eternal bliss the clear light of an endless day is shed on all around, and the children of the kingdom triumph in the joys which attend perfect holiness. Nothing that is unrighteous is done there; nothing that is polluted can enter there; no uncleanness, no impurity, is there found. All the dross of carnal desires is therefore consumed in the fires of purgatory, and purified by sufferings of various degrees as the Judge eternal ordains. So that as a vessel cleansed from rust and thoroughly polished is laid up in a treasury, so the soul, purified from all taint of sin, is admitted into Paradise, where it enjoys perfect happiness unalloyed by fear or care.

The priest, trembling at these appalling scenes, still rested on his staff, expecting apparitions still more terrible. And now there followed an immense army in which no color was visible, but only blackness and fiery flames. All were mounted on great war-horses, and fully armed as if they were prepared for immediate battle, and they carried black banners. There were seen Richard and Baldwin, the sons of Count Gilbert, who were lately dead, with so many others that I cannot enumerate them. Among the rest was Landri of Orbec, who was killed the same year, and who accosted the priest, and, uttering horrible cries, charged him with his commissions, urgently begging him to carry a message to his wife. Upon this the troops who marched before and after him interrupted his cries, and said to the priest: "Believe not Landri, for he is a deceiver." This man had been a viscount and a lawyer, and had raised himself from a very low origin by his talents and merit. He decided causes and affairs according to his own pleasure, and perverted judgment for bribes, actuated more by avarice and duplicity than by a sense of what was right. He was therefore justly devoted to flagrant punishment, and publicly denounced by his associates as a liar. In this company no one flattered him, and no one had recourse to his cunning loquacity. He, who while it was in his power had shut his ears to the cries of the poor, was now in his torments, treated as an execrable wretch who was unfit to be heard.

Walkelin having seen these countless troops of soldiers pass, on reflection, said within himself: "Doubtless these are Harlequin's people; I have often heard of their being seen, but I laughed at the stories, having never had any certain proofs of such things. Now, indeed, I assuredly behold the ghosts of the departed, but no one will believe me when I tell the tale, unless I can exhibit to mortal eyes some tangible proof of what I have seen. I will therefore mount one of the horses which are following the troop without any riders, and will take it home and show it my neighbors to convince them that I speak the truth." Accordingly, he forthwith snatched the reins of a black steed; but the animal burst violently from his hold, and galloped away among the troops of Ethiopians. The priest was disappointed at the failure of his enterprise; but he was young, bold, and light-hearted, as well as agile and strong. He therefore stationed himself in the middle of the path, prepared for action, and, the moment a horse came up, laid his hand upon it. The horse stopped, ready for him to mount without difficulty, at the same time snorting from his nostrils a cloud of vapor as large as a full-grown oak. The priest then placed his left foot in the stirrup, and, seizing the reins, laid his hand on the saddle; but he instantly felt that his foot rested on red-hot iron, and the hand with which he held the bridle was frozen with insupportable cold which penetrated to his vitals.

While this was passing, four terrific knights came up, and, uttering horrible cries, shouted to him: "What do you want with our horses? You shall come with us. No one of our company had injured you, when you began laying your hands on what belongs to us." The priest, in great alarm, let go of the horse, and three of the knights attempting to seize him, the fourth said to them: "Let him go, and allow me to speak with him, for I wish to make him the bearer of a message to my wife and children." He then said to the priest, who stood trembling with fright: "Listen to me, I beseech you, and tell my wife what I say." The priest replied: "I know not who you are, or who is your wife." The knight then said: "I am William de Glos, son of Barno, and was once the renowned steward of William de Breteuil and his father William, Earl of Hereford. While in the world I abandoned myself to evil deeds and plunder, and was guilty of more crimes than can be recounted. But, above all, I am tormented for my usuries. I once lent money to a poor man, and received as security a mill which belonged to him, and, as he was not able to discharge the debt, I kept the mortgage property and left it to my heirs, disinheriting my debtor's family. You see that I have in my mouth a bar of hot iron from the mill, the weight of which I feel to be more oppressive than the tower of Rouen. Tell, therefore, my wife Beatrice, and my son Roger, to afford me relief by speedily restoring to the right heir the pledge, from which they have received more than I advanced." The priest replied: "William de Glos died long ago, and this is a commission which no Christian man can undertake. I know neither who you are, nor who are your heirs. If I should venture to tell such a tale to Roger de Glos, or his brothers, or to their mother, they would laugh me to scorn, as one out of his wits." However, William continued still to persist in his earnest entreaties, and furnished him with many sure and well-known tokens of his identity. The priest understood very well all he heard, but pretended not to comprehend it. At length, overcome by importunities, he consented to what the knight requested, and engaged to do what was required. Upon this, William repeated again all he had said, and impressed it upon his companion during a long conversation. The priest, however, began to consider that he durst not convey to any one the execrable message of a damned spirit. "It is not right," he said, "to publish such things; I will on no account tell to any one what you require of me." Upon this, the knight was filled with rage, and, seizing him by the throat, dragged him along on the ground, uttering terrible imprecations. The prisoner felt the hand which grasped him burning like fire, and in this deep extremity cried aloud: "Help me, O holy Mary, the glorious mother of Christ!" No sooner had he invoked the compassionate mother than the aid of the Son of God was afforded him, according to the Almighty's disposing will. For a horseman immediately rode up, with a sword in his right hand, and, brandishing it over Roger's head, exclaimed: "Will ye kill my brother, ye accursed ones? Loose him and begone!" The knights instantly fled and followed the black troops.

When they had all passed by, the horseman, remaining alone in the road with Walkelin, said to him, "Do you not know me?" The priest answered, "No." The other said: "I am Robert, son of Ralph le Blond, and your brother." The priest was much astonished at this unexpected occurrence, and much troubled at what he had seen and heard, as we have just related, when the knight began to remind him of a number of things which happened in their youth, and to give him many well-known tokens. The priest had a clear recollection of all that was told him, but not daring to confess it, he stoutly denied all knowledge of the circumstances. At length the knight said to him: "I am astonished at your hardness of heart and stupidity; it was I who brought you up on our parents' death, and loved you more than any one living. I sent you to school in France, supplied you plentifully with clothes and money, and did all in my power to benefit you in every way. You seem now to have forgotten all this, and will not even condescend to recognize me." At length the priest, after being abundantly furnished with exact particulars, became convinced by such certain proofs, and, bursting into tears, openly admitted the truth of what he had heard. His brother then said: "You deserve to die, and to be dragged with us to partake of the torments we suffer, because you have rashly laid hands on things which belong to our reprobate crew; no other living man ever dared to make such an attempt. But the mass you sang today has saved you from perishing. It is also permitted me thus to appear to you, and unfold to you my wretched condition. After I had conferred with you in Normandy, I took leave of you and crossed over to England, where, by the Creator's order, my life ended, and I have undergone intense suffering for the grievous sins with which I was burdened. It is flaming armor which you see us bear, it poisons us with an infernal stench, weighs us down with its intolerable weight, and scorches us with heat which is inextinguishable! Hitherto I have been tormented with unutterable sufferings, but when you were ordained in England, and sang your first mass for the faithful departed, your father Ralph was released from Purgatory, and my shield, which was a great torment to me, fell from my arm. I still, as you see, carry a sword, but I confidently expect to be relieved of that burden in the course of a year."

While the knight was thus talking, the priest, attentively listening to him, espied a mass of clotted gore, in the shape of a man's head, at the other's heels, round his spurs, and in great amazement said to him: "Whose is this clotted blood which clings to your spurs?" The knight replied: "It is not blood, but fire; and it weighs me down more than if I had Mount St. Michael to carry. Once I used sharp and bright spurs when I was hurrying to shed blood, and now I justly carry this enormous weight at my heels, which is so intolerably burdensome, that I am unable to express the severity of my sufferings. Men ought to reflect on these things without ceasing, and to dread and beware, lest they, for their sins, should undergo such chastisements. I am not permitted, my brother, to converse longer with you, for I must hasten to follow this unhappy troop. Remember me, I pray you, and give me the succor of your prayers and alms. In one year after Palm Sunday I trust to be saved, and by the mercy of the Creator released from all my torments. And you, consider well your own state, and prudently mend your life, which is blemished by many vices, for know, it will not be very long. Now be silent, bury in your own bosom the things you have so unexpectedly seen and heard, and do not venture to tell them to any one for three days."

With these words the knight hastened away. The priest was seriously ill for a whole week; as soon as he began to recover his strength, he went to Lisieux and related all that had happened to Bishop Gilbert in regular order, and obtained, on his petition, the salutary remedies he needed. He afterwards lived in good health almost fifteen years, and I heard what I have written, and more which has escaped my memory, from his own mouth, and saw the mark on his face left by the hand of the terrible knight. I have committed the account to writing for the edification of my readers, that the righteous may be confirmed in their good resolutions, and the wicked repent of their evil deeds.

FROM THE LIFE OF ST. BRANDAN

Edited by Thomas Wright

SAYNT BRANDON, the holy man, was a monke, and borne in Yrlonde, and there he was abbot of an hous wherein were a thousand monkes, and there he ladde a full strayte and holy lyfe, in grete penaunce and abstynence, and he governed his monkes ful vertuously. And than within shorte tyme after, there came to hym an holy abbot that hyght Beryne to vysyte hym, and eche of them was joyfull of other; and than saynt Brandon began to tell to the abbot Beryne of many wonders that he had seen in dyverse londes. And whan Beryne herde that of saynt Brandon, he began to sygh, and sore wepte. And saynt Brandon comforted him in the best wyse he coude, sayenge, "Ye come hyther for to be joyfull with me, and therfore for Goddes love leve your mournynge, and tell me what mervayles ye have seen in the grete see occean, that compasseth all the worlde aboute, and all other waters comen out of hym, whiche renneth in all the partyes of the erth."

And than Beryne began to tell to saynt Brandon and to his monkes the mervaylles that he had seen, full sore wepynge, and sayd, "I have a sone, his name is Meruoke, and he was a monke of grete fame, whiche had grete desyre to seke aboute by shyppe in dyverse countrees, to fynde a solytary place wherein he myght dwell secretly out of the besynesse of the worlde, for to serve God quyetly with more devocyon; and I counseyled hym to sayle into an ylonde ferre in the see, besydes the Mountaynes of Stones, whiche is ful well knowen, and than he made hym redy and sayled thyder with his monkes. And whan he came thyder, he lyked that place full well, where he and his monkes served our Lorde full devoutly." And than Beryne sawe in a visyon that this monke Meruoke was sayled ryght ferre eestwarde into the see more than thre dayes saylynge, and sodeynly to his semynge there came a derke cloude and overcovered them, that a grete parte of the daye they sawe no lyght; and as our Lorde wold, the cloude passed awaye, and they sawe a full fayr ylond, and thyderwarde they drewe. In that ylonde was joye and myrth ynough, and all the earth of that ylonde shyned as bryght as the sonne, and there were the fayrest trees and herbes that ever ony man sawe, and there were many precyous stones shynynge bryght, and every herbe there was ful of fygures, and every tree ful of fruyte; so that it was a glorious sight, and an hevenly joye to abyde there. And than there came to them a fayre yonge man, and full curtoysly he welcomed them all, and called every monke by his name, and sayd that they were much bounde to prayse the name of our Lorde Jesu, that wold of his grace shewe to them that glorious place, where is ever day, and never night, and this place is called paradyse terrestre. But by this ylonde is an other ylonde wherein no man may come. And this yonge man sayd to them, "Ye have ben here halfe a yere without meet, drynke, or slepe." And they supposed that they had not ben there the space of half an houre, so mery and joyfull they were there. And the yonge man tolde them that this is the place that Adam and Eve dwelte in fyrst, and ever should have dwelled here, yf that they had not broken the commaundement of God. And than the yonge man brought them to theyr shyppe agayn, and sayd they might no lenger abyde there; and whan they were all shypped, sodeynly this yonge man vanysshed away out of theyr sight. And than within shorte tyme after, by the purveyaunce of our Lorde Jesu, they came to the abbey where saynt Brandon dwelled, and than he with his bretherne receyved them goodly, and demaunded where they had ben so longe; and they sayd, "We have ben in the Londe of Byheest, to-fore the gates of Paradyse, where as is ever daye, and never night." And they sayd all that the place is full delectable, for yet all theyr clothes smelled of the swete and joyfull place. And than saynt Brandon purposed soone after for to seke that place by Goddes helpe, and anone began to purvey for a good shyppe, and a stronge, and vytaylled it for vij. yere; and than he toke his leve of all his bretherne, and toke xij. monkes with him. But or they entred into the shyppe they fasted xl. dayes, and lyved devoutly, and eche of them receyved the sacrament. And whan saynt Brandon with his xij. monkes were entred into the shyppe, there came other two of his monkes, and prayed hym that they myght sayle with hym. And than he sayd, "Ye may sayle with me, but one of you shall go to hell, or ye come agayn." But not for that they wold go with hym.

And than saynt Brandon badde the shypmen to wynde up the sayle, and forth they sayled in Goddes name, so that on the morow they were out of syght of ony londe; and xl. dayes and xl. nightes after they sayled playn eest, and than they sawe an ylonde ferre fro them, and they sayled thyderwarde as fast as they coude, and they sawe a grete roche of stone appere above all the water, and thre dayes they sayled aboute it or they coude gete in to the place. But at the last, by the purveyaunce of God, they founde a lytell haven, and there went a-londe everychone. . . . .

And than they sayled forth, and came soone after to that lond; but bycause of lytell depthe in some place, and in some place were grete rockes, but at the last they wente upon an ylonde, wenynge to them they had ben safe, and made theron a fyre for to dresse theyr dyner, but saynt Brandon abode styll in the shyppe. And whan the fyre was ryght hote, and the meet nygh soden, than this ylonde began to move; wherof the monkes were aferde, and fledde anone to the shyppe, and lefte the fyre and meet behynde them, and mervayled sore of the movyng. And saynt Brandon comforted them, and sayd that it was a grete fisshe named Jasconye, whiche laboureth nyght and daye to put his tayle in his mouth, but for gretnes he may not. And than anone they sayled west thre dayes and thre nyghtes or they sawe ony londe, wherfore they were ryght hevy. But soone after, as God wold, they sawe a fayre ylonde, full of floures, herbes, and trees, wherof they thanked God of his good grace, and anone they went on londe. And whan they had gone longe in this, they founde a full fayre well, and therby stode a fayre tree, full of bowes, and on every bough sate a fayre byrde, and they sate so thycke on the tree that unneth ony lefe on the tree myght be seen, the nombre of them was so grete, and they songe so meryly that it was an hevenly noyse to here. Wherfore saynt Brandon kneled down on his knees, and wepte for joye, and made his prayers devoutly unto our Lord God to knowe what these byrdes ment. And than anone one of the byrdes fledde fro the tree to saynt Brandon, and he with flykerynge of his wynges made a full mery noyse lyke a fydle, that hym semed he herde never so joyfull a melodye. And than saynt Brandon commaunded the byrde to tell hym the cause why they sate so thycke on the tree, and sange so meryly: And than the byrde sayd, "Somtyme we were aungels in heven, but whan our mayster Lucyfer fell down into hell for his hygh pryde, we fell with hym for our offences, some hyther, and some lower, after the qualyté of theyr trespace; and bycause our trespace is but lytell, therfore our Lorde hath set us here out of all pyane in full grete joye and myrth, after his pleasynge, here to serve hym on this tree in the best maner that we can. The Sonday is a day of rest fro all worldly occupacyon, and, therfore, that daye all we be made as whyte as ony snow, for to prayse our Lorde in the best wyse we may." And than this byrde sayd to saynt Brandon, "It is xij. monethes past that ye departed fro your abbey, and in the vij. yere hereafter ye shall se the place that ye desyre to come, and all this vij. yere ye shal kepe your Eester here with us every yere, and in the ende of the vij. yere ye shal come into the Londe of Byhest." And this was on Eester daye that the byrde sayd these wordes to saynt Brandon. And than this fowle flewe agayn to his felawes that sate on the tree. And than all the byrdes began to synge even-songe so meryly, that it was an hevenly noyse to here; and after souper saynt Brandon and his felawes wente to bedde, and slepte well, and on the morowe they arose betymes, and than those byrdes began matyns, pryme, and houres, and all suche service as Chrysten men use to synge. . . .

And seven dayes they sayled alwaye in that clere water. And than there came a south wynde and drove the shyppe north-warde, where as they sawe an ylonde full derke and full of stenche and smoke ; and there they herde grete blowynge and blastyng of belowes, but they myght se no thynge, but herde grete thondrynge, wherof they were sore aferde and blyssed them ofte. And soone after there came one stertynge out all brennynge in fyre, and stared full gastly on them with grete staryng eyen, of whome the monkes were agast, and at his departyng from them he made the horryblest crye that myght be herde. And soone there came a grete nombre of fendes and assayled them with hokes and brennynge yren malles, whiche ranne on the water, folowyng fast theyr shyppe, in suche wyse that it semed all the see to be on a fyre; but by the wyll of God they had no power to hurte ne to greve them, ne theyr shyppe. Wherfore the fendes began to rore and crye, and threwe theyr hokes and malles at them. And they than were sore aferde, and prayed to God for comforte and helpe; for they sawe the fendes all about the shyppe, and them semed that all the ylonde and the see to be on a fyre. And with a sorrowfull crye all the fendes departed fro them and returned to the place that they came fro. And than saynt Brandon tolde to them that this was a parte of hell, and therfore he charged them to be stedfast in the fayth, for they sholde yet se many a dredefull place or they came home agayne. And than came the south wynde and drove them ferther into the north, where they sawe an hyll all on fyre, and a foule smoke and stenche comyng from thens, and the fyre stode on eche syde of the hyll lyke a wall all brennynge. And than one of his monkes began to crye and wepe ful sore, and sayd that his ende was comen, and that he might abyde no lenger in the shyppe, and anone he lepte out of the shyppe into the see, and than he cryed and rored full pyteously, cursynge the tyme that he was borne, and also fader and moder that begate him, bycause they sawe no better to his correccyon in his yonge age, "for now I must go to perpetual payne." And than the sayenge of saynt Brandon was veryfyed that he said to hym whan he entred into the shyppe. Therfore it is good a man to do penaunce and for-sake synne, for the houre of deth is incertayne.

And than anone the wynde turned into the north, and drove the shyppe into the south, whiche sayled vij. dayes contynually; and they came to a grete rocke standynge in the see, and theron sate a naked man in full grete mysery and payne; for the wawes of the see had so beten his body that all the flesshe was gone of, and nothynge lefte but synewes and bare bones. And whan the wawes were gone, there was a canvas that henge over his heed whiche bette his body full sore with the blowynge of the wynde; and also there were two oxe tongues and a grete stone that he sate on, whiche dyd hym full grete ease. And than saynt Brandon charged hym to tell hym what he was. And he sayd, "My name is Judas, that solde our Lorde Jesu Chryst for xxx. pens, whiche sytteth here moche wretchedly, how be it I am worthy to be in the gretest payne that is; but our Lorde is so mercyful that he hath rewarded me better than I have deserved, for of ryght my place is in the brennynge hell; but I am here but cer-tayne tymes of the yere, that is, fro Chrystmasse to twelfth daye, and fro Eester tyll Whytsontyde be past, and every feestfull daye of our lady, and every Saterdaye at noone tyll Sonday that even-songe be done; but all other tymes I lye styll in hell in ful brennynge fyre with Pylate, Herode, and Cayphas; therfore accursed be the tyme that ever I knewe them." And than Judas prayed saynt Brandon to abyde styll there all that nyght, and that he wolde kepe hym there styll that the fendes sholde not fetche hym to hell. And he sayd, "With Goddes helpe thou shalt abyde here all this nyght." And than he asked Judas what cloth that was that henge over his heed. And he sayd it was a cloth that he gave unto a lepre, whiche was bought with the money that he stale fro our Lorde whan he bare his purse, "wherfore it dothe to me grete payne now in betyng my face with the blowynge of the wynde; and these two oxe tongues that hange here above me, I gave them somtyme to two preestes to praye for me. I bought them with myne owne money, and therfore they ease me, bycause the fysshes of the see knawe on them and spare me. And this stone that I syt on laye somtyme in a desolate place where it eased no man; and I toke it thens and layd it in a foule waye, where it dyd moche ease to them that went by that waye, and therfore it easeth me now; for every good dede shall be rewarded, and every evyll dede shal be punysshed." And the Sondaye agaynst even there came a grete multitude of fendes blastyng and rorynge, and badde saynt Brandon go thens, that they myght have theyr servaunt Judas, "for we dare not come in the presence of our mayster, but yf we brynge hym to hell with us." And saynt Brandon sayd, "I lette not you do your maysters commaundement, but by the power of our Lorde Jesu Chryst I charge you to leve hym this nyght tyll to morow." "How darest thou helpe hym that so solde his mayster for xxx. pens to the Jewes, and caused hym also to dye the moost shamefull deth upon the crosse?" And than saynt Brandon charged the fendes by his passyon that they sholde not noy hym that nyght. And than the fendes went theyr way rorynge and cryenge towarde hell to theyr mayster, the grete devyll. And than Judas thanked saynt Brandon so rewfully that it was pité to se, and on the morowe the fendes came with an horryble noyse, sayenge that they had that nyght suffred grete payne bycause they brought not Judas, and sayd that he shold suffre double payne the sixe dayes folowynge. And they toke than Judas tremblynge for fere with them to payne.

ICELANDIC VISION

From the Poetic Edda. Tr. by Wright, St. Patrick's Purgatory, p. 177

> IN the Norni's seat
> sat I nine days;
> thence I was carried on a horse;
> the sun of the Gygiars
> shone grimly
> out of the apertures of the clouds.
>
> Without and within
> I seemed to go through all

the seven lower worlds;
above and below
sought I a better way,
where I might have a more agreeable journey.

I must relate
what I first saw,
when I was come into the palaces of torment:
scorched birds,
which were souls,
fled numerous as flies.

From the west saw I fly
the dragons of expectation,
and open the way of the fire-powerful;
they beat their wings,
so that everywhere it appeared to me
that earth and heaven burst.

The sun's hart
I saw go from the south,
him led two together:
his feet
stood on the ground,
and his horns touched heaven.

From the north saw I ride
the people's sons,
and they were seven together;
with full horns
they drunk the pure mead
from the fountain of heaven's lord.

The wind became quiet,
the waters ceased to flow;
then heard I a fearful sound:
for their husbands
shameless women
ground earth to food.

Bloody stones
those dark women
dragged sorrowfully;
their bleeding hearts hung
out of their breasts,
weary with much grief.

Many men saw I
wounded go
in the ways strewed with hot cinders;
their faces
seemed to me all to be
red with smoking blood.

Many men saw I
go on the ground
who had been unable to obtain the Lord's meal;
heathen stars
stood over their heads,
painted with fearful characters.

Those men saw I,
who cherish much
envy at other's fortune:
bloody runes
were on their breasts
marked painfully.

Men saw I there
many, without joy,
who all wandered pathless;
that he purchases for himself,
who of this world
is infatuated with the vices.

Those men saw I,
who in many ways
laid their hands on other's property;
they went in flocks
to Fegiarn's (Satan's) city,
and had burthens of lead.

Those men saw I,
who many had
deprived of money and life;
through their breasts
suddenly pierced
strong venomous dragons.

Those men saw I,
who would not
keep holy days;
their hands

were on hot stones
nailed tight.

Those men saw I,
who in much pride
magnified themselves too much:
their garments
were in derision
with fire surrounded.

Those men saw I,
who had many
words against another lied:
hell's ravens
out of their heads
cruelly tore their eyes.

All the horrors
you cannot know
which the hell-goers have.
Sweet sins
go to cruel recompenses;
ever cometh moan after pleasure.

Those men saw I,
who much had
given according to God's laws;
clear candles
were over their heads
burning brightly.

Those men saw I,
who magnanimously
improved the condition of the poor:
angels read
the holy books
over their heads.

Those men saw I,
who had much
their body lean with fasting;
God's angels
Bowed before all these;
That is the greatest pleasure.

Those men saw I,
who to their mother had

put food in the mouth;
their resting-places were
in the beams of heaven
placed agreeably.

Holy virgins
had purely
washed the soul of sins,
of those men
who many a day
punish themselves.

Lofty cars
I saw go midst heaven,
which had the roads to God;
men guide them
who were slain
entirely without fault.

O mighty Father,
most great Son,
Holy Ghost of heaven,
I pray thee to save
(who didst create)
us all from miseries!

ANGLO-SAXON DESCRIPTION OF PARADISE

From the Phœnix, a Paraphrase of the *Carmen de Phœnice*, ascribed to
Lactantius. Codex Exoniensis. Tr. by B. Thorpe, p. 197

I HAVE heard tell,
that there is far hence
in eastern parts
a land most noble,
amongst men renowned.
That tract of earth is not
over mid-earth
fellow to many
peopled lands;
but it is withdrawn
through the Creator's might
from wicked doers.
Beauteous is all the plain,
with delights blessed,
with the sweetest

of earth's odors:
unique is that island,
noble the Maker,
lofty, in powers abounding,
who the land founded.
There is oft open
towards the happy,
unclosed, (delight of sounds!)
heaven-kingdom's door.
That is a pleasant plain,
green wolds,
spacious under heaven;
there may not rain nor snow,
nor rage of frost,
nor fire's blast,
nor fall of hail,
nor descent of rime,
nor heat of sun,
nor perpetual cold,
nor warm weather,
nor winter shower,
aught injure;
but the plain rests
happy and healthful.
That noble land is
with blossoms flowered:
nor hills nor mountains there
stand steep,
nor stony cliffs
tower high,
as here with us;
nor dells nor dales,
nor mountain-caves,
risings nor hilly chains;
nor thereon rests
aught unsmooth,
but the noble field
flourishes under the skies
with delights blooming.
That glorious land is
higher by twelve
fold of fathom measure,

(as us the skilful have informed,
sages through wisdom
in writings show,)
than any of those hills
that brightly here with us
tower high,
under the stars of heaven.
Serene is the glorious plain,
the sunny bower glitters,
the woody holt, joyously;
the fruits fall not,
the bright products,
but the trees ever
stand green,
as them God hath commanded;
in winter and in summer
the forest is alike
hung with fruits,
never fade
the leaves in air,
nor will flame them injure,
ever throughout ages,
ere that an end
to the world shall be.
What time of old the water's mass
all mid-earth,
the sea-flood decked
the earth's circumference,
then the noble plain
in all ways secure
against the billowy course
stood preserved,
of the rough waves,
happy, inviolate,
through God's favor:
it shall abide thus blooming,
until the coming of the fire
of the Lord's doom;
when the death-houses,
men's dark chambers,
shall be opened.
There is not in that land

hateful enmity,
nor wail nor vengeance,
evil-token none,
old age nor misery,
nor the narrow death,
nor loss of life,
nor coming of enemy,
nor sin nor strife,
nor painful exile,
nor poor one's toil,
nor desire of wealth,
nor care nor sleep,
nor grievous sickness,
nor winter's darts,
nor dread of tempests
rough under heaven,
nor the hard frost
with cold chill icicles
striketh any.
There nor hail nor rime
on the land descend,
nor windy cloud,
nor there water falls
agitated in air,
but there liquid streams
wonderously curious,
wells spring forth
with fair bubblings from earth;
o'er the soil glide
pleasant waters
from the wood's midst;
there each month
from the turf of earth
sea-cold they burst,
all the grove pervade
at times abundantly.
It is God's behest,
that twelve times
the glorious land
sports over
the joy of water-floods.
The groves are

with produce hung,
with beauteous fruits;
there wane not
holy under heaven
the holt's decorations,
nor fall there on earth
the fallow blossoms,
beauty of forest-trees,
but there wonderously
on the trees ever
the laden branches,
the renovated fruit,
at all times
on the grassy plain
stand green,
gloriously adorned
through the Holy's might,
brightest of groves!
Not broken is
the wood in aspect:
there a holy fragrance
rests o'er the pleasant land.
That shall not be changed
forever throughout ages,
until shall end
his wise work of yore
he who at first created it.

A Note on the Type

The principal text of this Modern Library edition
was set in a digitized version of Janson, a typeface that
dates from about 1690 and was cut by Nicholas Kis,
a Hungarian working in Amsterdam. The original matrices have
survived and are held by the Stempel foundry in Germany.
Hermann Zapf redesigned some of the weights and sizes for
Stempel, basing his revisions on the original design.

MODERN LIBRARY IS ONLINE AT
WWW.MODERNLIBRARY.COM

MODERN LIBRARY ONLINE IS YOUR GUIDE TO CLASSIC LITERATURE ON THE WEB

THE MODERN LIBRARY E-NEWSLETTER

Our free e-mail newsletter is sent to subscribers, and features sample chapters, interviews with and essays by our authors, upcoming books, special promotions, announcements, and news.

To subscribe to the Modern Library e-newsletter, send a blank e-mail to: **sub_modernlibrary@info.randomhouse.com** or visit **www.modernlibrary.com**

THE MODERN LIBRARY WEBSITE

Check out the Modern Library website at
www.modernlibrary.com for:

- The Modern Library e-newsletter
- A list of our current and upcoming titles and series
- Reading Group Guides and exclusive author spotlights
- Special features with information on the classics and other paperback series
- Excerpts from new releases and other titles
- A list of our e-books and information on where to buy them
- The Modern Library Editorial Board's 100 Best Novels and 100 Best Nonfiction Books of the Twentieth Century written in the English language
- News and announcements

Questions? E-mail us at **modernlibrary@randomhouse.com**.
For questions about examination or desk copies, please visit
the Random House Academic Resources site at
www.randomhouse.com/academic